Labour Inside the Gate

Labour Inside the Gate

A History of the British Labour Party between the Wars

Matthew Worley

I.B. TAURIS

LONDON · NEW YORK

Published in 2005 by I.B. Tauris & Co. Ltd
6 Salem Road, London W2 4BU
175 Fifth Avenue, New York NY 10010
www.ibtauris.com

In the United States of America and in Canada distributed by St Martin's Press,
175 Fifth Avenue, New York NY 10010

ISBN: 1 85043 798 X (hardback)
EAN: 978 1 85043 798 7 (hardback)

A full CIP record for this book is available from the British Library
A full CIP record for this book is available from the Library of Congress

Library of Congress catalog card: available

Camera-ready copy edited and supplied by the author with the assistance of
൦ the spectacle press, Walthamstow, London

Printed and bound in Great Britain by TJ International Ltd, Padstow, Cornwall

Contents

To My Good Friend Scott King

Don't Stand Me Down

Acknowledgements

Many thanks to everybody who has helped with this book, particularly to Lester Crook at I. B. Tauris, and to Dominic Shryane for his expert help in proofing and formatting the text. A special thank you to Andrew Thorpe and Chris Wrigley for advice over the course of the project, and to Anne Curry for her constant support. Much love goes, as always, to Amelia, to Rosa (who arrived in time to be a premiership baby), and to mum and dad. Thanks, too, to Chris, Pete, Emma, Sue, Stan, Ed, Eileen, Scott, Tess, Simon N., Tizzy, Jo and Chris, Terry and Bob, Jane N., Patrick, Rachel, Alex, Nick, Jamie and Earl Brutus, Pete C., Katie, Emily and Tommy, Mark B., Anne, Joel, Hannah and George, Ben, Rupe, Nim, Dunc and Doreen, Steph, Katie, Melvin, Abi and Becks, Jon M., Cally, Richard and Joyce, Phil and Catherine, Andy, Dom W., Andrea, Pete B., Kath, Louise, John, Mike, Stu and Mel, Tom, Sarah, Dan, Keith, Simon W., Aileen, Mick, Thomas, Marty, B and Emma, Neil, Lisa, Viki, Jo B, Daniel, Steve, Jon Bell, David and everyone at Reading, Giles, Flice, Stuart, Eric, Toby Wolfe, Roger and Vin, Dave and Sally Smith, Alison and John Newland. For support in earlier life, my thanks go to the Heartsease Comprehensive School in Norwich, especially David Franklin, Colin Kay, Alan Spoors, Chris Husbands and Ann Carr. On the ball, City!

Introduction

The Labour Party: Origins and Early Development

> It is not so much socialism, nor the absence of it, which wins elections, as the fact that the candidate is representing a party which the average man who does not indulge overmuch in theories, understands and approves.[1]

> *Keir Hardie*

> The Labour Party owes its inspiration not to some economic doctrine or some theory of class domination. It has always based its propaganda on ethical principles. We believe that every individual should be afforded the fullest opportunity to fulfil his or her personality.[2]

> *Clement Attlee*

From its formation as the Labour Representation Committee (LRC) on 27–8 February 1900, the Labour Party has consistently fascinated historians, political commentators and students alike. Much ink has been spilt and many trees felled to explain the party's often turbulent history and character. In particular, Labour's relatively rapid rise to minority government in 1924 has prompted an on-going and hard-fought historical debate, as have the upheavals of the 1930s, 1950s and 1980s, the landslide victory of 1945, the governments of the 1960s and 1970s, and the advent of New Labour in the 1990s. Without question, the Labour Party has prompted an extensive historiography.

Surprisingly, however, there has never been a general history of the Labour Party concentrated specifically on the years between 1918 and 1939. While studies of the party in the pre-Great War and post-1945 eras have been extensive and increasingly explorative,[3] historians have, quite understandably, tended to treat the interwar years as two distinct periods: that up to 1931 and the collapse of the second minority Labour government, and that of the 1930s, with a primary focus on Labour's struggle with the socialist left and its response to the growing fascist threat. This is not to say that the party of MacDonald, Lansbury and Attlee has been neglected. Far from it: as outlined below, the historiography of the interwar Labour Party is typically wide-ranging. Nevertheless, it is the intention of this study to combine such research with an emphasis on the party's grass roots in order to construct a political history of Labour that reflects and, it is hoped, contributes to current estimations of the party's progress across the interwar period as a whole. In particular, it endeavours to be a history of the Labour *Party* rather than a history of the party in parliament, examining both the Labour leadership and the experiences of the men, women, trade unionists and socialists who built and sustained the party apparatus from 1918.

Looked at generally, studies relating to the interwar Labour Party can be divided into five 'types'. First there are the broad party accounts that outline the progress of Labour from its conception through to a particular 'time of writing'; second, there are the detailed examinations of a particular phase, or stage, in the party's history; third, Labour Party histories are intertwined with the biographies or autobiographies of leading party figures; fourth, historians have picked up on certain themes that run through Labour's history (gender, ideology), but which have been neglected by broader accounts; and fifth, the party has increasingly been examined in the context of a distinct region or locality. From each of these categories, important and often exceptional work has emerged.[4] However, the very diversity of such study – the range of focus and designated time spans – arguably makes necessary a complementary history that embraces and absorbs the apparent complexities of Labour's overall development between the wars. Most obviously, the bulk of general histories, (auto) biographies and 'key period' studies have tended to be histories 'from above' focusing on the Parliamentary Labour Party (PLP), utilising mainly central party documentation, and highlighting primarily the priorities and ideas of the party hierarchy. In so doing, the 'wider' Labour Party – its constituency level and local branches, its affiliated trade unions and socialist societies, its municipal 'Labour groups', women's sections, individual members and electorate – is frequently marginalised or ignored by such accounts. Of course, this is often necessary to meet the brief or objective of a particular study. But it should not be forgotten that the Labour Party was a multifaceted organisation, a federation of numerous affiliated bodies representing a wide range of views and opinions. While the PLP and the central party headquarters dominated the party's national profile, the Labour Party from 1918 actually comprised hundreds of local parties informed by far more than the political priorities and perspectives voiced from the front benches of parliament or the meetings of the National Executive Committee (NEC). Indeed, to Martin Pugh's recent observation that it is possible to talk of *two* Labour parties in the first half of the twentieth century (one radical–socialist, the other populist–patriotic), we could go further and suggest that we can actually talk of hundreds of Labour parties, all with similarities but all distinctive within their own geographical context.[5] To examine adequately the history of Labour, it is necessary to consider the priorities, perspectives and activities of those members who sustained the party in the localities; to assess the relationship between the PLP, the party centre, its affiliates and divisional organisations; and to recognise the differentiated contexts and ways in which the Labour Party emerged, developed and fought to represent its constituents.

To this end, some significant inroads have been made, and historians have more recently sought to include reference to regional and local party experience within their broader studies of Labour at a national level prior to 1945. With regard to Labour's emergence, Duncan Tanner's *Political Change and the Labour Party* (1990) brilliantly analyses the party's notable if uneven growth up until 1918 (although there is no comparable study for the period after the Great War). Similarly, David Howell's studies of the Independent Labour Party (ILP) and the Labour Party under James Ramsay MacDonald have demonstrated the multiple identities that informed and comprised Labour's development. Ross McKibbin's *The Evolution of the Labour Party* (1974) specifically examined the formation of local and constituency party branches from 1900 through to 1924, although this now classic study consulted just two local party minute books, relied primarily on the records of head office, and ends in the early stages of the interwar period.[6] More recently, Andrew Thorpe's broad sweep of the Labour Party's history from 1900 to 1997 refers to the author's wider research into Labour experiences and attitudes beyond the centre, although the scope of such a study obviously limited the extent to which such references could be pursued. Conversely, Neil Riddell's overview of the second Labour government (1929–31) makes extensive use of both national and local party records, but is concentrated on an extremely short period in the party's history. Beyond this, two recent centenary histories of Labour perhaps come closest to capturing the Labour Party in totality, exploring the party at a local, regional and national level in a series of contributed essays.[7]

Indeed, it is the more usual concentration on the party at a 'high' political level, in combination with the aforementioned debate as to just why the Labour Party emerged when it did and was able to overtake the Liberal Party as the main rival to Conservatism across much of the twentieth century, that has prompted a number of historians to turn their attention either to ignored themes of Labour history, or to regional politics. Such work is vital, and has helped recover key aspects of party life from the shadows of traditional male-centric, hierarchical narratives. The belated recognition, for example, that women played an integral role in the development of the Labour Party has been of particular significance.[8] Likewise, the numerous regional or local studies that continue to appear have brought to light the complexities of Labour's emergence. Taken as a whole, they warn against too generalised an appraisal of Labour's history – especially during the initial 'rise to office' between 1900 and 1924 – and demonstrate further the importance of local peculiarities on the experience (positive or negative) of the Labour Party in different parts of the country. In particular, the work of Mike Savage, Chris Williams, Duncan Tanner, Sam Davies, John Marriott and Catriona Macdonald has been instructive.[9]

Again, however, we can make certain qualifying remarks. An emphasis on previously ignored aspects of Labour history serves a purpose in bringing to light factors that *should* be an essential part of any more wide-ranging account. The next step is to carry out such integration in an attempt to construct a more precise depiction of the Labour Party's overall development. With regard to local studies, moreover, detailed accounts of particular localities, towns, cities and regions are vital as case studies delving into the party's grass roots and the 'dynamics' of Labour politics, but they must be compared, contrasted and assimilated if they are to challenge, complement or supplement established perceptions.[10] As Mike Savage has noted, political parties at a national and local level did not exist in a vacuum, but were affected respectively by a variety of influences, both general and specific.[11] Certainly, the varied and often tenuous levels of support that Labour achieved across the country during the interwar period should warn against too rash a reading of Labour Party progress.

This, then, is an attempt to construct a broad overview of the Labour Party's history between 1918 and 1939, taking into account the complexities and pitfalls noted above. In so doing, it is hoped that the difficulties of combining a local and national perspective, as outlined by Savage in his seminal article 'The Rise of the Labour Party in Local Perspective', will be avoided.[12] Thus, local developments will not simply be drawn upon to substantiate national trends, nor will it assume the exclusivity of either national or local political contexts, or suggest that the experience of one locality can be simply transplanted onto another. Rather, Labour's fluctuating fortunes will be seen to form part of a contested, contingent and overlapping history, in which a multifaceted organisation sought to construct a politics that both reflected and transformed the realities of everyday life.

COMPROMISE IS THE DEVIL TALKING?
THE LABOUR PARTY TO 1918

The Labour Party emerged from the Great War (1914–18) as a political organisation perceptibly different from that which had entered it. In August 1914, Labour was a federation of affiliated trade unions and socialist societies with no official means of individual membership and no set political programme or ideology. It had established itself as a notable presence in British politics, but it remained more generally in the shadow of the Liberal Party, with which it had formed an electoral pact in 1903 to gain a foothold in the House of Commons. Political representation, indeed, had been the principal objective of the LRC's formation: that is, to establish 'a distinct Labour group in parliament, who shall have their own whips, and agree upon their policy, which must embrace a readiness to co-operate with any party which may for the time being be engaged in promoting legislation in the direct interests of labour ...'[13] Thus, with Liberal assistance, the LRC registered 29 MPs at the general election of 1906 (so prompting the LRC's transformation into the Labour Party), a figure that had increased to 42 by the end of 1910. To this effect, Labour could certainly claim to have 'arrived' by the outbreak of war, with an organisational basis of support that had slowly but steadily grown, and with political representatives both nationally and locally. By 1914, Labour claimed 1,612,147 affiliated members, a presence in parliament, and an increasing number of elected municipal candidates.[14] Yet, the support that Labour had garnered by 1914 was unevenly dispersed across Britain as a whole, with its main bases located overwhelmingly in Yorkshire, Lancashire and among certain mining constituencies in South Wales and the North East.[15] Elsewhere, the Labour presence was slight. In Scotland, for instance, where Labour stood in a minority of seats, the party mustered just 3.6 per cent of the national vote in December 1910, bringing it three MPs.[16] As a party born, in Ernest Bevin's famous phrase, from the 'bowels of the trades union congress', Labour was sustained by trade union funds and often by trade union activists.[17] Of its affiliated members, 1,572,391 were trade unionists in 1914, themselves a minority of the wider British working class. The party's influence was evident but limited, therefore, and its continued progress far from certain.

Some four years later, in November 1918, Labour's position had changed significantly. The party boasted a developing national organisation of constituency-level parties with access for individual members, a political constitution committing the party to the 'common ownership of the means of production' (clause four), an apparent uniformity that contrasted with the divided and war-ravaged Liberals, experience in governmental office, and an affiliated membership of 3,013,129. Though it fared badly at the 'coupon' election of 14 December 1918, winning 57 seats, it had nevertheless put forward 361 candidates compared to just 56 in December 1910, and had withdrawn from its alliance with the Liberal Party.[18] As a result, Labour became the principal mainland opposition to a coalition government headed by Lloyd George but dominated by the Conservative Party.[19] On top of this, Labour proceeded to make strident gains in the municipal elections of 1919. Bradford became the first English city to claim Labour as its largest party; twelve

London boroughs were won for Labour; Glamorgan, Monmouthshire and Durham became Labour counties; and significant advances were registered in other British towns and cities. Though its 'second party' status was not immediately assured, it appeared by 1922 that the Labour Party at least rivalled the Liberals as the foremost alternative to the dominant Conservatives, a fact that was affirmed with the formation of the first minority Labour government in January 1924. Labour's eclipse of the Liberal Party was then made irrefutable with Ramsay MacDonald's return to office in May 1929, again as the head of a minority government but with 287 seats compared to the Liberals' 59.

For many historians, such an advance in Labour's position was well on its way prior to the outbreak of the Great War.[20] By August 1914, it is argued, the foundations of Labour's support had become firmly established, as more and more trades councils became electoral agencies for the party, and as locally contrived 'progressive alliances' with the Liberals began to strain and break. With the bulk of the British trade union movement affiliated to Labour, moves were further made to centralise and extend the party's organisation before the war, by which time two national organisers had been appointed, the London and Scottish parties were being established, and certain local parties had made provisions for individual members.[21] Furthermore, Labour's financial position had been stabilised by government legislation. First, the 1911 decision to enact payment for MPs took one obvious economic burden off the party. Second, the 1913 Trade Union Act allowed trade unions to hold ballots to establish political funds to contribute towards a political party.[22] In the meantime, the swelling ranks of trade union membership amidst the widespread industrial unrest of 1910–14 helped replenish the party coffers and further strain Liberal–Labour relations, suggesting that Labour may well have been willing and able to separate itself from its electoral pact had the war not intervened. Even the loss of four by-election seats between 1910 and 1914 was offset, in part, by the party's continued progress at local government level. From such a perspective, Labour's development has been portrayed as the product of a growing working-class consciousness embodied in the party's expanding trade union base.

Such interpretation has been challenged, not least by Duncan Tanner and Jon Lawrence.[23] The relationship between social and political change, and between class and voting, has been closely scrutinised, leading to a debate as to whether Labour's emergence was 'a product of changes in social relations or whether this central development in British politics was contingent upon Labour's construction of political images and strategies'.[24] For Lawrence Black, this has meant essentially a 'return to the "primacy of the political" approach', whereby it is argued that political parties gave meaning to the social, economic and political environments in which they functioned, and voters responded to such appeals in so much as they related to their own experiences and expectations. As a result, 'parties are seen not only to have a role in the making of their own fortunes, but in constructing social and political identities and redefining their audience'.[25] In fact, Professor Tanner's argument is rather more complex than this suggests. While indicating that 'the connection between social experience and political behaviour was something that had to be manufactured and maintained', he goes on to explain Labour's progress to 1914 as being 'contingent upon particular configurations of circumstances'.[26] As such, there was no guarantee that Labour would develop inevitably out of a growing class consciousness; indeed, both the Liberal and the Conservative Party remained an integrated part of British social-political culture at the outbreak of the Great War, thereby challenging Labour's potential advance as some sort of class-based alternative. In certain circumstances, however, where the Liberals were weak, where largely single-industry communities (mainly miners and railwaymen) had committed to labour representation, and where established local Liberal associations failed to adapt to the national party leadership's changing political programme, so Labour began unevenly to challenge the Liberal's position as the main anti-Tory force.[27]

Such differences of emphasis – essentially between the social and political – will no doubt continue indefinitely, but the observations of Tanner, Lawrence and others have certainly discredited any determinist formulation that a working-class constituency would lead inevitably to Labour Party support (even if Labour Party support was invariably located in a working-class constituency). Yet, in some ways, the debate has brought about an either/or argument that is something of a misnomer – a proverbial chicken and egg, reliant on too linear a notion of cause and effect.[28] That political change should be an uneven, protracted process would appear clear; the idea of some 'road to Damascus' working-class conversion to Labour absurd. Similarly, any notion of class (or class consciousness) as a precisely defined social entity ignores the essentially abstract and contested nature of such social definitions. People undoubtedly saw Britain as a class-based society in the early twentieth century – and this no doubt contributed to their political perspective – but they did so unevenly, inconsistently, and in competition with other intellectual and practical considerations.[29] Better, perhaps, to see the relationship between social-economics, politics, culture and the individual as a fluid, multifarious interaction in which a complex range of factors both fed off and affected one another. Ultimately, different determinants, including class, played different roles in defining Labour's progress in different places at different times; general, or national, developments coalesced with local peculiarities, customs and traditions. Equally, just as politics could shape a person's interpretation of his environment, so his environment, and changes within it (be it illness or industrial dispute, unemployment or marriage, working practice or habitation), could help to shape a person's political and social perspective. By adopting such an approach, the role of class in the development of the Labour Party is not lost but added to, while any emphasis on political agency, particularly political language, is balanced by the understanding that such discourse is given, received and interpreted in different ways, by different people, in different contexts.

Certainly, an approach embracing multiplicity rather than competing duality enables us to keep sight of a key reason why the Labour Party was formed in the first place: to allow working people – members of the working class – to speak, act and represent themselves. To cite Ernest Bevin again, in a quote from 1917 that sums up an important part of the Labour ethos:

> I had to work at ten years of age while my employer's son went to university until he was twenty … I was taught to bow to the squire and touch my hat to the parson; my employer's son was not. All these things have produced within me an intense hatred, a hatred which has caused me to organise my fellows and direct my mind to a policy to give my class a power to control their own destiny and labour.[30]

Within Bevin's thinking, the political is clearly integrated with the social. True, some historians have come to explain Labour's development as an extension of the 'radical tradition', emphasising continuities in Liberal and Labour thought that overrode expressions of class loyalty.[31] It is undeniable that Labour often displayed a radical heritage in its usurpation of Liberalism; many of its policies and ideas emerged from and formed part of the progressive movement of the late nineteenth and early twentieth centuries.[32] But any attempt to detach contested political reasoning from social place and class relations constitutes an artificial distinction, as Chris Williams has shown with regard to Rhondda.[33] If official Labour and Liberal policies were frequently indistinguishable before 1914, as was often the case, then what exactly was the initial appeal (or point) of independent labour representation?[34] Similarly, if Liberal associations sometimes showed willing to assume worker-friendly policies, and in some areas adopted worker candidates, then it was equally apparent that many Liberal elites and members did not want (and refused) to be represented by a member of the working class.[35] Subsequently, we should not lose sight of Stefan Berger's observation that 'the Liberal Party was becoming more and more of a hybrid' long before the outbreak of the Great War, suggesting that the progressive policies of New Liberalism should not let us forget the 'substantial parts of the Liberal Party [that] had more in common with the Tories than with Labour'.[36] Furthermore, for Labour to progress it also had to appeal to those sections of the working class previously attracted to Conservatism or repulsed by radicalism and/or Liberalism. Thus, if class by itself will never explain the Labour Party, to remove it from the equation is to remove the party from the social and political context in which it emerged; to place Labour too squarely in the radical tradition is to ignore the broader political beliefs and social preconceptions that the party had to compete against, absorb, and develop.[37] Accordingly, Labour grappled with such complexities throughout the interwar period. On the one hand, the party endeavoured to present its vision of a fairer and more just society to the British people, using imagery and language to shape identities and construct a social-political alternative (to 'make socialists'). On the other hand, the expressions, methods and priorities of Labour's mission were informed by and reflected the varied lives of those people who made up the local party branches and comprised their affiliates, as well as by the trade union, socialist and 'progressive' leaders who directed the PLP and NEC.

It is not intended here to pursue further the relative merits of a class- or non-class-based interpretation of Labour's development in the pre-Great War period. As outlined above, the Labour Party had established itself by 1914, but cannot thereby be seen as the guaranteed usurper of the still-powerful Liberals. What does seem to be certain is that the events and context of war helped Labour's advance, and they did so for a number of reasons. Though the party incorporated a wide range of opinion within its ranks, including both pro- and anti-war sentiment, it retained its underlying unity throughout the period of conflict, presenting itself at all levels as the defender of the workers' interests.[38] This contrasted with the serious divisions that wrought the Liberal Party apart during the war and, simultaneously, allowed Labour both to participate in and criticise government policy. While Liberal points of principle were rode roughshod by the war, Labour's less defined ideological basis – born more from a pragmatism and desire for worker representation than from any specific theory, socialist or otherwise – adapted itself to the circumstances of the time. This, in turn, allowed Labour to gain experience in office as part of the government coalition, with Labour members co-opted as a necessary means of keeping the trade unions (and their members) committed to the war effort. In the process, Labour's political perspective notably broadened, thereby enabling it to emerge as a feasible *national* substitute to a Liberal Party that had led Britain into war and fractured in the midst of it. In the wake of four years' hardship, Labour arguably surfaced as a viable and 'new' alternative to the old order, though such a position would have to be nurtured if it was to bring the party any long-term gains.

The Labour Party profited too from certain social-political by-products of the war. Most obviously, state control of key industries underlined important benefits to trade unions and workers alike, not least the miners.[39] The 'efficiency' of the wartime economy gave a legitimacy to the concept of 'common' or 'national' ownership, something that could appeal to trade unionists whether or not they subscribed to notions of socialism. At the same time, greater state intervention in industry – in the shape of workplace discipline, a legal freeze on industrial action, the 'dilution' of labour and fixed wage rates – prompted an increase in trade union membership, worker expectation and rank-and-file militancy. As should also be well known, there were regular instances of social unrest and public disillusionment during the hostilities in response to the Zeppelin raids, food shortages, price rises, rent increases and the unfolding horror of the war itself. State intervention ensured that rents were fixed and that profiteering was severely limited; political responses served to counter economic concerns. Ultimately, therefore, the Great War directly and greatly affected the British people at home and at the front. Given that it was the broad ranks of the British working class who suffered most, it is not unreasonable to assume that previously held convictions, loyalties and perceptions were at least challenged by the experience. Arguably, too, it brought the British working class more clearly under the umbrella of the 'nation', cutting across certain intra-class divisions and paving the way for a 'land fit for heroes'. Though the coalition victory of November 1918 allowed Lloyd George his election success, it similarly preceded an intense period of industrial militancy and further Labour Party advance as the country tried to return to the 'normality' of peacetime in a world that had changed irrevocably.[40] Conversely, of course, such national affinity may well have helped the Conservative Party maintain and win working-class support.[41]

If the events of 1914–18 provided a context, or 'space', into which Labour could progress, then the party had necessarily to adapt itself to the changed situation. This it did, in part, by withdrawing from the coalition government on 14 November 1918 (within days of the war's cessation), restructuring its organisation, adopting a new constitution, and formulating a distinct party programme. It also set its sights on those newly enfranchised men and women given suffrage by the 1918 Representation of the People Act, the majority of whom were believed to be working class. We shall look at the ramifications of these decisions in the following chapter. First, however, let us briefly outline the nature of Labour's organisation, the basis of the party programme that would become known as *Labour and the New Social Order*, and the question of franchise.

The Labour Party's organisation is best understood as a series of linked but distinct sections. From 1900, the LRC and then the Labour Party comprised affiliated trade unions and socialist societies (including the ILP), the aims and policies of which were devised through a system of delegates appointed to a national conference in relation to the size of their respective organisation. Within such an arrangement, the trade unions were clearly dominant. The LRC had been instigated on a trade union initiative; their mass memberships and block vote dwarfed that of the ILP and the other smaller party affiliates. Only in 1918 did the party constitution facilitate the formation of divisional parties at constituency level open to individual members, and these too affiliated to the national party and sent delegates to conference in accordance with their membership. Still, the trade union delegations continued to outnumber greatly those of the divisional parties and socialist societies. Even so, as David Howell has noted, each delegation brought with them a variety of traditions, cultures and priorities dependent on the geographical, economic and social peculiarities of their origin. All, however, subscribed to a basic notion of internal democracy and participation in the decision-making process.[42]

The central party organisation then extended to the PLP, consisting of all Labour MPs inside the House of Commons. Established in 1906, the PLP elected its own executive committee and chairman, and retained a degree of autonomy from the bulk of the wider party. Such a premise had been established by the first PLP chairman Keir Hardie at the 1907 party conference, where it was decided by 642,000 votes to 252,000 that although conference decisions were binding on Labour MPs, 'the time and method of giving effect to those instructions be left to the party in the House, in conjunction with the National Executive'.[43] This was ambiguous, but the general principle was reaffirmed in 1918. The new constitution declared that 'it shall be the duty of the party conference to decide, from time to time, what specific proposals of legislative, financial or administrative reform shall receive the general support of the party, and be promoted, as occasion may present itself, by the National Executive and the Parliamentary Labour Party'. Though conference sovereignty was clearly implied, the PLP was nevertheless instructed to 'give effect *as far as may be practicable* to the principles from time to time approved by the party conference' (my emphasis).[44] Moreover, the constitution went on to state that authority was only granted to a conference decision ratified by a two-thirds majority vote, thereby adding yet another qualification to policy adoption. In this way, the ambivalent relationship between the PLP and conference continued, with the parliamentary party developing its own traditions and identities amidst the changing contexts of the post-war world. Consequently, PLP or NEC defeat on policy at conference did not thereby lead inevitably to a change in the party's programme.

Overseeing Labour Party affairs between conferences and acting as a link between the PLP and the affiliated organisations was the NEC. This was elected by conference, although its more 'hands on' role in the day-to-day life of the party meant that it too 'acquired its own resources and established its own autonomy'. Accordingly, the NEC soon developed what Howell has described as a 'tutelary' relationship with the party, tabling resolutions at conference and co-ordinating the agenda.[45] In so doing, it retained an authority over the party conference, something that would sometimes lead to tensions within the wider party organisation. In adjunction, a Scottish Advisory Council (SAC) was established in 1914–15 to oversee Labour organisation north of the border. This retained a nominal autonomy from 1919, with its own secretary and sanction to discuss Scottish-related policy.[46]

At a local level, the Labour Party had developed primarily around already established trades councils, although a number of Labour organisations simultaneously existed in the form of Labour Representation Committees, local Labour parties and similar. These, like the national party, were initially federations of trade unions and socialist societies, and they functioned mainly as election committees prior to 1918. More often than not, the respective unions, socialist societies and trades councils retained their own organisational structures and carried out their own activities, co-operating only during municipal and parliamentary elections. Because of this, the ILP was able to cultivate its own special place within the Labour Party, propagating socialism and acting as a channel through which many prominent Labour leaders entered the party. In areas where trade unionism was weak and fractured, particularly in Scotland and parts of Yorkshire, the ILP effectively was the Labour Party to all intents and purposes. Consequently, the ethical socialism espoused by the ILP in countless rounds of lectures, meetings and publications across the country formed an integral part of Labour's identity up to and throughout the 1920s. Generally, however, Labour's structure was extremely loose, allowing a wide range of opinions and perspectives to coalesce around the basic objective of electing independent labour representatives to governing bodies locally and nationally.

Looming over all of this were the mass ranks of the Trades Union Congress (TUC), or – at least – those unions affiliated to the Labour Party. As noted above, the party structure ensured that the large industrial unions dominant in the TUC similarly formed the majority of the Labour membership, a fact reinforced by the conference vote being commensurate with the size of the affiliated body. At the party conference of January 1918, the unions cast 2,471,000 votes in comparison to the socialist societies' 48,000 and the local parties' 115,000. This had obvious repercussions with regard to votes on policy and the composition of the NEC, both of which reflected the unions' financial and numerical support for the party. Yet, as the German socialist Egon Wertheimer noted in 1929, what was striking about Labour was the extent to which the party, particularly the PLP, appeared to act independently of trade union domination.[47] While the unions could and did shape much of the culture of the Labour Party, while they constituted the bedrock of the party's support, and while they could act as a restraint on the party leadership, the PLP developed a distinct identity and retained a decisive influence over Labour's political development. How was this so?

For Lewis Minkin, the 'contentious alliance' between Labour and the trade unions was sustained by an evolving system of custom and tradition, of mainly unwritten 'rules' that 'embodied an acceptance of the permanent differentiation of functions and spheres – the political and the industrial'. Even in the 1920s and 1930s, certain trade unions (and trade unionists) retained an ambivalence towards the 'political', something that could be traced back to an innate distrust of the state and a history of self-reliance that formed the basis of British trade union development. The right to free collective bargaining – to an equal say in labour affairs – lay at the heart of trade unionism: political action was generated by threats to such a claim. At the same time, overt political loyalties could serve potentially to threaten the basic unity of the unions' objective, hence the lack of a specific Labour programme following the formation of the LRC in 1900. With the creation of a PLP in 1906, the distinction between the industrial and political was set, although the evident links between the unions and the party engendered a series of tensions and uncertainties that would inform Labour's progress throughout the twentieth century.

Generally, however, the TUC would continue to prioritise the industrial interests of its members during the interwar period, falling back on its traditions of unity and loyalty at times of would-be political division. In so doing, the TUC safeguarded its own points of interest, asserting its right to act independently within the realm of industrial relations. Simultaneously, it respected the Labour Party's need to prioritise and act within a political context, thus enabling the party, NEC and PLP to exist beyond the realms of trade unionism. Together, this formed a 'powerful, if ambiguous, demarcation of spheres which fed into the bloodstream of the [labour] movement and underpinned the values and rules of the union–party relationship'.[48]

A loose, federated structure had served Labour relatively well prior to 1914. Nevertheless, the social, political and economic changes affected by the war prompted a realignment of the party's organisational basis. Labour's new constitution – devised in 1917 and adopted on 18 February 1918 – was intended to establish the party as a national organisation, more uniformly structured but with a broader electoral appeal. Its principal architect was Arthur Henderson, party secretary from 1912, and it was designed to open Labour up to those outside of the trade unions' ranks, to all members of the working class and beyond. Accordingly, provisions were made for individual members to join the party and for divisional parties to be founded at a local level. These, in turn, were to include individual women's sections formed in recognition of the extension of the franchise to most women over 30 and the wartime increase in female trade unionists. As such, every parliamentary constituency was supposed to house a Divisional Labour Party to which trade union branches, socialist societies, co-ops and individuals could affiliate. Where divided boroughs existed, a Central (or Borough) Labour Party was formed to which divisional parties affiliated. Thus, to take one example, the Labour Party in Leeds was reorganised in April–May 1918 to comprise a Leeds City Labour Party to which six constituency parties were affiliated. These divisional parties then established ward parties formed in accordance with municipal electoral districts, each with the same structure as the larger party organisation. But although such changes were, in part, designed to signal Labour's emergence as something more than a parliamentary pressure group for the TUC, the dominant trade union influence was simultaneously reinforced by changes to the party's NEC.

The NEC had previously comprised sixteen members, eleven of whom represented the trade unions, three the affiliated socialist societies, one the trades councils, women's and local organisations, and a treasurer. After some debate, the NEC was expanded to 23 in 1918 to include thirteen representatives from the affiliated extra-party sections, five local party members, four women, and the treasurer. Not surprisingly, the affiliated positions were occupied predominantly by trade unionists, although Fred Jowett regularly represented the ILP and Sidney Webb the Fabian Society for much of the 1920s. While the unions could have taken all thirteen positions, due recognition was given to the role played by the socialist societies within the party; a piecemeal but significant concession that followed the abolition of separate socialist representation. More pointedly, the 1918 constitution ensured that the members of each NEC section were no longer elected directly by those they claimed to represent. Although the divisional parties could nominate candidates for the NEC, they were elected by the Labour conference as a whole; that is by the trade unions, whose delegates continued to make up the bulk of those in attendance. With regard to the NEC's female members, any affiliated body could nominate the women's representatives – one of many examples by which the interests of Labour women were circumscribed by the wider party – ensuring again that the unions exerted the deciding influence.

Historically, the constitution adopted by the party in 1918 has become famous for its commitment to 'secure for the producers by hand and by brain the full fruits of their industry, and the most equitable distribution thereof that may be possible, upon the common ownership of the means of production and the best obtainable system of popular administration and control of each industry and service'. In other words, Labour could be described – for the first time and by those who wished to do so – as a socialist party. Yet, the importance of clause four *at this time* should not be exaggerated. True, the Russian revolution had caught the imagination of some, and the impact of the subsequent Bolshevik revolution had convinced Henderson of the need for a parliamentary socialist alternative to Lenin's professional revolutionaries. But while clause four related to the Fabian influence of Sidney Webb and Labour's desire to mark a clear distinction between itself and the Liberal Party, it did not thereby turn Labour into a definite socialist organisation; its ideological basis remained broad over the 1920s. Indeed, nationalisation was an acceptable policy to many erstwhile Liberals and non-socialist trade unionists within the party.[49] The miners had begun to call for such a policy over the course of the 1890s, and the TUC had itself drawn up a 'wish list' of nationalised industries by the first decade of the twentieth century. The 1908 Labour Party conference had already committed Labour to the state ownership of the railways and, by 1912, to the mines, both at the bequest of the respective unions. From such a position, the adoption of clause four related as much to long-held trade union interests (confirmed by the experience of the wartime economy) and to notions of 'efficiency' and collective bargaining as it did to socialist ideology. Crucially, however, it married trade union objectives to a defining socialist aim in a formula acceptable to both; the trade unions could now use the label of socialism on their own terms.

Actual Labour policy was outlined in *Labour and the New Social Order*, 27 associated resolutions which were adopted at a further Labour Party conference held on 26–8 June 1918. Drawn up largely by Sidney Webb, the programme outlined the 'four pillars of the house of tomorrow' designed to form the basis of Labour's future vision: the establishment of a national minimum, the democratic control of industry, the revolution of national finance, and the redistribution of surplus wealth for the common good. In other words, Labour committed itself to full employment and widespread social reform, to the nationalisation of coal, the railways, electricity, land and liquor, to progressive taxation and a capital levy to pay off the national debt, and to the redistribution of wealth. In such a way, the 'new social order' envisaged by Labour was to emerge from state-enacted reform passed by a democratically elected Labour government. Though alternatives were around at the time – guild socialism within the Labour Party, broadly syndicalist and Marxist approaches outside of it – these were given short shrift by the party centre. Accordingly, Webb's basic model of Labour's 'parliamentary socialism' was initiated in 1918.

The adoption of such a programme was important. Prior to the Great War, Labour's alliance with the Liberal Party, not to mention the increasingly collectivist, state-interventionist policies of New Liberalism, had raised concern among some in the Labour Party that its own identity was being undermined. For many in the ILP, socialism was being buried beneath piecemeal Liberal compromise. Most notoriously, Victor Grayson stood and won as an 'independent socialist' candidate at the Colne Valley by-election of 1907 against the wishes of the NEC, his motivation stemming from Labour's reluctance to take a more combative position towards the Liberals. In similar fashion, Ben Tillett's *Is the Parliamentary Labour Party a Failure?* (1908), along with George Lansbury's resignation in 1912 over the PLP's compromise on the question of women's suffrage, were two further public manifestations of such dissatisfaction. Partly because of this, *Labour and the New Social Order* was a necessary component of Labour's coming out from the shadow of Liberalism and establishing its own 'ideological base', as Henderson described it.[50] Admittedly, on certain questions, including Ireland, free trade, land reform and social provision, the perspectives of the Labour Party and progressive Liberalism continued to remain close even after 1918. But *Labour and the New Social Order* endeavoured to articulate the differences between an emerging Labour socialism and a pre-established Liberalism, giving substance to Labour's political and ethical objections to capitalism while simultaneously offering an alternative. Indeed, it should be remembered that although the two parties had sometimes shared common policy, they often came to their conclusions from different starting points (as with the 'cheap loaf' of free trade). From 1918, Labour began to clarify such distinctions while absorbing that which continued to correspond to Labour's social-political vision.

Still, Labour's conception of socialism remained fluid. Just as the Labour Party was a coalition of affiliated unions and socialist societies, so its basic ideology encompassed a combination of priorities, concepts and perspectives that shifted over time. Given the structure of the party, it eventually articulated a socialism that conformed to – or could be interpreted as conforming to – trade union priorities. Officially, at least, it centred on the reorganisation of industry and the administration of wealth, with the commitment to public ownership being formulated in a way acceptable to the trade unions. At the same time, Labour continued to reference the didactic aspirations of its forebears, drawing on a range of often overlapping religious, radical and early socialist traditions. In such a way, 'socialism' arguably became a unifying *symbol* for the Labour Party from 1918, with the detail of its implementation and extent remaining open to interpretation at least until the 1930s. At its base, it could be defined as the independent representation of labour, the right of working people to participate in the shaping of their everyday lives. This, in turn, was envisaged as a collective response to social-economic circumstance and articulated in the notion of common ownership. Into this, the ILP helped inject a moral dimension that imbued Labour ideology with a distinctly ethical spirit. By the 1920s, it had become a parliamentary socialism, in which the state was acknowledged as the principal agency through which a practical government policy could be pursued. In the 1930s, the concept of a planned economy based on national boards of industry formed the bedrock of Labour's socialist objective. More widely, perhaps, socialism remained an abstract concept for many Labour supporters: it was that which was different to capitalism (yet another abstract term that implied low wages, poor working conditions and unemployment); something reaffirmed by the Tory insistence on labelling Labour the 'Socialist Party'. This is not to suggest that Labour members, leaders and intellectuals did not develop distinct ideological or political positions, but that these were drawn from a variety of sources, from the fluid political debates of the early twentieth century, and were never set into a rigid theoretical doctrine endorsed by the party as a whole.[51] In other words, Labour encapsulated a series of 'socialisms' that conformed more readily to a set of values, assumptions and instincts than to a comprehensive social-political theory akin to Marxism.

Taken very generally, Labour socialism associated itself with notions of 'justice', 'equality' and 'social improvement', an ethical socialism that asserted a moral certainty most closely equated with the ILP. The emotive appeals of socialists such as George Lansbury were very much informed by the inequities of capitalism and the promised even-handedness of a 'New Jerusalem'. Here, an emphasis was put on the transformation of social mores: the 'making of socialists'. This, on the one hand, placed socialism within the progressive tradition. Conversely, however, for those socialists who believed principle rather than expediency was the key to Labour progress, it meant that there could be no truck with an outdated and compromised Liberalism still tied to existing class, property and market relations. Moreover, many a Labour member's commitment to socialism and/or the party stemmed from a rejection of the poverty, toil and degradation into which they and others were born in the late nineteenth and early twentieth centuries. It was this that bred in them a desire to change themselves and society for the better; and it was this that was understood and accepted across the broad ranks of the labour movement.

Very often, the 'moral' strand of Labour socialism was notable for its religious foundation.[52] In particular, Labour support frequently found expression in nonconformist areas, although this should not obscure the wider religious and secular traditions that informed the party's development. Nor should it suggest that nonconformist chapel-goers became 'natural' Labour supporters. Many chapels and congregations retained an antipathy to Labour. As Peter Catterall has noted, 'the chapels may not have been generally Labour in sentiment, [but] they often provided a particularly good training ground for Labour politicians'.[53] In the case of Peter Lee and Jack Lawson, Methodist leaders of the Durham Miners' Association (DMA), socialism was an extension of their religious convictions, an ethical and communal ideal morally superior to the self-interest that informed Liberalism and Conservatism. From this came their belief in a municipal socialism that prioritised a collective response to the wider needs of society. A Labour administration, Lee promised in relation to the Durham County Council, 'would do collectively what had been before left to the individual'.[54] In such a way, religion and socialism often combined in the chapel or church to forge Labour members' wider social-political beliefs and expectations. Reverend Lang, in a speech to the Newport Labour Party in 1925, deliberately evoked the 'brotherhood of man' when he defined his socialism as 'an inherent right to equal opportunities … the placing the highest possible on human life [sic]'.[55] The secretary of the Coventry Borough Labour Party, George Hodgkinson, believed that 'Christ had socialism in him'; Alan Yates, a party member in Hampstead in the late 1930s, felt that there was little difference between 'a Christian outlook' and 'a Labour Party outlook'.[56] Wesley Perrins recalled the labour movement in the Black Country as being 'very largely a Christian crusade'.[57] More famously, perhaps, Philip Snowden's socialist morality, temperance and evangelical approach to public speaking were greatly informed by his religious beliefs, hence his lecture 'Socialism and the Sermon on the Mount'. Clearly, religious influences were absorbed and expressed in a variety of different ways across the party. If Arthur Henderson had from an early age been an active Wesleyan, then the political convictions of George Lansbury and Sir Stafford Cripps stemmed primarily from their Anglican Christianity. For John Wheatley, his socialist faith extended from his Catholicism.[58]

Simultaneously, of course, socialism was also expressed as a far more ideologically complex set of beliefs. Keir Hardie, speaking in 1894, suggested that socialist thought would develop from a reading of the New Testament, Carlyle, Ruskin, Mazzini, Blatchford and Hobson – a veritable mix of Christianity, Liberalism and humanism.[59] From similarly eclectic sources, Ramsay MacDonald conceived his socialism as a form of society that would develop organically, emerging from a capitalism that had 'ripened into a higher form of trade organisation'.[60] This was both teleological and gradual; socialism was a by-product of the moral ascent of humankind, the 'stage which follows Liberalism'.[61] MacDonald and Snowden in the ILP, along with Sidney Webb's Fabian Society, did much to develop Labour's approach over the first quarter of the twentieth century. This was – taken very generally – gradualist, collectivist and informed by the winning of existing state institutions to the cause of Labour. Socialism was to be introduced legislatively by degrees along an inevitable path of progress. Most importantly, it reconciled the objective of socialism with the piecemeal demands of the trade unions, thereby cutting across the obdurate outlook of the ILP's more staunchly ethical socialists and distinguishing Labour within the progressive milieu in which MacDonald, Webb and others were active. Yet, there remained clear differences between each of the aforementioned Labour theorists' worldview; a cohesive and accepted Labour socialism continued to be ill-defined.[62] For example, vagaries and inconsistencies were evident in Labour's conception of the state (both under capitalism and socialism), of its national and class interests, and as to what constituted the private and the public sphere.[63]

The overtly revolutionary theories of Karl Marx had only a limited impact in Britain.[64] Even so, the socialist emphasis on the inequalities and inefficiencies of capitalism, the basic LRC objective of independent labour representation, and the worker-based composition of the party, necessarily meant that Labour socialism was infused with a class dimension, as Hardie had always been aware. Again, this should not be read in too 'fixed' a way. Within such a paradigm, Labour socialism could be both patriotic and internationalist, pacifist and aggressive, ethical and pragmatic, class exclusive and socially inclusive.[65] Generally, however, Labour gathered its support and constructed its identity out of existing forms of working-class organisation.[66] Labour's political priorities – particularly at a local level, where they were based on issues of housing, employment, health and education – related directly to the lives, experiences, fears and aspirations of British working-class families. In the words of one young activist's father, it became for many 'a natural thing for a working man to be, is Labour'.[67]

Such ambiguities were evident in the extent to which the trade unions came to accept a socialist identity in the interwar period. This proved to be a protracted process, as there remained many within (and without) the trade union movement who retained suspicions of such (middle-class) intellectualism – J. H. Thomas being perhaps the most notorious.[68] To this effect, industrial and political questions were often considered on a practical 'right or wrong' basis: to what extent did a policy benefit the interests of working people. From the affiliates of the TUC, however, Labour socialism absorbed the principles of unity and pragmatism that informed the trade union movement and stood in contrast to the fissiparous nature of Britain's socialist societies. This, in turn, often served to stifle more radical conceptions within the party, but it brought to bear a resilience that could stand strong in the face of adversity. By the 1920s, therefore, many trade unionists accepted socialism as being synonymous with policies favourable to working people. In the words of Jeremiah Wooley, a Weavers' Union official from Preston, socialism represented a system in which 'a man should have work … he should be paid for his work … he should have a decent house … he should have clothes fit to wear, and … he should have a little spending money in his pocket'.[69] More than this, trade unionists such as Bevin saw socialism as a means by which his biographer has summarised as ensuring 'a change in the status of the worker, the end of exclusion from responsibility, the stigma of inferiority'; all of which was deemed integral to the improvement of industrial relations.[70] Though often regarded – disparagingly, intellectually and subjectively – as more 'labourism' than 'socialism', such an ethos defined what Labour socialism meant to many within the party ranks and to many of the voters to whom it appealed.[71]

Ultimately, of course, Labour politics informed and were informed by the social-economic and cultural circumstances of the time, by the interplay of 'formal' party politics and the 'practical' politics of everyday life.[72] The party's appeal was always set against people's wider concerns, interests and conceptions; against their family, work and neighbourhood relationships; against their interest or not in the party political. Though difficult to quantify, we have at least to bear in mind those people whose vote for (or against) Labour was but a minor part of their wider experience, whose political choice revolved around a single issue or a very generalised conception of what a party stood for; maybe even a like or dislike of a particular candidate. For Labour to progress, its policies – its socialism – had to have a resonance, and the party's advance depended partly on the extent to which it connected with and reflected people's insecurities, aspirations and self-perceptions. This meant appealing practically and emotively. Thus, the very successful Bermondsey Labour Party explained its objectives in the following way:

> Individually, we are hopeless to protect our health, to secure our life, to dispose of our dust and house refuse, to get rid of our sewage to ensure a pure and abundant water supply, or to obtain decent and proper housing. All together, acting as an organised community, utilising the resources of all for the benefit and service of each, we can provide all these things and we can make life fuller and richer and happier for everyone … every time you approve of these beneficent schemes you approve of socialism.[73]

For many others, Labour's appeal was more overtly materialistic. The Norwich Labour councillor, H. E. Witard, approached the electorate in starker class terms: 'Workers! Vote for yourselves by Voting for Witard'. He then made very simple comparisons: 'The landlord wants big rents for little houses … [and] the employer wants long hours for short wages … The worker wants big healthy houses for low rents and higher wages for shorter hours'.[74] This may seem crude, but Labour's electoral identity was arguably constructed more by such 'common-sense' reasoning than the theories of party intellectuals such as Cole, Dobbs, Tawney and

Webb. Labour's advance depended on showing that its socialism applied directly to the experiences of everyday life. Furthermore, such an approach suggests that the credibility of the people delivering Labour's message was an important, though not dominant, factor in Labour's development. A suspicion of (middle-class) intellectuals has already been noted, but there also remained a resistance in some areas to the almost self-righteous appeals of Labour's ethical socialists, to which the more forthright, patriotic or 'earthy' approach of members such as Thomas, Will Thorne, Jack Jones or Will Crooks became a possible antidote. Here, Labour's connection with the working class was forged through the collectivist impulses of the public house, football ground, betting shop and patriotic pride, a so-called 'Tory socialism' that stood in contrast to the cerebral concerns of many Labour leaders but often proved integral to the sustenance and extension of Labour's local appeal.[75] Hence, in the words of West Ham councillor Thomas Kirk, writing during the debate over the new Labour Party constitution in June 1918:

> Socialism was not pacifism, neither was it Fabianism with 'superior person' bureaucratic tyranny and government by experts policy … The workers' control of industry would follow naturally upon the realisation of their industrial and political power. Let them see to it that their power is used in coming elections for the establishment of a bona-fide working-class party, and above all let them beware of the intriguing politics and hypocritical middle-class friends of Germany.[76]

To sum up, Labour socialism encompassed a set of values, instincts and assumptions that drew from a wide range of sources and could be expressed in a variety of ways. The mechanics of transforming Labour's ideals into reality were less than certain: Labour unity relied on a broadly agreed objective and a shared dissatisfaction with the inequities of capitalism that cut across people's multiple identities as 'workers', 'men', 'women', 'socialists', 'trade unionists', 'Catholics' and so on. As we shall see, such vagaries allowed Labour to become a relatively 'broad church', but they would also provoke tensions within the party ranks and limit its ability to administrate significant change. And yet, even to begin to construct a 'new social order', Labour needed to be elected into power.

Until recently, Labour's limited progress before the Great War and its advance from 1918 had been linked to the Representation of the People Act. As applied from the first post-war general election, the Act widened the electorate from just 60 per cent of the adult male population to all men aged 21 and over and to most women aged 30 and over. In numbers, an electorate of 7,264,608 (1906) increased to 21,392,322 (1918).[77] Not unreasonably, historians tended to presume that because the franchise had been based on a property qualification it discriminated largely against the working class. Accordingly, the introduction of a broader working-class electorate was thought to have provided Labour with a pool of ready support. Latterly, such tidy assumptions have been challenged. As Duncan Tanner has persuasively argued, not all of those discriminated against pre-1918 were working class, and any suggestion that the working-class vote was 'naturally' a vote for Labour is simply unsustainable.[78] Certainly, the newly enfranchised were a potential source of support for a party whose horizons had expanded by 1918, and it seems fair to assume that amongst a population that was overwhelmingly working class, the *majority* of those disenfranchised were likewise.[79] Pre-war disenfranchisement often tended to be highest in working-class constituencies, as demonstrated in J. J. Smyth's study of Labour in Glasgow.[80] Furthermore, those who were working class and 'first-time' voters would certainly have been appealed to by a Labour Party that saw a workers' family as an integral part of its principal constituency. Political 'loyalties' and 'traditions' were not so ingrained in the formerly disenfranchised, as at least one failed Liberal candidate bemoaned following his defeat in the 1918 general election.[81] Nevertheless, the readiness of the newly enfranchised to vote Labour is debateable and hardly borne out by the party's electoral progress over the interwar period. Concurrently, boundary changes and the end of plural voting do seem to have benefited Labour. Perhaps, then, here is a site of local and regional variation with regard to the impact of such electoral reform? No doubt in certain areas, in certain circumstances, Labour gained most from the extension of the franchise, even if this was by no means a foregone conclusion.

Whatever the different permutations of franchise reform, social change and the appeal of Labour policy, the party undoubtedly made much progress between 1918 and 1923. The following chapter will endeavour to map this development, focusing on the growth of Labour organisation and the party's political response to both national and local concerns. These years were crucial to Labour's eventual eclipse of the Liberal Party, marking as they did the continuation of a shift away from working-class appeals for mere recognition towards a more proactive assertion of the Labour identity. It would, however, take developments throughout the whole of the 1920s to constitute such a recognisable change to Britain's political landscape.

Chapter One

Cultivating Political Space:
The Labour Party, 1918–23

Those who are inclined to blame us and say we stand for class distinction should remember it has been bred in us, not because our fathers had a desire for it, but because the educated and the rich left us largely alone in our village life.[1]

Peter Lee

The dominant note in present day labour work is the return to political effort. For several years, with unemployment non-existent or comparatively so, the trade unions were remarkably efficient in obtaining immediate results. With overwhelming numbers of unemployed, with capital armed with large resource funds and replete with carefully prepared machinery, the power of the strike can only be effective to an uncertain degree, and a growing realisation of this fact will swell the healthy development of the Labour Party.[2]

Edinburgh and District Trades and Labour Council, 1921

The signing of the armistice on 11 November 1918 brought to an end four years of hardship, horror and destruction. Even so, the celebrations, hopes and promises that followed the Great War were to prove short-lived for the majority of British people. A coalition government headed by Lloyd George was quickly elected on the back of much patriotic clamour, but the associated 'land fit for heroes to live in' and return to pre-war 'normality' were to prove illusive. In many ways, Britain was in a period of transformation, with political and economic realignments paving the way for the social and cultural changes that characterised the interwar period. On the one hand, the British political system emerged from the war with its time-honoured configuration in some disarray. The Liberals were divided, the Tories were in a coalition with their traditional foe, a Labour Party backed by a growing trade union movement had moved onto the national stage and, at the margins of Britain's body politic, the revolutionary stirrings of Europe were represented in the formation of the Communist Party of Great Britain (CPGB). On the other hand, Britain's industrial base, established over the nineteenth century on staple industries producing mainly for export (coal, textiles, iron and steel), appeared by the early 1920s to be floundering. Following a brief speculative boom in 1919–20, it became clear that markets had been lost amidst the war, that competition had increased along with production costs occasioned by wartime conditions, and that the pound was no longer the dominant international currency; a problem that would be exacerbated by the return to the gold standard in 1925. In such circumstances, a brief but intense flurry of industrial unrest gave way to simmering tensions and unemployment, to which the extended apparatus of the state struggled to find a solution whilst simultaneously enacting the decontrol of those industries that had come under its jurisdiction during the hostilities. It was, therefore, in such peculiar circumstances that the Labour Party endeavoured to augment its position as a major political force in Britain.

The following chapter will examine Labour's progress from 1918 until the end of 1923, plotting the party's growing parliamentary presence and associated political development. Simultaneously, the emergence of an extended local Labour Party organisation will be placed within the fluid social-political context of the time, before a brief survey of Labour policy will take us to the eve of the first Labour government. As throughout the book, an acknowledgement of regional social-political complexities will, it is hoped, override too generalised reasoning. It is only by recognising Labour's varied character and uneven growth that the party can be readily understood.

I. LABOUR INSIDE THE GATE

A Labour Representation Committee (LRC) cartoon published in 1903 shows a young Labour man, axe raised above his head, standing at the gate of parliament. The parliamentary door, which has been severely splintered, is adorned with the words 'landlordism', 'prejudice', 'low wages', 'rents and royalties' and 'misgovernment'. The picture is captioned 'Labour at the Gate', and clearly symbolises the fledgling LRC endeavouring to force its way into the citadel of governmental power. Three years later, in 1906, a further Labour cartoon shows a similar figure standing on the other side of a parliamentary gate still emblazoned with the five ills that the newly titled Labour Party had been set up to destroy. His axe remains raised, and he is festooned with broken ribbons bearing such words as 'promises', 'red tape' and 'closure'. Before him stand three larger figures, a fat and slightly bloated capitalist in a fur coat and top hat (labelled 'sweating'), a finely dressed landlord in his morning coat, and a monocled Tory Lord in 'monopoly' sash, each looking somewhat condescendingly at the young pretender. The caption – beneath the title 'Labour inside the Gate' – reads: 'The Three: "Well youngster, you've got in, but see how we tie you up". Labour: "You just wait. I still have my axe".'

Fast-forward another twelve years and the sense of mission suggested in such pre-war propaganda would appear to have some substance. By 1918, the Labour Party had not only increased its parliamentary representation, but had actually served as part of the wartime coalition government. At the Great War's end, moreover, the party had severed its ties with both the coalition and the Liberal Party, preparing to go before the expanded British electorate as an independent, national organisation with its sights fixed firmly on power. No longer was Labour to 'co-operate with any party … promoting legislation in the direct interests of labour': it was from here on to construct 'a new social order' of its own making. Accordingly, over the next five years, from November 1918 to December 1923, the party continued to make a steady but significant advance. In purely parliamentary terms, Labour grew from its pre-war 'pressure group' status to national opposition and then minority government in January 1924. Such a rise was unprecedented, altering the nature of British politics forever and helping to constitute the new age of mass democracy.

	Labour	Conservatives/ Coalition	Liberal	Other[3]
1910 (Dec.)	42	272	274	84
1918	57	473	36	141
1922	142	344	115	14
1923	191	258	158	8

Table 1.1 General Election Results, 1910–23

In many ways, such interpretation would appear to bear out the 'inevitability of gradualness' that Sidney Webb defined as Labour's 'scheme of change' at the party conference in 1923.[4] Yet, Labour's progress through the 1920s and 1930s was in no way as smooth as Webb's summation would seem to imply. When examined more closely, Labour's post-war history began far from surely, with the party winning just 57 seats at the election in December 1918 (61 if three unendorsed and one Co-operative candidate are included), somewhat less than anticipated. Furthermore, many of its leading members lost their seats – including such national Labour figures as Arthur Henderson, Ramsay MacDonald and Philip Snowden. To this effect, the Parliamentary Labour Party (PLP) retained its overwhelmingly male trade union bias between 1918 and 1922. All but eight of the Labour MPs elected in 1918 were sponsored by trade unions, and the party's four female candidates were all defeated. Geographically, the PLP comprised just six sitting Scottish members and nine Welsh MPs, with the English contingent being made up primarily of MPs from Yorkshire, Lancashire and the North East. Only four Labour MPs were based in constituencies south of the Severn–Wash line, three of which were located in or around London. In 122 constituencies, the National Executive Committee (NEC) reported, the result was 'so poor as to suggest that success is not likely'.[5] All in all, and despite much expectation and enthusiasm, Labour appeared to have improved its parliamentary position only slightly in comparison with 1910. Any thoughts of government continued to be focused some way in the future.

The 1918 general election result meant that the Labour presence in the House of Commons was limited in terms of both numbers and political ability; a deficiency that was regularly seized upon by Lloyd George and which raised concern within the wider labour movement. Not surprisingly, in an unstable post-war world and amidst significant industrial conflict, criticisms of the PLP's performance became evermore commonplace in the months leading up to the subsequent 1922 election. By as early as May 1919, Henderson had complained to Sidney Webb that the party was 'divided in [its] ranks' and 'leaderless in the House', suggesting that even the principal architect of Labour's reorganisation was not convinced of its 'inevitable' progress in the immediate aftermath of the Great War.[6] Although by-election victories and attempts to bolster the connections between the PLP and the NEC's political advisory committees promised to strengthen the party's position, little real progress was made. The majority of trade union MPs remained passive and sometimes in awe of the prime minister, while others appeared more concerned with their union business than their parliamentary responsibilities.[7]

Fittingly, perhaps, the core of the PLP during this time comprised four moderate, constitutionally committed trade unionists. Though the Labour Party did not have a designated 'leader' before 1922, the PLP chairman from 1917 until early 1921 was the secretary of the Fife miners' union, William Adamson, a man whose impact can be measured by the fact that he would not even receive a mention in the lavish three-volume party history published by Labour in 1948. Amongst the 40 profiles of Labour 'pioneers and founders', Adamson is conspicuous by his absence.[8] As this would suggest, he made a very poor impression on the party's more cerebral commentators, being described at different times as 'respectable but dull witted' and 'innocuous' by Beatrice Webb and G. D. H. Cole respectively. Even in the estimation of his equally forthright parliamentary 'brother', J. H. Thomas, he was simply 'useless as a leader'.[9] As a reputedly dour and uninspiring figure in his late fifties, Adamson proved no match for Lloyd George and surely did much to convince many in the party that a charismatic leadership figure was necessary if the PLP was to achieve all that was expected of it. Even Thomas Johnston, who worked with Adamson in the 1929 Labour government and later painted a slightly warmer portrait of 'Old Willie', described him as 'caution personified with a capital P'.[10] Nevertheless, Adamson was very much of a 'type' within the party, a conservative trade unionist of the 'old guard' who would go on to serve in both of Ramsay MacDonald's future cabinets.

Jimmy Thomas himself was a very different character. Born in 1874, he had worked on the railways from an early age, made his way in the Amalgamated Society of Railway Servants (ASRS) over the early 1900s, becoming assistant general secretary in 1910, before contributing to the formation of the National Union of Railwaymen (NUR) in 1913. By the end of the Great War, Thomas was the NUR general secretary. A skilled negotiator, his successful involvement in the industrial struggles of 1911 and 1919 was to be tarnished somewhat by accusations that he was behind the ruin of the triple alliance in 1921. Even so, he remained a respected, practical and effective trade unionist throughout the 1920s, overseeing his union's loyalty to Labour and safeguarding the sectional interests of his members. Politically, Thomas became Labour MP for Derby in January 1910 in agreement with the Liberals, though his political beliefs and social habits did not readily conform to Labour's supposedly radical tradition. While he proved a consistent advocate of nationalisation, Thomas was an unashamed patriot who supported the Great War and gave his fervent backing to the drink trade. In contrast to many in the PLP, Thomas was a larger than life character, known to be witty, sometimes crude, and a keen drinker, gambler and sports fan with something of a penchant for the fineries that came with social climbing. 'In many respects', he once claimed, 'the workers are even more conservative than the Conservatives', a view that tallied with his own deference to the British monarchy and empire. As such, Thomas was a Labour man for trade union rather than ideological reasons, but an important and charismatic one for all that. Unfortunately (or fortunately, depending on how Thomas's almost music hall style is appreciated), his union activities took up much of his time immediately following the war, thereby limiting his contribution to the PLP.[11]

In February 1921, John Robert Clynes took over from Adamson as party chairman, thereby bringing a slightly more assured, if politically moderate, approach to the Labour chair. It also gave the PLP a figurehead with notable government experience; Clynes had served as food controller during the war. Originally a textile worker from Oldham, he became a full-time organiser for the National Union of Gas Workers and General Labourers in 1891, becoming its president from 1916 and, subsequently, of the National Union of General Municipal Workers (NUGMW) in 1924. Inside the Commons, Clynes represented Manchester North East consistently from 1906 until 1931 (returning in 1935), exuding a patriotic Labour socialism that ensured he retained his seat at the 'coupon' election in 1918. In practice, Clynes was more administrator than leader, a loyal committee man who would keep the NUGMW block vote firmly at the disposal of the party leadership on all but the most specific of issues. In such a way, he maintained important ties between the PLP, NEC and the Trades Union Congress (TUC), becoming a stalwart of the party leadership throughout the interwar period. Again, however, if Clynes' autodidacticism and steadfast ability could earn him respect, his political sensibilities and deliberate amiability were hardly inspirational to all but the most perceptive parliamentary commentators.

Without doubt, therefore, the key figure in the Labour Party generally, and in the PLP from 1919 to 1922, was Arthur Henderson. Henderson was the well-respected party secretary, the architect of Labour's reorganisation in 1918, and the key link between the party and the TUC. Brought up in Newcastle, he became a foundry worker from the age of twelve and quickly made his way in the Friendly Society of Iron Founders, becoming a district delegate in 1892 and its delegate to the TUC in 1894. As an active nonconformist, temperance supporter and skilled unionised worker, his early politics took him into the Liberal Party, hence his appointment in 1895 as agent for Sir Joseph Pease, the Liberal MP for Barnard Castle in Durham. Somewhat ironically, Henderson was soon adopted as a parliamentary candidate for his LRC-affiliated union, a state of affairs that led to his winning the Barnard Castle seat for Labour in July 1903 following the death of Pease in June. He subsequently retained the seat until 1918, having become Labour Party secretary in 1912, and served in both the Asquith and Lloyd George cabinets during the Great War. Because of this, Henderson was arguably the most recognisable member of the PLP following his return to the Commons in August 1919 as MP for Widnes, although illness meant that he was largely absent throughout much of 1920. Moreover, his position as party secretary ensured that he was often preoccupied with the mechanics of the broader party organisation. Throughout his life, Henderson remained a moderate but tough, conciliatory but robust, politician. He was pragmatic, respectable and principled; the epitome of the skilled trade unionist and the man christened 'Uncle Arthur' by his party colleagues.[12]

Very clearly, Labour's progress between 1918 and 1922 was not the product of dazzling parliamentary repartee or sustained pressure mounted from the opposition benches. At the same time, the party's relatively disappointing display in 1918 should be qualified. The 'khaki' nature of the election, in which 'patriotic' candidates were 'couponed' for support, undoubtedly influenced the result, as did the party's running against a combined coalition of Liberals and Conservatives in many constituencies. The pacifism – actual or otherwise – associated with the Independent Labour Party (ILP) stood the wider Labour Party in contrast to the prevailing mood of the time, doing for MacDonald, Snowden and Fred Jowett as well as others whose support for the war effort had been far from equivocal.

Significantly, too, the election was held before many troops had returned from the front, meaning that just over 57 per cent of those entitled to vote were able to do so.

Whatever the peculiarities of the 1918 general election, the result did nothing to deter Labour from its broader mission. Following on from a sub-committee recommendation that Labour enter as many by-election contests as was 'possible' – that is, where support, finance or local political will allowed – the NEC in April 1919 resolved to permit local divisional parties to decide on whether to fight.[13] This was not always feasible; between 1919 and 1922, Labour contested 47 of a possible 81 by-elections. Nevertheless, Labour began to make significant progress from 1919, achieving a series of victories prior to the general election of November 1922. Among these were triumphs in Bothwell (July 1919), Widnes (August 1919), Norfolk South (July 1920), Penistone (March 1921), Heywood (June 1921), Southwark South East (December 1921, with a 39.7 per cent swing), Manchester Clayton (February 1922) and Leicester East (March 1922). In addition, a few erstwhile Liberals, such as Colonel Josiah Wedgwood, joined the PLP over the course of 1919–20. By the dissolution of parliament, the PLP comprised 75 sitting members.

Labour's victories, along with numerous unsuccessful contests, were informed by a range of social, political and economic factors, many of which were peculiarly local. Looked at from a national level, however, Labour's successes were no doubt facilitated in part by a growing disenchantment with the Lloyd George government. Where the PLP offered little in the way of capitalising on the tensions existent within the coalition, the party's extra-parliamentary forces were able to forge a noticeable opposition beyond the Commons. Industrial strife, councils of action, mass demonstrations and unemployed organisation would all become characteristic of 1919–21, before the recession began to stifle such activity and eat into trade union funds and membership. With the economic recovery apparently floundering, Labour positioned itself as the voice of those who suffered in its wake, offering an alternative to the economic insecurity and unemployment that had emerged in many places by the early 1920s.

Domestically, Labour continued to hold onto the baton of free trade and social reform, presenting itself simultaneously as the party of the cheap loaf and welfare provision. Given that the 'land fit for heroes to live in' had failed to materialise by the early 1920s, and with recession challenging the government's spending priorities, so Labour amplified its commitment to house building, healthcare and full employment in the face of Sir Eric Geddes' infamous axe.[14] Crucially, too, government policy conspired to alienate the trade union movement, arguably winning for Labour a number of union members previously unconvinced by the party. For the miners, in particular, the government's rejection of the Sankey report, with its endorsement of nationalisation, was no doubt integral to their political choice, as was Lloyd George's unwillingness to assist the evidently (if unevenly) crisis-ridden industry. Similarly, resort to emergency powers in response to industrial militancy and the rather half-hearted implementation of industrial courts for arbitration served only to rally union support behind the Labour Party and undermine further what was left of Lloyd George's Liberal credentials. With regard to foreign affairs, meanwhile, Labour was able to offer a persuasive critique of the 'compromised' peace settlements, reasserting its claim to be the party of peace, disarmament, and the League of Nations. From such a position, Labour put forward salient criticism of government policy in Europe, Russia, Ireland and the empire, to which much of the NEC's time was dedicated in 1918–23.

Of course, Labour's cause was also helped by the Liberal Party's continued disarray. Even with the cessation of the government coalition in October 1922, several Liberal associations around the country remained hopelessly divided. In effect, therefore, Labour spoke with two voices – one drawing on radical traditions already close to the party but now becoming distant from the divided Liberals, and one offering a new social order based on nationalisation, welfare reform and 'efficient' government. North of the border, the transfer of the Irish vote appears to have been beneficial in a number of instances, particularly on Clydeside where it accounted for twenty per cent of the vote. This brought with it associated tensions, both with the Catholic Church and from local Protestantism, but it also won for Labour an important constituency.[15] Elsewhere, as in Liverpool and parts of Lancashire, the Catholic and Irish vote would also prove important for Labour, but it was never unconditional and was in no way as uniform as has sometimes been supposed.[16] Recent research, too, suggests that generational factors must be taken into account when assessing Labour's emergence in the early 1920s. Younger voters formed a key part of Labour's electorate from 1918. It was they who had been largely disenfranchised in the pre-war period, and it was they who 'came of age' with a Labour Party that could, at times, 'tap in' to youthful idealism.[17] For such younger voters and members, too, Labour values were arguably understood, adopted and articulated in an increasingly secular and assertive manner.[18]

The actual extent to which Labour had advanced over the immediate post-war period was finally revealed at the general election held on 15 November 1922. Ultimately, the withdrawal of the Conservatives from the coalition meant that a Tory victory against a divided Liberal Party and the new Labour challenger was all but assured. Even so, Labour won 142 seats, a total that was more than the Asquithian and Lloyd George Liberals combined. Furthermore, Labour gained 29.7 per cent of the vote (4,237,349), consolidated its main bases of support, and broke new ground in some 86 constituencies. True, 39 of these were in mining districts, but advances were also registered in Scotland, Yorkshire and London. In Scotland, Labour made a clean sweep of the formerly Liberal coalmining constituencies and won ten seats in Glasgow. In Yorkshire, the party registered a net gain of fifteen seats to secure 21 MPs; in London, Labour claimed an improved nine seats, with a further seven in the capital's surround.

Such progress was obviously important. Most immediately, the election of a substantial PLP allowed Labour to establish its parliamentary credentials and confirm its ability to stand independently of the Liberals. With many of its charismatic figures back in the House of Commons, not least Ramsay MacDonald and Philip Snowden, so Labour was soon able to present itself as a more challenging opposition to Bonar Law's Conservative government. As this suggests, the PLP changed in tone and character from late 1922, with MacDonald keen to head a more assertive party in parliament. This was helped by the broader range of Labour MPs elected in 1922; known socialists such as George Lansbury and Fred Jowett returned alongside a clutch of middle-class intellectuals new to the party but deemed essential to the expansion of Labour's appeal. The 86 trade union-sponsored MPs in parliament by July 1923 continued to make up the bulk of the PLP, but the socialists and intellectuals arguably brought with them a wider conception of the party's objectives and capabilities. Notably, however, high-profile Labour women continued to be conspicuous only by their absence. It would not be until 1923 that the first female Labour MPs were elected: Susan Lawrence (East Ham North), Dorothy Jewson (Norwich), and Margaret Bondfield (Northampton).

The change in approach was soon apparent. Within days of the election, the PLP voted to appoint MacDonald as party chairman, a decision that would prove vital to the future history of the party. For the first time Labour had a designated leader, a public figure capable of broadening the party's appeal outside of the House of Commons as well as raising Labour's standard within it. His election was far from unanimous; MacDonald registered 61 votes to 56 for Clynes, suggesting some trade union resistance and a reluctance to remove the man who had, after all, chaired the party during its most impressive electoral performance to date. From here on, however, MacDonald was to become synonymous with the Labour Party of the 1920s, the man most closely associated with the party's objectives and aspirations. Although an intellectual and ambitious politician, MacDonald had begun life in 1866 as the illegitimate son of a Lossiemouth farm servant. Given such a background, his social mobility was fuelled by the autodidactic enquiries of his youth, leading him to Bristol and then London where he undertook clerical work and freelance journalism. Such a trajectory informed his view of socialism as a product of education and reason, though it was arguably his marriage to Margaret Gladstone in 1896 that finally sealed his 'ascension' into the well-connected world of the British middle class. Politically, he had briefly joined the Marx-inspired Social Democratic Federation (SDF) before finding a more congenial home in the Fabian Society and the ILP, from where he became the first LRC and Labour Party secretary from 1900 until January 1912. As party chairman between 1911 and 1914, MacDonald had breathed life into a somewhat lacklustre PLP, before the outbreak of the Great War led him to resign the position in opposition to British participation. On his return to parliament in 1922, therefore, MacDonald appeared temporarily as both a symbol of the socialist left who had opposed the war and a moderate political force able to complement the more pragmatic outlook of Henderson and the trade unions. As importantly, he was a powerful speaker with a rich and expressive oratorical style that commanded an audience. With MacDonald at the helm, the PLP looked at last to have found its voice.[19]

Returning to the Commons with MacDonald was Philip Snowden, a socialist pioneer from West Yorkshire who had encapsulated the evangelical style of the early ILP before being elected to parliament as member for Blackburn in 1906, a seat he held until 1918. He returned in 1922 as the MP for the ILP stronghold of Colne Valley. Snowden was a principled, ethical socialist whose beliefs were informed by his Methodism and a moral rejection of capitalism that was often articulated in a biblical language that invoked a contemporary Sodom and Gomorrah. Capitalist 'competition', he would claim, 'is largely responsible for insanity, suicide, and drinking'.[20] Despite this, he adhered to a reformist, evolutionary concept of social transformation, rejecting any revolutionary solution to the social ills occasioned by capitalism. Conversely, Snowden accepted the trade unions' objective of protecting the interests of their members, but remained critical and suspicious of their sectional concerns, preferring to see changes in the workers' condition as coming from consensual political reform. Though he would end his Labour career amid the acrimonies of 1931, Snowden's brief time as an insurance clerk in the 1880s earned him the role of the party's resident economic expert throughout the 1920s. This, notoriously, combined a belief in redistributive taxation and co-operation with the basic Liberal economic orthodoxies of free trade and balanced budgets.[21] Along with MacDonald's leadership and Henderson's organisational ability, Snowden's financial acumen formed a necessary component of the PLP's leading triumvirate. The three men were neither close nor similar in character, but their respective attributes complemented each other, providing Labour with a credible leadership inside the Commons.

At the same time, the return of George Lansbury as MP for Bow and Bromley added some left-wing bite to the PLP. Born to working-class parents in 1859, Lansbury was a hardened socialist campaigner and Christian pacifist whose principled stand on universal suffrage had led him dramatically to resign his seat in 1912 following the PLP's failure to persuade the Liberal government to implement such electoral reform. Significantly, Lansbury boasted a long career in local government, winning election to the Bow board of guardians in 1892, and to the Poplar borough council 1893. As editor of the *Daily Herald* between 1913 and 1922, he provided a socialist counter to the Labour Party's apparent moderation, while his imprisonment during the Poplar borough council's militant approach to the payment of unemployed relief (see below) made him something of a Labour martyr. But despite occasionally raising the hackles of his more cautious comrades during the early 1920s, Lansbury's popularity throughout the party suggests that his loyalty to the Labour cause was never in doubt. Indeed, on his election to the NEC chair in 1927–8 he revealed his conciliatory tendencies, moving to resolve disagreements as they arose and to defend party unity in the face of ILP and communist criticism.[22]

Beyond Lansbury, the emergence of a recognisable PLP left wing was located most obviously amongst the Clydeside ILP contingent of John Wheatley, James Maxton, David Kirkwood, George Buchanan and the Reverend Campbell Stephen. Seen off from Glasgow station by a large procession of workers amidst choruses of 'Jerusalem', 'The Internationale' and promises of socialisation, the Clydesiders instigated a string of 'parliamentary scenes' staged with deliberate irreverence to legislative procedure. 'We insist on our right to fight and to shock the fine ladies and gentlemen', Kirkwood would write later in 1926, 'and to have as little regard to their old institutions as they had for our mothers'.[23] Consequently, the 'Red Flag' was sung and abuse was hurled in the face of a Tory government that was perceived as the class enemy. This eventually culminated in the suspension of four members of the group in June 1923, following their accusation that the Tories' approval of cuts to local authority health grants was tantamount to murder. Maxton, whose wife had recently died whilst nursing their ill new-born son in Glasgow's Garngad, had directed his charge specifically at the Conservative member for the City of London, Sir Frederick Banbury, and was supported by Wheatley, Buchanan and Stephen amidst uproar across the Commons.[24] But although such tactics brought notoriety to the PLP, the vociferous left wing should not be seen as a viable alternative to the more conventional outlook that informed the party's wider ranks. The left would always remain a minority for whom there was sometimes sympathy but often very little patience.

The changing nature of the PLP was also evident in the composition of its executive from 1923, which included just three principal trade unionists (Thomas,

Adamson and Shaw) and a majority of members coming from ILP or intellectual backgrounds, including Snowden, Jowett, Lansbury, Webb and Morel.[25] At the same time, MacDonald's leadership status gave the party a far more focused parliamentary presence. This would become clearly apparent once MacDonald became Labour's first prime minister in 1924; prior to this, the PLP felt its way towards establishing its own customs and traditions, drawing on trade union notions of loyalty as it endeavoured to retain unanimity within the Commons. Such an approach was of course challenged by the aforementioned 'scenes' instigated by sections of ILP, but the majority of the PLP adhered to MacDonald's lead, seeking to familiarise themselves with 'parliamentary ways' in an attempt to demonstrate Labour's capability. As MacDonald himself insisted in an article of December 1922, the party was endeavouring to 'capture' parliament, not to 'destroy it'.[26] Though the PLP was to assert its opposition to the government, it was to do so by constitutionally acceptable means.

There were, however, evident limits to Labour's advance in 1922–3. Despite its increase, the Labour vote remained concentrated in specific areas, namely in the mining regions and working-class constituencies of certain (but not all) major cities. The progress made in and around London was notable but limited, while Labour support still proved patchy across much of the country. Important working-class centres such as Birmingham, Liverpool and Bristol continued to return no Labour candidates, while most rural and suburban constituencies stayed far beyond the party's reach. Labour hopes for the countryside had been briefly raised with the emergence of rural party organisations and an increase in the membership of the Agricultural Workers' Union towards the end of the war, only for a rural depression to combine with the deep-rooted social-cultural customs of many areas to scupper any potential Labour 'breakthrough'. Tory patronage, local identity and cross-class traditions all tended to hinder Labour's appeal, with many rural parties struggling to survive in the early 1920s. Even where Labour won votes, as in Cambridgeshire, the party initially found it hard to build a sustainable organisation.[27] In counties such as Leicestershire, several of the smaller villages became mini-fiefdoms of the local Conservative Association, complete with Tory women's branches that counted over half of the local female electorate among their membership.[28] Moreover, the logistical problems of covering such disparate areas made the propagation of Labour's message difficult, with only small bands of middle-class sympathisers (and some railwaymen) providing the nucleus of a sustainable party. Transport was expensive and beyond the means of most local parties and members, making meetings, canvassing and campaigning extremely difficult. One local activist in rural Wales summed up Labour's problem succinctly: 'Addressing four meetings after school last week I had to cover over 60 miles in a side-car'.[29] Not everybody would prove so dedicated. Only in certain nonconformist areas, such as North Norfolk, did Labour make any headway amongst overwhelmingly rural populations. As a result, Labour remained in 1922 a 'party based on the votes of the urban working class in certain towns and cities, plus the miners and a handful of others'.[30]

Little had changed by the following year, when Labour found itself unexpectedly involved in yet another general election battle. With the retirement of Bonar Law in May 1923, Stanley Baldwin had replaced him as prime minister only to announce his preference for protection as a means to solving the continuing problem of unemployment. As this contravened a Tory election pledge not to introduce tariffs, Baldwin resolved to dissolve parliament and call a general election for 6 December 1923. Consequently, the election centred squarely on the issue of free trade – a staple of both Liberal and Labour Party policy. In such circumstances, Labour was given the opportunity to campaign on a popular issue close to the party's basic beliefs, but also to do so in competition with a now unified Liberal Party. Accordingly, the result confirmed Labour's progress and paved the way for Ramsay MacDonald to head the first Labour government; but it simultaneously demonstrated the continued presence of Liberalism and the limits of Labour support across Britain as a whole. Despite the undoubted significance of the 1923 general election, therefore, it is necessary to offer some qualifying remarks before examining the ramifications of the first Labour government (see Chapter Two below).

First, Labour won 191 seats, but increased its percentage of the vote by just one per cent, up to 30.7 per cent compared to its 1922 figure. Second, the reunited Liberals won 158 seats and 29.7 per cent of the vote, suggesting that while Labour had overtaken the Liberal Party as the principal alternative to Conservatism, the Liberals were by no means a spent force. There remained many areas of the country, such as in Huddersfield, Halifax, Cardiff, East Wolverhampton, South Shields, and much of Devon, where Liberal candidates continued to garner notable support. Third, Labour appeared only to have made an advance of any real significance in Greater London, where it claimed 37 seats compared to sixteen a year earlier. Though important, there again remained parts of the country, including many working-class areas, where Labour had yet to make much headway.

This is not to underestimate Labour's development from 1918. Indeed, the party could point simultaneously to a general advance in its position at municipal level. Although this would sometimes prove erratic over the course of 1919–24, the first post-war local elections had seen impressive Labour gains. The people of Bradford, for instance, elected Labour as the largest party on the borough council in 1919, where 30 Labour councillors sat across from 26 Liberal and 28 Conservative representatives.[31] In South Wales, Labour took control of Monmouthshire county council and Glamorgan county council in 1919, winning the latter by securing 51 out of a possible 78 council seats. Thirteen Welsh urban district councils were also won for Labour in the same year, many of which – Abertillery, Bedwas and Machen, Brynmawr, Maestag, and Rhondda among them – would be Labour controlled throughout the interwar period (and beyond). In London, Labour first increased its representation on the London County Council (LCC) from five to fifteen (on a council of 124) in March 1919, before the November elections saw Labour's borough representatives win 572 seats compared to just 46 in 1912. Twelve London borough councils came under Labour control, including Battersea, Poplar, Islington, Fulham and Hackney, another two saw Labour emerge as the leading party, and breakthroughs were made in places such as Chelsea.[32] Elsewhere, too, Labour made notable advances or began to break new ground. In Durham, the party took control of the county council; in Sheffield, Labour gained 45 per cent of the vote and claimed twelve councillors; in Manchester, Labour secured a further seventeen council seats; in nearby Salford, where Labour had entered the war with just one councillor in 1914, the party boasted twelve by 1919; in Liverpool, Labour came out of the local elections with twenty council seats; in

Swindon, the local railway workers ensured that Labour won ten council places.[33] Again, such figures should be treated with caution – the turnout was often low, the municipal franchise continued to exclude certain voters (male and female), and the ward boundaries often served to concentrate or fragment support. Over much of the country, however, from Norwich to Preston to Birmingham to Falkirk, inroads were steadily being made.

Significantly, Labour's victories in 1919 were not necessarily decisive; municipal elections over the ensuing three years saw a mixture of gains and losses. After claiming those 30 seats on Bradford council in 1919, Labour representation fell yearly to 22 in 1922, before advancing from thereon until the end of the decade when overall control of the council was secured in 1929. In Leeds, too, the twenty seats held by Labour in 1919 had fallen to just thirteen by 1922. Labour lost outright control of its two Welsh county councils in 1922, although these were regained in 1925, by which time Labour also controlled eighteen urban and one rural district council in South Wales.[34] That said, the London Labour Party continued to make statistical progress in 1920–2. Although Labour won considerably fewer seats at the metropolitan borough elections in November 1922 (259), the party's vote increased from 185,600 in 1919 to 210,700. Similarly, Labour's representation on the LCC increased by just two (plus one extra alderman), but its vote leapt from 54,100 to 194,200.[35] Looked at nationally, every year from 1923 through until 1929 registered a net gain in the number of Labour members elected to represent their respective municipalities.

Quite clearly, Labour's municipal victories of 1919 and its improved performance in the general elections of 1922 and 1923 revealed the extent to which British politics had changed in the years after the Great War. Labour was by the early 1920s an established force; the party had developed to the extent of being considered able to take government office. In MacDonald, Snowden, Henderson, Thomas and Clynes, moreover, the PLP appeared to have an ostensibly cohesive and able leadership. All that remained was for Labour to prove that it was fit to govern.

II. ELEGANT CHAOS: REALISING A PEACEFUL ADVANCE

Let us look more closely at the circumstances in which Labour emerged to realise Ramsay MacDonald's ambition of becoming the main political opposition to the Conservative Party.[36] Taken generally, British politics entered into a period of flux over the course of the Great War, a situation that continued briefly in the immediate post-war years.[37] In the face of such unprecedented slaughter and upheaval, the relative certainties of the previous era were challenged and, temporarily at least, fraught with ambiguity. With the great Liberal Party split in two, with the spectre of communism gaining tangibility in the shape of the Bolshevik revolution, with Europe in ruins and many of its old elites overthrown, and with the social-economic dislocation affected by the war bringing with it widespread industrial and social unrest, so political configurations became somewhat fluid. The extension of the franchise and the advent of what could at last be described accurately as popular democratic politics only added to the potential mutability of Britain's political future. Certainly, it was a combination of Liberal division, franchise reform, and the need to construct a viable alternative to the revolutionary aspirations of Bolshevism that convinced Arthur Henderson to reorganise the Labour Party in the autumn of 1917.[38]

For some, the war had marked the end of the 'old order', paving the way for alternative political ideologies that would range from communism to socialism to fascism to syndicalism to overt nationalism. For others, the eventual termination of the war necessitated a return to normality, to the re-establishment of old certainties and continuities. In such circumstances, all three of Britain's major mainland parties suffered breakaways, realignments or divisions of varying degrees between 1914 and 1922. Most famously, of course, the outbreak of war put substantial pressure on the Liberals. This increased with the need for a 'war of engineers', not least with the coming of conscription. The party then split with Lloyd George's accession to the premiership in December 1916, before falling into two distinct 'coalition' and 'independent' camps at the war's end.

Less dramatically, the Labour Party also encountered disagreement at the outbreak of a war that offended pacifist and socialist sensibilities within its ranks. In the event, the party was able to hold its loose framework together, although it faced further schism following the decision to secede from the coalition in 1918. Such a course of action provoked terse discussion between the PLP and NEC, with Clynes warning that the party would face electoral disaster if it opposed Lloyd George's triumphant coalition.[39] But although Clynes and the bulk of the PLP bowed to the majority decision, the debate contributed to the formation of a National Democratic Party of 'patriotic labour' and the expulsion of four Labour MPs who refused to leave the government. Subsequently, George Barnes (a former PLP chairman) and George Roberts both retained ministerial office in the post-war coalition.

Labour was forced to confront threats from other directions too. In 1918, the possibility of a Trade Union Labour Party was raised by 'patriotic' trade unionists – primarily Crawshay Williams, W. J. Davies and Havelock Wilson – alarmed by what they regarded as Labour's socialist influence. Despite the rejection of such an idea by 3,815,000 votes to 567,000 at a meeting of the TUC in September, the fact that its three leading subscribers were each elected to the TUC's parliamentary committee suggests that it was not total political folly.[40] More durably, the Labour-affiliated British Socialist Party (BSP) constituted the basis for the CPGB that eventually formed in the summer of 1920 and comprised most of Britain's Marxist revolutionaries under its newfound Leninist banner. In its wake, the ILP also discussed affiliation to the Third International established by the Bolsheviks to disseminate the worldwide revolution, only to find the conditions for membership incompatible with its more peaceful and less disciplined political schema.

More surprisingly, perhaps, the Conservative Party faced the challenge of a breakaway Nationalist Party from August 1917. This would prove an irrelevance, but the focus on 'national politics' necessitated by the peculiar circumstances of the Great War and the formation of a coalition government combined to blur previous political distinctions, a development that obviously continued until 1922. Throughout much of the coalition government's existence, moreover, there was on-going talk of the need for a new 'centre party' – placed between the forces of reaction and revolution – gathered behind Lloyd George. In particular, the influx of new parliamentarians in 1918 included a number of younger members, many of whom were ex-servicemen committed to forging a new world in the aftermath of war. Although they had been elected as Conservative, Unionist or Liberal candidates, party labels were largely irrelevant to such patriotic idealists.[41] This, again, came to nothing, but such thinking was indicative of the fluid political circumstances of the time. More generally, Liberals and Tories perceived a common 'socialist' foe in such a period of social readjustment, industrial unrest and continental revolution, with political alignments at both national and local level shifting accordingly.

Though many of these initiatives proved short-lived and are now little more than historical curiosities, such political fluidity helped provide a 'space' into which the reorganised Labour Party of 1918 was able to move. In particular, the disagreements that continued to blight the Liberals following the Great War helped pave the way for Labour to usurp the former party's anti-Tory position. Nationally, the Liberals could be seen as the party that took Britain into war and split in the midst of it; a former champion of progressive reform now led a coalition government dominated by the Conservatives. The Liberals were both divided and, for many, politically bereft. In the words of the South Wales *Christian World*, commenting on the general election of 1922, 'the Liberal quarrel no doubt accounts for much of the landslide, but it is believed that the change has its origins mainly in discontent with the Liberal programme ... [On] the economic side especially, it does not meet the need of the post-war time ...'[42]

Locally, even a cursory glimpse at the surviving minutes of many a local Liberal Association reveals the uncertainties, divisions and contradictions that informed the Liberal Party in the immediate post-war world. From association to association, sympathy for alliances with either Labour or, more commonly, the Conservatives contested with a simultaneous insistence on local Liberal autonomy, confusing and alienating members and voters alike. So, for example, on his resignation as chairman of the Scottish Liberal Federation (SLF) in late 1920, Sir William Robertson described the Liberal Party as an organisation traditionally composed of 'men who held advanced views, moderate views, and what may be described as Conservative–Liberal views'.[43] In so doing, he left a federation that was nominally opposed to the coalition government but unable to retain a unity with which to confront it. By the time of the 1923 general election, the SLF proved incapable of nominating more than a handful of candidates, often facing difficulties in those constituencies where its representatives did manage to stand. Thus, in Edinburgh East, the Liberal candidate J. M. Hogge was opposed by a former vice-president of the local Liberal Association turned Tory, C. J. M. Mancor, who described his erstwhile friends as having 'a soul ... so dead that they prefer their Association before the interests of their country'.[44] Hogge held his seat, but the following year Labour contested the constituency for the first time and won, putting forward Dr T. Drummond Shiels on an essentially progressive platform. Here, as elsewhere, Labour could offer itself as the attractive heir to the progressive politics of pre-war Liberalism and the most viable alternative to Conservatism.

Similar problems confronted the Liberals in England. The Leicestershire Liberal Association was literally split down the middle in its attitude towards the coalition and the prospect of further co-operation with the Conservative Party. Within its ranks were divisional associations firmly opposed to the government and keen to approach the Labour Party with a view to adopting mutually acceptable candidates. Accordingly, the county association's decision in 1921 to endorse coalition Liberal candidates such as Sir Jonathan North was contravened by an annual meeting that voted by 93 votes to 85 against a resolution 'not to disturb' the coalition arrangement. The closeness of the vote says it all.[45]

Such realignments were also evident at a municipal level, where the formation of anti-Labour groups and Tory–Liberal electoral pacts – already evident before the Great War – became evermore common. Even as the national coalition began to strain at a rank-and-file level from 1920, municipal combinations remained. And although the various Moderate, Municipal Reform or Citizens' parties often retained the pretence of being 'non-political', they were typically forged from and sustained by local Conservative and Liberal members keen to represent the interests of property owners, ratepayers and employers. This, in turn, helped further to fragment the local Liberal associations, whose members divided over the language of class politics that sometimes informed such manoeuvres. In Leeds, for example, Liberals and Conservatives co-operated to block Labour's advance between 1920 and 1925, before the Leeds Liberal Federation belatedly withdrew having lost much of its identity and membership in the interim. In Durham, a Municipal and County Federation (DMCF) was formed to 'combat socialism in municipal affairs'. Typically, the DMCF proclaimed itself a 'non-party organisation' whilst boasting as its leading light Lieutenant Colonel Cuthbert Headlam, the Tory MP and/or candidate in Barnard Castle from 1924 to 1935.[46] Such alliances were at once recognition of Labour's progress and a defining moment – or so it turned out – in the future of the Liberal Party. In effect, they drew attention to the common interests of Conservative and Liberal members, while also acknowledging Labour's arrival as the principal political alternative. For many a Liberal voter, a choice had to be made as to where one's sympathies lay. As such, the fluidity of 1914–22 gave way to the polarities of the mid-to-late 1920s, 1930s and beyond.

In response to such developments, Labour and – more generally – the labour movement appeared to mount a significant, if not yet decisive, challenge to the former Liberal–Conservative hegemony of British politics. This occurred in very particular circumstances: in a period of social, economic and political readjustment from war to peace. Ironically, however, given the emphasis that Arthur Henderson placed on reorganising the party along constituency lines towards the end of the conflict, Labour's *initial* strength in 1918–23 lay outside the parliamentary sphere. As we have seen, the 1918 general election did not lead Labour to make the immediate progress that many in the party had hoped for; the PLP remained relatively ineffective prior to 1922. At the same time, the growth experienced by the labour movement during the war was extended in its wake, as a brief economic boom brought with it employment and an expansion of trade union membership. By 1920, the trade unions boasted some 8,253,000 members, representing nearly half of all male and a quarter of all female workers, 4,318,000 of whom were affiliated to the Labour Party.[47]

The financial implications of this undoubtedly benefited Labour's attempts to develop its organisational and electoral base. Although the unions resisted attempts by Labour to establish a central fund and increase subscriptions in 1919–20, the party eventually ensured that the unions' affiliation fee was raised from 2d to 3d per member per annum from 1921, bringing Labour £54,869 in 1921–2, compared to £30,244 in 1919–20.[48] With such increased income, Labour extended its apparatus centrally and across the country. We shall look at the emergence of party branches in the following section. Meanwhile, the central party established a number of standing sub-committees in the summer of 1918 to review and perfect party activity, focusing on: (a) organisation and elections; (b) policy and programme; (c) literature, research and publicity; and (d) finance and general purposes. These were to be appointed annually, contained between seven and eleven members, and were initially headed by, in order, Arthur Peters, J. S. Middleton and Herbert Tracey, with Middleton further overseeing the last.[49] Second, Labour head office was transferred to the TUC building at 33 Eccleston Square, thereby facilitating greater day-to-day contact between the two labour leaderships. It also provided space for a party that was employing a growing number of centrally appointed staff, with some 47 men and women working under the auspices of head office by June 1919. Alongside Arthur Henderson, Jim Middleton (assistant secretary), Arthur Peters (national agent) and Marion Phillips (chief women's officer), a number of organisers, clerks and typists oversaw party work in Eccleston Square, the House of Commons, Scotland and the regions.[50] Though such changes by themselves did not ensure Labour success, they helped strengthen the party's central apparatus and gave Labour the means by which to build its organisational and electoral presence.

Despite the apparent financial and numerical benefits of a burgeoning trade unionism, the upsurge in industrial militancy in 1919–21 brought mixed fortunes for Labour. The impetus for the widespread unrest was varied. On the one hand, the trade unions emerged from the war in a position to demand the reorganisation of sections of the economy, an objective that tallied with Labour's new constitution. The case for nationalisation appeared far stronger following the Great War, particularly with regard to the railways and the mines. From this, and in the context of a post-war world, the trade unions reflected and informed Labour's desire for a 'new social order'. At the same time, the restocking of British industry and overseas demands prompted successful union campaigns for increased wages, improved conditions and shorter working weeks. On the other hand, as Chris Wrigley has demonstrated, the social and industrial unrest of the period was also driven by fear and insecurity. On the industrial front, the unions feared mass unemployment with the return of some five million conscripts and the termination of the 'war economy'. Concerns over changed working practices similarly informed the unions' perspective, arousing a 'justified anxiety as to whether the government would honour its repeatedly made pledge to restore trade union conditions at the end of the war'.[51] As a result, 2,959 stoppages were recorded in 1919–20, amounting to some 61,537,000 days lost to industrial action.[52] Concurrently, union unrest was complemented by broader working-class protests regarding poor housing conditions, food shortages, price increases and profiteering, many of which had gained momentum during the war years. This was clearly evident in places such as Clydeside and London's East End, where Labour's importance arguably related more to its embrace of social concerns than to industrial struggle.[53] As we shall see, housing, welfare, education and health formed the basis of local Labour politics from 1919, thereby healing the divisions of wartime and providing the party with a programme applicable to the principal concerns of many in the post-war period.

Such militancy, along with the heightened and evidently uncertain political climate of the time, could not but have an impact on the Labour Party. Debate over the relative merits of 'direct action' informed party discussion throughout 1919–20, with even MacDonald, during the heady days of 1919, seeming to consider such strategies under certain conditions. 'We must strike industrially with good effect', he wrote somewhat uncharacteristically in his diary in April, only to return to his more typically constitutional position soon after.[54] Indeed, the party did briefly involve itself in 'direct' extra-parliamentary activity, joining in August 1920 with the trade unions to threaten a general strike in opposition to allied intervention in the Russia–Poland war.[55] Consequently, Labour agreed to establish a council of action to oversee and assess British government policy, instigating a series of demonstrations and forming local councils to co-ordinate the workers should they be called upon. To this effect, some 350 councils were formed across the country. Even before this, the 'Hands off Russia' campaign had excited many local parties, prompting members to pass resolutions urging the government to establish full diplomatic relations with Russia and in protest against 'the actions of Poland invading Russian territory'.[56] Most famously, workers on London's East India docks refused to load munitions onto the Russia-bound 'Jolly George' in May 1920; a demonstration of 'direct action' in which David Adams, a Poplar Labour councillor and secretary of the Dock, Wharf and Riverside Workers' Union, took a leading part.[57]

Ultimately, the councils of action established in 1920 proved to be the high point of Labour's dalliance with direct action at a national level. From the end of that year the economy moved into recession, bringing with it the inevitable associated problems. The cost of living index fell from December, wage rates diminished, industrial production declined by 18 per cent to the middle of 1921, exports fell by 30 per cent and unemployment began to rise, reaching nearly 2,500,000 by the summer of 1921. In such circumstances, the trade unions' position was no longer so dominant; membership began to fall and the threat of industrial action proved increasingly ineffective. By 1923, trade union membership had dropped to 5,382,000, while the number of days lost to strike action fell from a high of 85,872,000 in 1921 to 10,672,000. Simultaneously, of course, union finances suffered as income both fell and/or was paid out in unemployment benefit. In the meantime, both the government and the employers moved to economise and reclaim the initiative they had seemingly lost over previous months.[58] Conditions differed across the TUC and the economy generally, but the general mood was one of retreat from the 1921, symbolised most acutely by 'Black Friday', 15 April 1921. As the government instigated its decontrol of the mines on 31 March 1921, so a lockout began that led the mineworkers to call on the support of their partners in the 'triple alliance', the NUR and the National Transport Workers' Federation (NTWF). Formed originally in April 1914, the triple alliance supposedly ensured co-ordinated action on the part of the Miners' Federation of Great Britain (MFGB), NUR and NTWF; indeed, it had contributed to the miners' successful strike action in 1919. In the changed circumstances of 1921, however, the NUR and NTWF chose belatedly to hold back from their promise to mobilise their members in defence of the miners, thereby bringing the period of assertive post-war militancy to an effective close.

The recriminations surrounding 'Black Friday' were bitter, but the more general 'retreat' from direct industrial confrontation was seen by many Labour politicians and trade unionists, including Arthur Henderson, to be in the best interests of the Labour Party. Labour's association with industrial militancy and direct action had tallied with the mood of the immediate post-war months, but it had simultaneously unsettled many of its more moderate members; the militancy expressed at the end of the war could only be tolerated within certain limits.[59] Henderson was explicit in his desire to guide the 'mass movement along the path of constitutional change' devoid of 'violence and disorder'.[60] Thus, if the unity encapsulated in the councils of action could provide succour to Henderson's hatred of war and his vision of fusing the 'two wings' of labour, then the extension of such strategies to the mainstream political arena remained anathema to him. Militancy did little more than alienate potential support, the party secretary believed, and this at a time when Labour's priority was to broaden its appeal and prove its moderation and efficiency. In this, he received ready support from MacDonald, Clynes and others in the PLP, including the Edinburgh Central MP William Graham, who bemoaned in May 1920 the 'harm they [left-wing militants] are doing to the Labour Party'. Such an approach was often deemed counter-productive and, more resonantly, was not seen to 'accord with the temperament of the men and women who make up the great body of our people'.[61]

By the end of 1921, therefore, the more cautious voices within the Labour Party had also become the most dominant. As unfavourable economic conditions ensured that the trade unions began once more to look to parliament as a means of protecting and advancing their interests, so the Labour Party regained the ascendancy within the wider labour movement. Evidently, TUC influence within the PLP and NEC was already extensive. The circumstances of war and the divisions in the Liberal Party had helped consolidate the party–union alliance, with Henderson commenting that such 'close co-operation' was greater in 1917–18 than at any previous time in the party's history.[62] Politically, the TUC parliamentary committee and the trade union representatives on the NEC had been happy to follow Henderson's lead so long as they were consulted on matters deemed to be of interest. Although the industrial unrest of 1919–21 had temporarily diverted the unions' attention, the party records show that close contact was maintained between the PLP, NEC and TUC. Regular meetings were held and discussion was spread across a wide range of issues, from the peace settlements and foreign affairs to industrial and domestic concerns.

From late 1920, Henderson moved to ensure that such alliance was extended further. Monthly meetings between the NEC and the newly formed TUC general council were convened in 1921, while a National Joint Council (NJC) that comprised representatives of the PLP, NEC and TUC general council was instigated to co-ordinate the wider activities of the labour movement.[63] The old TUC parliamentary committee had already come in for criticism by this time, and its replacement by the general council was designed to better direct trade union action and opinion.[64] In addition, a number of 'joint departments' were set up, focusing attention on press and publicity, research and information, and international affairs. For the immediate future, at least, party activity was regularly discussed through the joint departments, NJC memorandums detailed Labour policy, and the Labour Party's election manifestos were co-signed by the TUC chairman and secretary in 1922, 1923 and 1924.[65]

Despite Henderson's best efforts, this relationship was sometimes tense if always underpinned by recognition of mutual need. Certainly, in the early 1920s, even before the Labour Party formed its first government in January 1924, a distinction remained between the political and economic spheres. Leading trade union officials were far more likely to ascend to the TUC general council than to the PLP, and the unions in no way saw their commitment to the Labour Party as a replacement of the industrial struggle. As Ernest Bevin made clear in the third month of the first Labour administration, 'If we rest on the industrial side for one moment, it will be fatal to our progress ... we must therefore go on with the economic war, waging it the whole time, and utilising every available opportunity, on behalf of the class we represent'.[66] Similarly, the TUC proved suspicious of Henderson's attempts to develop joint sub-committees and oversee co-operation with the Fabian Research Department from 1918, no doubt fearing political interference in overtly trade union matters.[67] For the TUC, industrial disputes continued to be seen as the preserve of the trade union involved, with the Labour Party being expected to be supportive at best. In return, the trade unions lent their numerical and financial backing to the Labour Party (and PLP), but left political decisions to the NEC and PLP leadership. Here, the trade unions and their respective MPs could push for their interests to be prioritised, but they claimed no control over the NEC or PLP agenda. And while the trade union block vote made such a relationship apparently uneven, it would be misleading to assume that the party's industrial affiliates formed a monolith. Different unions fashioned different relationships within the Labour Party, revealing different priorities and political perspectives. The federated and diverse nature of the MFGB, the conservative outlook of the cotton unions, the loyal moderation of the NUGMW, and the assertive interventions of Bevin's Transport and General Workers' Union (TGWU) distinguished as well as complemented the Labour Party's trade union basis.[68]

Locally, too, trade union branches began to pay more concerted attention to the fledgling divisional party organisations from approximately 1921, a shift consolidated by the party's relative success in the general elections of 1922 and 1923. Thus, in 1922, the Hornsey trades council wrote to deplore 'the apathy, inactivity, and lack of political sagacity exhibited by the Hornsey Labour Party in not taking steps to enable the workers of Hornsey to vote for a Labour candidate at the last two elections'.[69] More positively, trade union donations to the Norwich Labour Party and Industrial Council increased dramatically between 1918 and 1924, rising from £133/4/10 to £1,392/13/10, by which time all of the city's trade unions had affiliated to its industrial council. In Durham, a miners' party such as that in Houghton-le-Spring was guaranteed financial assistance from the DMA. Even so, the party's income had increased from £35/12/5 in 1918 to £151/14/6 by 1925, primarily as a result of trade union contributions. In Edinburgh, meanwhile, the trades council's special election fund saw a fall in trade union contributions over the non-election years between 1920 and 1922, but increased from £68/9/6 in 1919–20 to £137/1/6 in 1923–4.[70] The only real downside from the Labour Party's point of view was that a focus on electoral activity and all that it entailed (manifestos, canvassing, etc.) did not provide the immediate participatory appeal of an extra-parliamentary campaign. From 1921 onwards, local parties began regularly to note 'a lack of enthusiasm' amongst their members and constituents. This was initially attributed to the trade depression, but was in fact to be a perennial problem for many parties throughout the interwar period.[71]

Clearly, the organisational, financial and numerical basis that the trade unions provided the Labour Party was consolidated between 1918 and 1924. However, Labour needed to gain the support of a far wider constituency if it was to mount a realistic assault on parliament, particularly as union membership began to decline from 1920. By 1924, 3,158,000 trade unionists (from a total of 5,463,000 members of the TUC) were affiliated to Labour, a fall of over a million from its post-war peak.[72] The wartime experience and industrial unrest of 1919–21 had secured Labour support in those areas where it had already made headway pre-1914, but it was essential that Labour recruited votes beyond as well as amongst the organised working class if it was to become a party of national proportions. Accordingly, a variety of strategies, configurations and approaches were apparent across the country, revealing different priorities and attaining different results.

On one important level, Labour's advance depended on its ability to supplant the Liberal Party as the main progressive force in British politics. It was often in former Liberal strongholds, such as South Wales, Durham and parts of Yorkshire, that Labour forged its early 'heartlands'. As noted in the Introduction above, the move from Liberal to Labour was not necessarily a dramatic leap given the ambiguous nature of Labour socialism and the party's radical heritage. Despite representing a variety of traditions, several erstwhile Liberals 'won over' by Labour, including Sidney Arnold, H. B. Lees-Smith, Cecil Wilson, Josiah Wedgwood, Charles Trevelyan and Arthur Ponsonby, strayed little in their basic political beliefs. In Leicester West, the former radical and suffrage campaigner Frederick Pethick-Lawrence won against Winston Churchill in 1924 by appealing to voters as the 'true heir to the Liberal tradition'.[73] Similarly, Noel and Charles Roden Buxton made the journey from Liberal to Labour without any dramatic change in their basic political or ideological perspectives. Their Methodist links proved easily transferable; this, in part, explains Noel Buxton's successful shift from Liberal to Labour member for North Norfolk. Writing in mid-1918, Buxton referred to his general agreement with Labour's 'aims', but simultaneously of his wish 'that Liberal and Labour ought not to split at all'. Soon after the war's end, however, he evidently deemed the Labour Party to be the more suitable vehicle for his own particular beliefs.[74] Yet, while many such recruits became close associates of Ramsay MacDonald, they generally had little contact with the party's trade union (proletarian) elements. It was primarily the Labour Party's adoption and maintenance of a progressive foreign policy that attracted these former Liberals to 'socialism', many of whom had been members of the wartime Union of Democratic Control.[75]

Of course, several Labour leaders and members had previously worked with and/or supported the Liberal Party. Some, such as Arthur Henderson, had transferred to Labour in the context of their union affiliation.[76] During his Widnes by-election victory of August 1919, moreover, Henderson continued to draw on his Liberal heritage, fighting a 'progressive' campaign and openly acknowledging Liberal support.[77] In the case of Arthur Peters, his position as national agent made him integral to Labour's standing a record number of candidates in 1918, yet he also faced criticism from within the party for signing the nomination papers of the Liberal candidate in North Croydon.[78] Not surprisingly, given such on-going connections, concern as to Labour's 'independence' was raised intermittently within the party over the early 1920s.[79] Generally, however, Labour set about severing the 'progressive alliance' in all its possible forms, standing against Liberal candidates wherever possible and resolving in 1921 and 1922 against any pact with the Liberal Party. Though there remained rumours of the two parties coming to some kind of agreement, Labour recognised that its future development depended on the extent to which it could displace its former ally. Where Liberal–Labour ties remained apparent, as in Oxford, Newark and Huntingdon, the NEC sought increasingly to undermine such arrangements.

But Labour's potential appeal did not rest solely on its usurpation of progressive Liberalism; the reorganisation of the party was partly carried out to present Labour as a distinct political and ideological entity. To those committed to socialism, clause four gave Labour a socialist objective that could be interpreted as marking a clean break from its Liberal past. At the same time, it served as a bulwark against the revolutionary aspirations of the CPGB, providing an alternative and more peaceful route to socialism. From a different perspective, Labour had to appeal to disgruntled Conservatives, particularly those whose belief in Tory social reform could be transmitted to Labour objectives, and whose patriotism had an obvious affinity with Robert Blatchford's influential *Merrie England* (1894). Just as the Labour MP for Leeds South East between 1918–24, James O'Grady, could claim himself certain that his 'socialist ideal [was] not in any sense anti-national', so one Tory recruit to Labour (Sir John Sankey) could assume the classless socialism advocated by MacDonald to be of benefit to the national interest. Here was the flipside to Labour's radical heritage, a Tory socialism built on an amorphous and often incoherent set of customs, loyalties and traditions. At a parliamentary level, Martin Pugh has listed 31 notable 'Conservative Recruits to Labour' between 1904 and 1930 (including those from Tory families, such as Attlee and Dalton), the motives of whom varied.[80] Without doubt, these well-heeled individuals brought with them finance, a potentially wider electoral appeal and, in some cases, government experience, all of which complemented MacDonald's conception of the Labour Party. Equally, some would join MacDonald in his journey to National government in 1931, while others – Mosley, Cripps, Strauss and Strachey – could often position themselves on the maverick or far left wing of the party. Although Attlee, Dalton and Cripps would go on to dominance, the majority of those listed by Pugh sat uneasily with their Labour 'identity'.

More importantly, Labour had to assert itself in localities where working-class Toryism was dominant, most obviously in the West Midlands, parts of Lancashire, the south coast, and in areas of London. This could often prove problematic. Given that Labour's political thought owed much to a synthesis of radical Liberalism and moderate socialism, its practical appeal necessitated a more versatile approach towards working-class Conservatism/conservatism. Without doubt, the ingrained morality of much Labour socialism, from temperance to an almost stoic dedication to 'the cause', often sat uncomfortably with working-class priorities and cultural traditions in parts of Britain. Yet, it must be remembered that the trade unionism of men such as Jack Jones, J. H. Thomas and John Hodge was also imbued with a proud patriotism and a conception of 'labour' distinct from Hardie's ethical appeal. Their sense of 'pragmatism' and 'realism' shared something with the Conservatism that they later opposed and did not preclude certain socialist solutions to the problems of the day. Their extra-political lives, like many Labour supporters, comprised the pubs, sports and humorous irreverence so loathed by many of Labour's more cerebral activists.[81] To this effect, political support could come as much from a shared identity, union loyalty or class allegiance as from any distinct ideology; a commitment to independent labour representation did not inevitably entail wider 'progressive' beliefs.

As Pugh, Tanner, Howell and others have shown, Labour often absorbed Tory policies and outlooks in working-class areas where the Conservatives represented the party's main opposition. Thus, in towns such as Preston and Blackburn, 'where Labour recognised that Liberal policies alienated working-class support, Labour backed rate aid for voluntary schools, supported compensation for publicans who lost their licences, and opposed disestablishment'.[82] In and around Birmingham, certain divisional parties adopted erstwhile Tory supporters (Oswald Mosley, John Strachey, Oliver Baldwin), espoused popular patriotism, and secured members' places on local charitable bodies to win over working-class loyalties.[83] Essentially, the party had to reconcile itself to local political and social cultures, the 'nature' of which varied from and within town to town, city to city and region to region. For this reason, Labour could – and did – find it difficult to 'convert' such constituents. For many workers, a suspicion of interfering state legislation, religious divisions, patriotism and parochialism all continued to hinder Labour's generally interventionist, moral appeal. For others, Labour failed to meet their aspirations and remained a socialist 'other' detrimental to their individual interests.[84] Moreover, the Conservative Party proved itself able to maintain much working-class support across the interwar period. Yet, there were places – as in parts of the East End – where Labour could evidently override such preconceptions to present itself as the political expression of the local working-class community.[85]

A similarly versatile approach was necessary with regard to others previously disenfranchised or immune to Labour prior to the 1918 Representation of the People Act. In particular, the party leadership began to target three important sections of the population. First, the extension of the vote to the majority of women aged 30 and over forced Labour to turn its attention towards its female constituents.[86] Officially, Labour stood for sexual equality, though this was typically articulated in a language that suggested and reflected distinctive roles for men and women in wider society, particularly within the working-class homestead. In the words of *Labour and the Nation* (1928):

> The party welcomes the influence of women in politics, not only in the sphere of the social services, where their knowledge, experience and aspirations are indispensable, but in the world of international relations and world peace. Its policy is based on the belief that women have common interests with their husbands, sons and brothers, and that its principles and ideals appeal to citizens irrespective of sex. But it realises also that women are specially concerned with the development of the social services – with care for the mother and infant, for the child and the sick, for the bereaved, the aged and the workless; with the general conditions of home life, and with the preservation of peace.[87]

Subsequently, there was no attempt to give women equal representation on the party's decision-making bodies before or after the Great War. Even so, significant moves were made to incorporate women more securely within the party apparatus following the party's reorganisation in 1918. Thus, women received four seats on the NEC, a National Labour Women's Annual Conference was convened, the Standing Joint Committee of Industrial Women's Organisations (SJC) became an NEC advisory committee, and a number of women organisers were employed from head office to help rally women to the Labour cause. Indeed, much effort was made to establish individual women's sections in the localities, though these represented more an attempt to harness female support than to secure a means by which to give women a specific voice within the party. Reports to the NEC gave figures of meetings held and numbers in attendance; little mention was made to resolutions passed or the views of women members. More broadly, references to women became a staple feature of party election material, regular campaigns were launched to widen the circulation of *Labour Woman*, pamphlets directed at potential female members were published (*Women and the Labour Party*), and women were recruited to participate in Labour campaigns at a national and municipal level.[88]

Overseeing all this was the party's chief women's officer, Dr Marion Phillips. Phillips had emerged as a leading figure in the Labour-affiliated Women's Labour League (WLL) before the war, becoming its secretary in 1912 and editor of *Labour Woman* from 1916. Throughout the 1920s, she maintained a staunch loyalty to the party leadership, by whom she was appointed and to whom she was directly answerable. Beyond the immediate party apparatus, links with non-party organisations were maintained via the SJC, originally formed in 1916 and comprised of representatives from nationally organised trade union, Labour Party and co-operative women. From 1918, it was charged with carrying out detailed research into such issues as housing and maternity hospitals, with Margaret Bondfield taking over from Mary Macarthur as chair in early 1921. The ubiquitous Phillips was its secretary.[89]

Despite the lack of equal representation within the Labour apparatus, the party's women's department discussed, formulated and presented a wide range of policy issues. International, social and domestic politics were all given coverage, although the latter tended to preoccupy the party's approach to the female electorate. One early campaign inherited from the WLL, *The Working Woman's House* (1917), was intended to interest 'working women in planning their own houses' and 'developing public opinion about dwellings'. In response, 86 meetings had been held by November 1918, and 10,000 questionnaires completed.[90] Later in 1918, the first women's conference agenda focused on: (a) the rights of women; (b) the Child Welfare Act; (c) housing; (d) the political organisation of women; (e) the prevention of venereal disease; and (f) food problems after the war.[91] This, in brief, encapsulated the political world inhabited by Labour women between the wars: a mixture of gendered, electoral, social and domestic policies deemed broadly to complement a 'typical' woman's life experience. That said, the SJC arguably maintained a wider brief and retained a degree of independence from the Labour Party. In particular, it regularly discussed international affairs, corresponding 'directly with external organisations such as the League of Nations and the Labour and Socialist International'. Representatives took their place on government commissions, and advice was given to the NEC on a variety of government initiatives, including the Criminal Amendment Bill, the Unmarried Parents Bill, and the Juvenile Courts Bill of 1921.[92] As we shall see, however, discussion among the female party membership did not guarantee a ready or receptive audience on the NEC or at the party conference.

Beyond the women's conference and meetings of the SJC, Labour's approach to its female members and potential electors was infused with the gender preconceptions of the time. Essentially, Labour believed that socialism would function in the common interest of both sexes; the common interests being similarly indivisible. In practice, this often led to distinct spheres of activity and concern being designated. Electorally, Labour appealed to women primarily as housewives, mothers and consumers, presenting Labour as a 'gateway' to improved living conditions, cheap food and fair rents. 'On the women lies the burden of high prices and overcrowded homes, of unemployment and the empty cupboard', exclaimed MacDonald's Woolwich by-election address in 1921, a view that mirrored Labour's 1918 description of women as the 'chancellor of the exchequer of the home'.[93] By 1929, the party had honed its appeal to women into nine key points – that is, that Labour put children first, promoted the welfare of mothers, promoted shorter hours and better conditions 'for workers in the workshop and women in the home', provided better housing, offered better pensions for widows and mothers, reduced prices and taxes on food, offered work or maintenance for the unemployed, supported equal civil rights for men and women, and believed in peace between nations. 'It is the children's party; it is the peace party; therefore it is the women's party'.[94] For this reason, perhaps, Jean Mann recalled her own candidacy as a prospective ILP councillor in Glasgow as gaining support primarily on the premise that the party 'must have housewives' rather than on any commitment to gender equality.[95] Thus, while women were recognised and approached as a part of the wider social-political constituency, they were often done so within a clearly defined remit.

Second, the extended franchise of 1918 forced Labour to present its vision of a 'new social order' to the 'unorganised', non-union working class. This could sometimes prove difficult, and many Labour officers and supporters retained a rather condescending attitude towards the 'mass' of unskilled, casual, rural and unemployed workers. In particular, certain working-class cultural pursuits, such as drinking, gambling and what MacDonald described as a love of 'gaudy ornament and sparkling anything', clearly rankled the more high-minded socialist.[96] In such a way, limited Labour progress was often put down to the shortcomings of the workers themselves. Snowden, for example, would claim disdainfully that 'the people for whom [the socialist] works are often indifferent and seldom show any gratitude'.[97] Not dissimilarly, Labour's new middle-class recruits after 1918 would regularly bemoan those who E. M. Latimer described as the 'drink sodden, coarse folk' that they were now forced to canvass for votes.[98] Certainly, Morgan Philips Price would blame his failure to win a Labour seat in the early 1920s to the 'fickle mobs in Gloucester'.[99] And even among the trade unionists on the NEC, the middle-class Fabian socialist Susan Lawrence reputedly claimed to discern 'drunkards and nitwits', a comment that arguably reveals more about Lawrence than it does about Joe Compton, Jimmy Walker, George Lathan et al.[100]

But there was also antipathy between the 'respectable' skilled trade unionist and the non-unionised or unskilled worker. For the Leith trades council, reporting on the limited gains made by Labour in the municipal elections of 1920, it remained 'a pitiful reflection on the intelligence of the working class that an election should find them such simple victims as to be influenced in any way by those who are naturally opposed to all such questions as effect the interests and lives of the workers'.[101] In Glasgow, J. J. Smyth has demonstrated how the ILP prior to the Great War focused overwhelmingly on the 'respectable' working-class vote. It was due partly to the social-industrial changes affected by the war, Smyth argues, along with the emergence of housing issues from approximately 1910, that such an approach was discarded, thereby allowing Labour to make its breakthrough. Even so, Smyth shows how some, including Tom Johnston, continued to retain a disregard for the poorer electorate. Writing in 1921, the future secretary of state for Scotland maintained that the 'slum areas are represented by capitalists', despite evidence beginning to point to the contrary.[102]

Similar attitudes were evident in England. In Manchester, as Tony Adams has confirmed, Labour's support prior to the Great War was extremely area specific, winning council seats in skilled working-class neighbourhoods but failing in certain 'slum' areas where issues of religion and drink were dominant.[103] Although exceptions can be found, Labour's trade union basis frequently combined with the party's links to Liberalism to estrange or neglect sections of the working class. Very often, as in Nottingham or cotton Lancashire, dominant unions could focus the Labour agenda on sectional interests of little concern to the wider community.[104] In Oxford, the trades council – which remained divided over the formation of a local Labour Party in the 1920s – ensured that the party prioritised the needs of skilled workers rather than cultivate support among the semi-skilled within the developing motor industry. So, for example, the divisional party campaigned for better quality housing rather than responding to the shortage of accommodation that had begun to afflict the expanding university city.[105] In Salford, too, there existed a number of obstacles to the extension of Labour support among its poorest inhabitants. Progress was made post-1918, when housing questions began to top Labour's local electoral programme. But even then, religious tensions, a Liberal–Conservative alliance formed after Labour became the largest group on the council, and the threat of increased rates and rents, appear to have limited the party's appeal in the town's 'slum' districts.[106] More widely, Labour's rather dim view of a certain 'type' of worker was clearly discernable throughout the interwar period (and beyond) in the hapless cartoon figure of Henry Dubb, who featured in the *Daily Herald, Forward!* and other Labour publications. Dubb was an 'incorrigible fool', always exploited, always gullible to the capitalist press and the demands of his employer, and always drinking, gambling or sporting rather than improving his mind via socialism.[107] Despite all this, Labour's focus on housing, social welfare and unemployment was obviously designed to appeal to all sections of the working class, though the extent to which the party succeeded in this undoubtedly varied.

Third, Labour endeavoured to attract middle-class professional members and voters from 1918. This, to a certain extent, was indicative of Labour's Liberal heritage; its general election manifestos were often an 'appeal to the people', a term inherited from the radicalism of the previous century. For MacDonald, Webb and others, socialism was not a class-based ideology, but a belief in moral citizenship that transcended sectional or individual interest. Alternately, the party leadership recognised the importance of middle-class support in purely electoral terms. This was particularly true in London, and was famously articulated in a series of articles by Herbert Morrison, Sidney Webb, Emile Davis and W. J. Brown for the *London Labour Chronicle* in 1922.[108] Earlier, in the immediate aftermath of the 1918 general election, Hugh Dalton had privately linked the party's need for middle-class recruits with its political limitations, suggesting that Labour required 'an influx of brains and middle-class, non-crank membership. It is very weak now in knowledge on foreign and imperial policy, and army and navy. Also it will want some good lawyers (but not too many)'.[109] Political precision, not to mention the party coffers, was to benefit from middle-class recruitment.

Nevertheless, appeals to the middle class were not always popular. On hearing of the Glasgow Central constituency party's decision to nominate the former

Liberal – and deliverer of many an anti-socialist speech – Craigie Aitchison KC as its parliamentary by-election candidate in May 1929, the Scottish Advisory Council (SAC) executive complained that:

> [Now], when the work, tears and lives of people who have gone give us the chance to take control of our own conditions, we are informed that 'legal efficiency' is indispensable ... and offers come thick and fast from people who are willing to ease the financial burdens entailed in an election, provided they are selected as candidates. We feel that in many instances it would be far better for local organisations to refuse such offers and carry on as those before did, allowing the inspiration of independence that has carried us so far to finish the job ...[110]

Similarly, George Milligan of the Liverpool dockers' union had in 1918 stated his opposition to individual Labour Party membership on the grounds that he 'did not want middle-class or higher-class leaders to come and tell them what to do, or theorists like Mr H. G. Wells and Bernard Shaw'.[111] In West Ham, too, local Labour members would protest against the party taking in 'faddists or theorists', preferring instead 'practical, hard-headed industrial workers who understand the workers' aims and desires'.[112] Such a suspicion of middle-class intellectualism was rampant in the Labour Party and trade union movement. Even so, Labour's central electoral appeals attempted to speak across the class divide, referring to 'organised labour' and the 'workers', but also to those who 'labour' in the 'laboratory' and 'office'. And while mention was made to the 'parties of privilege of birth and privilege of wealth', Labour presented itself as the party of 'the nation', speaking to 'men and women of good will in all classes' with a commitment to the 'service of all'.[113]

Despite the concerted efforts of Labour's sub-committees, the party's ability to extend its appeal was neither uniformly nor quickly achieved. Moreover, potential areas of support were not wholly realised. This was certainly the case with regard to the co-operative movement, wherein a shift towards political representation and the formation of the Co-operative Party did not lead to affiliation with the Labour Party. While, in places such as Kettering and West Ham, the co-op could form an important part of the labour movement and contribute to Labour Party success, elsewhere hostility to formal political activity prevented effective collaboration.[114] As this suggests, Labour strategies and perspectives varied in response to local circumstances and conditions. Because of this, the construction of a coherent, uniform and independent party organisation was one of the major challenges of the 1920s, and it is to this that we now turn.

III. THE HOUSE THAT ARTHUR BUILT

Labour Party support and organisation was spread unevenly across Britain prior to the Great War. Very briefly, the party had by 1914 an estimated official presence in 158 British localities, based either on a trades council or local Labour organisation.[115] In addition, there were 672 ILP branches of varying size affiliated to Labour, the crusading activities of which had often proved integral to the party's early development. In Scotland, where the 1903 Lib–Lab pact had not applied, Labour boasted just three parliamentary seats after the December 1910 election, in Dundee, Glasgow Blackfriars and West Fife. Despite the leading role played by many a Scottish activist in Labour's early history, from Keir Hardie onwards, Liberalism remained dominant throughout much of the country in the pre-war years, with the mining divisions being staunchly Liberal, and with the progress of the ILP in the urban centres proving notable but inconsistent. This was partly due to the fact that trade unionism remained relatively weak north of the border, with socialism in Scotland drawing from an eclectic mix of radicalism, anti-landlordism, Irish nationalism, the 'doctrinal exclusiveness and disputatiousness ... fundamental to the Scottish Calvinist tradition', and 'a value system which derived its strength from temperance and religion'.[116] Even so, with 31 (of 150) trades councils affiliated to Labour by 1914, and with a vibrant if argumentative socialist movement making ground, a potential Labour challenge to Liberal hegemony was at least evident. In such circumstances, the impact of the Great War and the social-industrial unrest that succeeded it would prove vital to Labour's continued emergence in Scotland.

In Wales, Labour had begun to make progress in the south of the country before the outbreak of war, although its organisation beyond the mining lodges was rudimentary. There were five Welsh Labour MPs by 1914, all in the south, and all but one had succeeded against exclusively Conservative opposition. Only in Gower did Labour defeat a Liberal in December 1910. Similarly, at a municipal level, Labour councillors had become a feature of certain southern town, borough and urban district councils (Abertillery, Rhondda, Merthyr Tydfil and Swansea), but remained noticeably absent throughout virtually all of central and northern Wales. As such, Labour's challenge to Liberal domination in Wales as a whole was limited before the Great War. In the south, however, the transition of trade union support from Liberal to Labour was clearly underway, most obviously via the South Wales Miners' Federation (SWMF).[117] Here, as Chris Williams has shown with regard to Rhondda, the independent organisation of workers in the coalfield – in trades councils, union lodges and ILP – allowed 'the rights of labour' to be more overtly understood and expressed in class terms, paving the way for a local Labour Party built on such loyalties firmly to establish itself within the region's communities.[118]

Labour's English bases of support were found overwhelmingly in the north. Thus, in Lancashire and Cheshire, where 42 local affiliated trades councils or Labour parties had been established by 1914, the Manchester and Salford Labour Representation Committee (MSLRC) was amongst the most advanced in the country, with associated divisional parties and an affiliated membership of 17,959 by 1910.[119] Here, cracks were beginning to show in the Liberal–Labour alliance, with the Manchester Liberal Union's unwillingness to run working-class candidates having acted as the spur to the MSLRC's formation in the first place.[120] Even so, the Lancashire textile belt continued to contain mainly Liberal strongholds, wherein 'a nonconformist inspired sympathy for religious, political, and individual liberty, and for self-development, was reinforced by a perception of economic progress through free trade, co-operation between labour and capital, and "sane" reform'.[121] Concurrently, the county further included several bastions of working-class Toryism, such as Preston, Bury and Oldham, where trade loyalty often overrode class or political fidelities.[122] In the west of the region, most obviously Liverpool, religious sectarianism cut across Labour's comparatively secular appeal. As a result, potential Labour progress was blocked on the one hand by a politically relevant and progressive Liberalism, and by an entrenched working-class Toryism on the other. Even in Manchester, what appeared to be a strong party organisation registered just two MPs and fifteen local councillors (on a council of 105) by the eve of the war. Consequently, as Tanner has shown, the progressive alliance that had facilitated Labour's advance throughout much of the north west remained relevant, despite the fact that tensions were beginning to characterise such a relationship in many places.[123]

In Yorkshire, there were twenty Labour affiliated trades councils and party organisations by 1914, with a strong ILP presence in towns such as Bradford. Here, the birthplace of the ILP, Labour antipathy towards an entrenched Liberal Party was clearly apparent, and this was equally true in places such as Leeds where Liberal elites proved equivocal to the demands of labour. Given such a context, the Labour Party was able to build a basis of support upon its trade union affiliates, with progress being made primarily as a result of materially related campaigns specific to the industrial conditions of the relevant town or city. Accordingly, Labour's prospects varied across Yorkshire, but the potential for a Labour heartland was apparent. In the northern counties, moreover, Labour had made notable progress in the coalfields and urban centres of the region by the eve of the Great War, though this had generally been achieved in tandem with the Liberals. As in South Wales, nonconformist traditions within the North East mining constituencies merged into the trade union culture, meaning that Labour politics were largely informed by Liberal ideas and progress tended to be reliant on Liberal–Labour co-operation. Yet, such solid Liberal constituencies would prove receptive to Labour's appeal by 1918. As in the North West, tensions between Liberal and Labour were palpable by 1914, and these would become decisive over the early 1920s. Within many non-mining industrial centres, working-class demands had begun to necessitate a realignment of Liberal politics that certain Liberal associations appeared loath to carry out, thus provoking fractures in the Lib–Lab accord. Significantly, however, Labour progress in such circumstances would prove more reliant on practical appeals informed by prevailing ideas than the propagation of an overtly socialist alternative. As Tanner's exhaustive study has again demonstrated, the Labour Party needed to absorb and supplement previous traditions (rather than wholly supplant them) if it was to supersede prevailing Liberal support.[124] Across the north of England as a whole, Labour boasted 21 MPs in 1914.

Elsewhere, Labour organisation was far patchier. Throughout the Midlands, as G. D. H. Cole has noted, there were just 23 local Labour parties or trades councils carrying out political work in 1914. The coalfields and cities of the east remained primarily Liberal, and there were but six Labour MPs in the region as a whole.[125] Though socially and economically varied, the West Midlands remained a Conservative stronghold, with a tradition of paternal Toryism that had proven accessible and responsive to working-class needs and insecurities. Here, Liberalism was notoriously weak, suggesting that a practical and materially relevant Labour Party had room to emerge as a feasible alternative. However, Labour remained some way from becoming the dominant political presence in the region.[126] East Anglia, with just one MP and developing but limited Labour organisations in Norwich and Ipswich, was largely a Labour desert. Equally, the South and South West had little Labour organisation outside of the large urban centre of Bristol. Beyond Britain's industrial localities, Labour pioneers were rare indeed, often comprising just a handful of converts meeting secretly and 'fearful of being victimised and rough handled'.[127]

Finally, in London, Labour progress was apparent but slow. A capital-wide party organisation had not been formed until May 1914, only three London parliamentary seats had been secured by Labour in December 1910 – Deptford, Woolwich and Bow and Bromley (along with one in greater London, West Ham South) – and, given the capital's diverse social-economic composition, Labour faced socialist, Liberal and Tory competition for the working-class vote. It would, in part, take generational changes to break this deadlock, thereby helping to pave the way for a young Herbert Morrison to embark on a prestigious political career.[128] In the meantime, Labour appeared by the outbreak of war to have made inroads into those parts of the East End and South London where the Liberal Party was weak and Labour offered a salient alternative to the Tories, but the party elsewhere remained very much cast in a Liberal shadow.

Overall, therefore, Labour's organisational and electoral development was irregular and incomplete on the eve of the Great War. Labour had clearly gained a political foothold, but the party generally appeared reliant on the progressive alliance to maintain its progress; its comparative strength often depended on Liberal weakness rather than a distinctive Labour or socialist appeal. In Tanner's words:

> After 1910 Labour consolidated its strength in particular areas, most notably those inhabited by miners and railwaymen. In such places, and in parts of the country where the Liberals had traditionally been weak (like the West Midlands and Merseyside), Labour was often becoming the main anti-Tory party. Elsewhere, limited Liberal enthusiasm for their party's national programme could create opportunities for Labour. Where the opportunity was grasped, Labour sometimes developed a substantial political base, although generally without replacing the Liberals as the main anti-Tory force.[129]

As we have seen, Liberal–Labour tensions were exacerbated by the events of 1914–22, opening a political space into which Labour could move. As such, the organisational reforms introduced by Arthur Henderson in 1918 were designed to take advantage of the changed circumstances occasioned by the war and considerably to extend the basis and nature of the Labour Party's support. This was seen to be integral to the party's sustained challenge to both the Liberals and the Conservatives over the 1920s and beyond. To this effect, the party made fairly rapid progress; by 1924, with 626 divisional parties and trades councils affiliated to Labour, only three British parliamentary constituencies could not boast a party organisation of some form or other.[130]

In logistical terms, following the adoption of the party's new constitution in 1918 and the basic formation of divisional Labour parties throughout much of the country, Henderson produced over the next year a 'general scheme of organisation' that divided Britain into seven 'regional' sections. After much discussion, this was extended to nine – North Eastern, North Western, Midlands, Southern and Home Counties, London, South Western, Eastern, Wales and Monmouth, and Scotland – with a paid organiser appointed to each region. These were, in order, Messrs Gibbin, Standring, Drinkwater, Shepherd, Windle, Robinson, Holmes, Mardy Jones, and Shaw. By 1925, Harold Croft had replaced Shepherd in the Southern and Home Counties, C. C. Jones had taken over the South Western region, and T. C. Morris had become responsible for Wales and Monmouthshire. Both the organisers and the regions remained firmly under the remit of the party centre; the organisers were paid from London, had no regional offices, and functioned as co-ordinators rather than political decision makers. Subsequently, they served to take many of the day-to-day administrative responsibilities away from head office; acting as a point of contact between centre and locality, while more generally undertaking the management of election campaigns and ensuring the maintenance of the regional party apparatus in-between times. The regional organisers solved local problems, helped with appointments, and advised local agents and officers. In short, they sustained the party apparatus below the realm of head office.[131]

Important in all this was the promotion of Egerton Wake to national agent. Born in Chatham in 1871, Wake was a trained law clerk and accountant who had joined the ILP in the late 1890s, eventually becoming the Labour Party agent-organiser in Barrow-in-Furness in 1908. His evident abilities were noted by the party centre, leading to Wake's appointment as organisational secretary in the summer of 1918. From such a position, he managed the party reorganisation in Scotland and Wales, taking over as national agent from Arthur Peters in October 1919.[132] As a keen centraliser and close ally to Henderson, Wake directed the extension of the party across the country, orchestrating a series of regional and local conferences to consolidate party organisation and disseminate central party policy. These would seek to rally local support via the appearance of a known party leader – often Arthur Henderson – and simultaneously allow head office to circulate (and ensure the adoption of) a broadly uniform political perspective. From his position as secretary to the NEC sub-committee on organisation, Wake endorsed and recommended Labour candidates, reported on the party's by-election preparations, and helped in the selection of local party agents. Accordingly, the party had appointed 112 full-time agents by 1920, in addition to a further 24 appointed by affiliated organisations.[133]

On paper, at least, Labour's reorganisation appeared to have quickly established the party on a nationwide scale. Equally, of course, there were limits to Labour's expansion. Labour did not become a mass membership party in the early 1920s, and its support remained unevenly distributed. Most local Labour parties continued to have a largely affiliated membership, the majority of which played little active role in maintaining the party on a day-to-day level. As before the war, trade union support was both financially and numerically important for many a borough, constituency and ward party. The 'winning' of local trade unionism away from the Liberal Party, or from its own independence, was therefore an important factor in the party's initial development. But this too brought its own problems, particularly if a trade union or trades council sought to dominate the local Labour organisation. Too tight a union control over a local party could hamper the widening of Labour's appeal, alienating the party from those beyond the dominant union's ranks. A lack of individual male members remained a concern for the party throughout the decade, while the ever-expanding number of female members was not matched by an equal distribution of power. Furthermore, a lack of trade union organisation could reduce a local Labour party's financial and organisational scope, leaving a core of dedicated activists to maintain a Labour presence. Typically, therefore, the Labour Party reflected the attitudes, objectives and traditions of those who formed its organisational basis. In the words of Chris Williams, 'it is possible to argue that in certain critical respects there was no British labour movement, but that there were a series of projections from the localities and regions onto an ostensibly national stage of the principles, priorities and preferred policies of the movement, which had been determined at a local level'.[134] At the same time, attempts to build up the party organisation necessarily went hand in hand with the forging of distinct

Labour identities, loyalties and priorities. In this way, Labour sought to augment and extend its support by combining local concerns with a nationally contrived vision of a 'new social order'. Because of this, the experiences of Labour members and the nature of the Labour Party varied across Britain as a whole.

Durham provides an apparently classic example of post-war Labour organisation. Here, the Labour Party was based largely upon the DMA, a union that was gradually won over from Liberal to Labour in the decade prior to and during the Great War as a younger generation of socialist checkweighmen began to usurp the union's older Liberal agents.[135] Typically, Durham party members articulated a socialism that was forged from within the county itself; these men – and the party hierarchy was dominated by men – were primarily miner Methodists located in small self-reliant pit villages with beliefs that comprised moderate socialist, Liberal, trade union and Methodist traits. They would often hold a variety of offices within the community, as was the case with Jack Lawson, the MP for Chester-le-Street from 1919, whose 'curriculum vitae' listed him as miner, checkweighman, county councillor, DMA executive officer, ILPer and chapel member. Appropriately, then, when the Durham Divisional Labour Party was inaugurated on 9 February 1918, it was so at the Miners' Hall with the DMA as the host organisation. Will Whiteley, miners' agent and Methodist, was elected president, while Methodist miners and checkweighmen such as Lawson, Jack Swan and Joe Batey dominated the party executive and candidate list. By 1922, DMA-sponsored candidates filled six of Durham's eleven county seats, with the union financing both the election campaign and the political agents. The union's political fund for 1922–3 spread its services widely, spending £1,018/9/4 on agents' salaries and contributing to the expenses of eight divisional parties.[136] Certainly, the DMA did not always get its way – the Seaham Labour Party deliberately sought non-mining candidates, snubbing the DMA to win the services of Sidney Webb in 1922[137] – but the union and its representatives undoubtedly shaped the party's character and perspective throughout the region.

Within such a context, class politics could sometimes play an important role. The county's municipal election contests effectively pitted the 'colliery managers, undermanagers and engineers against checkweighmen, store managers, club secretaries and committee men'. So, in 1919:

> In Willington the sitting member Llewelyn Weeks, a mining engineer, was defeated by Matthew Reed, a coal miner, who polled three times as many votes as his opponents. In Hetton another miner, Thomas Glish, polled five times as many votes as J. B. Dixford, the local science teacher. In Birtley, Jack Gilliland, a checkweighman, polled 1,837 votes while his opponent, a retired building contractor, polled just 639. In Ryton, Thomas Addison, a miner, beat the local colliery manager … This pattern of electoral contests was repeated at the more local levels of district and parish councils as the social structure of the coalfield became politicised.[138]

Although Labour veterans such as Peter Lee continued to insist on a class-inclusive socialism, such views were by the 1920s being challenged by a more assertive socialism that emphasised the right of the worker (and the working class in general) to participate in society and affirm their own identities, objectives and priorities. Here, 'the tradition of miners was expressed in a language in which "communities" and "class" were interchangeable as ideas of solidarity'.[139] Indeed, the formation of a Moderate Party in 1921 to unite Conservatives and Liberals against Labour seemed to confirm the extent to which Durham politics came to reflect the two sides of the coal industry. Partly because of this, and despite the DMA's domination of the county's Labour parties, Labour lost control of the county council in 1922, only to regain it in 1925.

As the above synopsis suggests, Labour activity in Durham was often mobilised through the miners' lodges, guaranteeing the party a firm basis of support across the county. At the same time, so overt an affiliation served as a potential block on the party's wider appeal; constituency organisation was rudimentary beyond the lodges, individual membership of the Labour Party remained low, and although women's sections were established in Durham county after 1918, their members were denied access to the higher echelons of the local party. Of the 56 Labour councillors who took control of Durham county council in 1919, making it the first English county to come under Labour authority, none were female and the overwhelming majority were members of the DMA. For this reason, DMA domination was a source of tension in some constituencies (including South Shields and Bishop Auckland), while many voters remained unconvinced of Labour's political credentials.[140] Consequently, Liberalism continued to form a viable, if generally unsuccessful, alternative to Conservatism in a number of places. Labour growth was not so secure in certain county seats wherein the miners' influence was diluted and thereby less dominant. Sedgefield, a large and newly formed constituency that encompassed both mining and rural populations, was won for the Conservatives in 1923 and 1924, before the opening of a new chemical works in 1929–31 brought with it an influx of workers that affected a change in the constituency's social-political make-up. Likewise, the small but scattered population of Barnard Castle, where the Tories were able to squeeze out the once dominant Liberals (largely by appealing to the farmers, landowners and coal owners on anti-socialist lines), elected a Conservative MP in 1922 and 1924. Similar observations can be made with regard to the county's six borough constituencies. Even in those that were overwhelmingly working class, such as Gateshead and South Shields, Liberal resilience made Labour's progress uncertain in the early 1920s; Labour won the former in 1922 and 1924, but lost in 1918 and 1923, while South Shields remained Liberal until 1929. Hartlepool, meanwhile, proved immune to the charms of Labour until 1945, despite the party's growing presence there. In Darlington, it would take a concerted effort by the railwaymen finally to break the hold of the Pease family on the town in a by-election in 1926, only for Labour to lose the seat again between 1931 and 1945.[141]

Yorkshire, as another emerging bastion of Labour support, saw a flurry of activity in 1917–22. Thus, in the West Riding, divisional parties were quickly formed, full-time agents were appointed in Bradford, Leeds, Huddersfield and Spen Valley, and local party newspapers were developed, most famously the *Bradford Pioneer*. The recruitment of women members appears to have taken a little time, although the Advisory Council of Labour Women for the West Riding of Yorkshire comprised 119 organisations by the turn of the decade, 42 of which were local Labour parties. Leeds, in particular, soon boasted a relatively flourishing women's section of some 500 members, not to mention a female assistant secretary, Clara Adams, who retained her position for much of the interwar period.[142]

Labour's basis of support in the region had been built on a combination of mainly woollen trade unionism and the moderate socialism of the regional ILP, but it was consolidated over the early 1920s amidst the realignment of political relationships that occurred during and following the Great War. Thus, a once

Liberal stronghold became a battleground in which Labour fought against a Conservative Party reliant on Liberal support. As always, there were complexities. Leeds and Wakefield encompassed far more mixed economies than their woollen satellites, while the intricacies of the wool trade saw disparities across the region, from the fine woollen cloths of Huddersfield to the worsteds and artificial silks of Bradford to the low-quality used wool produce of Morley, Dewsbury and Batley. Equally, as in Durham, the readymade foundation of support within the trade unions immediately informed the party's wider identity, but its progress would depend on its ability to extend its appeal beyond such parameters. To this effect, Labour evidently made much headway in the early 1920s. Although Labour domination of West Yorkshire municipal politics would be continually blocked by a series of local Conservative–Liberal alliances, Labour had become the dominant party in the region by 1924, with its eleven MPs comparing to eight Conservatives and four Liberals.[143]

In South Yorkshire, Sheffield was quickly to emerge as a Labour stronghold following the Great War. Here, an entrenched working-class Toryism previously sustained by a number of (Conservative) workingmen's clubs, local economic conditions and municipal paternalism had by the early 1900s been challenged by a moderate Liberalism closely linked to the city trades council. Such contact caused division, however. Demands for worker representation pushed many Liberals into an anti-socialist alliance in 1909; Liberal moderation persuaded the city LRC to establish a rival trades council in 1908 and opened up a space that Labour could exploit after 1918. Accordingly, the city's two trades councils had combined by 1920, the already practical focus of Sheffield Labour politics, based around such issues as school meals, education and housing, was given sustenance by the impact of war, while close links with the co-op and the city's trade unions facilitated an institutional base on which the party could build. By 1926, Labour formed a majority on the council that would lose control for just two years over the interwar period and beyond.[144] Elsewhere in Yorkshire, the mining areas around Barnsley, Rotherham and Doncaster (which further included a significant number of railway workers) boasted solid Labour bases of support, although the largely rural East Riding proved rather less conducive to Labour progress outside of York and, by the later 1920s, Hull.[145]

In Wales, the coalmining region of the south became a committed Labour stronghold from 1918. As in Durham, the basis for such support centred primarily on the coalminers' union lodges, the agents and checkweighmen of which held special status among the mining communities. Like Durham, too, certain mining villages became known for their socialist militancy, although the majority of communities retained a political moderation broadly in line with (and loyal to) the national Labour leadership. As Duncan Tanner has explained, Labour politics in Wales were informed more by the pragmatic and the practical than the ideological militancy associated with certain 'Little Moscows' in the Rhondda Valley. This, in turn, should neither be underestimated nor dismissed for its perceived incompatibility with more overtly left-wing interpretations of socialism. Labour support was certainly understood in class terms, while the social-economic problems of Welsh mining and other industries provided Labour with 'fertile ground for Labour propaganda' that began to resonate beyond the pit.[146] Generally, Labour established and built its support via the close-knit social and industrial loyalties of the mining communities, wherein the links between party, union, lodge and chapel often overlapped. This made some of the divisional parties mining fiefdoms, with wider party membership rarely extending much beyond the union affiliates. This mattered little given the concentrated nature of the industry; in many places, the SWMF operated as 'a social institution providing through its local leaders an all round service of advice and assistance to the mining community on most of the problems that could arise between the cradle and the grave. Its function became a combination of economic, social and political leadership in these single industry communities'.[147] Though the CPGB occasionally challenged for working-class loyalties, the SWMF effectively functioned as a branch of the Labour Party in a number of localities.

Beyond the mining regions, certain Welsh industrial towns – Llanelli, Swansea and Wrexham – did become relatively safe for Labour from the early 1920s. Others, however, including Carmarthen, Carnavon, Newport and Cardiff, boasted a sizeable Labour presence/vote, but regularly failed to provide Labour with a parliamentary seat. Though trade union support underpinned these local parties, it was not so concentrated as in the mining areas; the union's function was not so intertwined in the everyday lives of the community. The effect of this was evident with regard to local government. Although Labour soon controlled a number of county, borough and district councils from 1919, Williams has suggested that 'the limits to Labour control of local government ... were set, more or less, by the geographical boundaries of the South Wales coalfield, with its associated industries of iron, steel and tinplate'.[148] Labour's development at a municipal level was, therefore, rather more uneven and protracted than suggested by its general election success. In many places, Labour's progress was notable but ambivalent. To take one example, dock, steel and railway workers in Newport existed alongside a sizeable commercial and service sector. Given such a context, Labour developed extensive and active party support but proved unable to gain either a safe parliamentary seat or a council majority. There was, primarily, stiff Tory opposition throughout the interwar period, with the town council's relatively progressive housing policy going some way to deflect one of Labour's principal campaigning issues. In addition, many trade unions in the town continued to harbour Liberal sympathies and outlooks.[149] Over Wales as a whole, Labour's electoral progress was evident and significant but stuttering, with the party winning ten seats from 36 in 1918, peaking with 25 in 1929, only to fall to sixteen in 1931. Just two further seats were gained in 1935.

The example of Newport is informative. Urban centres with mixed occupational and class populations revealed Labour's progress to be less than certain. In Edinburgh, where distinct working-class areas contrasted with those occupied by a large professional class, the variety of worker occupations negated a dominant trade union hold over the fledgling Labour Party. Indeed, many of the prominent early Labour leaders who emerged in the city came from middle-class backgrounds, such as John Young (dentist), Gerald Crawford (mechanical engineer, musician and composer) and William Graham (journalist).[150] Consequently, the Edinburgh trades council responded slowly to Arthur Henderson's plea for concentrated Labour organisation. Prior to 1914, the trades council had affiliated to the ILP-dominated Labour Party for electoral purposes but continued to pursue many of its activities independently. As the unions then began to make gains without Labour Party input during the late and immediate post-war period, so the political appeals of the party made little headway. Only as boom gave way to slump in 1920–1, did the city's working-class organisations begin to converge around the Labour Party. This worked on two levels. First, unions began to look for political support as their industrial position weakened, as memberships declined, and as rising unemployment and 'rationalisation' undermined the bargaining positions achieved between 1917 and 1920.[151] Second, those leaving the unions or affected by unemployment began, to an extent at least, to consider political explanations and solutions to their circumstances. Partly for this reason, plans for the formation of an Edinburgh and District Trades and Labour Council were not agreed before October 1919; it did not actually meet until the following April; and little attention was paid to Labour Party organisation until 1921.[152] From here on, the influence of trade union organisation and finance became manifest, as the party appeared better co-ordinated, more financially stable, and made notable political progress. Even so, there were regular attempts to separate Edinburgh's industrial and political organisations into the 1930s, suggesting Labour's steady growth related to more than simply trade union support. A broadening party agenda and a divided Liberal Party that allowed Labour to take up its radical lead both assisted Labour's advance.

Glasgow was a more obviously working-class Scottish city, and one in which ten of its fifteen parliamentary seats had been won for Labour by 1922. Indeed, the notion of 'Red Clydeside' was born from a history of widespread wartime militancy and the subsequent election of socialist candidates such as Wheatley, Maxton and Kirkwood.[153] As Smyth has argued, the experience of war did much to realign Glasgow's political composition, forcing the ILP to concentrate on immediate social concerns such as housing (already an issue pre-1914), rents and prices.[154] Because of this, ILP members provided the 'nuts and bolts' of the various strikes and social protests of 1914–22, thereby enabling the party to form the basis of the Labour presence in the city.[155] ILP strength ensured that individual Labour Party membership remained low in Glasgow throughout the post-war decade, with ILP cardholders occupying fourteen of the eighteen seats on the Glasgow Labour Party executive committee in 1920. In addition, Labour established and consolidated much support amongst Glasgow's large Irish community after 1918. Yet, there was a limit to Labour's appeal. The city corporation remained in the hands of the Moderate Party (Tory) until Labour's breakthrough in 1933; the party typically boasted between 40 and 50 councillors on a council of 111 over the 1920s. It was, therefore, the Moderates who built the municipal estates that increasingly housed a substantial part of the Glasgow electorate. Thus, many tenants retained their support for Moderate policies, and it was not until the Scottish Protestant League endeavoured to split the Moderate vote that Labour was able to establish municipal control in the 1930s.

The policies and approach of the ILP evidently provided a pool of ready support within Glasgow during the 1920s. But despite the avowedly socialist politics associated with Maxton, Wheatley et al., we should not assume that the Glasgow population thereby subscribed completely to their relatively militant outlook. Glasgow comprised a 'mixed economy' with varied occupational and social structures, and although the industrial unrest in and surrounding the war had aided the Labour cause in the city, it was more the combination of wartime experience, the widened franchise, and the party's focus on the insecurities of working-class families that enabled Labour finally to establish itself. Indeed, the Glasgow ILP incorporated a wide range of opinions within its ranks. Alongside Maxton's militancy, Patrick Dollan articulated a far more moderate ILP perspective; one that was arguably more representative of Glasgow Labour opinion. Dollan was the chairman of the Glasgow ILP from 1917 until 1926, whereupon he became chairman of the party's Scottish Divisional Council. Though never elected to parliament, Dollan was the ILP's 'city boss' in Glasgow, with close links to the trade unions and co-op. He served as councillor for the Govan ward from 1913 to 1947, remained loyal to MacDonald in the face of his fellow Clydesiders' criticisms between 1924 and 1931, and resisted the ILP's disaffiliation from Labour in 1932. When the ILP finally left the Labour fold in 1932, only eight of the 40 ILP members on the city council followed Maxton and his comrades, the vast majority remaining with Dollan. Organisationally, too, Glasgow demonstrated the apparent anomalies of Labour's development. Often, areas that boasted large ILP memberships and much activity rejected the party's approach (Partick and Govanhill), while small party organisations in such 'slum' areas as Gorbals and Cowcaddens oversaw Labour strongholds. Though important, the links between organisation, membership and electoral success were not consistent.[156]

Labour support in the Midlands continued to vary greatly from 1918. In the east, the progressive alliance had often worked well and largely harmoniously before the war. In Derby, with its relatively stable industrial infrastructure, a moderate trade union movement had been co-opted by the local Liberals to bolster their already strong hold over the town. Partly because of this, there had been few attempts to update Liberal policy prior to 1914, allowing Labour to move into the vacuum occasioned by the Liberals' wartime divisions. With a strong trade union base and a charismatic and patriotic MP in J. H. Thomas, Labour dominated Derby politics over the 1920s (and for much of the 1930s).[157] Yet, Labour's separation from the progressive alliance did not guarantee it success; many unions in the region retained their Liberal tendencies, even within the MFGB.[158] Moreover, while Labour clearly supplanted the Liberals as the main alternative to Conservatism in the East Midlands, it did so without fundamentally altering its essentially moderate position. Labour stood for the right of working people to represent themselves and conduct their own affairs; attempts by socialists to extend that agenda were generally given short shrift. Thus, in Nottingham, the lace makers and miners who initially dominated the trades council at the war's end generally retained their Lib-Lab perspective, creating problems for Labour that were exacerbated once newer industries (Raleigh, Players' cigarettes, Boots) and unskilled unionisation brought about inter-union rivalries that challenged the city's existing social-industrial structures and relations. Though a growing band of socialists sought to break through such 'moderation' and actually took control of the trades council by the mid-1920s, the obvious importance of the miners and the diminishing influence of trades council organisation over the 1920s meant that the Nottingham labour movement continued to resist any attempt to stray too far from its essentially sectional and Liberal roots.[159]

In the West Midlands, Labour initially suffered badly for its perceived pacifism during the war, with many fledgling local parties being ill-prepared for the 1918 election contest. More generally, many predominantly working-class cities, towns and localities remained aloof from Labour during the 1920s, preserving instead their commitment to working-class Toryism. Classically, Birmingham retained its attachment to the Chamberlain family well into the 1930s, responding to a paternal Unionism that ensured the Tories won 82 of the 90 parliamentary vacancies of 1918–44 and retained control of the city council. Although Birmingham changed notably over the interwar period, as its population increased, 'new' industries developed, existing industries combined and expanded, and electoral boundaries were redrawn, its traditionally weak trade union movement remained scattered over 'a thousand trades' until the end of the 1930s. With little Liberal competition, Labour made some progress over the 1920s; the Borough Labour Party issued the *Birmingham Town Crier*, adopted former Tory 'notables' as candidates, and claimed 36 seats on the city council by 1928. Yet, the Birmingham Labour Party was a tempestuous mix of moderate trade unionists, dyed-in-the-wool socialist militants and middle-to-upper-class intellectuals (including Sir Oswald Mosley). Although Labour won six parliamentary seats in 1929, the combined impact of bitter in fighting, expulsions and Labour government crisis served to demonstrate the tenuous and conditional nature of the party's support in the city. By competing on the same terms as the Conservatives, Labour had made some headway, only for the fallout of 1929–31 to undo ten years' hard work. It would take the rearmament of the mid-to-late 1930s to place the city's unions in a better financial and bargaining position, with the NUGMW, Amalgamated Engineering Union (AEU) and Electrical Trades Union (ETU) helping to forge a more homogeneous city labour movement. Appeasement, of course, would finally lay the ghost of Chamberlain to rest.[160]

In places such as Liverpool, Labour progress was challenged and its identity informed by an array of social-economic, political and cultural obstacles. Traditionally, religious sectarianism was recognised as a principal reason for Labour's apparent weakness in a city that was predominantly working class. As one Labour councillor, Jack Braddock, later recalled, 'every March 17 when the Irish paraded to celebrate St. Patrick's Day, the Protestants would batter them; and on July 12, when the Protestants marched through the city in the Orangeman's Day celebrations, it was Ireland's turn to attack'.[161] Without doubt, religious division helped shape political loyalties and hampered Labour's progress in Liverpool. Recently, however, a rather more complex pattern of political support has been suggested. Though Labour came to dominate the city's Catholic wards over the 1920s, a sectarian response was far from uniformly expressed in Liverpool's predominantly Protestant areas. Other determinants were clearly apparent, the import of which shifted and varied over time, and were complemented by wider regional and national developments. First, Labour's traditional trade union base was less readily established in a mixed-industrial and dockyard city that employed much casual labour. On its formation in 1921, the Liverpool Trades Council and Labour Party comprised some 52 trade unions alongside a variety of ILP, Labour and Fabian organisations. Generally, Labour support was less forthcoming in areas where dock-related employment was predominant, with wards populated by craft union members offering a rather more fruitful return. In addition, working-class Toryism, financed and sustained in part by the local brewing industry and representative of the city's 'native' population, remained ingrained within parts of Liverpool. Second, as Sam Davies has shown, the party proved unable to establish a functioning party apparatus throughout much of the city, with religious and craft loyalties often hampering development. In particular, the Liverpool Labour Party was only partially successful in mobilising the city's female voters, often neglecting the neighbourhood campaigns that helped develop the party in other localities. All these factors – religious, gender and occupation difference – cut into and across the Labour Party, thereby limiting the party's constituency presence and subsequent appeal to the Liverpool electorate. Third, Davies has further demonstrated how Labour suffered as a result of the city's electoral boundaries and a peculiar mix of aldermanic manoeuvring and franchise anomalies. Ultimately, Labour clearly usurped the Liberals as the main opposition to the Conservatives, but it tended only to offer a serious challenge to the working-class Tory vote if it suppressed its pacifist, moralistic and sectional tendencies in favour of a more practical approach applicable to prevailing local traditions, cultures and circumstances. As Davies concludes, structure and agency intertwined in explaining the nature and experience of Liverpool Labour.[162]

In certain Lancashire cotton towns, too, Labour found itself confronted by a variety of trade, religious, gender and distinctly local peculiarities. Sam Davies and Bob Morley, in their comparative study of Blackburn, Bury, Bolton and Burnley, have shown how the 'politics of place' could contest Labour's fortunes. All four towns were mill towns, all were predominantly working class, and all were of approximately similar size. Yet, while Burnley proved to be relatively susceptible to Labour's appeal, with the party winning the parliamentary seat throughout the interwar period bar 1931 and gaining overall control of the borough council in the 1930s, the Bury electorate consistently rejected its Labour candidates. Labour failed to win a parliamentary contest in the town between 1918 and 1935, and its municipal representatives never secured more than a fifth of the available seats. Blackburn and Bolton, meanwhile, saw Labour advance to win parliamentary seats in 1923 (Bolton) and 1929 (both Bolton and Blackburn), but prove unable to gain overall control of either local council. The reasons for such disparity in what appear ostensibly to be similar towns are many, but Davies and Morley denote certain key factors. Patterns of employment varied: between spinners and weavers, workers and employers, and different 'types' of workers. Though cotton predominated, Burnley was home to 3,000 miners as well as cotton workers; Burnley and Blackburn were generally weaving towns, while Bury and Bolton tended towards spinning. There were also differences in the extent and nature of women's employment, with weaving providing a higher percentage of female workers. Interestingly, however, Davies and Morley 'tentatively' suggest that – unlike weaving towns such as Nelson – the role of women in the shaping of Labour's political progress (or lack of it) was restricted. This would suggest that the male-dominated unions retained control of the local Labour parties, thereby marginalizing Labour's appeal, inclusion and adoption of issues relevant to female voters. More decisively, attention is drawn to the relatively compact and long-established employer–worker relations that contributed to the 'paternal' or 'popular' Toryism characteristic of Blackburn, Bury and Bolton. By contrast, Burnley's smaller, less-integrated employers exerted less of an influence on a workforce that drew instead from Liberal traditions. Certainly, the strength of Anglicism in Bury, Bolton and Blackburn contrasted with Burnley's nonconformism. Finally, the relative ability (and willingness) of the various political parties to forge and maintain social-cultural links with their constituents appear to have had a significant influence on patterns of support, be it the Conservative clubs in Bury or the 'neighbourhood politics' of Labour in Burnley. Of course, such relationships were challenged by the interwar decline of the cotton industry, but it is notable that the four towns were affected in different ways, with Bury being hit less severely than Burnley.[163]

Outside of the industrial centres, Labour initially found it difficult to establish itself after 1918. In largely rural areas, some cities and towns could boast something of a Labour tradition, but elsewhere the party was literally beginning from nothing. The Norwich Labour Party was built on the city trades council, particularly the contribution of the National Union of Boot and Shoe Operatives (NUBSO), though a sizeable ILP contributed most of the party's active membership. Until 1932, the ILP club acted as a meeting place for the Labour Party and several trade union branches, cementing the 'harmonious' relationship between the two that reportedly existed in the fine city. By 1925, the party's fifteen wards boasted some 2,600 members.[164] By contrast, the Peterborough constituency encompassed a large rural area that combined with the city's Unionist heritage to keep a Labour Party based on a relatively weak trades council at bay. Though a divisional party was formed in October 1918, it remained ineffective prior to 1925, when a special party meeting sought to solve what had proven to be a perennial problem of adopting a sufficiently wealthy parliamentary candidate (J. F. Horrabin) and full-time organiser (George Watson). With the formation of a Labour club in 1927, moreover, the party succeeded in forging a more sustained presence in the city, although Horrabin's victory in 1929 proved to be something of a 'false dawn'. The surrounding village membership remained small, and the party's development was wracked with internal wrangling for much of the 1930s. Significantly, the party minutes suggest tensions between its rural and city members, with the divisional committee ruling in 1923 that it would only accept an affiliated (i.e. trade union) parliamentary candidate if no financially 'independent' nominee was forthcoming.[165]

The minutes of the East Grinstead Labour Party offer a fascinating glimpse into one of the newer Labour Party organisations formed towards the end of the Great War. The divisional party was inaugurated on 20 July 1918, with initial support coming from the NUR, Workers' Union and Agricultural Workers' Union, along with various middle-class Labour sympathisers such as W. H. Syme (a local architect), Reverend H. W. Layng and Lady De La Warr. With limited funds and members, the party nominated Major David Graham Pole as its parliamentary candidate, who continued to help finance the party after the 1918 election, buying the party premises at 12 Railway Approach in 1919. Even so, the party evidently took time to find its feet. Active women's sections were quickly formed, but there was much debate over where and when to hold party meetings. Following the formation of the local Hayward's Heath party in a country pub on 8 September, the East Grinstead executive resolved that it was undesirable ever to hold meetings on licensed premises or on a Sunday. At the same meeting, Mr Pay objected to the holding of 'irresponsible' open-air gatherings that may antagonise would-be supporters. Despite this, various local campaigns concentrating on education and housing conditions were launched, often with the women's section – particularly Violet Nash – in the vanguard. By February 1919, the division consisted of five local parties and numerous polling committees, although the rural nature of the constituency meant that poor transport services and scattered villages made meetings difficult to arrange. Middle-class enthusiasm knows no bounds, however, and eager Labour members launched an Arts League of Service that toured local towns and villages across East Sussex, reporting in 1919 that 'though the audience did not always appreciate the beauties of dancing or the pathos of *The Price of Coal*, the reception invariably accorded to the performers showed that there is a demand for first class entertainments in the rural areas'. From all this, the party organisation continued to extend into the villages over the course of 1919–20, with the odd party member winning election to a local government body, before a combination of lacklustre trade union support and financial deficiency threatened to kill the fledgling organisation.[166] Ultimately, East Grinstead offers an example of a party that relied on the hard work and dedication of few active members to keep the red flag flying. At the same time, the 'nature' of the party clearly reflected its membership, if doing little in the short term to entice farm workers or trade unionists into the Labour fold.

Finally, there is London, which boasted a central London Labour Party (LLP) with an affiliated membership of some 371,260 by 1926, scattered across 61 constituencies.[167] As this suggests, the LLP remained something of a political mosaic. Indeed, the differing approaches to Labour politics pursued by the London party secretary Herbert Morrison in Hackney and the hardened socialist campaigner George Lansbury in Poplar in 1919–22 provide a glaring example of the polarities that could exist beneath the Labour Party umbrella. Where Morrison had resorted to charitable methods to offset the effects of unemployment, acting within the legal limits of office and rebuking the methods of the borough's organised unemployed representatives, Lansbury's Poplar borough council gained notoriety from its disregard of established governmental precedents. In response to the growing number of unemployed workers applying to the local board of guardians, the council launched its own work scheme, employing some 300 men in December 1920, before refusing to pay its levy to the LCC and granting relatively generous payments to those applying for relief. As a result, the LCC undertook a legal action that led to the arrest and imprisonment of 30 Labour councillors in September 1921, with the 62-year-old Lansbury among them.[168] Though this raised much sympathy, with J. R. Clynes visiting the councillors in prison, the Labour leadership, including Morrison, were appalled at Poplar's methods.

Lansbury led a Labour council that in 1919 occupied 39 of an available 42 seats. Located in the East End, Poplar comprised primarily dock and transport workers living in close (often overcrowded) proximity to each other. Though based on trade union support (Poplar housed over 70 trade union branches), the Poplar Labour Party incorporated a relatively wide range of opinions within its ranks; something that Lansbury has been credited with forging into an effective and purposeful organisation. From this, both the party and the local council established and retained strong links to their constituents. Certainly, the demonstrations following the councillors' imprisonment were well attended, but Labour was further able to mobilise large attendances for more routine party meetings. Individual party membership in South Poplar numbered 2,300 by 1923.[169] As such, Labour's status depended as much on its communal as its class identity, though the two necessarily coalesced in such quarters of London. The borough party campaigned in its constituents' interests, benefiting from the gradual extension of local and national state intervention into areas of casual labour and unemployed relief in the early twentieth century. In such circumstances, Labour in Poplar, Stepney and Bethnal

Green appeared to intervene 'positively' on behalf of its working-class constituents, providing relief, jobs and protection in the midst of economic uncertainty.[170]

But despite Lansbury's reputation, Morrison was the leader, 'architect and inspirer' of London Labour.[171] Born in Brixton in 1888, Morrison reacted to his hard-drinking Tory policeman father by adopting an almost puritanical socialism that encompassed temperance, vegetarianism and, most unusually for a Labour man, non-smoking. Though he had dropped such principled positions by the 1930s, he always retained a commitment to hard work and an unquenchable thirst for political detail. He was known for his boundless energy; a typical portrait of him would provoke images of books and leaflets spilling from his pockets as he harried and hurried his party colleagues to the Labour cause. Having been exempted from the war on account of his being blind in one eye (he declared himself a conscientious objector in any case), Morrison became secretary to the newly formed London Labour Party in 1915.[172] From 1920, and despite some reservations at head office, London was recognised as one of Labour's nine regional centres, with an appointed regional organiser, Richard Windle, and women's organiser, Miss Somers, funded by the NEC. Windle, who was promoted to assistant national agent in 1929, worked closely with Morrison, building up the local party organisations, prompting trade union affiliation, and assisting in the selection of parliamentary and municipal Labour candidates.

Financially, the LLP received significant backing from the TGWU, despite the legendary animosity that existed between Ernest Bevin and Morrison. The party was also assisted by the decision of the Royal Arsenal Co-operative Society (RACS) in 1921 to affiliate to the party nationally and locally. With a membership of some 320,000 and an annual trade of £8,000,000, RACS members and finances proved integral to the progress of Labour politics in the capital. By the 1930s, the RACS was paying £400 annually to the LLP, while annual grants of £40 were made to those constituency parties employing full-time agents, and a further £600 was distributed to constituency parties in relation to the society's membership within the division.[173] Accordingly, the London party organisation continued to expand over the 1920s. In 1925, there were five clerks assisting the two party organisers, and a growing band of volunteers who Morrison oversaw with his customary efficiency. Contact with party members was maintained via the monthly *London News* (known as the *London Labour Chronicle* pre-1924), in which Morrison again took a leading role. In the meantime, his fondness for organisation was expressed in his own punctiliousness and his belief that 'the silent visionary with a card index beside him … is not less important than they who move in the limelight'.[174] Although Morrison sought to emulate and encourage the social-political ingenuities of the German Social Democratic Party (SPD), his real predilection was found in the minutiae of organisation.

In the working-class communities of South London, Labour was clearly able to build a foundation of support among the organised (though not necessarily skilled) workers in the area. Although Southwark stretched from Waterloo Bridge through Dulwich, Elephant and Castle, Bermondsey, Camberwell and Peckham, its various industries were often interlinked and employed workers who lived in close proximity to each other. Throughout the 1920s, the local trades councils provided the hub of Labour politics in Southwark's nine constituencies, and these retained a practical character that appeared relevant to the wider electorate. Attention was focused overwhelmingly on local concerns, particularly housing, health and relief for the unemployed. By 1924, seven of the nine parliamentary seats had been won for Labour, by the 1930s all three of the Bermondsey, Southwark and Camberwell borough councils were controlled by the party. As Sue Goss has demonstrated, the Labour Party in these areas became a centre for social and political life. The West Bermondsey party had a social club, swimming club, youth club and football team; it organised regular socials, outings and dances, including trips to the seaside for the local children. More practically, surgeries and legal advice centres were run from the party offices, while Labour Party newspapers were maintained and delivered door-to-door. In such a way, the party became an entrenched part of the local community, offering help, advice and entertainment.[175]

As these varied examples suggest, the Labour Party continued to develop in a diverse and uneven manner in the immediate post-war period. Different factors accounted for Labour's advance, or lack of it, in different places. As well as the localities listed above, there were still areas – mainly rural villages and small towns – where Labour was unable to contest elections in the early 1920s, due primarily to a lack of organisation, finance or perceived support.[176] The Chichester Divisional Labour Party, for example, established in April 1919 and comprised of an eclectic mix of agricultural labourers, railwaymen, builders, general workers, sympathetic clergy and middle-class socialists (such as Ralph and Bertha Morley), was unable to put forward a candidate at the general elections of 1923 and 1929.[177]

Consequently, the house that Arthur Henderson began to build in 1918 had solid foundations but was far from complete by the mid-1920s. Despite head office's endeavour to co-ordinate Labour Party activity and organisation, its efforts were inevitably refracted through a combination of circumstance, interpretation and implementation on the part of local members and voters in an array of different locations. Clearly, traditional explanations for Labour's growth, based primarily on trade union developments either in the workplace or with regard to the state, only take us so far. Generally, the trade unions continued to form the basis of the Labour Party's organisation in the early 1920s and throughout the interwar period. In areas of concentrated industry and strong union traditions, moreover, they maintained a loyal Labour Party support that would prove resilient even to the devastations of 1931. Yet, there were places where the trade unions were weak – particularly in Scotland – in which the ILP continued to play a central role in the extension of Labour politics. There were places, too, where mixed economies contested trade union domination, necessitating a broader party appeal beyond union ranks. In rural areas and parts of the south, Labour began to be maintained and nurtured by individual memberships, the size and import of which varied. As we shall see, Labour's 'breakthrough' was finally cemented at a time of declining union membership, suggesting that further progress was dependent on Labour's approach to the wider community and its projecting a viable political identity to which the electorate could relate and respond.

Before looking at the ways and means by which Labour endeavoured to do this, however, let us first consider the local parties' reaction to a key aspect of the changing political landscape in 1918, that is the emergence of a female electorate. As noted above, the central party moved quickly to appoint Marion Phillips as chief women's officer and to make arrangements for the inclusion of individual women members within the party. In order to give such provisions a practical expression, the party further appointed a number of women organisers from head office, all of whom were immediately dispatched across the country to visit the newly established constituency parties in order to help organise the female members into women's sections. Not all divisional parties had to be cajoled, or encouraged, to do this. In explicit reference to the extended franchise, the Bedwellty party decided in September 1918 to send a 'personal invitation signed by the secretary of the women's group' to prospective members and voters.[178] Even so, by the end of 1918, Phillips, alongside Mrs Fenn, Mrs Chettle, Mrs Hardie, Miss Thompson and Miss Basnett, had covered vast swathes of the country in the name of Labour women. From July through to October, they visited some 69 constituencies in England and Wales, with Hardie further taking responsibility for Scotland. And although they reported that many male members took 'too small an interest in the work of women organisers', their efforts evidently proved useful.[179] Following further reorganisation in 1920 and the appointment of women organisers to each of the nine regional sections outlined in Henderson's 'scheme of organisation', the party claimed to have over 100,000 female members gathered in some 800 women's sections by 1922, increasing to 120,000 the following year. True, only twelve sections boasted a membership over 200, with the vast majority registering members in the tens rather than hundreds.[180] But Labour's efforts were significant in that they at least demonstrated a willingness to absorb women into the party apparatus. In addition to the almost *de rigeur* 'appeal to women' made in party election material, the party organisers formed a series of advisory councils to give a more coherent voice to its female members.[181] Only in Scotland, where the ILP defended its traditional 'mixed' sex organisation and harboured reservations about individual Labour membership, did the party find any undue resistance to its objective.[182] By 1920–1, the nine women organisers were Mrs Hardie (Scotland), Mrs Andrews (Wales), Mrs Anderson (North West), Mrs Fenn (North East), Mrs Fawcett (Midlands), Miss Francis (Eastern), Miss Fraser (South East), Mrs Townley (South West) and Miss Somers (London).

The role of these women has traditionally been underplayed in histories of Labour. Yet, their influence was important in the future development of the party. On becoming women's organiser for Wales in March 1919, Elizabeth Andrews, a miner's wife and executive member of the Rhondda Labour Party, contributed greatly to the extension of Labour support in the country, working tirelessly for the party through to her retirement in 1948.[183] In between encouraging local parties to form women's sections and visiting women's groups to disseminate party policy and oversee their progress, Andrews sought to rally female electors during municipal, general and by-elections, ensuring that issues relevant to the lives of Welsh women were recognised and addressed by the party. In such a way, Andrews perceived the women's sections to be 'the working women's university', emphasising the role that the party played in the self-image and aspirations of its members. For her efforts, women made up 45 per cent of individual party membership in Wales by 1933 (9,160).[184]

The women's organiser for the North East region, Lillian Fenn, made similarly impressive progress, helping to establish some 118 women's sections in Durham alone by 1925, though her remit also included Yorkshire and Northumberland.[185] While often appearing to operate beneath the surface of the various male-dominated Durham Labour parties, the county women's sections maintained a functioning

Labour Women's Advisory Council, an annual summer school to which a number of scholarships were awarded, and an annual women's gala around which much of the sections' activity was based. Amongst all this, Fenn was very much to the fore, acting as steward and speaker at the gala rally, encouraging regular activities within the often small and scattered local women's sections, organising speakers' classes, and ensuring that women were involved in election campaigns.[186] She was succeeded by Margaret Gibb in 1929, who continued to encourage a wide range of women's activity throughout the region. A former teacher, Gibb served the party until 1957.

Through its instigation of women's sections, Labour endeavoured to offer a political home to the recently enfranchised female electorate. Despite this, different points of interest and activity often distinguished male and female members of the party in the 1920s. In the words of one Labour activist, Winnie Smith, it appeared as though 'men were the masters and women were left to do the soppy things'.[187] Where men forged, discussed and maintained the party's focus on industrial-economic issues, foreign affairs and working-class living standards, activity amongst the women members was generally concentrated on matters deemed to be of particular relevance – health, childcare, education and domestic life. There were increasingly 'grey areas' – most obviously, the question of working-class housing, welfare reform and unemployment – but a division of labour was notable within the local parties. Taken generally, male members dominated official party positions and set the terms of debate within the executive and general committee meetings, while the party women concentrated on maintaining the party machinery via canvassing, fundraising and organising party socials.

Yet, to assume that women were thereby insignificant to the Labour Party's development would be extremely misleading. As we shall see, women played an important role in the preservation of Labour's organisation and the extension of the party's appeal in the 1920s and 1930s. Moreover, as Pat Thane has noted, the Labour Party's consistent association of women and the home was not simply 'the expression of a male-dominated "false consciousness"'; it was also born from a 'conviction that the home should and could provide the base for the liberation of women rather than their insuperable bondage'. Though some women referred to their being sidelined or ignored within the party, most Labour women did not seem to perceive their role as inferior, but as their shared contribution to broader party activity, seeking in the process to ensure 'equal status for domestic and other social roles'.[188] Even more pragmatically, Labour's attitude was informed by the fact that the home was exactly where a large proportion of working-class women were located in the early twentieth century. What Labour often failed to do – along with other political parties and organisations – was to appreciate that women comprised multiple identities: housewives, workers, mothers, consumers, wives, lovers, Catholics, and so on. The political lives of many Labour women were often interspersed with the 'responsibilities' of home, with Labour ready to accept rather than question such a status quo. Thus, the South Shields Labour Party could 'explain' its lack of active female members in 1927 as 'owing to the added work in the home through the operation of the eight hour day in the mines'.[189] Lastly, therefore, we should not read gender differences in too 'fixed' a way. The 'identity' of Labour women was not simply created out of their party involvement, but was informed by – and would inform – the wider social-cultural environment from which they came. Class and occupational status cut across gender distinction, and such differentials were evident both within the Labour Party and with regard to Labour women's relationship with non-party women's organisations.[190]

The minutes of various party women's sections reveal much about the extent, nature and effectiveness of female activism within the party in the 1920s. Often, the newly established sections began with a relatively wide political-organisational brief. Thus, in one local Scottish women's section, formed in January 1924 after the party's women organiser for Scotland (Mrs Hardie) had visited Hawick, the allocation of 'tray holder' duties at a forthcoming party 'soirée' was juxtaposed with a discussion of the housing problem, the meaning of socialism, and government foreign policy with regard to France and Egypt.[191] Too often, however, the increased regularity of party activity over the 1920s served to blunt such diversity. The same local (Hawick) was reporting there being 'no correspondence or business of any importance' by 1927, as whist drives, jumble sales and the odd recitation headed the section agenda.

Such a pattern of development was broadly evident elsewhere. In Newport, 53 women had joined the divisional party as individual members within four months of the party's reorganisation in 1918. A women's section was duly formed, three women were elected to the party's executive committee, and a women's representative – Mrs Wyatt – presented the party with a list of female candidates for the town council elections.[192] But although female membership continued to grow to 'over 1,000' by 1924, the party soon developed 'traditional' patterns of activity. Within little over a year, the women's section had been instructed to act as a committee to arrange whist drives and party socials; its first annual conference in 1920 was held following a bazaar. Similarly, although Labour women candidates were adopted and elected to the board of guardians, Mrs Bartlett was soon complaining to the party's general committee about the absence of female candidates for the 1920 municipal elections.[193] Moreover, if the Newport party, as elsewhere, did at least concentrate on issues of direct concern to female and male constituents, then it continued initially to do so in a gendered way. To take one example, the party's 1919 municipal election manifesto described improvement in the town's housing as being necessary 'to give women a fair chance of living a life of reasonable leisure in an atmosphere of comfort and security'.[194] Again, however, it would be wrong to conclude that Newport women were thereby passive party members. The party's female executive members later grew to have some notable influence; Newport delegates to the Labour conference were mandated to support policies promoted by the women's sections, and the general committee was persuaded in 1933 to listen to a talk given by Mrs Daniels of the National Birth Control Association. This caused some controversy, with a letter being sent to the NEC for guidance, before the talk was duly given with necessary reference to the 1925 Labour conference resolution that 'no decision as to birth control shall be taken by any party meeting as the position of the party ...'[195]

In St Helens, meanwhile, Margaret Lloyd recalled the local women's section thus:

> I started a little, well, we had a few up and down, just a home meeting. We didn't call it political, we was just, every week, about a dozen people came to visit me ... [made] it a little saving club, I think, more than anything. We would put half a crown a week in a box and then, after that, we'd another tin. We had a raffle and each one of us in turn made sandwiches, and I made tea ... anything that went on at Labour Club, we none of us went

in a club but only for the ladies' meetings. And Mrs Shard was there. She was another born organiser and she could get us to do anything. And there'd be big meetings. And there'd be a Labour Party women's rally all from the North West. And it would be held here in the Co-op ... We'd a marvellous section.[196]

Not dissimilarly, the ten to thirteen members of the Crook Labour Party women's section recorded a number of 'sociable evenings' in the mid-to-late 1920s, consisting primarily of tea, cake and conversation. The section met fortnightly, with members giving talks on 'industrial peace' or 'trade unionism', preparing social activities for the wider (Spennymoor) party, and singing songs.[197]

While hardly the cut and thrust of political struggle, such activity should not simply be dismissed as 'soppy'; much of the Labour women's activity was integral to the maintenance and extension of the party's support. At election time, women soon began to take on much of the practical work of electioneering.[198] Writing in 1922, following his election to parliament as member for West Stirlingshire, Tom Johnston commended the way in which local female party members had 'hustled the indifferent to the booths; they lent shawls and held babies: they carried the sick and dying to the polls on mattresses – and they won'.[199] In many places, women members staffed the party offices or campaign rooms, undertook extensive canvassing via the distribution of leaflets and the calling on potential voters door-to-door. Margaret Lloyd was only sixteen when she began working as secretary to her father, the full-time election agent in St Helens and Labour Mayor in 1926. Looking back on the 1920s, she recalled how she 'had to get all these women (we got women, more or less, not so many men with us) and we did all the canvassing', before her brother then lent his car to take people to the polling booths.[200] Speaking at the 1929 party conference, moreover, Mr Broad from the Edmonton Divisional Labour Party admitted that the 'bulk' of the money raised by the party was done so by the women's section, a claim that could have been echoed by many non-trade union funded parties.[201] To take one example, the Peterborough party's discussion on raising funds for a full-time organiser in 1925 led one of its two female executive members, Mrs Dale, to exclaim that 'the women had done the work in the past, it was now time for the men to get on with it'.[202]

Ultimately, the activities and policies taken on and instigated by Labour's women members would become vital to the preservation of many divisional Labour parties – their involvement gave Labour a physical female presence that informed its development at a local or community level. As such, the existence of women's sections did not mean that the party's female members were continually detached from the men; the party's social and election activities increasingly brought co-operation and interaction. Furthermore, the political and social worlds of many local parties began to blur amidst the regularly organised socials and sub-committee meetings. Although women tended to remain in the minority on the central decision-making organs of the party, they would become integral to the party's local character and, in due course, influential in shaping or extending the party's breadth of interest.

Looked at generally, therefore, Labour had established itself nationally by 1923, though the extent and form of its organisation varied from place to place. True, the Labour Party in the early 1920s continued to be largely dependent on trade union finance and support. Nevertheless, such a pattern of organisation was evidently beginning to change by the middle of the decade, as the constituency party apparatus became more established, as membership broadened, and as local Labour attention to social-political matters combined to extend the party's relevance and appeal.

IV. FROM THEORY TO PRACTICE: FORGING LABOUR POLICY

Labour's reorganisation in 1918 was not confined to the extension of the party apparatus. Equally important was the broadening of Labour policy, encapsulated in the publication of *Labour and the New Social Order* and the formation of a distinctive foreign policy relevant to the immediate post-war world. Domestically, meanwhile, the party developed a series of social welfare policies that would increasingly inform both Labour's municipal and national election campaigns. Of course, social and welfare issues had been an essential part of Labour politics prior to 1918, most obviously via the broadening of educational opportunities and improved health care, though it was through the provision of work and a decent standard of living that Labour had more commonly envisaged social improvement.[203] By accession to parliament, Labour could use the state 'efficiently' to provide opportunities and assure equality for all. For this reason, Labour had encouraged and supported Liberal reforms such as free school meals for the poorest children, compulsory medical inspections in state schools, and the 1908 Old Age Pensions Act. True, certain Liberal measures including the introduction of labour exchanges and the National Insurance Act had proved controversial, primarily because of their encroachment into the realm of trade unionism. But the Great War helped convince many in the labour movement of the state's responsibility for social welfare. In the short term, industrial-economic concerns and foreign policy issues attained priority status, but it was arguably Labour's developing social policy that would help serve eventually to widen the party's support beyond that of the organised working class and disgruntled former Liberals.

This need to extend the party's appeal was recognised within the constituencies, where it related first to efforts to ensure maximum trade union affiliation, the enlistment of individual members, and the establishment of women's sections. Thus, soon after the formation of the Bedwellty Divisional Labour Party in April 1918, its prospective parliamentary candidate Charles Edwards underlined the importance of recruiting individual members and the need to provide for the 'body of labour' outside of the trade union movement. Similarly, the Colne Valley Divisional Labour Party urged its members in early 1920 to take more interest in local election contests in an effort to 'spread the light'; the party was to utilise the press and ensure that regular meetings were held to attract individual members.[204] Yet, simply 'opening the doors' of the Labour Party was not in itself a guarantee of success. Clearly, Labour policy had to relate to the wider (expanded) electorate. To this effect, both the NEC and the various divisional party executive committees across the country sought to construct electoral appeals that reflected and confronted the fears, concerns and aspirations of their respective constituents. Not surprisingly, the results varied.

Labour articulated its political vision most explicitly in *Labour and the New Social Order* (1918), with its 'four pillars' comprising a national minimum, the democratic control of industry, the 'revolution' of national finance, and the distribution of wealth for the common good. The first of these, the national minimum, referred to the principle of assuring a minimum standard of living for all.

In effect, this meant a minimum wage, but it also pushed Labour towards a commitment to full employment and the safeguarding of workers' conditions. In the meantime, the unemployed were to be assured of an adequate standard of living, with the state taking responsibility for initiating national and local government works and services (houses, schools, roads etc). Second, the democratic control of industry was a commitment to the public ownership of industry, or 'socialisation' in the words of the resolution adopted at the party conference in June 1918. This was clearly couched in terms of efficiency and morality rather than overt ideology, and was placed in contrast to capitalism's 'evil shadow' of low wages. More specifically, *Labour and the New Social Order* referred to the 'immediate nationalisation' of the railways, mines and electrical power, along with the 'common ownership' of land, canals, harbours, shipping, roads, post and telegraphs. Logistical details were vague, although the 'steadily increasing participation of the organised workers in the management' of communication and transport industries was envisaged. Third, the commitment to a 'revolution of national finance' comprised an overhaul of the taxation system to safeguard the national minimum, to ensure a 'graduated scale' of taxation, to allow a revision of inheritance and land taxation, and to develop a national banking system. More immediately, Labour called for a capital levy to meet the war debt. Lastly, the fourth 'pillar' represented Labour's commitment to a 'new social order' in which equality of opportunity was assured. This entailed educational, social and welfare reforms, including the removal of privilege in the education system, the funding of public housing schemes, the abolition of the poor law, and the 'public provision for the prevention and treatment of disease'. It reaffirmed Labour's commitment to the 'complete emancipation of women', specifically to equal pay, entry to the professions, an equal franchise, and eligibility for election to all public bodies. In addition, *Labour and the New Social Order* envisaged notable constitutional reform. Thus, Home Rule for Ireland and separate legislative authorities for Scotland and Wales were proposed, along with the extension of local government powers and the abolition of the House of Lords. The objective was a society 'based not on internecine conflict, inequality of riches, and dominion over subject classes, subject races, or subject sex, but on the deliberately planned co-operation in production and distribution, the sympathetic approach to healthy equality, the widest possible participation in power, both economic and political, and the general consciousness of consent which characterise a true democracy'.[205]

Beyond the broad objectives of *Labour and the New Social Order*, Labour policies were further considered by a number of advisory committees under the jurisdiction of the NEC. Nine of these were established in March 1918, and included committees on international questions, industrial policy, education, local government and 'drink traffic'.[206] Initially, at least, these proved ineffective, leading to their reorganisation in 1920. Subsequently, eleven committees reported irregularly to the NEC, offering comments on government policy, forwarding suggestions for future Labour programmes, consulting with the PLP, and advising Labour's local government representatives. Two further committees were established in 1923 (housing and science), although they continued to function erratically and with an apparent autonomy that unsettled the TUC.[207]

Given the post-war context, foreign affairs dominated much of the NEC's time between 1918 and 1923. The party's general election manifestos of 1918 and 1922 both led on Labour's commitment to peace, the League of Nations, an Irish Free State and international conciliation, policies inherited from the party's (Liberal) radical tradition but also synonymous with its socialist internationalism.[208] Across a myriad of issues, four took priority: the peace settlements, Russia, Ireland, and the refounding of the Second International. From late 1917, the NEC worked closely with the TUC parliamentary committee to define the party's post-war aims, the basis for which were endorsed at a joint conference on 28 December. On the one hand, Labour conceived a number of broad objectives, specifically that there should be no more war, the 'complete democratisation of all countries', the 'abandonment' of imperialism, the 'suppression' of secret diplomacy, the abolition of compulsory military service, the limitation of armaments, and the 'entire abolition of profit-making armament firms'. Simultaneously, Labour called for more concrete measures, such as the formation of a League of Nations, for territorial adjustments to be achieved by allowing 'the people to settle their own destinies', and an end to economic aggression in the form of tariffs, trusts and monopolies.[209] Such aspirations were to be echoed by President Wilson's 'fourteen points', which Labour warmly welcomed, but which would too often be absent from the eventual treaties drawn up in an atmosphere of victorious jingoism from 1919. From here on, Labour offered its full support for the League of Nations, through which it hoped for the peaceful revision of the 'compromised' peace settlements.

With regard to Russia, Labour opposed allied intervention, going so far as to endorse the call for direct action made during 1919–20. Though openly critical of Lenin's Bolsheviks, Labour refrained from supporting any moves designed specifically to undermine the fledgling workers' republic. Rather, Labour proposed diplomatic recognition and the establishment of trade relations with Soviet Russia, measures that the party reasoned would facilitate peace and help bolster economic recovery in Britain. By taking such an approach, Labour became open to almost hysterical Tory and press claims of Bolshevik sympathies, the impact of which were resonant if difficult to gauge. So, for example, on the eve of the first Labour government, warnings of bloody revolution coalesced with more specific scaremongering, such as the possibility of a socialist administration introducing 'free love'.[210] Significantly, such claims were made at all levels. During the 1922 election, the Conservative Association in Tiverton presented voters with a stark choice between 'a parliament elected on the most representative and democratic basis', or a 'soviet with industrial conscription under socialist officials' which 'only a revolution can remove'. Even Noel Buxton, an erstwhile Liberal, was forced to dismiss claims that he was a 'red revolutionary' during the same election. Appealing to local propertied interests in North Norfolk, his opponent, Captain Crewdson, claimed that Buxton would stop people from buying their own homes.[211] Of course, such claims were absurd; the NEC and PLP line on Bolshevism remained consistently critical, and the transferral of revolutionary labels to men such as Arthur Henderson, Jimmy Thomas and Ramsay MacDonald – not to mention Noel Buxton – was ridiculous to all but the most jaundiced of political observers. Nevertheless, the potential damage inflicted by such claims did help to shape Labour's development over the interwar period, ensuring that the party kept its distance from the CPGB and formed a constitutional alternative to Bolshevik communism. Rejecting the 'old bogey' of socialist revolution became another staple of party propaganda over the 1920s.

Labour was less consistent in its response to the worsening situation in Ireland, though it always retained a commitment to some form of Irish autonomy. Initially, this was conceived via the enactment of Home Rule, a policy that kept Ireland within the British Isles and proved consistent with Labour's wider conception of empire, for which it proposed self-government and equal rights within existing imperial boundaries.[212] As the situation deteriorated, however, Labour responded to the government's brutal repressions by moving eventually to a position of supporting Irish independence through self-determination. This was somewhat equivocal, and was prompted, in part, by an indigenous Irish pressure most obviously articulated at the Stockport by-election of March 1920, where the intervention of a Sinn Fein candidate helped to block a Labour victory. By this time, Labour had already sent a delegation to Ireland in January 1920, before establishing its own inquiry into the government's 'law and order' policy, the results of which were published as the *Report of the Labour Commission of Inquiry into the Present Situation in Ireland* (1921). A conference and national campaign ensued, recommending the withdrawal of British troops and the formation of a constituent assembly to devise 'without limitations or fetters' a new Irish constitution.[213] From such a position, Labour was able to develop close – if always conditional – links with Irish communities in places such as Liverpool, Glasgow, parts of London, Lancashire and elsewhere. Even so, Labour endorsed the eventual partition of Ireland, lending Lloyd George support in the face of substantial Conservative and Unionist opposition to a settlement which provided Nationalists with a significant part of their aims.

Finally, the Labour Party took a leading role in the refounding of the Second International following its disintegration at the outbreak of war in 1914. Both MacDonald and Henderson contributed to the protracted discussions that took place from 1917, particularly once the Bolshevik revolution had paved the way for a revolutionary alternative. To this end, Henderson formed part of a three-man permanent commission appointed at the Berne conference of European socialists in 1919 to prepare for the reconstruction of the Second International, the headquarters of which were temporarily transferred to London in 1920. Eventually, the new Labour and Socialist International was formed in May 1923.

Domestically, the broad sweep of *Labour and the New Social Order* ensured that Labour appeared clear as to its aims. Concurrently, Labour policy remained less certain with regard to its implementation. Such discrepancy was especially relevant at a municipal level, where Labour was closest to the levers of power in the immediate post-war era. Accordingly, a series of social-political priorities came to inform Labour propaganda in the early 1920s, though these were often interpreted in a variety of different ways. First and foremost, Labour sought to ensure that it had a say in the administration of its constituents' everyday lives. That, after all, was the objective of the Labour Party: 'to promote the political, social and economic emancipation of the people, and more particularly of those who depend directly upon their own exertions by hand or by brain for the means of life'.[214] As such, practical policy tended to follow on from this, and was informed by a variety of determinants particular to each constituency and divisional party. In such a way, Labour policy could reflect different priorities and encapsulate different forms in different places at different times.

For Mike Savage, a number of factors combined to shape the Labour Party's objectives and procedure at a local, or municipal, level in the period following the Great War. First, employment differentials could inform the 'nature' of a local Labour party. This was clearly evident in certain mining and textile villages, but could prove more complex in 'mixed' economic localities. Thus, in Savage's case study of Preston, the interests of the town's skilled cotton workers initially informed the party's composition and priorities in the immediate post-war years, arguably to the detriment of the party's broader advancement. Here, the pursuit of essentially sectional interests appeared initially to alienate the party from those it more broadly endeavoured to represent, particularly working-class women. Second, patterns of gender relations came to influence Labour's progress and identity. This, in turn, was informed by local employment patterns, trade union domination of divisional and ward party structures, and local socio-cultural traditions. Third, therefore, social configurations shaped Labour policies; that is, class relations, housing patterns and associated 'cultures'. In particular, Savage points to the emergence of distinct working-class neighbourhoods as being integral to Labour's ability to progress over the interwar period. More widely, Labour's identity was informed by the ways in which it was portrayed both by the party itself and its political opponents. In this, the importance of local (and national) newspapers, party activists and local Liberal and/or Conservative organisations should not be underestimated.

In specific relation to Preston, Savage dissects the town's occupational and social patterns to explain Labour's progress, focusing especially on the differentiated and gendered nature of the town's cotton industry, on changes in workplace relations and structures, on the town's topography (the migration of the town's elite and the formation of distinct working-class environs), and on the impact that broader 'national factors' had on the town's political, economic and social composition. Quite clearly, the conversion of the cotton unions to Labour helped establish the party in Preston. But local Labour activists necessarily had to broaden the party's appeal in order to make a significant challenge to the dominant Conservative Party. This it did in the 1920s by refocusing its attention onto the emerging working-class neighbourhoods, establishing Labour clubs, ward organisations and social activities, and applying Labour policy to the concerns of the (largely) working-class community. Significantly, Preston's populace were not converted into avowed socialists. Rather, the Preston Labour Party sought to address the insecurities and needs of the wider community, campaigning for better housing, health facilities, education and public amenities. In so doing, the party broke from the constraints of essentially economistic trade union concerns, winning support that was encapsulated in the burgeoning women's section of the mid-to-late 1920s. By 1929, Labour held seven of the twelve council seats and both the town's parliamentary seats. Ultimately, therefore, 'different elements of the local social structure [provided] various capacities for the maintenance of particular forms of collective action', of which the Labour Party was one.[215] The aim and subsequent progress of the Labour Party was reliant on its ability to reflect and harness these elements in a way that was relevant to the needs and desires of the local community.

To expect to find exact patterns of development elsewhere would be naive, but Savage's approach is certainly instructive. If we take Coventry as an example, we can see how Labour's fortunes in the city ebbed and flowed over the interwar period in response to internal and external changes and pressures.[216] Coventry was a city in transition during the first half of the twentieth century, with a developing industrial base centred on 'new' engineering industries such as motor cycles, cars, aircraft and various associated works. The city's workforce was overwhelmingly male, some 48 per cent of whom were engaged in skilled employment over the 1920s and 1930s. Female employment was concentrated primarily in the Courtauld silk factory and the General Electric Company, and was largely unorganised. Industrial tensions were not uncommon, although relatively harmonious workplace relations tended to complement paternal employment traditions that diminished only slowly. At the same time, Coventry's population was growing, from 128,152 in 1921 to 220,000 in 1939, prompting difficulties with regard to housing, education and the provision of social services. And yet, despite an overwhelmingly working-class population and problems associated with Coventry's changing topography, the ruling council 'shopocracy' of retailers, manufacturers, professionals and petty bourgeoisie maintained a commitment to low rates and low public expenditure that retained support. As a party, Labour remained weak over the 1920s, winning the occasional general election contest but in no way securing a Labour stronghold. Why was this?

Several factors can be posited in terms of explanation. First, the city hierarchy had developed a social as well as political leadership. In particular, savings banks and building societies ensured that home ownership was not the preserve of the few, providing opportunities for building contractors and ensuring that a significant minority of the working class owned their own homes. Though a need for municipal housing was evident, it was not imperative; neither municipal nor statist solutions to Coventry's problems were necessarily apparent. Moreover, many of Coventry's social centres – its clubs, pubs, cinemas, dance halls and sports attractions – were private or professionally owned, and were available to a young and relatively affluent population. Second, the council coalition – which saw the Liberals and Conservatives openly co-operate from 1919 – combined to block Labour's progress throughout the 1920s. The obligatory anti-Labour disposition of the *Midland Daily Telegraph*, the Tory owner of which sat on Coventry council, merely reinforced this. Third, the Labour Party was initially subordinate to the city's trade unions, which had acted independently during the wartime disputes and themselves faced a challenge from a militant shop stewards' movement that eventually fed into the fledgling CPGB. Somewhat paradoxically, Labour was linked to a sectional trades council focused on immediate industrial-economic concerns and deemed to be the preserve of skilled engineer, while also being portrayed as the political expression of the post-wartime militancy evidenced in the CPGB and the unemployed demonstrations of 1920–1. Despite divisions within the once-dominant Liberal Party, a combination of workplace militancy and sectionalism coalesced to lose potential Labour support to the Conservatives. Only with the decline in union strength in the early-to-mid 1920s did the party begin to breakaway from the trades council's predominantly workplace politics. A ward-based organisation was finally established under the direction of George Hodgkinson, along with a women's section that brought with it an increase in individual party members; electioneering took priority, and the breadth of membership and support widened. In addition, the council's 'Achilles heel' – its unwillingness to invest in social amenities and services – was targeted by Labour and eventually brought dividends. After the setback of the second Labour government's collapse in 1931, the Coventry party won a steady stream of municipal seats to take control of the council in 1937. Again, Labour's slow and essentially limited development was not a natural expression of some abstract class-consciousness, but a product of the local and national party's ability to respond to and articulate the concerns and aspirations of its constituents within a particular set of circumstances.

But what does all this tell us – in general terms – about Labour's progress in the immediate post-war period? How did Labour endeavour to court the local electorate? Most obviously, Labour tended to advance in industrial areas where manual workers dominated the electorate and Labour could present itself as the party 'of the workers'. Election propaganda often made much of a candidate's labour, class and local credentials. Chris Williams has given the example of James James's 1925 election address in Rhondda, which made it clear (in a language telling of the time and place) that 'James is a collier – one of yourselves. Workingmen be true to your own class. Vote like men for your own man'.[217] Indeed, similar examples are to be found elsewhere. Across the country, Labour candidates were presented with a list of their local titles, positions and credentials – the combined point of which was to entrust the local electorate with their vote. The example of Durham has already been cited, but we could also look to the election leaflet of Edward Henry Brown, a Labour municipal candidate in Norwich, whose credentials included his service as secretary of the NUR branch (No. 2), or A. E. Pummell, a Norwich city councillor, local Labour executive member, and secretary of the Norwich Railway Clerks' Association (RCA) for twelve years.[218] Alternatively, in areas with a radical tradition, Labour nominees were often erstwhile Liberals or middle-class candidates campaigning on an essentially progressive programme, as in parts of Edinburgh or Leicester. Similarly, in suburban and Tory areas, middle-class candidates were selected to woo the local electorate, as in East Grinstead, Lewisham or Birmingham. The objective was to present a Labour identity applicable to the relative constituency.

Secondly, the establishment of an effective party apparatus and leadership able to present an identity relevant to local interests and conditions was a Labour priority from 1918. This, again, had to be combined with the adoption of appropriate candidates and organisational schemes to canvass and recruit members if Labour was to advance.[219] Yet, while such an observation is undoubtedly true in many instances, there remained places where Labour organised well but failed to secure regular parliamentary or municipal success. In Wales, Newport was a classic example; elsewhere we could point to the large divisional party memberships in Cambridge, Ilford, and Reading over the 1920s. Conversely, there were many Labour 'strongholds' that were managed by parties with very basic organisational structures beyond the local trade unions, such as Ebbw Vale and Bishop Auckland. We shall look in more detail at such organisational concerns in Chapter Two below.

Third, the Labour Party began to formulate a politics that increasingly related to and sought to improve the lives of people beyond the workplace. Locally, and despite the centralisation of Labour organisation from 1918, the divisional parties retained a degree of flexibility in their portrayal of Labour's objective, particularly in relation to municipal politics. Equally, at a national level, the importance of social welfare issues gradually and unevenly began to eclipse the 'high' political and often religious-associated issues of the Victorian and Edwardian era. This would take time, but it is clear that Labour candidates, councillors and activists focused evermore attention on the living conditions of working people in their constituencies, highlighting in particular issues of housing, health and education. For instance, the Edinburgh trades council listed housing, unemployment and the feeding and clothing of necessitous school children as its foremost political (non-industrial) concerns in 1923.[220] Local Labour candidates, councillors and council groups across the country agitated and reported primarily on such subjects, believing that Labour could alleviate such social ills through its more efficient – and morally superior – running of society. In the words of the *Daily Herald* in 1919, a vote for Labour was ostensibly a vote for 'better education, better housing, better sanitation; in fact better everything that concerns our everyday life'.[221] To this effect, divisional parties in London offered local versions of Labour socialism, appealing in different ways in different areas to women electors, Jews, Catholics, skilled and unskilled workers.[222] In Glasgow, as noted above, Labour made progress largely as a product of the ILP's concentration on local social-political issues such as housing and rents, something that was sustained during general election campaigns. In 1922, for example, the official Labour Party programme appears to have been ignored in favour of a series of manifestos drawn up by John Wheatley. For Wheatley and Patrick Dollan, men who had honed their political skills in the council chamber, it was essential to combine local and national perspectives. In Wheatley's case, his rise to parliament came after ten years as a councillor in Shettleston, where his knowledge of local housing problems and active support for tenants turned him into something of a 'local hero'.[223]

Not surprisingly, housing became one of Labour's most prominent and consistent concerns from 1918. Following the Great War, there was an estimated shortfall of some 800,000 homes, not to mention the continued existence of overcrowding and dire inner city slums. In response to Lloyd George's promise of 'homes fit for heroes', Labour gained a handy piece of negative propaganda around which the party was able to make some political headway. So, in those areas of London where Labour borough councils were elected in 1919, the party moved quickly to improve the living standards of its constituents. Thus, in Camberwell, the Labour council of 1919–22 built 450 council houses, although the coalition government's repeal of the Addison Acts prevented it meeting its target of 2,000 new homes.[224] In Poplar, the Labour council quickly introduced a house-building programme, applied pressure to landlords to make necessary repairs, and extended the borough's electricity undertaking.[225] Linked to this, Labour programmes made much of health and welfare issues. These could comprise appeals for state intervention, as in Sheffield, where the Labour Party portrayed the question of health and medical services as a national question, or schemes of 'mutualist' co-operation, as in Tredegar, with its Medical Aid Association to which 90 per cent of the town's population belonged by 1944.[226] Elsewhere, extensive health reforms would be enacted in Bermondsey from 1922, while Poplar again instigated wide-ranging measures, including the opening of a tuberculosis dispensary, the opening of public baths on Sundays, the initiation of a scheme for free milk, the expansion of library services, and the organisation of social events on Saturday nights.[227]

By 1921, unemployment had also become a key issue for Labour, both nationally and locally. In the economic circumstances of the time, trade unions existed in what John Holford has described as 'shifting and different terrains', as industries responded to the variegated affects of the post-war economy.[228] At root, however, unemployment was now recognised by many Labour supporters to be 'an ever-present feature of capitalist society, and will not be satisfactorily solved until the capitalism system is abolished'.[229] In response, a joint Labour–TUC conference held on 27 January 1921 endorsed *Unemployment – A Labour Policy*, in which the party called for the provision of work or adequate maintenance, the restoration of European trade relations (including with Russia), and the removal of restrictions on local government expenditure. Simultaneously, unemployment began to inform Labour election campaigns. During the Newcastle East by-election of 1922, Labour members successfully backed Arthur Henderson's re-election under banners declaring 'Fighting 1914: Starving 1922', in direct appeal to the city's jobless ex-servicemen.[230] Finally, the divisional parties campaigned around specifically local concerns. In Newport in 1920, council plans to borrow £1,641,000 towards new water works led to a Labour campaign to spend money on new housing. In Gloucester, the local elections of 1923 were fought exclusively on the question of vaccinations and municipal control of the small pox epidemic.[231]

To sum up, while the basis of Labour's organisation, finance and support was reliant on the trade union movement, its future development was dependent on its ability to appeal beyond the realm of organised labour. This the party began to do in the early 1920s, and did so to some success; Labour extended its organisation, increased its vote, and rose to government at a time when its trade union base was shrinking. To an extent, these two trends were linked: as the room for industrial action to secure improvements in working-class living standards diminished, so workers and unions looked to the political arena for progress. Alternatively, Labour's political priorities developed in accord with its broadening organisation, an expanding electorate, and its increased parliamentary presence. This, in turn, was engineered partly by the party leadership, but also by local Labour Party officers and members, who retained much scope in the articulation and projection of Labour policy. Taken generally, the trade unions gave Labour a financial and organisational base, but the party's development relied on the construction of policies, institutions and identities that reflected and connected with communities throughout the British Isles. At root, Labour's advance marked a shift from earlier trade union attempts to seek recognition and equal status to a broader working-class aspiration to gain control over their environment and the running of their everyday lives.

Even so, actual Labour policy often remained vague. Its objectives and values were clear, but the party lacked a coherent practical programme. The official Labour vision, as articulated in *Labour and the New Social Order*, continued to be centred on an ethical, collective basis: it viewed capitalism as a morally deficient system that needed to be infused with the ethics of socialism. Moreover, the industrial bias of party policy remained apparent. In the immediate post-war period and early 1920s, Labour advocated the extension of wartime collectivism, recognising the need for greater state intervention while calling simultaneously for a society informed by a collective responsibility and action. Just how this was to be achieved remained open to question. Come the 1923 general election, and the principal point of issue was that of free trade. It was, however, presented in a context linked directly to the problem of unemployment. In such circumstances, *Labour's Appeal to the Nation* usurped a traditional Liberal cause and applied it to a specifically Labour concern: a section headed 'tariffs are not the answer' was followed by the call for 'work or maintenance'. Practical solutions were proffered – national schemes, public works, full education – alongside commitments to improved social provisions. By January 1924 and the formation of the first Labour government, material circumstances, a relatively solid organisational foundation, and a more focused political approach had enabled Labour to maintain the impetus it had received over the course of the Great War. The question now was: could Labour deliver?

Chapter Two

Preparing for Responsible Government:
Labour's Breakthrough, 1924–9

The political progress of the Labour Party … is mainly trade union political progress … The political organisation is kept running by trade union funds, and the Political Labour Party in this country can be referred to as a Trade Union Labour Party, if we wish to use that term.[1]

Fred Bramley, Secretary of the TUC, 1924

So soon as a parliamentary party subordinates itself to the edicts of any non-parliamentary body, it ceases to be responsible. It must consider public opinion and the conditions under which it has to work, but its decisions must be taken on broader grounds than those held by any outside body. Its duty is not to take orders, but to consider advice. The political organ in society, to me, must ever be the supreme organ and its responsibility belongs to itself.[2]

Ramsay MacDonald, diary entry, 4 July 1926

The Conservative Party dominated British politics throughout the 1920s. Having formed the majority of Lloyd George's coalition government, the Tories won the 1922 general election only to lose power to Labour for the first time following the election of 1923. A year later, and Stanley Baldwin once again led his party to victory and remained prime minister until May 1929 Even then, despite Labour's winning the majority of seats to form a minority government, the Conservatives gained a higher percentage of the national vote than their rivals: 38.1 per cent to Labour's 37.1 per cent. During this time, the British economy stabilised but in many instances under-performed as the country's staple industries continued to struggle in the face of overseas competition and an over-valued pound. Most obviously, British mining suffered as a combination of government policy, competition and the recalcitrance of the mine owners led to unemployment, wage cuts and longer working hours across much of the industry. Similarly, the textile industry confronted severe difficulties during the 1920s, with tariffs and competition hampering progress and once again paving the way for high levels of unemployment and mounting workplace tension that 'boiled over' towards the end of the decade. British shipbuilding, along with iron and steel, faced equally damaging problems, with unemployment, low productivity and falling exports combining to keep the industry depressed. Over the decade, unemployment never fell below 1,000,000, with the bulk of those looking for work coming from the pits, mills and shipyards of Britain's industrial heartlands.[3] In such circumstances, industrial tensions simmered to varying extents throughout the 1920s, peaking with the 1926 lockout and General Strike.

The short-term causes of the General Strike stemmed from the mine owners' decision in July 1925 to reduce wages in response to declining coal exports and Britain's return to the gold standard in April of the same year.[4] Following concerted trade union pressure, the government agreed to a temporary nine-month subsidy on 31 July 1925 ('Red Friday'), during which time a royal commission headed by Sir Herbert Samuel was set up to examine the troubled coal industry. Come April 1926, however, and it was clear that the temporary concessions of the previous year were but a prelude to confrontation. When in March 1926 the Samuel Commission endorsed, among other things, the reduction of the miners' minimum wage, a strike seemed inevitable. In the event, both the employers and the Miners' Federation of Great Britain (MFGB) rejected the commission's findings. Consequently, after a final round of negotiations broke down, the owners implemented their lockout and the Trades Union Congress (TUC) sanctioned, from one minute to midnight on 3 May 1926, a General Strike that lasted for nine days and was supported solidly throughout by up to 3,000,000 workers, before the TUC unconditionally ended the action on 12 May. As the miners fought on, the labour movement began to assess the implications of such a dramatic defeat.

Of course, such industrial drama forms only part of the story. The problems sketched above would be offset, in part, by the growth of demand-led consumer industries, the service sector, and the gradual emergence of 'new industries' based on motor cars, artificial textiles, chemicals and electricity. Ultimately, however, change was slow and British economic development was still conceived with regard to the staple industries on which its industrial might had been forged. Subsequently, rationalisation – the creation of larger, more efficient and modernised units of production – became the buzzword of the decade, although it more practically entailed longer intensified working hours and cuts in the workforce than purposeful investment. Moreover, the problems that beset the British economy were compounded by the world economic depression that came in the wake of the Wall Street 'crash' in October 1929.

Within such a context, Labour's development over the 1920s was informed by its brief experience in government, by the events surrounding the 1926 General Strike, and by what it perceived as a series of social-economic circumstances maintained by a Conservative administration that had 'stabilised luxury and squalor, private waste and public parsimony, idleness and the disorganisation of productive industry ...'[5] Significantly, however, the Labour Party's politics were themselves focused primarily on Britain's staple industrial base. The party organisation and finances continued to be maintained largely by the unions of the staple industries, and this ensured that Labour continued to prioritise the interests of the 'older' rather than 'newer' industries throughout the 1920s. At the same time, the processes outlined in the previous chapter continued; Labour sought to extend and co-ordinate its organisation, broaden its political programme in an effort to integrate its identities and values with those of the British people, and to prove itself as a viable – a moderate, efficient and reliable – alternative to Baldwin's Conservative government.

I. A NEW DAWN FADES?
THE FIRST LABOUR GOVERNMENT

The first Labour government lasted just nine months, from 22 January 1924 until its dissolution on 9 October.[6] Noticeably, Labour did not immediately take office following the general election of December 1923. Given that the Conservatives had won the majority of seats, Stanley Baldwin initially retained his position as prime minister only to deliver a protectionist king's speech that was rejected by the House of Commons on 21 January 1924. It was on the following day, therefore, that George V called James Ramsay MacDonald to Buckingham Palace and invited him to form Britain's first (minority) Labour administration.

The significance of Labour's success should not be underestimated; Labour had travelled far in a relatively short period of time, becoming the first and only party to upset permanently Britain's otherwise relatively stable political configuration. The poignancy of the event was later captured in an oft-quoted – if rather romanticised – passage from J. R. Clynes' memoirs, in which he describes 'MacDonald the starveling clerk, Thomas the engine driver, Henderson the foundry labourer and Clynes the mill hand' standing before royalty and 'making history'.[7] Indeed, the miners' MP Jack Lawson later asked rhetorically how it could be that 'men of the mines and factories, the multitudes from the long lines of brick streets, [could] hope to stand beside the makers of a science, a literature, and a mechanical world which was the wonder of all men?' Nevertheless, he continued, in 1924 'the thing was done', insisting that the very existence of a Labour government brought 'succour to the masses'.[8] Without doubt, it was a historic and momentous achievement. Despite this, the sight of Labour's representatives in ceremonial court dress on their knees to the king brought both resentment and mirth, especially given Stephen Walsh's (minister for war) reputed difficulty in keeping his sword from entangling with his legs.[9] For George Lansbury, the episode raised doubts in his mind as to the extent to which Labour could achieve socialism by demonstrating 'how adaptable we are and how nicely we can dress and behave when we are in official, royal, or upper-class circles'.[10] More symbolically, John Wheatley and Fred Jowett – both appointed to the cabinet – refused to comply, attending the palace in their customary suits and hats (though both still bowed before the king).[11] Yet, the majority of ministers' willingness actively to observe parliamentary custom was in many ways a precursor to the generally conventional nature of Labour's tenure in office.

The decision to form a Labour government was taken by MacDonald in consultation with the Parliamentary Labour Party (PLP), the National Executive Committee (NEC) and the TUC general council. Though sections of the party were uncertain as to the opportunities offered by a minority administration, the labour movement leadership resolved at a series of meetings on 12–13 December 1923 to support MacDonald's premiership if called upon, a decision that was marked by a large and well-orchestrated victory rally held four weeks later at the Albert Hall on 8 January.[12] To refuse office, MacDonald had argued persuasively, would have allowed the Liberals the possibility of returning to the government benches, with the Conservatives becoming the principal opposition. In short, refusal could have led to Labour being accused of shirking its responsibilities; its position 'in the country' and in the Commons may well have become marginalised.[13]

In contrast to the collective spirit that facilitated and celebrated Labour's assumption of government office, the composition and character of the first Labour cabinet was deemed the responsibility of the PLP leadership and, specifically, the prime minister himself. To this effect, MacDonald was keen that Labour uphold what he saw as the best traditions of the British parliament, an adherence that was born as much out of genuine respect as by a determination to prove that Labour was 'fit to govern' Writing in his diary on 10 December 1923, following a meeting over dinner with Henderson, Webb, Thomas, Snowden and Clynes, MacDonald recorded a consensus that 'moderation & honesty were our safety'.[14] This was no doubt sensible given the minority status of the government and the hostility and trepidation registered by the wider British establishment. With the press talking of England's ruin and the king harbouring severe misgivings, MacDonald's unwillingness to personify these 'bogeys' was understandable if prone to lead to disenchantment amongst sections of his own party. Accordingly, perhaps, MacDonald would become increasingly intolerant of those who sought to repudiate his methods or stymie the parliamentary process, asserting repeatedly the government's national responsibilities in the face of those who wished to pursue more overtly socialist agendas.

Such concern for moderation and respectability was apparent in MacDonald's cabinet, although the new prime minister evidently found the personal politics of choosing his 'team' a rather painful experience. Lists were drawn and redrawn, negotiations ensued, bitter letters were received, before MacDonald finally completed what he described as 'the most horrible job in my life'.[15] Ultimately, the cabinet's twenty members included seven moderate and loyal trade unionists, four erstwhile Liberals, the former military attaché Lord Thomson, one ex-Conservative, two Fabians, and a core leadership of experienced Labour parliamentarians.[16] Thus, MacDonald doubled as foreign secretary, Henderson became home secretary, Snowden took up the chancellorship, Clynes became lord privy seal, and Thomas secretary of state for the colonies. The Independent Labour Party (ILP) left wing secured just two cabinet positions – Fred Jowett as commissioner for works, and John Wheatley as minister for health. The position of first lord of the admiralty was appointed to Lord Chelmsford, a Conservative. Notably absent from MacDonald's eventual short-list was George Lansbury, whose recent imprisonment and avowed sympathy for the Soviet Union ensured that the prime minister regarded him as something of 'loose cannon', a conception that was apparently reinforced by conversations with George V. Although Arthur Henderson had raised the question of a cabinet position with Lansbury in early 1924, MacDonald's concern for 'respectability' once again held sway. In the prime minister's estimation, Webb later recalled, 'Lansbury was always speaking so wildly and indiscreetly at meetings that he would injure the government'.[17] Wheatley's inclusion, meanwhile, was perhaps an attempt to tame the Clydesiders.

Taken generally, MacDonald's cabinet was intended to represent a government that was 'safe' in Labour hands. Somewhat appropriately, perhaps, its first meeting began with a lecture by Viscount Haldane on the fineries of ministerial etiquette.[18] At the same time, with no women or co-op members in its ranks, and with trade unionists in the minority, it was hardly representative of the party as a whole.[19] Indeed, the formation of a Labour government further brought a new organisational question to the fore: that of the relationship between the PLP and the government. In effect, the PLP executive now acted as a link between the cabinet and the parliamentary party, seeking to reaffirm the traditions of loyalty and unity that were coming to characterise the Labour Party more widely. This was achieved to only a limited extent in 1924, with the PLP executive complaining to the NEC that it had 'no more authority and frequently not much more information than the [NEC] with regard to government policy'.[20] Even so, when anxieties did emerge within the parliamentary party, they tended to remain confined inside the PLP ranks. Only the emerging pattern of ILP criticism broke from this to any notable extent. In such a way, the moderate character assigned to the government was broadly accepted within the party on its taking office in January.

In terms of domestic policy, the first Labour government achieved relatively little. John Wheatley's Housing Act has generally been seen to be Labour's most striking success, allocating subsidies to local authorities in order to build houses for rent, stipulating improved housing standards, and removing the provision that local authorities could only supply accommodation to fill the 'gaps' in the private market. Simultaneously, certain measures were introduced to protect tenants from eviction.[21] Without doubt, this was to have the most far-reaching impact on Labour's working-class constituents, enabling local councils to improve the living standards of many working-class families. Moreover, it connected with a key political priority of local Labour organisations. But beyond this, Labour's reforms were limited. Increased expenditure was secured for health and education, and the benefit system was liberalised, but such measures were piecemeal at best. Evidently, too, there was some disquiet in the PLP that the government's response to the problem of unemployment was largely inadequate.[22]

Economically, Philip Snowden's fiscal orthodoxy held sway; the government oversaw cuts in taxes and tariffs, remained committed to restoring the gold standard, sought a balanced budget, and endeavoured to bolster the economy via improved international relations. Given Labour's minority position, no moves towards public ownership were attempted beyond a private members' bill to nationalise the coal industry. This, inevitably, was rejected in the Commons, while John Guest's attempt to amend the 1912 Minimum Wage Act was similarly sidelined under the excuse of inadequate parliamentary time.[23] Furthermore, the capital levy remained notable only for its absence. In accord with his belief that socialism would develop from capitalist prosperity, Snowden erred on the side of caution. Public work schemes were moderate, as were benefit increases, and although Snowden envisaged the balanced budget as a means by which to transfer the economic burden from the poorer taxpayer to the rich bondholder, this meant very little in the adverse conditions of the 1920s. At the same time, of course, Snowden's moderation may have done much to convince many Liberals that Labour was now the standard bearer of its treasured ideals.

Disappointing, too, was the performance of Henderson as home secretary. Henderson lost his seat in December 1923, before returning to the Commons following a by-election in Burnley in February. Even so, the party secretary had wanted initially to head the foreign office, only to be thwarted by MacDonald's own diplomatic ambitions. Instead, Henderson proved a cautious minister, unable to overcome the prevarications of his civil servants and consistently committed to the formalities of his office. Most obviously, Henderson placed his governmental responsibilities ahead of his Labour, or class, loyalties, conferring rarely with the TUC and showing himself willing to use existing 'emergency' legislation in response to various strike actions, much to the consternation of fellow trade unionists such as Bevin. Not dissimilarly, Henderson disappointed the TUC and many in his party by refusing to reinstate those policemen dismissed following the 1919 police strike, despite Labour's previous commitment to do so. Although he agreed to an inquiry, following pressure from the NEC, Henderson retained a principled distinction between the rights of 'ordinary' trade unionists and those workers in the disciplined services.[24]

On a number of issues, Labour appeared reluctant to act with any decisiveness. To take one example, the NEC's opposition to Conservative plans to reform London transport in favour of Lord Ashfield's private combine was ignored by the PLP, with the minister of transport, Harry Gosling, bowing to pressure from civil service officials and the Transport and General Workers' Union (TGWU) to support the already drafted Tory bill. With Ashfield's bus workers receiving better pay than those employed by the London County Council (LCC), and with Bevin opposed to Morrison's alternative plan for wider municipal control of the capital's transport, Gosling and the cabinet plumped for inaction. Gosling, of course, was 'on leave' as president of the TGWU while representing the government. In the event, the logistical implications of the bill dragged on throughout the decade, with Morrison fighting it all the way, first in the LCC, then in the PLP, and finally – as minister of transport from May 1929 – in government. Only then was the bill killed and the 'London tramways were rescued from the grip of private monopoly'.[25]

As for MacDonald, his premiership affirmed many of the criticisms that had been levelled against him prior to his forming a government. As party chairman in 1912–14, his close relationship with the Liberals had raised concern both in and out of the PLP; similarly, his political caution and apparent aloofness had already become apparent in the years up to 1924. In office, therefore, he appeared a weak delegator, not close to his cabinet colleagues, and preoccupied with foreign affairs. Though there was no question of re-establishing formal ties with the Liberals, the prime minister's vain egocentricity lost rather than gained him admirers within the party hierarchy. Certainly, his notoriously tenuous relationship with Henderson was not improved by their time in government, though both continued to recognise the other's worth. Equally, allegations of impropriety surrounding the granting of a baronetcy to MacDonald's close friend and benefactor Alexander Grant did little to help bolster the prime minister's standing.[26] More widely, his government's insensitivity towards the trade union movement that had sponsored Labour's rise to power provoked tensions that impinged on Labour's development for much of the remaining decade. That said, kudos was garnered by MacDonald's activities as foreign secretary, particularly the implementation of the Dawes Plan to revise German reparation payments following the French occupation of the Ruhr. Due respect was shown to the League of Nations (though not to the extent that Henderson would have wished), with MacDonald appearing to fulfil capably his position as a British statesman.[27] More controversially, discussions towards a trade agreement were undertaken with Soviet Russia, a move that further jeopardised the Liberals' already tepid willingness to support the government. Although MacDonald officially recognised the Soviet Union in February, the Liberals chose to defeat the proposed commercial agreements negotiated by the government. Overall, therefore, MacDonald appeared a capable if evidently flawed prime minister. While effective in cabinet and on the international stage, he had shown himself simultaneously to be prone to errors of judgement and uncongeniality. Behind closed doors, his vain bouts of anxiety and disillusion no doubt contributed to his apparent detachment.[28]

Ironically, given the government's evident moderation and limitation, its brief lifespan was to be terminated amidst claims of Bolshevik sympathy and revolutionary conspiracy. These were fallacious, but summed up the furore that even the slightest hint of socialism could inspire amongst the British establishment.

The government had been willing to absorb the charges of Bolshevism that accompanied its negotiations with Soviet Russia – such a policy was very much in line with Labour's belief that economic stability would stem from peace between nations. But the PLP proved less robust when the accusations related to events at home, hence the government's attempt to demonstrate its anti-Bolshevik credentials by prosecuting the editor of the communist *Workers' Weekly* (Johnny Campbell) for an article that appealed to British soldiers not to fire on their fellow workers. This quickly proved to be an overly hasty judgement, but the cabinet's subsequent decision to drop the prosecution led only to Tory and Liberal charges of conciliation. A Liberal motion in favour of an inquiry was then passed with Conservative support, leading MacDonald to tender his government's resignation on 9 October.[29]

Not surprisingly, perhaps, the general election that followed saw Labour defending itself against charges of surrogate Bolshevism, culminating in the *Daily Mail's* publication of the 'Zinoviev Letter'. This was supposedly a communication from the president of the Communist International instructing British communists to prepare for revolution; but although the letter was in all probability a forgery, it nevertheless added to the general hysteria of the election campaign. That said, the extent to which the letter contributed to the election result is questionable. In fact, the peculiarities of the British electoral system did as much to unseat the Labour government as the media-induced climate of a 'red scare' While Labour lost over 40 seats, its percentage of the vote actually increased to 33.3 per cent (from 30.7 per cent). Progress was also made in certain areas where Labour had previously made little impact, including the Midlands. Baldwin's return to office, it seemed, was linked as much to the collapse of the Liberal vote as it was to the supposed failings of the Labour government. In the end, the Conservatives won 412 seats, Labour 151, while the Liberal presence in the Commons declined to just 40 (with 17.8 per cent of the vote). As such, the 1924 election suggested that the British electorate, particularly those who had previously voted Liberal, now perceived their choice to be set more clearly between Conservative and Labour.

By the end of 1924, therefore, the Labour Party could look back on its progress with qualified satisfaction. Given the circumstances in which Labour came to office, the government's limitations were hardly surprising. Not only was it heavily reliant on Liberal support, but the PLP was evidently short on ministerial experience beyond those such as Henderson and Clynes who had served in the wartime coalition. As already noted, MacDonald's principal objective was to demonstrate that the country was 'safe' in Labour hands. To this end, he was relatively successful, as the government prompted neither the revolution nor the social-economic collapse that many predicted. In the estimation of Sir Maurice Hankey, the cabinet secretary who had served under four prime ministers, Labour had formed a 'businesslike government' that soon won 'a great deal of good will from the British people'.[30] Accordingly, the NEC report to the 1924 Labour Party conference commented on the speed of Labour's rise to office and the 'political education of the people'. Erstwhile critics of the party had been silenced by Labour's performance, it insisted, with Labour proving 'it can undertake the task of government as seriously, as sincerely, and as successfully as any of its predecessors'.[31] Although Labour's first term in office had been short-lived, the party had not disgraced itself. Its relatively cautious performance could be balanced against its minority status, while the subsequent election result could be explained as much by the Machiavellian manoeuvres of the Tory party and press as by the record of the government itself. Looking back, Margaret Bondfield, who served as parliamentary secretary to Tom Shaw in the ministry of labour, felt 'amazed that the first Labour government made so few blunders and reaped so many successes'.[32] Certainly, the confines of Labour's minority status appear to have been acknowledged by most divisional parties. In Edinburgh, where the financial secretary to the treasury William Graham was an MP, the party accorded 'many achievements' to the Labour government. Not dissimilarly, in Yorkshire, the Leeds party praised the government's 'educational advances', while the *Bradford Pioneer* welcomed the 'safety' of Snowden's budget.[33]

But despite such loyal praise, the record and experience of the 1924 Labour government soon led to questions being raised with regard to the evident limitations of Labour policy. Minority or not, Labour had appeared uncertain in its response to unemployment, and there had been few signs as to just how Labour was to oversee the evolution of socialism via parliamentary reform.[34] Yet, the criticisms and concerns that did emerge in 1924–5 were important but contained (see below); the vast majority of the wider party remained committed to both the party and Ramsay MacDonald. Accordingly, Labour's general election manifesto for 1924 was based on a defence of the government's achievements with regard to peace, housing and social reform.[35] To a notable extent, the government had realised its own principal objective: that is to have formed a competent Labour administration serving clearly in the national interest. In the process, however, it had revealed certain shortcomings in Labour's preferred 'scheme of change'.

II. ORGANISATION AND CONTROL

Despite Labour's continuing electoral progress and the formation of a Labour government in 1924, it was clear that the party still had to widen its appeal if it was finally to condemn the Liberals to the political wilderness and, simultaneously, present a definite challenge to Baldwin's Conservative Party. For all its progress, Labour continued to be a party based largely on trade union and urban working-class support, and even this was far from evident in a number of British towns and cities.[36] Accordingly, the means by which to propagate Labour's message remained at the top of the party's agenda; efforts were made to consolidate the support already achieved, preferably within an expanding party organisation, and to entice middle-class, female and rural voters to Labour. This, in turn, meant an emphasis on Labour's moderation, on its national appeal, and on its rational (and ultimately moral) argument. To this effect, organisational and political initiatives were instigated to tighten the centre's influence over the party at all levels, before a new party programme was finally introduced at the 1928 party conference. The following section will examine the ways in which the Labour Party secured and extended its organisational base between 1924 and 1929. This will be followed by an overview of Labour's efforts to contain and/or expel potential sources of tension within its ranks during the mid-to-late 1920s. An examination of the party's political programme will then form the final section of this chapter.

Over the course of the 1920s, the balance of power and influence inside the Labour Party shifted in accord with the party's general development. Most obviously, the standing of the PLP within the wider party increased with its size, with its brief sojourn in office, and with the simultaneous decline in trade union membership and industrial leverage. By the end of the 1920s, the PLP exerted a notable influence over both the NEC and the party conference, relying on the block vote of a trade union movement that recognised the need for a parliamentary presence and was committed to electing a Labour government. This was achieved in a variety of ways. First, patterns of authority became established, with politicians dominating the NEC. The most prominent of the NEC's trade union representatives – who formed almost half of the executive – tended to be politicians first and foremost, and were not generally the leading figures within their respective unions.[37] J. R. Clynes, as representative of the National Union of General and Municipal Workers (NUGMW), was perhaps the most notable example of the primarily political trade union member, and he took his place alongside a variety of trade union MPs or parliamentary candidates, including Frank Roberts, Joseph Compton and C. G. Ammon. Such members tended, too, to bring with them the traditions of unity and loyalty that were entrenched within the union movement, so proving reliable advocates of the party leadership. This is not to say that important trade union figures did not feature, but that members such as Charlie Cramp (National Union of Railwaymen (NUR) and the mercurial Frank Hodges (MFGB) were not necessarily typical of the NEC's trade union contingent. Similarly, PLP members and/or prominent Labour politicians, such as Herbert Morrison, George Lansbury, Ben Spoor and Sir Charles Trevelyan, continually formed the divisional party section; and the same was true of the women's section. Susan Lawrence, Ethel Bentham and Agnes Dollan were each regular NEC members during the 1920s.[38]

Second, while the trade union presence was evident and potentially overriding, the labour movement generally continued to distinguish between the 'industrial' and the 'political', with due propriety given to the political context in which the Labour Party functioned. In such a way, the NEC was distinguished by its unanimity over the 1920s, administrating the party's affairs as it sought to extend Labour's electoral appeal. Finally, the core leadership of the Labour Party – already recognisable by 1924 – was further consolidated within the PLP by the end of the 1920s.[39] Alongside Ramsay MacDonald and Arthur Henderson, as chairman and secretary respectively, the composition of the PLP executive remained fairly constant between 1926 and 1929, comprised overwhelmingly of moderate parliamentarians such as Snowden, Webb, Graham and Dalton, all of whom were generally loyal to MacDonald's leadership (if not the man). Indeed, all but two of the PLP executive elected in 1927–8 and 1928–9 would form part of the Labour cabinet that split in August 1931.[40] Accordingly, the opportunity for one or more of the trade unions to direct the PLP was tempered as the parliamentary party expanded. Though still significant, the number of miners' MPs increased by just one between 1924 and 1929, while the PLP increased by 136.[41] At the same time, the ILP left wing in the Commons became increasingly estranged from the bulk of the PLP over the course of the 1920s (see below), with its representatives' constant criticisms being seen as divisive rather than constructive. Ultimately, this apparent cohesion would be first augmented and then destroyed by the experience of the 1929–31 Labour government. Over the decade as a whole, however, the continuity of party leadership reflected the unified sense of purpose that generally characterised the Labour Party at this time.

Not surprisingly, this consolidation of the party centre's authority was reflected in the constitutional changes implemented in 1929. From here on, the affiliated societies' section was reduced from thirteen to twelve, becoming a specifically trade union section; the socialist societies gained their own section of one; and the women's section was increased from four to five, with representatives continuing to be elected by the conference as a whole. Simultaneously, the stipulations regarding the 'duty' of a Labour MP – that is to act 'with a view to giving effect to the decisions of the party conference as to the general programme of the party' – were removed, allowing the link between the PLP and conference to be further diluted.[42]

As this suggests, the party leadership's growing authority extended to the party conference. Of course, grumbling was always evident. The report of the 1928 party conference by the Bedwellty Labour Party president, Lewis Lewis, highlighted the concerns of those who felt Labour's new party programme, *Labour and the Nation*, was 'not sufficiently socialist'; Philip Snowden, in particular, had been criticised for the limits of his financial policies, Lewis noted.[43] Yet, the party conference became ever more orchestrated from 1924, with the NEC setting the agenda and Arthur Henderson supervising its schedule. Where pre-war conferences have been described as 'assertive and often recriminatory', those taking place from the mid-to-late 1920s were surprisingly devoid of conflict and increasingly formal. So, for example, the 1925 conference debate on the NEC sub-committee's draft proposals for a new party programme was deliberately conducted after the question of Communist Party affiliation had designated clear lines of loyalty within the Labour Party.[44] More commonly, the conference was characterised by its attention to formal party matters, with little to no detailed discussion of specific policies or strategies.[45] This was partly logistical; conference attendance had grown considerably since the Great War, before which fewer than 500 delegates were annually present. Between 1924 and 1929, there were often more than 1,000 delegates on the conference floor, prompting recommendations that the party lengthen the conference to five days and, later, reduce the number of delegates eligible to be present.[46] But the objective was also to marginalize those who MacDonald labelled as 'silly, agitating, brainless', specifically those on the party left who sought to radicalise or challenge the leadership's moderate course.[47] By 1928, MacDonald felt able to assert openly to the party conference that he and his parliamentary colleagues would not take 'instructions from an outside body', perhaps the clearest statement to that date of the PLP's perceived autonomy.[48]

Such developments were widely accepted over the 1920s. Not only was the necessity of political and parliamentary advancement recognised by the vast majority of trade unionists, but there was a similar recognition of the achievements of the existing party leadership. Labour had, after all, risen to government in less than a quarter of a century. Although concerns and criticisms were sometimes broached on specific issues while Labour was in and out of government, these were not extended into a broader critique of the party as a whole. The trade unions, even in the bleak days of 1931, would stay loyal to the Labour Party, even if they proved willing to disown the Labour government. Despite some TUC detachment from the middle of the decade (see below), connections with the important trade union hierarchies were maintained, with Henderson often providing a convivial bridge between the party and the respective union. Customs and traditions continued to shape the party–union relationship; the unions would lobby and apply pressure on key issues whilst retaining a wider loyalty to the party centre. So, for example, if the NUGMW would typically abide by party decisions on issues such as communist affiliation or birth control, then this must be recognised in accordance with the union's close interaction with the party leadership and the understanding that it would defend its interests where threatened, as it did over the 1929 Unemployed Bill drawn up by one its own members, Margaret Bondfield.[49] Such quid pro quo become less evident in the immediate aftermath of the second Labour government, but the links established previously would do much to 'save' the party from an even worse fate.

Following on from this, party headquarters hoped to oversee a well-orchestrated and extensive divisional party apparatus. Alongside a recognised 129 safe (and some 'impregnable') Labour constituencies, the party report on the 1924 election highlighted a further 192 divisions where Labour held no seats and where the Conservatives maintained a secure majority. In response, special organisational conferences were recommended, with an emphasis on individual members, propaganda, and tea-table gatherings to enlist 'the service and enthusiasm of the women'.[50] Concurrently, divisional Labour Party activity across the country tended to became more uniform and co-ordinated over the 1920s. Local and constituency parties endeavoured to meet regularly and work efficiently, establishing various sub-committees and departments better to direct activity. Executive and general committee meetings became more formal and administrative, model standing orders were circulated (if not always adopted), and correspondence to and from Eccleston Square (later Transport House) was consistent and extensive. Most importantly, visits from the male and female regional organisers appointed by party headquarters were regular and served greatly to maintain the party apparatus at a local and constituency level, while the publication of *Labour Organiser* from 1921 further helped circulate ideas and information.[51] In such a way, the organisational progress made by Labour from 1918 was consolidated and extended throughout the 1920s. In practical terms, meetings usually began with a reading of correspondence, followed by the reports of ward organisations, Labour council groups, women's sections and other 'special' committees dedicated to finance, May Day, or party socials. The party structure, as outlined in the 1918 constitution, was occasionally realigned, but general patterns of office holding soon became evident. Men dominated the party committees, though their political outlook and background varied from place to place and from party to party. Even so, the roles of the chairmen, secretaries, agents and organisers were defined over the decade: chairmen co-ordinated party meetings, secretaries applied themselves to the day-to-day administration of the party, and agent-organisers – many of whom doubled as secretaries – familiarised themselves with electoral law and sought to direct party members in their activities.[52]

Yet, we should not overstate Labour uniformity. Although a model party organisation was supposed to be adhered to, anomalies continued to exist. In Leicester, for example, the formation of three constituency parties, as outlined in the party constitution, was quickly eschewed in favour of remaining as one borough party. Elsewhere, as we shall see, the call to build a mass party membership was sometimes ignored, while intra-party tensions often hampered progress and efficiency. Furthermore, while the NEC was evidently willing to intervene decisively into local affairs, it did so rarely and usually in a consultative manner. It was, primarily, communist involvement that prompted a draconian response from the party centre. Communication between headquarters and the localities more commonly took the form of circulating party literature and information than disciplined instruction. Essentially, divisional Labour parties saw themselves as an integral part of the national organisation, but they retained a degree of autonomy within a somewhat loosely defined political and organisational paradigm.

Across the country, Labour relied on a core of committed volunteers to sustain its organisation. In McKibbin's phrase, 'what Labour lost in cars and money it more than made up by volunteer support and energetic canvassing'.[53] Countless examples exist of individuals who helped raise and maintain the Labour banner. Nick Tiratsoo has cited the selfless dedication of Mr and Mrs Harris in Lowestoft between the wars, whose help for the local poor and unemployed later earned them a reputation as secular 'saints'.[54] Yet, we could also point to Ernie Gompertz, a Labour pioneer, shop assistants' union activist and borough councillor (later alderman and mayor) in South Shields, who acted as party secretary-agent from 1928, and continued to do so for eight successive general elections. Not surprisingly, he was known throughout the town as 'Mr Labour'.[55] Certainly, the vast majority of Labour supporters and members remained passive sympathisers rather than activists. But Sidney Webb's comment that it was the 'fanatics and cranks and extremists' who maintained most local parties was as condescending as it was unfair.[56] That said, some divisional parties retained a remarkably continuous leadership. The Bedwellty party revolved around the troika of its president Lewis Lewis, its secretary-agent James Panes and its MP Charles Edwards almost throughout (and beyond) the interwar period. In Huddersfield, Arthur Gardiner would act as the party agent from 1926 into the 1950s; in Barnsley, the veteran campaigner Edward Sheerien (president), Andrew Wright (secretary) and Joseph Jones (Yorkshire Miners' Association) came to dominate the constituency party across the interwar period. Sheerien edited the local party newspaper, acted as agent to the town's first Labour MP in 1922 (John Potts), before being elected to the borough council in 1923. Predictably, he then led the Labour group, becoming mayor in 1929.[57] The Penistone party was presided over by Jack Trickett and Jim Hibbert from the 1920s.[58] Of course, this could and did breed political cliques and encourage nepotism. The sponsorship of John and Patrick Wheatley has sometimes been referred to as a necessary means by which ambitious Labour activists advanced on Clydeside into the 1920s. As Christopher Howard has also pointed out, a combination of enthusiasm and ambition allowed many union or party activists to dominate their respective locals in the 1920s and 1930s, among them James Griffiths in Llanelli, Jack Mansfield in Peterborough, and George Hodgkinson in Coventry.[59]

A peculiar situation occurred in North Lambeth. Here, George Strauss struggled to take firm control of the divisional party in the early 1930s, asserting his authority as his star rose within the London Labour Party (LLP), LCC and PLP. Strauss was a wealthy metal broker who for some time had given notable financial assistance to the divisional party, acquiring it both premises and a billiard table in the process. Yet, Strauss also sought to remove the party's popular and long-serving secretary-agent, Sidney Harford, reportedly telling him in the wake of his 1931 general election defeat that 'I am absolutely convinced that there will never be a strong and active party in North Lambeth so long as you are here'. Initially, the party refused to accept Harford's resignation, but Strauss continued to offer financial incentives – £150 in April 1932 – to ensure the secretary's departure. Harford, in turn, took up his case with the National Union of Labour Organisers and Election Agents, rejecting Strauss' financial offers as 'unworthy' In the event, Strauss held the trump card; his financial contributions to the party in fact paid Harford's salary. Strauss therefore threatened to stop contributing to Harford's wage, leading the general council finally to accept his demand by eleven votes to six. Harford then had his membership refused (along with his wife and son), before an unseemly row broke out as to how much the party owed Harford for his former services. By the end of 1932, the party's annual report admitted that the dispute had split the party ranks and contributed to a drop in membership, before Strauss then agreed to pay half the salary of the party's new secretary-agent, Ray Roberts, and all rates and taxes on the party premises.[60]

But although examples of party cliques and individual fiefdoms exist, the wider turnover of party membership was often brisk and many parties saw (and ensured) regular changes in the ranks of party office holders. As we shall see, the bulk of the party membership rallied around specific events, particularly at election time, when individuals and affiliated trade unionists could be mobilised to deliver Labour's message. So, for example, the South Wales Miners' Federation (SWMF) raised some 750 canvassers and 1,000 polling scouts to propagate Labour's by-election campaign in Abertillery in 1920.[61] Beyond the committed volunteers, councillors, candidates and office holders, there existed a body of actual and potential support that Labour endeavoured to attract, utilise and complement. Loosely speaking, therefore, we can denote four types of party supporter in the interwar period: the passive, the supportive, the active, and the electoral. The first of these paid their subscriptions when asked, voted accordingly in elections, but generally remained detached from the party organisation. The supportive member similarly subscribed to and voted for the party, attending perhaps the odd social and annual meeting, but only really lent their assistance at election time. Third, the active members were those men and women who sustained the party organisation throughout the year, attending a constant round of meetings, helping at the local and divisional office, and organising events associated with the party. Finally, the electoral supporter voted Labour but was neither a member nor involved in wider political activity. Ultimately, all played their part in advancing the Labour cause, in maintaining its organisation and local presence, and in shaping Labour's identity.

Within the divisional parties, electoral work took priority. In the words of the Edinburgh and District Trades and Labour Council, the party was 'not a debating society, an economic class, or a school of sociological philosophy. It is a machine! We are not schoolmasters; we are mechanics!'[62] By 1926, the trades council had formed a central election committee to direct activity within the city, to allocate speakers, distribute election material, distribute finances, place adverts in the press, and even supply motor cycle corps for electioneering purposes.[63] As this suggests, the objective was to forge an effective electoral organisation that retained contact with its constituents, proved able to mobilise support, and visibly projected the perspective of the Labour Party at a national and local level. Such an approach was echoed elsewhere. The Norwich Labour Party instilled in its members the idea that 'strong membership reflects itself in adequate electoral machinery, and after all, that is the main object of our party'.[64] Given this, much of a divisional party's time was taken up by the selection and promotion of municipal and parliamentary candidates. Such choices depended on a number of factors, although finance was often the primary consideration. Where trade union support was forthcoming, the selection, financing and promotion of a Labour candidate all but looked after itself. As we saw in the previous chapter with relation to Durham, the overriding influence of a particular industry could lead to union domination of a divisional party and its associated functions and priorities. This was similarly true in South Wales, where the strong ties between union lodges, party and community led the SWMF to nominate candidates, print badges, photos and posters, and employ full-time agents.[65] In many Scottish mining villages, where miners had often taken the initiative in forming constituency Labour parties after the Great War, union members, support and finance formed the bedrock of Labour's electoral challenge. The adoption of the National Union of Scottish Mine Workers' political organiser for Fife, Joe Westwood, as parliamentary candidate by the Peebles and South Midlothian Divisional Labour Party was a case in point. Local miners had formed the divisional organisation, the Arniston miner Robert Burnside led the party, and Westwood was duly elected to parliament in 1922.[66] As Alan Campbell has shown, such developments were mirrored throughout the country's mining regions.[67]

Even where 'mixed' economies existed, the very structure of the Labour Party tended to ensure that the affiliated trade unions had the dominant influence over the appointment of a parliamentary candidate. For instance, Labour candidates in Manchester came from a variety of sources, including the NUR, MFGB, NUGMW, National Union of Vehicle Builders (NUVB) and the Railway Clerks' Association (RCA), but only occasionally directly via the divisional party. This would become less apparent over the interwar period, as parties increasingly financed their respective candidates (in Manchester and elsewhere), but many 'safe' Labour seats continued to be union-sponsored and union delegates continued to comprise the majority of the divisional party executive, general committee and party officers in urban or industrial areas.

Occasionally, however, tensions could exist between different unions within a constituency. The outwardly 'safe' Labour seat of Bishop Auckland had to contain rivalries between the miners, railwaymen and teachers that comprised the local party. Here, Will Davis, as a school master, miner's son and party secretary, was regularly at odds with Bob Middlewood, the fiery leader of the Labour council and former train driver. At the same time, the railwaymen of Shildon clashed bitterly with the more numerous miners of West Auckland, Cockfield and elsewhere. Partly for this reason, the constituency party met rarely, with Labour's support being secured more effectively through the respective union branches.[68] Even in the 'model' party of Barrow, the Workers' Union executive protested in 1918 that the divisional party's reluctance to endorse Charles Duncan as parliamentary candidate was due to craft union hostility towards the labourers' organisations. In reality, the controversy was complicated by Duncan's committed support for the war, but the Workers' Union complaint is suggestive of supplementary antagonisms. The union reminded the NEC that it could return such 'hostility' elsewhere, before Henderson visited the constituency to sort things out.[69] More damagingly, the Nottingham labour movement was hampered by disagreements between the skilled Lace Workers' Society and the Workers' Union in the early-to-mid 1920s, the sectional detail of which no doubt coloured and impinged upon the activities of the city

Labour Party.[70] Significantly, too, many union branches and members continued to remain aloof from Labour. In Lancashire, several cotton union branches and members refused to affiliate to Labour, even where the local party organisations emphasised the 'labour' rather than the 'socialist' aspect of Labour membership. Following the 1927 Trade Disputes Act, which ensured that union members had to 'contract in' to the Labour Party, the Spinners' Union affiliated only a third of its members to the party.[71]

Elsewhere, in parts of Scotland, the south of England, rural areas, and commercial centres, the influence of the ILP and certain middle-class individual members could be more readily detected. In such instances, those who could best contribute towards their own election costs contested seats where union support was not sufficiently forthcoming. David Graham Pole, for example, contributed much money, time and effort to the East Grinstead Labour Party and, later, the South Derbyshire constituency. Once in Derbyshire, Pole paid for an agent – including his moving expenses, house deposit and car – subsidised the constituency office, and contributed to the party's annual subscription.[72] At the same time, middle-class, aristocratic or well-connected candidates were a way of extending Labour's appeal beyond its trade union base, something that was important in a number of constituencies.

Yet, such 'philanthropy' could bring problems, leading occasionally to allegations or suspicions of impropriety. If so, party–individual relationships soon broke down. One of the first controversies surrounding Sir Oswald Mosley's Labour Party career came, in part, from allegations of his 'buying' his candidacy in Smethwick and financially controlling his local party in Birmingham Ladywood. If Mosley was lauded by many in his Birmingham division, where he helped fund *The Birmingham Town Crier*, contributed to party costs, and paid for Allan Young to become party organiser, he would later be criticised for neglecting his constituents and using the party for personal advancement.[73] Similarly, in Nottingham South, the party's wealthy barrister MP, G. W. Holford Knight, had personally financed his election campaign in 1929, only to refuse further to bankroll the party on his taking his seat in parliament. After rejecting the local party's demand that he pay £100 per annum towards its 'fighting fund', Holford Knight finally agreed to pay £50 in March 1931, provoking severe divisions in the party in the process. Come August and he supported MacDonald's formation of a National government, no doubt confirming the local party members' prejudices against him.[74] Clearly, although middle-class candidates could offer a financial lifeline to divisional parties, and could further help spread Labour's appeal into previously untapped areas, they could also be a source of embarrassment.

Notwithstanding such associated problems, the selection of a parliamentary candidate was nominally the preserve of the constituency organisation, with the NEC generally giving immediate approval to the locally appointed nominee. Only occasionally did party headquarters try to impose a candidate upon a constituency, leading to varied responses from the divisional parties involved. In the aftermath of the 1918 general election, Widnes and Woolwich East were both persuaded to abandon their preferred by-election candidates to allow Henderson and MacDonald to stand for parliament. Similarly, during the second Labour government, Sir Stafford Cripps – only recently enrolled into the party – was nominated by Ramsay MacDonald to contest the January 1931 by-election in Bristol East. Unfortunately, the divisional party had already given its support to Leah Manning, necessitating that Henderson, Dalton and Shepherd (as national agent) apply pressure to both the party and the candidate before Manning finally agreed to stand down.[75] As a result, Cripps was adopted and elected amidst much local bitterness at the party centre's foisting a 'rich man' upon them.[76] On the other hand, the NEC had sometimes to bow to local party determination. Thus, the NEC had initially proved reluctant to stand a candidate in the Rusholme by-election of September 1919, in spite of the constituency party's desire to contest the seat. After sending a delegation (Jowett and Cameron) to discuss the matter with local leaders, the national executive duly reversed its decision and lent its support. Generally, however, national party 'interference' was unusual; only when a communist was selected as a Labour candidate was the NEC minded to intervene more definitively.

In the event of election success, Labour MPs were expected to retain regular contact with their respective constituency party and constituents. In the case of George Lansbury, his close relationship with Bow and Bromley formed perhaps the principal foundation of his popularity. Lansbury's home at 39 Bow Road was the political hub of the community, where callers were welcome and regular.[77] Here as elsewhere, the parliamentary representative was often the 'star turn' at party events, while many MPs issued reports to their divisions explaining party objectives or, as in 1924 and 1929–31, government policy. The latter, more often than not, began with the disclaimer of Labour's difficult position as a minority government, suggesting that Labour MPs in the 1920s were far happier reporting from opposition.[78] That said, Chuter Ede's regular reports to his South Shields constituency party arguably helped placate potential uncertainty as to the government's direction in 1930. By the same token, divisional parties could on occasion raise concern at the lack of contact offered by their respective MP during the same period.[79] As this suggests, the rapport between divisional party and parliamentary member could break down. One example was in Aberdeen North, where the sitting MP Frank Rose clashed with local members over his opposition to the General Strike, to nationalisation, and to Labour criticism of the 1927 Trade Disputes and Trade Union Act. From 1926 through to Rose's death in 1928, the local party repeatedly endeavoured to replace him as its parliamentary candidate.[80] Another example was Evan Davies, MP for Ebbw Vale between 1920 and 1929, whose forced resignation for inactivity paved the way for Aneurin Bevan to succeed him.[81] In particular, financial disputes could sour relations. Rennie Smith's tenure as MP for Penistone was characterised by an on-going dispute over his refusal to pay election expenses incurred by his party in 1929.[82]

While parliamentary elections were obvious rallying points for divisional parties, the round of annual and triennial local government elections offered Labour more regular opportunities to propagate its vision of a better society and establish its social-political identity within a respective locality. As Williams has suggested in relation to Wales, municipal elections acted as 'marker of progress' for local parties, both in terms of seats won and votes polled.[83] They further served as both a point of focus upon which to build support and as a training ground for future Labour leadership. Moreover, the functions of local government provided Labour members with experience in power. During the 1920s, municipal authorities were responsible for the maintenance of various services, including gas, lighting, transport, and electricity.[84] Authority was permissive rather than mandatory, but access to the council chamber would enable Labour to prove the efficiency of socialist administration. Equally, it allowed Labour the opportunity to improve the lives of its constituents through a range of municipally implemented social policies, including free milk for school children, free school meals, maternity clinics, health care and housing. To this effect, much divisional and ward Labour Party activity revolved around such local election contests, although parties occasionally found it difficult to recruit municipal candidates. This was rarely for lack of members, but more for a lack of members' time. Council work was unpaid, and most Labour members had jobs that necessarily limited their availability for serving in – or standing and campaigning for – municipal office. In the case of Albert Baker, a Poplar councillor elected in 1919, his day began at 6 a.m. at the railway goods yard and ended in the late evening following either a council or board of guardians meeting. Of his 38 colleagues on the Poplar council in 1919, 26 were manual workers and four were housewives. All of them made sacrifices to represent Labour and further 'the cause'.[85]

In connection with such electoral activity, the work of a divisional party was increasingly concentrated on devising campaigns, on canvassing, raising funds and propagating the Labour Party programme. So focused was the party on its effective campaigning, that the *Labour Organiser* was even publishing hints on how best to address envelopes by 1923.[86] Essential, therefore, to the co-ordination of an effective election campaign was the secretary-agent (or organiser), whose primary role was to ensure the party's readiness to contest elections at all political levels, to manage and direct party activity, and to cultivate a divisional party's organisation and membership. Such agents were later described by Herbert Morrison as the 'field officers of the Labour Party', a party activist who could 'radiate confidence, cheerfulness and a joyful fighting spirit'.[87] Thus, D. B. Foster, the agent for Leeds South became a well-known figure throughout the city in the 1920s and 1930s.[88] In Peterborough, the appointment of George Watson as full-time organiser (along with J. F. Horrabin as the city's parliamentary candidate) evidently breathed life into a latent party organisation. Watson had previously worked in Norfolk, where he had formed a Labour choir, organised village concerts, and worked as agent for Noel Buxton. With his arrival in Peterborough, a divisional party that met only fitfully and was almost solely preoccupied with election contests began at last to co-ordinate and extend its activity. Accordingly, Horrabin was elected as the member for Peterborough at the general election in 1929.[89] In Norwich, Jack Brooksbank's appointment as full-time agent in late 1923 helped cultivate the city Labour Party's relatively large membership (2,600 in 1924), forging buoyant ward organisations that cultivated a successful method of 'house-to-house' canvassing. In 1924 alone, the party distributed 43,750 circulars covering over 100 subjects, while Brooksbank maintained the party organisation through the difficulties of 1931–2. Despite the Labour government's defeat and the disaffiliation of the ILP, which meant the loss of the party headquarters, the party 'held its own' to take control of the city council in 1933.[90]

Very rarely, as in Leeds, a female agent was simultaneously recruited to mobilise women to the cause, although such a 'luxury' was beyond the means of most parties. Indeed, the cost of appointing just one agent could prove problematic; by 1923, there were only 111 across the Britain as a whole, rising only to 123 in 1933.[91] As such, Labour relied on a number of trade union-sponsored (and later co-op-sponsored) agents to undertake such responsibility. More often, part-time agents were appointed for the duration of an election contest, while many parties relied on the centrally appointed regional organiser to help co-ordinate and manage their affairs.

Again, such arrangements could be problematical. For this reason, Herbert Morrison also noted that an agent could spread 'pessimism, cynicism and depression' within a party's ranks, as appeared to be the case with regard to the Roxburgh and Selkirk Divisional Labour Party. First, the party employed John Airlie as a full-time organiser in 1925, only to receive various complaints from local party and executive members in response to Airlie's lack of effort, his using the party motor car for personal errands, and his attempt to secure a parliamentary candidature for himself while supposedly working in support of George Dallas. For his part, Airlie complained of too much clerical work, working 'twelve to fourteen hour days', and facing an organisation committee that was 'working against' him. Eventually, following a series of letters to and from Egerton Wake, Airlie was forced to resign.[92] Not surprisingly, the party resisted the temptation to appoint a replacement (despite Dallas' initial insistence and later resignation as parliamentary candidate), only then to accept an offer from a Mr Scott to act as organisational-secretary in return for out-of-pocket expenses. For the second time, the party inadvertently hired a 'misfit', who within weeks of his assignment had bought a car with the insurance money from a previous party motor, crashed it, and left the party with a series of garage bills. Two years later, a 'skeletal committee' was appointed to run the party between elections and membership fell from approximately 1,000 in 1927 to 450 in 1932. The party was eventually reconstituted in 1935.[93]

Given the electoral focus of the Labour Party, the method and character of local party activity changed in emphasis over the 1920s. This was a slow, protracted and incomplete process, but there was evidently a move away from the mass demonstration and street-corner meeting towards door-to-door canvassing and distribution of literature. Following the 1924 general election, W. B. Lewcock – the Newport party agent – urged his members to replace demonstrations with doorstep canvassing and party teas and socials. Under his direction, canvassing classes were established within the party, while membership campaigns were initiated, sometimes with prizes being awarded to those sections that could recruit the most members.[94] Similar developments were evident in London. By as early as 1921, the London women's organiser Annie Somers was convinced that T. E. Naylor's Walworth by-election victory was won 'on the doorstep', concluding that 'the most important duty of the election worker is that of canvassing'. In so doing, she echoed Herbert Morrison's belief that the 'new school of Labour politicians is a scientific school. It knows that noisy tub-thumping does not make up for careful organisation'.[95] Such a refrain became ever more common. In 1930, the Loughborough Borough Labour Party unanimously agreed 'that no useful purpose would be served' by open-air meetings; that it would be better to concentrate on 'canvassing and getting personal contact with the electors'.[96] Although 'star' speakers remained important as a means of rallying the party faithful, the *Labour Organiser* continued to insist that 'hard doorstep work' was more beneficial to party progress than 'showy enthusiasm'.[97] Equally, such a focus of party energy arguably helped to broaden Labour's appeal and, in some instances, enabled Labour to ingratiate itself within a particular community, constituency or locality. As Dan

Weinbren has suggested, Labour supporters were thereby able to take Labour or socialist values into the homes of their family, friends and neighbours.[98] Links were made between the party and the prevailing concerns and perspectives of a particular community; civic, kinship, class and ethnic loyalties could be drawn upon and transformed into political support.

In order to sustain and further the party's electoral ambition, much attention was placed on fund-raising and canvassing. Whist drives, raffles, cigarette machines, football pools and sweepstakes were among the most popular means of bolstering the party coffers. Indeed, whist drives became almost an obsession with some parties. Weekly, monthly, divisional, ward and regional drives were frequently organised to raise money, despite the fact that whist was also played habitually at socials, dances, after meetings, and sometimes instead of meetings, all year round. In addition, bazaars, jumble sales, teas and dances became standard and often profitable points of party activity. More unusually, the Norwich party raised money from the weighing machine kept at its party headquarters, while the North Islington Divisional Labour Party sold matchbooks.[99] Linked to such activity, divisional and local parties formed social committees to arrange events and outings for members, supporters and constituents. Significantly, these tended to be based on the party women's section, whose members organised, supplied and staffed such public events, sometimes at the specific bequest of the constituency party.[100] In addition to simple social gatherings, musical activities such as brass bands, orchestras and choirs were often initiated and sports clubs were established. As a result, political and social activity began to coalesce, with social gatherings doubling as fund-raising schemes that further included political speeches and dissemination of propaganda. Obviously, such events were designed to draw members into the party, both for social and political reasons, but they also attracted publicity and gave the party or association a public profile that extended beyond its offices, clubs or rooms.

This was important. Yet, such activity could sometimes encroach on the party's principal electoral objective. Many local parties appeared to spend at least as much time organising social activities as they did promoting the party cause. In between the general elections of 1924 and 1929, the Merton and Morden Labour Party entertainments committee had come to dominate party business by 1928, culminating in an executive meeting that consisted of 'half an hour's talk and discussion with regard to the ward's social activities' followed by 'a most pleasant and interesting evening' in which members recounted 'amusing incidents and experiences with regard to politics and acquaintances'. Come the general election, only fourteen of the party's 80 members helped with the campaign. Even in the late 1930s, when the question of Spain had excited some activity among party members, Mr Davis called for one hour of every alternate meeting to be open to discussion of party policy 'as he did not think enough attention was given to this part of the business'.[101] Despite this, the positive function of locally organised social activities no doubt overrode any negative connotations, as did the services established by locals to advise and assist members and constituents. The North Lambeth party, for instance, set up a free legal advice service, at which a solicitor (Mr Harwood) was stationed at the party headquarters each Tuesday night. Similarly, the gradual formation of Labour clubs in established and developing working-class neighbourhoods began to allow the party to become synonymous with sections of a local community.

More disarmingly, perhaps, the fine-tuning of Labour's 'electoral machine' over the 1920s arguably occurred at the expense of broader political discussion and activity. This is not to say that Labour members did not engage in political debate on a wide range of issues, but that the priorities of the party served to marginalize, or emasculate, areas of contention. The logistics of this will be explored further below. Generally, however, where the immediate post-war period saw an array of topics debated and resolved upon, such breadth of deliberation had narrowed conspicuously by the late 1920s. So, where the Newport Labour Party discussed and issued resolutions on the peace treaties, Welsh devolution, the Russia–Poland war, Indian home rule and Irish self-determination in 1918–21, it soon became more fixed on organisational issues – selecting candidates, renting party rooms, canvassing support, collecting funds, etc. If policy was discussed, it more commonly centred on social welfare and local governmental matters from the mid-1920s. Of course, broader questions would still arise, such as China in 1927, but they no longer formed so central part of executive or general committee debate.[102] In Colne Valley, the divisional party actually raised concern as to party members' lack of interest in local election campaigns, while simultaneously noting that members were not attending public meetings 'to the extent that they did previous to the war'.[103] Consequently, Labour's evident 'evolution' – from a party based on the trade unions to one located also in the wider community – prompted a concentration of its political effort. This was beneficial in that it made Labour appear more immediately relevant to the electorate and its potential supporters, but led simultaneously to concern among some party members that Labour was lacking in ideological rigour. For those brought up with an 'ethical' or strictly socialist inclination, such as Syd Bidwell, a Labour recruit from 1930s Southall, the Labour Party spent 'a lot of time on explaining how to run elections', but it 'never [took] political education seriously'.[104]

Given such activity and initiative, the recruitment and retention of something approaching a mass party membership was deemed essential to Labour's continued development. In 1925, the NEC instigated a national drive to increase its individual membership and shore up its local organisation. A 'model scheme' was drawn up, detailing arrangements for the regular collection of party dues and instructions for the formation of local ward organisations. In addition, a by-election fund was established – to which each party made a small contribution – and a party badge scheme was introduced to give members a 'keener sense of belonging to a united national movement'.[105] This was important, because the collection of subscriptions was the bête noire of many a party. Not all adopted the party's model scheme, and a variety of methods were tried and tested. Ultimately, however, the collection of 1d a week was the most popular option for the perennially cash-strapped organisations, allowing a steady if unspectacular income while simultaneously encouraging regular contact between party representatives and members. Typically, the party's approach could vary from place to place, but such activity became more systematic over the 1920s. In Darlington, for example, the party agent prepared a 'scheme of organisation' to augment the national party directive to appoint 'street captains' by which to maintain contact with individual members. The objective, the executive recorded, was to have a captain in every Darlington street.[106] Indeed, such schemes were reproduced at a local level. The Hebburn Labour Party (affiliated to Jarrow) formed a sub-committee in 1924 to ascertain the best ways in which to maintain the machinery to conduct election contests and to encourage new and active members. To this effect, meetings and debating classes were to be held, volunteers were to collect subscriptions, check the voting lists and advertise the *Daily Herald*, and ward co-operation was encouraged to bolster weaker areas of support.[107] Unfortunately, the precarious existence of the local party throughout the 1920s suggests that even the best laid plans could not always be relied upon to produce the desired result.

Lastly, local Labour activity was geared towards the propagation of Labour's political and social vision. Most obviously, the importance of establishing local party newspapers was raised regularly from the early 1920s, with Patrick Dollan arguing in relation to the Labour group on the Glasgow city council that 'unless municipal Labour can maintain a local press it will not hold ruling power for more than year'.[108] Unfortunately, the necessary funds to produce and maintain such a publication were not always available. Despite the establishment of a Labour news service at Eccleston Square, headed by Will Henderson, only thirteen local parties were reportedly using its insert by 1924, leading to its dissolution by 1926.[109] Even when the Edinburgh trades council rescued the ILP-initiated *Labour Standard* in 1927, it was forced to cease publication in 1930, despite having increased its circulation by some 50 per cent. The problem, it seemed, was a failure to secure adequate advertising.[110] Elsewhere, a number of Welsh parties set up Labour papers only to see a combination of financial, logistical and circulation problems scupper their plans. By 1929, the Swansea Labour Party had recorded a debt of £1,028 on its *Labour News*.[111] More successfully, the London party published *London News* and the *Citizen* newspaper, both of which were recognised as a means by which Labour could broaden its appeal in the capital. Significantly, local editions were produced and distributed by party volunteers.[112] Elsewhere, the *Bradford Pioneer* remained an important local paper; the Barnsley Trades and Labour Council published its own *Barnsley News* to counter the hostile local press; the East Lewisham party managed to publish an eight-page *Monthly Herald*; the *Oldham Labour Gazette* secured distribution of 5,000 a month in the mid-1920s; and, in Glasgow, *Forward!* remained an important Labour periodical.[113] Generally, however, the production of a party press proved difficult over the 1920s, with the revamped *Daily Herald* eventually providing a more sustainable means for Labour to spread its appeal.

Despite these moves to extend the party's profile and efficiency, progress could be slow. Large individual memberships were rare in the 1920s, although they did develop in certain localities across the country. By 1929, Labour's larger divisional parties included Reading, which claimed 2,500 members, Norwich with 1,818, Romford with 1,742, and Greenwich with 2,435. The Woolwich Labour Party, meanwhile, boasted 4,355 individual members in 1929, cultivated on a basis of systematic canvassing, sports clubs, bazaars and newspapers.[114] Generally, however, such mass-member parties were the exception rather than the rule.

Gaining accurate membership figures for many divisional parties is difficult, as there exist no official statistics for the period before 1928. From 1930, it was simply 'assumed that all constituency parties had a minimum of 240 members and figures were compiled and published on this basis'.[115] In most cases, it would appear that constituency parties found it difficult to recruit and retain large numbers of active supporters. The five divisional Labour parties in Edinburgh generally had memberships of below 180 between 1924 and 1929, with only the party in Edinburgh West bucking the trend with some 330 registered members in 1926–7, and 422 in 1928–9.[116] The party's focus on electioneering meant that wider activity was generally left to the ILP. But although this could provide the impetus for important initiatives, such as the aforementioned *Labour Standard*, the unions sought simultaneously to limit the ILP's influence within the party.[117] Indeed, Labour's Scottish divisional parties remained extremely weak; only six constituencies boasted more than 200 individual members in 1929, although the strength of the ILP in places such as Glasgow should be remembered.[118] Even among Labour supporters, selfless political activity after a long working day for low-to-moderate pay did not have an immediate appeal.

For some, moreover, the building up of a 'members' party' was of little consequence. Given his apparent security as candidate and MP for the Durham Miners' Association (DMA) dominated constituency of Bishop Auckland from 1929, Hugh Dalton believed that a 'healthy party is an inactive one'. 'Too many members might upset the applecart', he once said, 'and bring in militants'.[119] Here, the guaranteed vote of the overwhelmingly working-class mining community was enough, allowing Dalton to remain detached from the constituency beyond a brief sojourn in the parliamentary recess and an annual appearance at the miners' gala. Beyond this, the party retained its dominance through networks of individuals whose position largely relied on the patronage of – and the support mobilised by – the DMA. In such circumstances, a constituency party was hardly deemed necessary. Indeed, the party secretary (Davis) sometimes managed to allow a whole year to pass without a single executive meeting, claiming there was simply nothing for the party to discuss![120] At the same time, Dalton's beliefs were shaped by his previous constituency experience in Peckham, where he had clashed disastrously with the local party. His attempts to 'advise' the local party organisation were resented by his agent, Ernest Baldwyn, while many in the party reputedly found Dalton's social background difficult to accept. Ultimately, after public rows and much Machiavellian manoeuvring, Dalton opted to leave Peckham for the more tranquil party base in Durham County.[121]

As Dalton's experience suggests, there was no obvious correlation between party membership and electoral success. For example, the Doncaster Labour Party had just 178 individual members in 1921 and a reputedly apathetic approach that extended even to its elected officials. Nevertheless, Wilfred Paling was returned as Labour MP from 1922 until 1931.[122] By contrast, the large memberships of parties in Reading, Norwich or Oldham saw only sporadic election victories. Often, where Labour support was evidently deep-rooted, the impetus for continued Labour organisation was sometimes lost or deemed unnecessary. Bessie Braddock, a hard-talking Liverpool councillor and later MP, tellingly recalled that:

> Local Labour Party organisations are rather like local divisions of unions. Where a branch of industry is trouble free and the workers are well looked after, the union organisation is likely to wither, for it's extremely difficult to keep the soldiers at their peak of efficiency when there isn't any war. Conversely, if one looks at a strong Tory constituency where Labour hasn't a dog's chance of winning, one often finds that the Labour Party there is virile, well organised, and supported by strong funds. In places like [Liverpool] Exchange, or Ebbw Vale, the Labour Party hardly exists except at election times, or at times when it is part of the social life of the area.[123]

A glimpse through the party membership figures bears this out. Ebbw Vale and Liverpool Exchange regularly recorded the party minimum individual membership from 1928. Yet, constituencies where Labour struggled to win electorally could often boast relatively impressive individual memberships. So, for example, the Cambridgeshire party could claim 1,091 members in 1929, and the Mitcham party 1,038.[124]

Throughout the 1920s, Labour endeavoured to construct a united, coherent and efficient party organisation. To this end, the party made evident progress, though with severe limitations. Certainly, Labour did not become a 'mass party' to compare with its foreign counterparts, most obviously the German Social Democratic Party. Constituency parties often relied on a committed band of volunteers and functioned most visibly only at election times. In such a way, the character and identity of a divisional party was arguably informed as much by its local composition as it was by the wider party structure and programme. Even so, Labour undoubtedly consolidated and extended its organisation in a number of places, working through an already established trade union base and/or integrating the party within local neighbourhoods and communities. As the organisation extended, as party policy widened, as social functions were organised, and as Labour members gained experience in municipal government and became more attuned to the needs of the local community, so Labour became more integrated into the everyday lives of those the party claimed to represent. As always, the scope and 'success' of Labour organisation varied from place to place and depended on an array of social, political, economic and cultural factors. Looked at generally, however, the 1920s saw the party become more centralised, disciplined and uniform. The prestige of the PLP leadership rose in tandem with its electoral progress, the slowly shifting political focus of the party was reaffirmed via the relative limits of trade union activity during the decade, and Labour generally appeared unified in its effort and purpose. At the same time, of course, tensions were always evident, and the party leadership at all levels was forced to work hard to maintain an appearance of gradual and steady progress.

III. KEEPING UP APPEARANCES

Although Labour aspired to function as a unified party with a loyal and committed membership, there were always rumblings of discontent within its 'broad church' during the mid-1920s. After all, Labour was in many ways a coalition of distinctive but overlapping identities that included socialist, trade unionist, radical, feminist and less clearly defined individual and affiliated members. Inevitably, therefore, the apparent limitations revealed by the 1924 Labour government raised concern among sections of the party. Most obviously, the moderate, or partial, nature of Labour policy had become clear during the party's turn in office, thereby leading almost immediately to attempts to construct a more precise and applicable political programme. The official outcome of this would be 1928's *Labour and the Nation*, but alternatives were also posed, most coherently from within the ILP and, beyond the party ranks, the Communist Party of Great Britain (CPGB). Simultaneously, from a trade union perspective, the need to develop a new relationship – between the trade unions and a Labour government – had brought questions relating to labour movement priorities to the fore. As well as the apparent inability (and seeming unwillingness) of a minority government to deliver policies reflecting trade union interests, there appeared to be a divergence between the government's perceived national responsibilities and the unions' primarily industrial concerns. These were overtaken, to an extent, by the events of 1926; the defeat of the General Strike and the implementation of the 1927 Trade Disputes and Trade Union Act refocused the need for a Labour government in the minds of many a trade unionist. Even so, the strike had itself raised points of contention within the labour movement, provoking old concerns as to the validity and purpose of industrial action. By the mid-1920s, too, sections of the party's female membership endeavoured to broaden Labour's social-political perspective in relation to gender relations and issues such as birth control.

Given such tremors of potential and actual discontent, the Labour leadership resorted to a series of organisational measures and compromises to enforce and further shape its essentially unified and moderate course. From 1924 through until the demise of the second minority Labour government in 1931, the most consistent and concerted internal criticism of prevailing Labour policies and methods came via the ILP. Although the ILP had necessarily reinvented its role within the Labour Party following the constitutional changes of 1918, it had nevertheless become somewhat marginalised by the mid-to-late 1920s. Both the formation of divisional Labour parties open to individual members and the removal of socialist society representation on the NEC had threatened to reduce the ILP's influence, the former by creating an alternative point of admission to the Labour Party for party members, the second by limiting the ILP's access to the decision-making process. Furthermore, Labour's adoption of clause four arguably challenged the ILP's distinctive place within the party.[125] In many areas, the erstwhile functions of the ILP were steadily taken over by the newly formed constituency organisations from 1918. At the same time, the loose but complex federal structure of the ILP, in which local sections varied considerably in terms of their political and social character, meant a coherent ILP policy and strategy was both difficult to discern and implement. Initially, at least, such problems were partly offset by a rise in ILP membership following the war; in 1921, the ILP affiliated to the Labour Party with some 35,000 members, though this had fallen to 30,000 by 1925.[126] Within certain areas, including much of Scotland and parts of Yorkshire, ILP members remained the 'public face' of the Labour Party, often with a presence on the local council. In the House of Commons, too, the ILP could claim to form a significant part of the PLP in the early 1920s. Indeed, the election of ten ILP MPs in Glasgow in 1922 was understood by some as a triumph of ILP socialism, though it should be remembered that the political outlook of this 'Clydeside contingent' varied – the leftist perspective of Maxton, Wheatley and Kirkwood was not necessarily complemented by the moderate politics of George Hardie and Manny Shinwell, for instance.[127] Nevertheless, the PLP included 39 ILP-sponsored members among the 191 MPs sitting in the Commons by October 1924, alongside several other ILP cardholders (including MacDonald, of course). It was from such a basis, therefore, that Clifford Allen – the Cambridge-educated former Fabian elected ILP treasurer in 1922 and chairman in 1923 – conceived the ILP as a 'socialist think tank' within the wider Labour Party; a mechanism by which Labour could develop a truly socialist policy.[128]

But despite Allen's best intentions, the ILP increasingly became a site for left-wing discontent inside the Labour Party over the 1920s. In this, the ILP's left credentials were associated most publicly with John Wheatley, James Maxton, and certain fellow MPs whose combative approach to parliamentary procedure and penchant for creating 'scenes' had already led to their suspension from the Commons in 1923. Following Maxton's election to the ILP chair in April 1926, the leftward drift was set in place, coinciding with a continued decline in ILP membership and the further limiting of ILP influence within the Labour Party. By the end of the decade, Labour's divisional parties had more firmly established themselves, while new and younger Labour members could and did enter straight into the constituency party rather than via the ILP, particularly outside of Scotland. Very crudely, something of a 'catch-22' began to develop for the ILP in such circumstances: as ILP members began to merge into the Labour Party, so the existing ILP organisation was utilised increasingly by the more active left wing; as the left wing became more active, so many ILP members began to merge into the Labour Party. As this suggests, ILP perspectives were not uniform. In Yorkshire, for instance, widespread ILP loyalty to MacDonald jarred notably with the militant pronouncements of a minority of regional members. In Glasgow itself, moreover, the ILP under Patrick Dollan represented a far more temperate strand of socialism than that voiced by some of the city's representatives in the Commons. As such, it would be wrong to presume that the views put forward by a vociferous contingent of ILP MPs in Westminster and on the ILP's National Administrative Council (NAC) were necessarily representative of the party as whole. Even so, the complex interaction of loyalties felt by ILP members cannot be easily discounted. Many in the ILP continued to believe that their party had a special role to play within the wider Labour Party as the keeper of the socialist flame and the distributor of socialist wisdom.

ILP criticism came, primarily, from two directions: strategically through members in the PLP and, politically, through the debate on party policy that ensued following the October 1924 general election. In both cases, Clydesiders were to the fore. Among the most prominent was James Maxton, a distinctive parliamentary figure with a shock of black hair and taut facial features. As a former teacher in his constituency of Bridgeton, Maxton had witnessed the poverty of the Glasgow working class via his classroom: an experience that fed into his evangelical speeches and robust political style. Alongside him was the popular David Kirkwood, an engineer and leader of the Parkhead shop stewards who had joined the ILP on the outbreak of the Great War at the bequest of John Wheatley. Wheatley himself was originally a mineworker from Lanarkshire, although he had become the successful owner of a printing firm by the outbreak of the Great War. A self-proclaimed 'Catholic socialist', he was also a leading advocate of the ILP's confrontational parliamentarianism before his experience in government served further to radicalise him.[129] By the mid-1920s, his avocation of protectionism and suggestion that 'trade unionism has been mortgaged to its enemies' meant that his views had begun to drift some way from the Labour mainstream, although he remained a well-respected and inspirational politician.[130] George Buchanan, described with the Reverend Campbell Stephen as 'the most extreme Clyde men' by Arthur Ponsonby, was a former pattern worker, while Neil Maclean was a Workers' Union official and former member of the Marx-influenced Socialist Labour Party. Clearly, the Clydeside left was a relatively diverse group, but one with a shared experience of the industrial and social unrest that had broken out in

Glasgow over the war years and a fierce commitment to ending the often severe poverty that existed around them. From this, the group maintained a remarkably close working and social relationship while at Westminster.[131]

Inside the PLP, as noted in Chapter One above, this section of the ILP was committed to the utilisation of parliament for largely confrontational purposes. This had proven controversial in 1922–3, and would continue to do so throughout the 1920s. During the period of the first Labour government, however, the Clydeside MPs agreed, initially, to lend their support to MacDonald's administration, especially given the inclusion of Wheatley in the first Labour cabinet. Such reticence would soon prove difficult, as concerns over MacDonald's moderation and observance of parliamentary niceties began to surface. By April, Campbell Stephen was warning MacDonald that ILP support was not unconditional, although it appears that more overt criticism was restrained for fear of damaging the wider Labour cause.[132] This would change following the 1924 general election. Almost immediately, Maxton and others in the PLP openly questioned the limits of Labour's achievements in office, criticising MacDonald's leadership and going so far in December 1924 as to nominate George Lansbury as a replacement party leader. In the event, such a proposition was refused by Lansbury – despite his harbouring similar reservations about Labour's recent record in office – and MacDonald was easily re-elected.[133] Yet, the lessons of 1924 for the ILP left were summed up in a purported Maxton quote that 'the sooner they are out of office the better, as every day they were in led us further from socialism [sic]'.[134] In the Commons, Maxton and Wheatley, along with other 'backbench rebels' such as Lansbury and Wedgwood, returned to the offensive. As well as the continuation of parliamentary 'scenes', moves were made to tighten ILP organisation inside the PLP and, in December 1925, an inner executive of seven established to direct ILP strategy.[135] The 1925 ILP conference, too, included much criticism of the recently removed Labour government.

Labour's parliamentary party leadership responded quickly to such criticism from late 1924. Most obviously, the PLP committee on party organisation moved to control more effectively the livelier members of the PLP, with Henderson replacing the ill and ineffective Ben Spoor as chief whip. Indeed, such measures appeared initially to have had the desired effect with the election of a more moderate PLP executive in 1925, before the anxieties occasioned by the General Strike brought renewed tensions to the party in 1926–8.[136] Looked at generally, the PLP was characterised more by its unanimity than its division during the 1920s. By 1927, the PLP executive was committed to MacDonald's leadership and Labour's moderate path; even Lansbury had emerged from a period of disenchantment to act as a loyal and effective party chairman in 1928.[137]

In terms of policy, the ILP sought to construct a more practicable socialist alternative to the gradual and relatively general programme of the wider Labour Party. To this effect, the ILP had established a number of commissions by 1925, the most significant of which – consisting of J. A. Hobson, E. F. Wise, H. N. Brailsford and A. Creech Jones – was to forge a plan for the 'abolition of poverty and the realisation of socialism' based on Hobson's theory of 'under consumption'.[138] From this, the commission developed a series of policies under the title of 'the living wage'. Significantly, however, and despite such initiative, Allen's standing within the ILP had begun to wane from late 1924; his background, relative moderation and essential (if not uncritical) loyalty to MacDonald contrasted with the Clydesiders' growing antipathy. After a series of disagreements, the ailing Allen resigned in late 1925, paving the way for Maxton to become ILP chairman in April 1926.

The Living Wage, which was eventually published in late 1926, had been propagated by the *New Leader* and was adopted – in the form of an interim report entitled 'Socialism in our Time' – at the 1926 ILP conference in April. In this, the ILP called for a high-wage economy in which those firms failing to pay a state-set minimum were to be nationalised or brought under the control of a state-appointed industrial commission. The objective was to raise consumer demand via the purchasing power of the working class, a conception that included the introduction of family allowances, redistributive taxation, and credit control to prevent inflation.[139] In response, Maxton, Wheatley, Fenner Brockway and others on the left of the ILP quickly built on the premise of a 'living wage', utilising its basic conceptions as the means by which to implement immediate socialist measures. Only under socialism, the ILP now argued, could a living wage be secured. In such a way, as David Howell has made clear, the original 'living wage' programme 'was blurred to some extent by the fact that prominent individuals within the ILP were propagating their own agendas which had affinities with *The Living Wage* but also differences of content and style'.[140] In short, a sense of urgency and militancy was added to the policy by the Maxton leadership, thereby accentuating its challenge to the official Labour Party programme, strategy and leadership.

Because of this, perhaps, the policies advocated by the ILP were easily deflected by the Labour Party conference in 1926. Not only could the programme of 'Socialism in our Time' be accused of contradicting itself – it offered a solution to the capitalist affliction of unemployment (as intended by Hobson) whilst simultaneously appearing to envisage imminent capitalist collapse – but the trade unions did not take kindly to socialist attempts to intervene into the industrial sphere, i.e. wage rates. While MacDonald was not unfamiliar or wholly unsympathetic with the economic basis of the policy, he fundamentally opposed the political assumptions that Maxton and the ILP left had drawn from Hobson's original thesis, namely that socialism would emerge out of conflict and capitalist collapse.[141] Even so, the party conference's dismissal of 'the living wage' did not thereby curtail the ILP's steady drift to militancy. The events of 1926 had only served to fuel both the ILP's socialist ire and the unions' obstinacy. ILP criticisms of the TUC's handling of the General Strike prompted Bevin to condemn – in a speech aimed at the Henry Brailsford-edited ILP paper *New Leader* – the 'superior class attitude' that 'people in your category in the movement' showed to the 'trade union leader who comes from the rank-and-file'.[142] And although the NEC discussed the ILP's policy proposals, it never considered them as a feasible alternative to *Labour and the Nation* For MacDonald and many trade unionists, the ILP had become an irritant, and it was with much gravity that the then prime minister finally decided to allow his own ILP membership (taken up in 1894) to lapse in 1930.

The ILP left's final attempt to alter the Labour Party's political course prior to the formation of the second Labour government in 1929 was based upon the so-called Cook–Maxton campaign forged with the miners' leader Arthur Cook. Such an initiative had been instigated by John Wheatley in the spring of 1928 and was intended to propagate a socialist agenda within the wider labour movement. This amounted to a manifesto of limited demands that insisted Labour act a 'class party' rather than 'a party representing all sections of the community', including capitalism.[143] The manifesto made little progress, exciting only modest support within either the unions or the Labour Party. Even the CPGB, members of which had helped draft the manifesto, soon distanced itself from the campaign, arguing that it merely gave the working class the misplaced hope that change could be affected through the 'reformist' Labour Party. Accordingly, when Maxton once more entered parliament following his re-election for Glasgow Bridgeton in 1929, he did so with few expectations as to the potential for Labour-sponsored socialist change (see Chapter Three below).

Of course, tensions involving the ILP could, and did, exist at all levels of the party. Given the ILP's historic role within the Labour Party, these often concerned the remit of ILP activity within the newly constituted organisation. In an archetypal example, the ambiguity of the ILP's position was revealed in Newport during the spring of 1923, when the local ILP challenged the divisional Labour Party's right to organise a visit by Ramsay MacDonald. Although a trade union-dominated executive committee resolution not to recognise the authority of the ILP was later deleted in an attempt to retain party unity, one ILP delegate to the executive resigned and a meeting with Arthur Henderson was necessarily arranged to reassert 'wholehearted' ILP support for the town's parliamentary candidate J. W. Bowen.[144] More damagingly, disagreements between the ILP and the trade unions in Sunderland contributed to the resignation of the entire divisional executive in 1929.[145] At a grass-roots level in Glasgow, Patrick Dollan ensured that the ILP remained loyal to the national Labour Party, but he simultaneously resisted moves to increase the Labour Party's individual membership or subordinate the ILP's dominant position within the city.[146] In Newcastle-under-Lyme, Josh Wedgwood's adoption as an ILP Labour candidate in 1919 was initially opposed by a group of local trade unionists who favoured 'common sense trade unionism' over the 'rabid socialism' of the ILP. In this instance, the NEC ensured that Harold Drinkwater (as Midlands organiser) forced the issue and secured the seat for the popular radical.[147]

The ILP, too, provided the base for Sir Oswald Mosley to launch his Labour Party career. Having been elected as a Unionist candidate for Harrow in 1918, the young aristocratic war hero quickly turned into an ardent critic of the government, eventually 'crossing the floor' of the Commons in November 1920 following heated exchanges over Ireland. After standing successfully as an Independent candidate in 1922 and 1923, Mosley joined the Labour Party in March 1924, quickly teaming up with John Strachey to form a formidable intellectual force based in the Birmingham ILP (where they had both been adopted as prospective Labour candidates). Here, the two men devised a series of 'proposals' that formed the foundations of Strachey's *Revolution by Reason* (1925), the novelty of which was its emphasis on the nationalisation of the banking system and its fusion of proto-Keynesian economics with socialist objectives. Significantly, MacDonald had much time for Mosley; he had welcomed such a notorious and well-heeled politician into the party with open arms and spent much time with 'Tom' and his wife 'Cimmie' thereafter. Even so, the 'Birmingham proposals' were dismissed by Labour's more established financial experts such as Dalton, Pethick-Lawrence and, of course, Philip Snowden. Throughout the mid-to-late 1920s, Mosley's and Strachey's concepts of credit expansion, state control of finance and increased purchasing power were countered by fears of inflation and an entrenched commitment to the orthodox balanced budget.[148] Nevertheless, Mosley's reputation was such that he was involved in the drafting of Labour's party programme prior to the 1929 general election (see below).

Taken generally, the ILP's influence within the Labour Party declined in tandem with the consolidation and extension of a nationwide Labour organisation. This was a contentious and, for many, traumatic experience. Many ILP members maintained an almost indistinguishable loyalty to both the Labour Party and the ILP. Several MPs, meanwhile, were sponsored by ILP funds; some – including Hugh Dalton – had joined the ILP specifically to benefit from such a resource. But while the militancy of Wheatley, Maxton and others could at times raise some sympathy within the wider party in the mid-1920s, it never projected the predominant concerns or opinions of Labour members within the ILP or the labour movement as a whole. By 1928, even erstwhile sympathisers such as George Lansbury had lost patience with the methods and trajectory of the ILP.[149] The socialist 'think tank' was becoming a 'party within a party', regarded increasingly by the bulk of the Labour leadership and trade union affiliates as more a hindrance than a help to Labour's electoral mission.

Ultimately, a lack of trade union support and the minority position of the ILP left wing made it possible for the Labour leadership to marginalize and contain such a challenge to the prevailing party agenda. With regard to the CPGB, more overtly disciplinarian measures could be utilised to repel communist influence within the party. Formed in 1920, the CPGB endeavoured to supplant the Labour Party as the principal working-class party in Britain and lead the workers to revolution. This it intended to do by working inside the Labour Party (and trade unions), pushing the party to the left but, more importantly, preparing the ground for the time when material circumstances facilitated a revolutionary challenge to capitalism. As such, the CPGB offered 'critical support' to Labour, worked for the return of a Labour government, and even put forward its members as Labour parliamentary candidates. In such a way, Shapurji Saklatvala was returned as Labour MP for Battersea in November 1922, despite his being a CPGB cardholder. In the same year, J. T. Walton Newbold won Motherwell as an out-and-out communist but endorsed by the Labour-affiliated trades council. Communists, such as Harry Pollitt, Arthur Horner and Aitkin Ferguson, were regular speakers at Labour conferences as union or trades council delegates, while many communists held joint membership with the Labour Party or via their trade union affiliation. The objective, as Lenin had put it in his pamphlet *Left Wing Communism*, was to support Labour 'in the same way as a rope supports the hanged – that the impending establishment of a Henderson government will prove that [the communists are] right, will bring the masses over to [the communists'] side, and will accelerate the political deaths of the Hendersons and Snowdens as was the case with their friends in Russia and Germany'.[150] To this effect, the CPGB made repeated attempts to affiliate to Labour between 1920 and 1928, only to be rebuked decisively on each occasion.[151]

Labour's reasons for rejecting such advances were clear. From the perspective of the NEC and the wider party conference, the insurrectionary aspirations of the CPGB did not conform to the constitutional approach of the Labour Party. Nor too did the 'dictatorship of the proletariat' established by Lenin's Bolsheviks and supported by the CPGB complement the gradualist and peaceful conception of social transformation envisaged by the vast majority of Labour members. Not surprisingly, Labour also viewed with suspicion the CPGB's affiliation to the Bolshevik-instigated Communist International. This, Labour reasoned, meant the CPGB was 'signed, sealed and delivered, mind, body and soul to whatever instructions they got from Moscow'.[152] Internationalism did not come into it; Labour simply regarded the CPGB as an appendage of the Soviet regime. More pragmatically, such 'insuperable differences' could not be easily overcome, particularly at a time when the so-called 'reformist' Labour leaders were regularly harried in the national and local press for their 'Bolshevist tendencies'.[153] As this suggests, electoral considerations informed Labour's rejection of CPGB 'support', although we should not underestimate the genuinely fierce anti-communism of leading Labour members such as Henderson, MacDonald, Clynes, Bevin, Morrison and Snowden. Across the 1920s, therefore, moves were made to contain and then expel all remnants of communist influence within the Labour Party.

First, a resolution sponsored by the Wallasey Labour Party at the Edinburgh conference in 1922 insisted that delegates accept the constitution and principles of the Labour Party, although an attempt to disallow delegates from being members of 'any organisation having for one of its objectives the return to parliament or to any local governing authority, a candidate or candidates other than such as have been endorsed by the Labour Party' was simultaneously dropped. Such a measure was contentious, especially given the federated nature of Labour organisation. Despite the TUC's general antipathy to communism, trade unionists raised concern about what appeared to be the NEC's impinging on their right to appoint delegates to conference. As this suggests, such equivocation was more a point of principle than a sign of sympathy for the CPGB. Eventually, however, such scruples were put aside as communist influence within the trade union movement became more apparent over the mid-1920s. In 1924, therefore, the screw was further tightened. Thus, the party conference declared communists ineligible for both political candidacy and individual Labour Party membership, decisions that were reaffirmed the following year in Liverpool with an 'appeal' to trade unions to act against communists within their own apparatus. From 1926, moreover, Labour began a process of disaffiliating those divisional parties deemed to be under communist influence. Finally, in 1928, the banning of communists attending conference as trade union delegates closed off the final point of entry for communists into the Labour Party. By the end of the decade, the CPGB and a variety of associated organisations, including the National Unemployed Workers' Movement (NUWM) and the League Against Imperialism (LAI), were deemed to represent interests and objectives incompatible with Labour Party membership. Divisional parties were neither to include communists within their ranks nor co-operate with communists in wider political activity.[154]

The national party's rejection of the CPGB was generally accepted at a local level. Given the CPGB's small numbers, such proscriptions were hardly relevant to many a constituency organisation.[155] Where communists were active, many divisional parties applied party discipline. So, for example, the Edinburgh trades council consistently rejected local communist appeals for affiliation from 1921, as did the South Shields Labour Party.[156] In Colne Valley, communist participation in the 1922 May Day prompted a letter from Snowden and a local executive decision to have no part in the annual procession.[157] More unusually, the North Lambeth

Divisional Labour Party refused to attend meetings of the Borough Labour Party from July 1926, complaining to head office of communist domination. The NEC advised that the divisional party continue to be represented at borough level, before further communist agitation led the party to again withdraw, and the NEC to disaffiliate the borough organisation.[158]

Elsewhere, several local Labour parties recorded their opposition to the arrest of the CPGB leadership in 1925 as part of the government's preparation for the forthcoming General Strike, while sympathy was sometimes registered for individual communists. To take one example, the Merton and Morden Labour Party noted its regret that its secretary, Mr Fidler, had to stand down his position owing to the rulings of the party conference.[159] In the early 1920s, sympathy for the Russian revolution, prevailing traditions of co-operation across socialist organisations, and communist commitment to trade union work and the plight of the unemployed, ensured that cross-party activity continued in some localities. Communists were often known and valued activists within their respective communities, meaning that the NEC's proscriptions were never fully applicable in many places. On occasion, communist members continued to be proposed as parliamentary candidates, prompting the NEC to move somewhat uncertainly to prevent their adoption, particularly following Aitkin Ferguson's controversial defeat as a Labour candidate in the Kelvingrove by-election of 1924 and the Bolshevik scare-mongering that accompanied the general election of the same year.[160] More dramatically, a number of divisional parties in which the CPGB exerted an influence rejected the conference ruling on communist membership. As noted above, the NEC came to act decisively in such instances, eventually disbanding 27 divisional parties in London, Scotland, South Wales, Birmingham and Southport between 1926 and 1929. Yet, the 'problem' of the CPGB consistently took up much of the NEC's time throughout the 1920s, revealing the concern with which the party viewed the relatively small CPGB. Indeed, Labour's perceived need to move against communist influence was both cause and effect of an organisation that was becoming increasingly centralised and disciplined, if in a rather circumscribed way.

Rather subtler, if no less hard-headed, organisational measures were used to forestall matters deemed potentially divisive or harmful to the electoral fortunes of the party. This was particularly the case in response to issues raised by the Labour's expanding women's section throughout the interwar years. By 1928, the party claimed 1,791 women's sections and between 250,000 and 300,000 female party members.[161] As we have seen, individual women members could sometimes outnumber their male comrades, as in Newport and Cardiff, and Labour women across the country were becoming an increasingly visible and integral part of Labour's wider identity Nevertheless, despite their growing numbers and the (limited) organisational recognition given to women by the 1918 constitution, Labour women consistently struggled to get their voices heard within the party apparatus during the 1920s.

Several 'obstacles' were placed in the way of women's advancement within the party. First, in terms of women standing as Labour candidates or attaining official positions within the party, the predominance of trade union seats and the related industrial nature of many divisional parties served to limit opportunities. Even as Labour began to adopt a wider and more communally focused politics, the party's identity generally continued to be infused with the masculine signifiers of organised labour: the factory, workplace and flat cap. Whatever the references to 'hand and brain', and despite the influx of both female and middle-class members, Labour remained a party built on the trade union movement. As Pamela Graves has suggested, even issues directly relevant to women, such as equal pay and the right of married women to work, were often interpreted in relation to trade union concerns.[162] Second, as noted in the previous chapter, prevailing gender assumptions contributed to the creation of male and female 'spaces' and priorities within the party. Women candidates and officers were, of course, breaking much new ground, and the process of gaining the confidence, respect and trust of what was an overwhelmingly male political world took some time. Those women who did break into the upper ranks of the party in the 1920s tended to be middle class and/or socially mobile (and usually unmarried). More commonly, Labour continued to portray women as wives or mothers, the empowerment of whom was perceived within existing social structures. This, in turn, was not simply imposed by male members, but was part of what Martin Francis has called the 'complex matrix of identities' that characterised both Labour and the society of the time.[163] Third, specifically organisational factors were important. We have already observed how the women nominees to the NEC were selected and voted for by the party conference as a whole, that is by the trade union-dominated block vote rather than by the women's sections themselves. Additionally, such marginalisation was reinforced by the apparently 'toothless' nature of the women's conference, the resolutions of which were regularly overlooked, sidestepped or discounted. The conference had no policy-making powers, and attempts to ensure its resolutions were considered by the main Labour conference were rejected. Similarly, the women's advisory committee to the NEC was restricted to offering advice and providing information; it too had no policy-making powers. Accordingly, perhaps, Dorothy Thurtle – who campaigned hard on the issue of birth control throughout the 1920s – complained in 1926 that the NEC only had 'use for women so long as they have no opinions of their own but are willing to do the donkey work of the party'.[164]

Evidently, such a view was not without foundation. The NEC refused the regular attempts made by the women's sections to change the constitution over the 1920s, while certain issues near the top of the women's conference agenda, such as birth control, were dismissed as 'personal questions' likely to prompt division within the wider party. However, the reasons for such apparent disregard were varied. From a practical point of view, fear of alienating the Catholic vote informed Labour's arms-length approach to questions of contraception. Indeed, the experience of Glasgow, wherein the party became embroiled in a controversy over the placing of *Birth Control News* in municipal libraries that impinged negatively on Labour's 1927 local election result, no doubt reinforced such concern.[165] At the same time, many in the party related questions of birth control to eugenics; anti-Malthusianism, which saw contraception as an alternative to social reform, retained an appeal among Labour members and was used by MacDonald to undermine related issues.[166] Of course, the party's blatantly male perspective also tended to subjugate such issues beneath more overtly political-economic priorities; even when the NEC and women's conference did find common ground, the trade unions could block further progress. Thus, party agreement on the payment of family allowances raised trade union fears that such a policy would lead to an associated drop in wages, and the policy was duly buried.[167] In similar fashion, such a question as equal pay for equal work, a policy that formed part of Labour's election manifesto in 1918, remained largely rhetorical in the 1920s and 1930s.[168] Ironically, perhaps, women organisers in the party were paid less than their male equivalents.[169] Finally, the party's insistence that issues such as birth control and abortion were 'private' issues related partly to embarrassment in discussing such matters, and partly to a prevailing belief in designated spheres of interest and activity – in this case, the 'personal' and the 'political' Throughout the party, issues that encouraged 'sex antagonism' were consistently avoided in favour of what were defined by the male leadership as 'the common interests of both sexes'.[170]

Such inequalities were clear at a divisional level. Although women were included on the general committees and executives of the divisional parties, they were always in the minority. Similarly, while women were selected as candidates in municipal election contests, their number was few in comparison to male Labour candidates. On occasion, divisional parties received resolutions from their respective women's sections demanding greater female representation on the municipal lists, but it would appear that women's sections and candidates were more typically overlooked, underrepresented, or not consulted by their male counterparts.[171] Meanwhile, in terms of a party's direct appeal to the female electorate, we can only imagine what South Edinburgh women made of Arthur Woodburn's suggestion that women should vote Labour out of 'gratitude' to the party's previous support for women's suffrage.[172]

Inevitably, the priorities and opinions evident within the divisional women's sections and expressed at the annual women's conference varied. To state the obvious, women did not form a homogeneous bloc within the Labour Party; their views covered the gamut of Labour opinion on a range of different issues. Even with regard to the so-called 'women's questions', the party's female members and women's conference rarely displayed unanimity. Those women who had broken into the higher ranks of the party tended to subordinate issues of gender to issues of class or the wider community. As such, Margaret Bondfield and Ellen Wilkinson, from different perspectives, were not known primarily for their stance on gender issues. Bondfield, in particular, was concerned that the party should not be divided along gender lines via the discussion of specifically 'women's issues'. Wilkinson, while keen to promote women's interests on her election to parliament, insisted that she did not want to be seen 'purely as a woman's MP'. While her maiden speech to parliament in 1924 included reference to equal suffrage, widow's pensions and the rights of unemployed women, she saw her commitment to the industrial constituency of Middlesbrough as overriding specifically gender concerns. '[Men] voters predominate in Middlesbrough East', she remarked, 'thousands are unemployed and I mean to stand up to the gruelling work for all their sakes'.[173] As such, there remained much debate as to whether women should retain a separate status within the party, or whether Labour's women members should simply join and act alongside their male comrades. In fact, the question as to the desirability of individual women's sections was raised at the national women's conference in 1919, with some delegates reporting that male and female members wished to meet together. Certainly, for long-serving women activists such as the ILP's Hannah Mitchell, it soon appeared as though the women's sections had been set up primarily to become the 'official cake-maker to the party' Similarly, as an experienced NEC member, Susan Lawrence argued against separate organisation, encouraging women instead to fight and scrap alongside male members 'on terms of perfect equality'. Indeed, Lawrence had in 1921 insisted that she be arrested and imprisoned with her fellow Poplar Labour councillors for 'representing a principle which we have the right to defend as well as the men'.[174] Conversely, those women new to politics appeared to welcome the individual sections as a place to hone their political views and skills. To this effect, the majority of Labour's female members chose to join a separate women's section despite the fact that the party constitution allowed women to attend both 'regular' party and women's section meetings.[175] In the context of the 1920s and 1930s, sexual equality was broadly – but by no means exclusively – interpreted in terms of 'separate-but-equal', with distinct male and female 'spaces', concerns and responsibilities. That these began to blur is certain, but the process was protracted and uneven, reflecting the workplace, home and community lives of the men and women who informed Labour's membership.

Nevertheless, attempts were made to challenge inequalities within the Labour Party. In 1921, the women's conference resolved to approach the NEC with regard to, first, extending its authority in order to submit statutory resolutions to the party conference and, second, to assume the right to elect its own representatives to the party executive Despite some support, the conference rejected the proposals, with Henderson arguing that they would encourage sectionalism.[176] Still, the basis for such a resolution remained pertinent, and a renewed offensive was made towards the end of the 1920s. A number of women's sections passed resolutions supporting changes to the election of the NEC women's representatives; in 1928, the women's conference resolved that the party allow three resolutions a year to be presented to the national conference.[177] The party's response was ambivalent. The reorganisation of the NEC in 1929 allowed an extra woman representative on the NEC, but there was no compromise on the method of election or the power of the women's conference. In addition, where the 1918 party constitution had allowed constituency parties with over 500 women members to send a female delegate to conference, the 1929 party conference resolved to make this applicable only to parties with a female membership of over 2,500.[178] As a result, women continued to be massively under-represented at conference throughout the interwar period.

If a combination of organisational procedure and the basic structure of the Labour Party was enough to repel the CPGB and to contain disquiet among the ILP left wing and party women's sections, then discontent within the ranks of the trade union movement in the immediate wake of the first Labour government posed a more potent threat to the MacDonald leadership. The opportunity for union–party conflict was an ever-present characteristic of the Labour Party, with Lewis Minkin recognising four broad areas of potential division: ideology, priorities, social affinities, and strategies.[179] These, in turn, provide a neat paradigm through which to consider Labour–union relations in the mid-to-late 1920s. Ideologically, the definition of Labour socialism as expressed by the party centre caused relatively little concern within the TUC. Throughout the 1920s, Labour's ideological basis remained ill defined but broadly applicable to trade union interests. Of course, tensions and suspicions would remain between trade unionists, politicians and socialists, but the basic premise of piecemeal, parliamentary reform remained a point of convergence for the PLP, NEC and TUC. As such, the trade unions continually backed the party leadership against its critics in the ILP, CPGB and, later, the Socialist League. Far more problematical was the question of political and industrial priorities.

At its conception, the Labour Party had been formed in the pursuit of 'trade union ideals and aims', and although the party's stated objectives had widened following the Great War, the protection and advancement of trade union interests remained integral to most members' understanding of Labour.[180] Consequently, the experience of the first Labour government caused some concern among sections of the TUC. Most obviously, Ramsay MacDonald – a man always wary of the non-political struggle – had revealed himself unresponsive to trade union demands. '[If] strikes went on', he reputedly told Hugh Dalton, they would 'knock us out'.[181] Accordingly, miners' attempts to renegotiate wage agreements in the wake of a brief upturn in the industry that accompanied the Ruhr crisis were sidelined by the MacDonald government under the guise of inquiry and negotiation, while the prime minister was provoked to criticise a dockers' strike in February before threatening to resort to emergency powers when the London tramwaymen struck in March. At a time when unions were again pushing to advance their members' positions, the Labour government was unwilling to respond in a way that appeared subservient to union demands. For MacDonald, reflecting the outlook of many within the PLP, a Labour government's principal obligation was to the national rather than the sectional interest. Even the trade unionists inside the cabinet, such as Henderson, Thomas and Clynes, had pointedly placed their national responsibilities above those of their union representation in 1924.

Not surprisingly, some in the TUC expressed disquiet at the Labour government's unwillingness to consult adequately with its union sponsors. For example, the TUC general council had refused to take part in the Balfour Committee on industry and trade due to the 'failure' of the government to consult with the unions over its composition. By September 1924, the TUC president Alf Purcell was informing his members that even the formation of a Labour government left 'us confronting capitalism in the field', further suggesting that a 'well disciplined industrial organisation is the principal weapon of the workers'.[182] In 1925, too, the TUC conference made pointed reference to 'the mistaken view of regarding the political labour movement as an alternative instead of an auxiliary to the trade union movement ...'[183] This, in turn, was a lesson that Ernest Bevin would not readily forget. Later, in 1933, he recalled how he knew all about emergency powers, how 'the first Labour government had rushed down to Windsor to get them signed in order to operate on me'.[184] Indeed, the emerging force that was the TGWU proved to be the Labour Party's most potent union critic in the immediate wake of 1924; it was Bevin who moved the 1925 Labour Party conference resolution against the formation of another minority Labour government.[185] Even so, Bevin was not yet the power he would later become and the proposed resolution was defeated. As Hugh Clegg has commented, the actual extent of industrial unrest in 1924 was modest, with fewer days lost to strikes than any year since 1918.[186] If the experience of a Labour government had revealed that the trade unions and a Labour government had different priorities, it did not raise the question of the unions' more general commitment to the party. As we shall see, the TUC moved to realign its position with regard to Labour from 1925, but it did not question its support for the party; nor did this diminish the trade unions' desire for a Labour government.

With regard to 'social affinities', the common social basis of the Labour Party and the trade unions remained throughout the 1920s; the majority of Labour members, officers and voters were working class, predominantly male, and usually union cardholders. However, such 'affinity' was less evident within a PLP that continued to expand with each general election. Although the number of trade union MPs increased over the 1920s, so too did those sponsored by their divisional party and without overt union backing, many of whom came from outside the working class. Thus, the 1929 general election saw 172 non-union sponsored Labour MPs enter the Commons (60 per cent of the PLP), compared to 90 in 1923 (47 per cent), meaning that the percentage of Labour MPs (and candidates) from non-working-class backgrounds grew notably over the 1920s. By the end of the decade, the Tilletts, Thornes, Jones' and Lunns were sitting alongside a growing number of Malones, Buxtons, Picton-Turbervills and Ponsonbys. Such a shift was clearly apparent within the party leadership. Both Labour cabinets appointed in 1924 and 1929 included a disproportionate number of aristocratic and upper-middle-class members, while names such as Wedgwood, Trevelyan, Mosley and Dalton had begun to appear on the NEC by the mid-to-late-1920s. Of course, such class distinctions did not lead inevitably to conflict, although they added grist to the mill of many a trade unionist's suspicion of intellectuals, party politicians, and those somehow detached from the 'realities' of working-class life.

In terms of strategy, the attempts of the early 1920s to co-ordinate more firmly the activities of the TUC and the Labour Party appear to have stalled by the end of the first Labour government. This was symbolised most acutely by the TUC general council decision to dissolve the joint research departments in 1926. Practical and administrative problems played a part in this, but so too did the experience of Labour's minority administration.[187] Labour's term in office had seemingly reinforced the impression that the TUC and PLP had different roles to perform within the wider labour movement. Thus, according to the TUC general council's functions committee in July 1925, 'it was impossible for the work of the Congress adequately to be carried on by joint departments. The identity of the trade union and political Labour Movements is kept entirely distinct both nationally and internationally, and while the closest collaboration between the two is necessary, the work of each necessitates its own machinery'.[188] Such thinking was confirmed by the TUC's refusal to partake in a party investigation into tariff policy on the grounds that it was an industrial matter that should be left to the unions.[189] Indeed, the National Joint Council (NJC) proceeded to meet rarely, often just once a year, between 1926 and 1929. For the Labour Party, meanwhile, its continued growth – which occurred in tandem with falling trade union membership – meant that its own responsibilities and objectives no longer simply overlapped with the TUC. A priority for Labour from 1918 and throughout the 1920s was to present itself a party of the 'people' and the 'nation', not just of the organised working class.

The 'new direction' of the TUC was closely associated with Walter Citrine, its general secretary from September 1926. For Citrine, a former assistant secretary to both the TUC and the Electrical Trades Union (ETU), the experience of the Labour government and the General Strike reaffirmed his belief in the need for a more professional, co-ordinated and strategically minded TUC. To this effect, Citrine began from 1926 to ensure that the trade union movement became 'an integral part of the economic machinery of society', an objective that received the important backing of Bevin, Pugh (Iron and Steel Trades Federation) and Hayday (NUGMW) among others.[190] As noted above, this did not thereby lead to an ideological split between Labour and the TUC. By the mid-1920s, however, the TUC under Citrine had distinguished distinct trade union areas of concern, from industrial disputes and campaigns to union recruitment and policy development. Beyond the Labour Party, the TUC pursued its own strategies, first in response to the coal dispute of 1925–6, and then in the form of collective bargaining and greater accommodation with employers (the Mond–Turner talks). The TUC's priorities remained firmly connected to its own interests and those of its affiliates and members. Henceforth, the TUC claimed the right to lobby governments of all political persuasions, developing in the process its own increasingly complex bureaucratic structures. Such distinction was to be reinforced at individual union level. In 1926, for instance, calls from the local Labour parties for 'closer working arrangements' between party officers and the unions during industrial disputes were only 'welcomed' by the TGWU, with the caveat that 'the direction and scope of the strike' remain under union control.[191] Concurrently, the bastions of the TUC continued to respect the Labour Party's need to pursue its own political priorities and responsibilities. In such a way, the 'contentious alliance' continued within what Minkin has described as a 'framework of mutual restraint', in which distinct roles were more clearly apportioned to the respective wings of the labour movement.[192]

The most explicit threat to labour movement equilibrium in the period between 1924 and 1929 occurred in the build up, execution and immediate aftermath of the 1926 General Strike. In many ways, the strike was the culmination of on-going economic problems facing Britain and its coal industry in the wake of the Great War. Yet, as confrontation between workers, unions, employers and government became more likely, so different approaches to such a conflict could be discerned. For MacDonald, if the unions sought to take on the state they would fail and possibly do more harm than good to the wider labour movement.[193] In the intensified economic climate of 1925–6, however, this did not fall readily on trade unionist ears. The TUC had appeared to take a more militant stance in 1924–5, while the CPGB-instigated National Minority Movement (NMM) was able to mobilise notable support among left-wing trade unionists in the months leading up to the outbreak of the strike. This should not be overstated. The TUC may have been committed to defending the miners' interests, but this was *industrial* militancy and not the revolutionary challenge to British capital that some in the NMM and CPGB desired. Following 'Red Friday', a belief in trade union strength had been reaffirmed, and it was in such a spirit that the TUC responded to the Samuel Commission and the coal owners' threats in 1926.

Not surprisingly, the ensuing nine-day struggle has gone down in labour history folklore, its defeat seemingly irrelevant to the strike's demonstration of working-class solidarity. That the strike was terminated by the trade union leadership – rather than the breaking of the workers' resolve – is not in doubt. Simultaneously, however, the strike's cessation led to accusations of 'betrayal' across sections of the labour movement. While miners' leaders such as Arthur Cook made excited pleas for the workers to remain resolute in their struggle, so the bulk of the TUC general council sought to resolve the dispute in the face of government charges that the strike posed a threat to the British constitution. In between, the PLP leadership and NEC looked on the events of 4–12 May with uncertainty. As Clynes later recalled,

'Thomas, Snowden, Henderson, MacDonald and I moved behind the scenes, trying to find some way out of the impasse, hindered on the one hand by the armed preparations of the government, and on the other by the ferocious statements and wild promises of Cook and his following'.[194] Accordingly, the Labour Party's official response to the dispute juxtaposed an undoubted sympathy for the miners' plight with disquiet at the unions' methods.

Yet, just as the methods of the TUC and the Labour Party looked at their most divergent, so the wider ramifications of General Strike exemplified their reliance on each other. First and foremost, once the dust had settled, the strike's defeat can be seen to have reinforced both worker and trade union commitment to the return of a Labour government. Trade union support for the Labour Party in the mid-to-late 1920s would never be unconditional; tensions remained and the concerns raised by the first Labour government were never completely forgotten. But the moderate and conciliatory approach endorsed by union politicians such as Henderson, Clynes and Thomas re-emerged as the foundation stone of trade union policy from late 1926. As the staple industries stagnated, as unemployment remained above one million, and as trade union membership fell, so the unions pursued a far more accommodating strategy, part of which centred on its support for Labour. Thus, Joseph Sullivan declared to the MFGB conference in 1927 that 'for the time being, our salvation lies in the leadership of MacDonald'; a sentiment echoed in the estimation of the union's president, Herbert Smith, who equated loyalty to the Labour Party with loyalty to the MFGB.[195] In return, Labour leaders welcomed the unions' rapprochement with the employers. Henderson, for one, endorsed the Mond–Turner talks.

Such a change of tack was evident in the TUC's endeavour to enter into more congenial industrial negotiations from late 1926. In effect, the General Strike's failure proved to be the final nail in the coffin of union-sponsored direct action, ushering in a period of limited industrial unrest. Just 1,174,000 and 1,388,000 days were lost to strike action in 1927 and 1928, a lower figure than at any time during or following the war.[196] Even erstwhile militants, such as Will Lawther from the 'little Moscow' of Chopwell, recalled that following 'the bitter experience in 1926 … we made up our minds that in our lifetimes there'd never be another one [general strike]'.[197] Yet, this should not be seen as some kind of watershed in trade union history. As noted above, the unions were placed in an increasingly unfavourable position over the 1920s: with the economy continuing to stagnate so the unions' bargaining position became ever more limited. Recourse to defensive action and arbitration was a pragmatic response to the circumstances of the time. Equally, it should be remembered that most trade unionists regarded industrial action as a last resort; a number of trade union leaders had shared the apprehensions of their parliamentary 'brothers' on the outbreak of the General Strike. In such circumstances, although the distinctions between the 'industrial' and the 'political' were reaffirmed in late 1926, the perspectives of the TUC and the Labour Party continued to complement each other.

Second, the passing of the Conservative government's Trade Disputes and Trade Union Act in 1927 further underlined the need for a trade union-backed Labour Party. Not only did the Act outlaw sympathetic strike action and force civil service unions to disaffiliate from the TUC, but it also instigated a direct challenge to the trade unions' and, therefore, the Labour Party's, financial solidity. By replacing 'contracting out' with 'contracting in' – meaning that workers had actively to choose to pay a political levy to their trade union – the Act brought a period of financial hardship upon the unions and Labour Party alike. Thus, as Labour's affiliated trade union membership fell from 3,352,347 to 2,025,139 between 1926 and 1928, so the party's income from affiliation fees fell from £40,622 in 1927 to £28,955 in 1929.[198] It was, of course, to defend the unions against such legislation that the Labour Party had been formed. To do this, the party relied on trade union finance and support in order to apply pressure inside parliament.

As would be expected, Labour immediately instigated a nationwide campaign against the Trade Disputes and Trade Union Act. Local committees were set up, such as in North Lambeth where the party formed a Trade Union Defence Campaign in May 1927, although the results were more generally disappointing. Divisional parties were also instructed to consider ways to raise the necessary funds to keep the party running and, more importantly, to contest elections. Numerous ideas were offered as a result, inspiring weekly door-to-door canvassing, propaganda campaigns and membership schemes. Simultaneously, appeals were made to those union branches not affiliated to their respective constituency party to bolster Labour membership and finances in any way that they could. At a national level, the 1929 party conference authorised a special levy of 2d to be spread over three years, while the regular affiliation fee was eventually raised to 4d.[199] Moreover, contributions to agents' salaries were reduced in 1932–3, funding for the *Daily Herald* was discontinued, and the party's central organising staff was trimmed: all four of the party's propagandists were dispensed with between 1929 and 1932.[200] Some changes were resisted. In an attempt to extend the party membership further, the NEC proposed in 1929 to allow a third 'type' of member to join the party by affiliating nationally to head office. For George Shepherd, who had become national agent following the death of Egerton Wake in March 1929, this was to allow professional people who felt they could not be too closely associated with Labour to join the party.[201] However, strong opposition from the conference floor prompted the NEC to withdraw such a suggestion. Fears of untrustworthy and unaccountable members evidently overrode whatever financial and numerical benefits such an arrangement could have brought.[202]

Third, the failed militancy of the strike united the TUC and Labour Party against the CPGB and its militant sympathisers inside the labour movement. While the Communist Party endeavoured to rally support for those miners who fought on after 12 May, the more common response to the strike's defeat was disillusionment and recrimination. Just as the left and the CPGB blamed the TUC and Labour Party leaders for 'betraying' the working class, so the labour movement hierarchy accused the militants of having pushed the miners into an intractable struggle. Simultaneously, the CPGB was subjected to extensive criticism from the bastions of the TUC during the various inquiries that followed the strike.[203] Thus, Charlie Cramp – steadfast NEC member and secretary of the NUR – blamed not the TUC general council for the events in May, but 'our people who for years made it impossible for the General Council to resist the General Strike' This was followed by the TUC's declaration that affiliation to the NMM was 'not consistent with the policy of the congress'. Accordingly, both the TUC and a number of individual trade unions undertook a series of measures designed to restrict the influence of the

CPGB inside the union apparatus. Most immediately, the NUGMW declared membership of either the NMM or CPGB to be 'inconsistent' with 'loyal attachment' to the union from late 1926. As a result, several of the 61 NUGMW members who attended an NMM meeting on 6 February 1927 against the orders of the union were disqualified, five London branches were disenfranchised, and the union executive insisted that no communist or member of the NMM should hold an official position within the union. In 1927, the Amalgamated Engineering Union (AEU) blocked the payment of affiliation fees to the Minority Movement, instructed local branches to ignore any circulars issued by the NMM, and warned against sending delegates to NMM conferences. The Boilermakers' Union voted in 1927 to deny communists the right to act as union delegates; the NUR and the TGWU sought to block correspondence between the NMM and the local union branches; the Painters' Union ruled affiliation to the NMM out of bounds; the Printers' Union denied CPGB or NMM members the right to stand for official union positions; and even the MFGB condemned the activities of the CPGB and the NMM at its annual conference in 1928. At a more general level, the TUC general council issued a circular on 25 March 1927 that withdrew recognition of those trades councils affiliated to, 'or associated with', the NMM. Accordingly, some 22 trades councils had disaffiliated from the NMM by the end of the year, while the London Trades Council, in which five NMM members had served on an executive of twelve, was purged of its communist element via a series of organisational procedures.[204]

Ultimately, therefore, it may be argued that the experience of the General Strike helped to advance the Labour Party's electoral fortunes. Superficially, at least, such reasoning would appear to be borne out in the municipal election contests that followed the unrest, as the party made considerable gains between 1926 and 1929. To take a few examples, the number of Labour councillors in Edinburgh more than doubled in November 1926, increasing to fourteen compared to just six the previous year. Over South Wales as a whole, Labour gained control of Swansea county borough council in 1927, and won or regained five urban district council majorities in 1926–9 (taking its total to 23).[205] Even more immediately, the strike caused such anti-Conservative hostility during a municipal by-election in the working-class Tory heartland of Birmingham Ladywood in 1926, that Labour won the seat after the Unionists felt forced to abandon canvassing.[206] Further north, in Barnsley, Labour had gained equal representation on the council in 1921, but finally took control of the council in 1927.[207] Similarly, Sheffield was won for Labour in 1926. In Nottingham, meanwhile, Labour gained five seats in November 1926 to at last deny the Conservatives overall control; from here on, the Tories relied on Liberal support as the Nottingham Labour Party continued to make a steady advance and become the largest party on the city council in 1928.[208] Finally, in London, Labour won 459 seats at the metropolitan borough elections of 1928, compared to 364 in 1925.[209]

In the context of falling union membership and diminishing industrial disputes, the ballot box now appeared the most effective means by which to advance the labour interest. Yet, we should not overestimate the strike's impact on the Labour vote; broader factors – of both a local and national character – also contributed to Labour's progress over the mid-to-late 1920s. In many places, Labour's municipal fortunes within certain working-class communities had been advancing well before

1926. As Mike Savage has suggested with regard to Preston, Labour's progress was arguably a response to the party's extension of its organisation into working-class neighbourhoods and the broadening of party policy beyond the immediate needs of the organised working class. This, indeed, was a characteristic of many divisional parties over the 1920s. Perhaps, therefore, the local and general elections of 1926–9 brought the two strands of Labour's appeal together: the election of a Labour government would both overturn Tory legislative limitations on trade unionism and improve the lot of working people in general. Whatever the combination of forces, the improvement of Labour's local electoral performance from 1926 was clear. Although Labour had gained 307 seats on provincial borough councils in England and Wales between 1923 and 1925, it won 389 between 1926 and 1928, and a further 219 in 1929.[210]

To sum up, Labour's moderate and constitutional identity was consolidated by a variety of factors over the mid-to-late 1920s. Organisationally, the party became more centralised, while its struggle against the CPGB and potentially divisive elements within its own ranks initiated greater NEC intervention into local political affairs. The party's approach became more orchestrated over the 1920s, although we must be careful not to overstate such a development. In this, party headquarters had the support of the trade unions, despite certain tensions that existed in the period 1924–6. From here on, however, the 'contentious alliance' was secure in its ultimate objective of establishing a second Labour government. If union-party co-operation was loosened and the separate industrial and political spheres reaffirmed, then both the party's and the TUC's commitment to practical, constitutional and moderate reform was similarly compounded by the events of 1926 and the material circumstances in which the labour movement perceived itself to exist.

IV. LABOUR AND THE NATION

If Labour's experience in government had revealed anything, it was the need for a more detailed account of just how Labour intended to initiate its vision of social change. As Andrew Thorpe has made clear, 1918's *Labour and the New Social Order* had been written in very distinct circumstances, with its basic objective amounting as much to a defence of the labour movement's wartime gains as it did to enacting realisable social transformation.[211] Thus, its commitment to 'public ownership' applied to those industries brought under state control during the war, its emphasis was focused on post-war reconstruction, and its wider perspective was shaped primarily by notions of continued capitalist development and increased production. By 1924, many of its concepts and objectives had become open to question. For instance, the capital levy was no longer so readily perceived as an option in the less favourable economic conditions of the early-to-mid-1920s, with doubts about its efficacy and its potential electoral impact being enough to convince Snowden and MacDonald of its inexpediency. Subsequently, the policy had all but been abandoned by the time that Labour took office. Similarly, Labour plans for public ownership had not progressed much beyond it being a stated objective. The NEC's industrial policy committee had remained largely dormant from its establishment in 1918, meeting rarely and producing very little. Only in the coal industry was nationalisation seen as an immediate and possible solution, and this was largely due to the MFGB's policy initiatives and the legitimacy given to such an idea by the experience of the Great War and subsequent Sankey commission. If anything, Labour policy retreated over the period between the armistice and the first Labour government, with respectability and caution replacing social transformation as MacDonald's overriding priority. This, in turn, had served its purpose in proving Labour 'fit to govern', but had simultaneously helped curb the potential impact of a 'socialist' government.

Partly for these reasons, the Labour Party resolved to fight the 1929 general election on a revised political programme. The process of producing such a document had begun in the spring of 1925, following the appointment of a sub-committee by the NEC on 7 April.[212] The committee's findings were then reported – and accepted – by the party conference of the same year, beginning with a six-point resolution introduced by MacDonald. This briefly outlined Labour's commitment to the 'extension of industrial organisation, political democracy, and popular education' in opposition to capitalism's failure to provide employment for over a million people. 'Only upon avowedly socialist principles can the claims of the workers for a fair and decent standard of living be met', the fourth point of the resolution asserted. As such, the necessity of bringing the 'larger and more widely-used public services' under national ownership and democratic control was determined, before a series of 'co-ordinated' policies of reconstruction and reform were placed before the conference. These included resolutions on unemployment, housing, banking and credit, foreign policy, land reform, agriculture, and various health and educational matters.[213] Significantly, however, there continued to be little detail as to the extent or practical application of Labour policy, particularly with regard to national ownership. Moreover, the emphasis on social welfare policy evident at a local Labour level was not so obviously apparent, although conference reiterated the party's commitment to extend the powers of municipal government. Clearly, while the party conference ratified with few objections the substance of a new Labour programme, this would necessarily have to be refined in preparation for the next general election.

Such a process was no doubt encouraged by the emergence of the ILP's more detailed 'living wage' policies in 1926. Thus, at the Blackpool conference in 1927, MacDonald moved a resolution to develop 'broad proposals' for a general election programme outlining 'legislative and administrative action for a Labour government'.[214] In response, the NEC obliged by appointing a sub-committee in October 1927, comprising MacDonald, Henderson, Lansbury, Cramp, Roberts, Morrison, Mosley, Wilkinson and Trevelyan.[215] Although ostensibly a diverse group, it was one made up primarily of PLP members in which the inclusion of Roberts, Henderson, Cramp and Morrison ensured that MacDonald's political position was dominant. Different points of emphasis were raised during discussion, and different versions of the party programme prepared, but the draft eventually presented to the NEC in March 1928 bore the obvious influence of the Labour leader.[216] This, according to Sidney Webb, was 'properly vague, and comprehensive without anything new'.[217] Indeed, attempts by Mosley, Wilkinson and Trevelyan to produce a more detailed and incisive statement of Labour government policy had been rejected. MacDonald's initial reference to 'broad proposals' was deliberate, allowing him to maintain a strategy of 'cautious leadership' that avoided specific commitments that would limit or compromise future government action.[218] The NEC concurred, and a final draft was then completed with R. H. Tawney in June and distributed to the party nationally in preparation for the 1928 party conference in October.[219]

In the event, *Labour and the Nation* was adopted with relative ease. Potential dissent had been blocked by the NEC's decision in May to disallow any amendments to the proposed programme, allowing only specific paragraphs to be referred back.[220] Though Maxton, Wheatley and others criticised the programme's evident gradualism, and some delegates felt the programme too broad in its scope, the conference was overwhelmingly committed to providing a united front as the general election loomed on the horizon. The criticisms of the ILP left were expected and easily overcome. More generally, the programme had been structured not only to avoid potential dissent within the party, but also to appeal as broadly as possible to the British electorate. It was for this reason that Tawney would later describe *Labour and the Nation* as 'a glittering forest of Christmas trees, with presents for everyone'.[221] That, in many ways, was exactly what MacDonald intended it to be.

So, what exactly did *Labour and the Nation* entail? Ostensibly, it outlined a series of policies designed to transform 'capitalism into socialism'.[222] The opening sections provided a general critique of the Conservative government and Lloyd George's Liberal Party, along with a typical reassertion of Labour's constitutionalism. Labour demanded a 'peaceful revolution' in the transition to a 'new era', the programme maintained. Following this, five principles were established by which Labour pledged to use its power in office. These were to 'secure to every member of the community the standards of life and employment which are necessary to a healthy, independent and self-respecting existence'; to 'step by step' convert industry into a 'co-operative undertaking, carried on for the service of the community and amendable to its control'; to 'extend rapidly' social reform in education, health, housing, pensions and unemployment; to adjust taxation so that surplus wealth could be used 'for the good of all'; and to establish international 'peace, freedom and justice' by renouncing war and promoting economic and political co-operation through the League of Nations. To this effect, a number of pledges were then outlined with regard to the fixing of a 'minimum standard of life' for all.

Significantly, Labour's vision of society was shaped primarily by the organisation and administration of the economy. Accordingly, a series of industrial measures were perceived as necessary to safeguard the workers and increase economic efficiency. To this effect, Labour pledged to repeal the Trade Disputes and Trade Unions Act, to implement more effectively existing welfare legislation (such as the Factory Acts and provisions about pensions, hours, etc.), to recognise the Washington Convention on the 48-hour week, and to ensure fair wages via the extension of the Trade Boards Act. At the same time, the on-going problem of unemployment received much attention, with pledges to provide 'humane' and 'adequate provision for unemployed workers' Beyond this, an increase in the school leaving age, co-operation with other nations, and inquiries into 'financial methods and credit policy' were to be complemented by the formation of a National Economic Committee to advise the government on the organisation of industry and the best means of increasing economic efficiency. Such a committee was to be directed by the prime minister, with the objective of ensuring that economic policy was adjusted 'to the needs of the moment'. Linked to this, *Labour and the Nation* promised the formation of an Employment and Development Board to provide work schemes for the unemployed, including clearing slums, building houses and satellite towns, ensuring adequate 'national drainage', afforestation, and building roads.

With regard to the 'democratic control of industry', Labour reaffirmed its commitment to common ownership, presenting the electorate with a choice between industry as a 'public service, democratically owned and responsibly administrated', or as 'the private economic sovereignty of the combine, the syndicate and trust'. Even so, any policy of nationalisation was to be achieved 'without haste and without rest', and with 'due compensation to the persons affected'. Beyond this, however, a detailed analysis of just what public ownership actually entailed was still lacking; the sections on bringing mining and transport under public ownership were general rather than specific. Evidently, Labour continued to conceive of socialism as emerging from a burgeoning industrial capitalism. The party's immediate economic priorities focused on helping the beleaguered staple industries, supporting industrial rationalisation, and improving international trade relations. Linked to this, much space was given to 'the nation's housekeeping', with plans for a more efficient economy, progressive taxation, increases on death duties for large estates, surtaxes on large incomes from property, and the taxation of land values. Significantly, however, the issue of nationalising the Bank of England was qualified rather than made explicit, something that was commented on during the conference discussion. Thus, while the conference resolved to 'control the Bank of England by a public corporation', even this was dropped from the final publication of the programme in favour of a commitment to 'more stringent control of banking and credit'.[223]

In terms of social welfare policy, *Labour and the Nation* responded to the 'women electors' by advocating an equal franchise and the 'fullest equality of opportunity, both political and economic, for men and women alike'. While insisting that 'the foundation of social reconstruction must be the reorganisation of the economic system', Labour claimed also to recognise the need for education, 'health, personal decency and comfort'. Expenditure on social services was therefore seen as a contribution to the wider wealth of the community, and Labour promised a variety of measures to prevent disease, provide better housing, protect mothers and children, and improve health insurance. The widening of educational opportunity was introduced as the basis of 'the nation of tomorrow'. Constitutionally, Labour's previous proposal to abolish the House of the Lords was substituted in favour of reforming the second chamber and ensuring the supremacy of the Commons. With Labour now inside the gate, the party sought to reform rather than overturn. Similarly, as Miles Taylor has demonstrated, Labour's approach to devolution and local government was modified as the party began to plan in terms of efficient central government. Here, perhaps, the experience of Poplar had raised central party suspicions of relinquishing too much responsibility: increasingly, 'national problems required nationwide solutions'.[224] From here on, such reform was considered primarily in so far as it took a burden off Westminster and Whitehall.

Finally, the foreign policy outlined in *Labour and the Nation* centred on the 'six pillars of peace': the renunciation of war, disarmament, international arbitration, economic co-operation, publicity, and political co-operation. In achieving this, Labour committed itself wholeheartedly to the League of Nations and the establishment of diplomatic and commercial relations with the Soviet Union. Such principles were extended to the British Commonwealth, with Labour advocating close co-operation between Britain and the Dominions, self-government for India, and the establishment of safeguards against capitalist exploitation.[220]

As MacDonald intended, the broad principles and objectives of *Labour and the Nation* were acceptable to most members of the party. Questions of detail remained, but it was a programme behind which the party could rally its support. Most divisional parties discussed the programme relatively uncritically, with only eleven parties contesting the NEC's decision to limit the debate at the 1928 annual conference. Indeed, the general air of approval was reinforced by the carefully orchestrated nature of the programme's presentation, in which MacDonald, Clynes and Snowden all played a leading role.[226] Ultimately, however, *Labour and the Nation* would go on to suffer from problems similar to its predecessor. Although the programme had been referred to a further sub-committee of Snowden, Shaw, Graham and Webb in the wake of the conference discussion, it remained a list of objectives rather than a programme of practical political policies. While certainly more comprehensive than *Labour and the New Social Order*, it did not offer policies that could be readily implemented by any subsequent Labour government. Belatedly, this would become all too apparent.

In the meantime, Labour's eventual general election manifesto was drawn from *Labour and the Nation*. Entitled *Labour's Appeal to the Nation*, it was also the longest and most wide-ranging set of proposals to date. The problem of unemployment took priority, with Labour pledging to assist those out of work 'immediately and practically' – words that would soon come back to haunt the PLP. Plans for national development were then detailed, including slum clearance, the reorganisation and improvement of transport, electrification, afforestation, and land drainage. The nationalisation of the mines was promised if Labour became a majority government, but this was applied to none of the other industries listed in *Labour and the Nation* Social policies and a graduated income tax were then outlined, before the principles of Labour's foreign policy were further restated. Caution, once again, was the order of the day; the term 'socialism' was barely used.[227]

The extent to which the policies and aspirations outlined in *Labour and the Nation* contributed to Labour's success in the 1929 general election is open to question. Well before the election was held on 30 May 1929, there were clear signs that Labour's electoral advance over the decade would continue apace. Thirteen by-election victories had been registered since October 1924 (alongside one defeat), with the yearly 'swing' to Labour increasing from 4.9 per cent in 1925 to over 12 per cent in 1929.[228] Accordingly, party members and supporters across the county were mobilised in the attempt to return a second Labour government. In Bristol East, for example, the party used some 700 volunteers over the course of May. Here and elsewhere, leaflets and newspapers were directed at the local electorate, sometimes as a supplement to the party's national manifesto.[229] The effort proved worthwhile. For the first time, Labour won the majority of available seats, claiming 287 to the Conservatives' 260 and the Liberals' 59. Equally, the party had 'broken through' in important urban areas that had previously resisted Labour's appeal, most obviously in Liverpool and Birmingham. In the latter, the party won six out of a possible twelve seats. Elsewhere, Labour strongholds were confirmed. In Durham,

Labour consolidated its control over the county by winning all eleven county seats and five out of the six borough seats. In West Yorkshire, Labour won nineteen of a possible 23 parliamentary seats, taking 39 seats over the county as a whole. Forty-one victories were recorded in Lancashire, compared to 22 in 1923; 37 seats were won in Scotland. In Wales, Labour now held 25 parliamentary seats. As for those elected, the number of MPs sponsored by divisional parties for the first time outnumbered those sponsored by the trade unions: 128 compared to 115. Once again, however, women remained a tiny minority within the PLP. Of the 30 female candidates adopted by Labour, only nine were successful.

Equally, of course, Labour remained a minority party; its vote was located in industrial areas, but many working-class electors continued to vote against the party. To a notable extent, and despite the attempts of party headquarters to prove otherwise, Labour's identity continued to be closely associated with the sectional interests of the trade unions and the 'extremities' of socialism. This, certainly, was the portrayal of Labour evident in the national press and the propaganda of most Tory and Liberal organisations. Here, Labour was presented as a threat to the status quo, allowing Labour's rivals to play on the fears, prejudices and aspirations of the middle class and large sections of the working class.[230] Women, in particular, retained an ambiguous place within the party's actual and projected worldview. At the same time, the Tories themselves viewed the enlarged electorate and unfolding political climate with uncertainty, thereby endeavouring to extend its organisation and appeal positively to the 'new' electorate as the embodiment of the nation and social order. The Conservative Party, just as much as Labour, had to construct and maintain its relationship with the British people between the wars, and the Tories put much effort into training its activists and articulating its policies to the electorate.[231] As such, Labour's identity was forged and countered by external forces, contexts and traditions as well as by its own policies, language, personnel and image.

Throughout the 1920s, Labour had believed that history was on its side; that the party's role was to channel and unify the British people towards social progress. Caution and moderation had become characteristic of MacDonald's party, and this was augmented in the pages of *Labour and the Nation*. Attempts to divert the party along more radical, socialist or revolutionary lines had been diverted or contained; issues of potential division buried beneath the need for party unity and the principal objective of electing a Labour government. In the meantime, the party organisation was consolidated and extended, with the growing number of individual members helping to widen both the party's potential appeal and its social-political priorities. In May 1929, such a strategy appeared to have brought success. Within months, however, many of the preconceptions that lay at the base of such political beliefs and strategies were exposed by the onset of a worldwide economic depression. In such circumstances, a party that believed socialism would emerge from prosperous capitalist development and more efficient social-economic administration was ill equipped to cope. Within just two years, a combination of mounting unemployment, economic crisis and political impotence would appear to undo all that the Labour Party and its members had strived to achieve over the first third of the twentieth century. Perhaps gradualness was no longer inevitable?

Chapter Three

In Search of a Solution:
The Fall and Partial Recovery of Labour, 1929–35

Is there a man or a woman here who does not know that the unemployment which started last October and November is an unemployment of a totally different nature from that which we faced at the last general election ...[1]

Ramsay MacDonald, 1930

It is essential that socialism should be sound public business as well as being healthy in its social morality.[2]

Herbert Morrison, 1933

Final victory and *final* power can never be achieved by the workers politically without the full co-operation and active support of the Trade Unions.[3]

Labour Party, Victory for Socialism, 1933

Put bluntly, the period between the general elections of 1929 and 1935 was one of crisis and change for the British Labour Party. Having formed a second minority government in the summer of 1929, the party was quickly overtaken by a worldwide economic depression for which it was clearly unprepared. In the process, the image of Ramsay MacDonald was transformed from Labour figurehead to Labour 'traitor' following his decision in August 1931 to head a coalition government with his former Conservative and Liberal opponents. While the vast majority of the Parliamentary Labour Party (PLP) chose to move into opposition rather than countenance proposed cuts in the rate of unemployment benefit, MacDonald, Snowden, Thomas and a handful of other Labour members continued to sit on the government benches. Nevertheless, an electoral massacre soon followed, leaving Labour with just 46 members in parliament and a long period of rebuilding ahead. Although some progress was made over the early 1930s, as the party developed a far more detailed policy programme and recovered some ground at a municipal level, Labour's political instability was reaffirmed by the resignation of its leader, George Lansbury, on the eve of the 1935 general election following a dispute over foreign policy. In the event, the election revealed Labour to be still some way from regaining the political initiative.

What had caused such an apparent retreat from Labour's self-determined path of progress? On the one hand, the party was arguably the victim of circumstances beyond its immediate control. Within a year of Labour's taking office, the relative stability that had characterised the British economy for much of the previous decade had clearly been undermined.[4] In particular, the economic upheaval prompted by the Wall Street crash of October 1929 served to plunge Britain into a severe economic crisis. If export orders had been falling since 1928, then the problems that beset the US economy in the following year quickly accentuated Britain's decline. The deterioration of the old staple industries intensified, unemployment continued to rise, and the balance of trade proceeded to deteriorate. Across Britain as a whole, the number of registered unemployed workers rose from 1,534,000 in January 1930 to 2,783,000 in July 1931.[5] Simultaneously, the collapse of the Austrian and German banks in the summer of 1931 helped add European political instability to the existing economic turmoil. Given such a context, and given the government's minority status, MacDonald and his colleagues were in an unenviable position. On the other hand, the vagaries of Labour's political approach were revealed in the face of such a crisis. The essentially traditional economics of Snowden and the cautious policies of the prime minister were simply unable to respond to the events unfolding around them.[6] More damagingly, perhaps, the government appeared unwilling to listen to alternatives from within its own ranks, responding instead to the financial forecasts and strategies emanating from appointed financial 'experts' and the opposition benches.

Following the government's collapse and the ensuing general election defeat, Labour endeavoured to reinvent itself. Notions of economic planning and assertive references to socialism began more readily to characterise party policy; the vagaries of MacDonald were replaced by the 'practical socialism' of Dalton, Morrison, Attlee, Bevin and Citrine. Yet, problems remained. The small PLP was largely ineffective in the years up to 1935, while Sir Stafford Cripps' Socialist League soon took up the baton of the critical left wing dropped by the Independent Labour Party (ILP) on its disaffiliation in 1932. As this suggests, the early 1930s encompassed difficult times for Labour. Yet, the continued support of the trade union movement, the persistence and commitment of party members at the grass roots, and the construction of a more precise socialist programme distinct from an apparently ailing capitalism combined to ensure Labour's survival and pave the way for its revival over the decade as a whole.

I. INTO THE MAELSTROM: THE LABOUR GOVERNMENT, 1929–31

The problems sketched above did not descend immediately. Indeed, the first parliament of the second Labour government opened on 2 July 1929 and brought with it much optimism and expectation. Not surprisingly, the extent of Labour's advance from 1924 had excited scenes of jubilation amongst its supporters. Neil Riddell has cited the example of Nelson, where Arthur Greenwood was mobbed during his victory speech to the textile town; 'tears of joy' trickled down a watching old man's face, the local newspaper reported, 'for he knew that his work had been worthwhile'.[7] And such scenes were replicated elsewhere. In Derby, Jimmy Thomas and William Raynes were reputedly escorted to the party headquarters by a crowd of thousands following their retaining Labour's two parliamentary seats. Similarly, James Chuter Ede's victory in South Shields saw the town's first Labour MP carried on the shoulders of two Labour councillors amidst a hat-throwing and cheering crowd.[8] As for MacDonald, his train journey from the North East back to London on 31 May was greeted by delighted supporters at each of its stops, before an estimated 12,000 people swept him off his feet on arrival at King's Cross.[9] From across the country, local parties sent their backing to the prime minister in expectation of the promised change ahead. Thus, party members in Darlington gathered to register their 'great satisfaction' at the election result, while the divisional party in York passed a resolution urging the newly formed government to 'go forward encouraged by the knowledge that the workers are behind them in their efforts to deal with this great problem [unemployment]'.[10]

As in 1924, MacDonald found the task of appointing his cabinet a troublesome and personally difficult affair, although the end result brought a familiar mix of moderate politician-trade unionists (Thomas, Henderson, Shaw, Adamson, Clynes), middle-class former Liberals (Wedgwood Benn, Buxton, Trevelyan), intellectuals (Webb), and 'mild' ILPers (Graham).[11] In the principal posts, Snowden was again appointed to the chancellery, Henderson acquired his chosen position of foreign secretary, Thomas became lord privy seal charged with 'special responsibilities for unemployment', and Clynes took the post of home secretary. Given Wheatley's continued criticism of MacDonald's leadership post-1924, the prime minister ensured that neither he nor any of his ILP comrades were appointed to the cabinet. The nearest left wing equivalents were George Lansbury, appointed as the first commissioner for works, and Charles Trevelyan for education. More notably, Margaret Bondfield became the first woman to hold a cabinet position, thrust into the baptism of fire that was the ministry of labour. The co-operative movement was also represented this time round, with Albert Alexander being appointed first lord of the admiralty. Outside the cabinet, Herbert Morrison was assigned minister of transport (he joined the cabinet in 1931); Dalton became parliamentary secretary to the foreign office, Shinwell financial secretary to the war office, Johnston parliamentary secretary to Adamson at the Scottish office, and Mosley chancellor of the duchy of Lancaster.[12] Although there was much internal wrangling over who was appointed where, particularly with regard to the foreign office, MacDonald appeared to have behind him an ostensibly able cabinet, if one that was conservative in outlook and biased towards the PLP's more elderly figureheads.[13] Beneath the surface, moreover, personal animosities and uncertainly within the leadership were never far from view.[14]

Of course, the government hoped that it could rely on the steadfast support of the wider PLP. To ensure this, the retiring parliamentary party executive formed a consultative committee to liaise between the government and the backbenches, although this would appear to have been geared more towards reaffirming government policy than actually 'consulting' with Labour members.[15] As such, the increased ranks of the PLP remained an overwhelmingly loyal group (or 'Loyal Lump', as Dalton called them), just over a third of whom were trade union members described by Jennie Lee as 'decent, well-intentioned, unpretentious' and committed to MacDonald. 'Again and again', the North Lanark MP recalled, 'an effort was made to rouse their inertia. On every occasion they reacted like a load of damp cement'.[16] Beyond the small group of ILP 'rebels' gathered around Maxton (Wheatley died in 1930), the vast majority of the PLP continued to adhere to the leadership's gradualist approach and to keep faith in a man whose considerable reputation was then at its peak.

Unfortunately, any sense of Labour enjoying a political 'honeymoon' did not last for long. Despite much expectancy and declarations of party unity, signs that the government was out of its depth were soon apparent. As in 1924, Labour had ⟨ ⟩ office with a number of objectives but with little to no idea of how to achiev⟨ ⟩ Furthermore, Labour had for the second time elected to form a minority gov⟨ ⟩ whose guiding light was the 'inevitability of gradualness', believing that ⟨ ⟩ would emerge from a combination of buoyant capitalist development a⟨ ⟩

social and moral reform. Consequently, both the government's agenda and its room for application were limited from the outset. Even by as early as the party conference in October 1929, the continued problem of unemployment was beginning to cause concern. Indeed, Hugh Dalton was confiding to his diary in February 1930 that he agreed with his then constituency secretary William Hodgson's description of MacDonald as 'a frightened man'. With the government appearing uncertain as to its response to Britain's mounting economic difficulties, Dalton was left to consider secretly the benefits of 'an early and crushing defeat'.

> The cabinet is full of overworked men, growing older, more tired and more timid with each passing week. Pressure from below and from without is utterly ineffectual. High hopes are falling like last autumn's leaves. There is a whisper of spring in the air, but none in the political air. One funks the public platform, and one wishes we had never come in. We have forgotten our programme, or been bamboozled out of it by officials.[17]

Dalton was not alone. Almost simultaneously, Philip Noel Baker was reporting to MacDonald's son, Malcolm, how the Coventry Labour Party members had 'said that there was the greatest anxiety and discontent in all sections of the Coventry party, and that outside the party, confidence and support were falling very rapidly'.[18] From within the PLP, too, Charles Edwards was forced to report gloomily to his Bedwellty constituency in April 1930 on the problems of minority government, complaining rather helplessly – if with some justification – that the Liberals were holding the government's proposed Coal Bill to ransom. Come November, and he was openly raising his contention that MacDonald was spending too much time on foreign affairs at the expense of the more pressing issue of unemployment.[19] Given such a change in mood, Leah Manning's record of her election to parliament in February 1931 is apposite.

> I arrived at Westminster fresh and euphoric from a totally unexpected bye-election victory, and I walked into an atmosphere which stung like a cold lash. Bitter hostility there was where there should have been comradeship. I was hurt by the cold contempt of old ILP friends, such as Jimmy Maxton, who treated me as a criminal for having dared to stand, let alone win; everywhere I found frustration and defeatism in place of hope and constructive ideas ...[20]

Manning's autobiography reveals her as a supportive party member keen to give her 'life for education' rather than embark on a political career in parliament. Even so, her account is one of many detailing disquiet throughout the Labour Party some time prior to the full-blown crisis of 1931.

The reason for this growing trepidation was clear, of course: the problem of unemployment became even more acute following the Wall Street crash of October 1929. Labour's election campaign had concentrated heavily on the plight of the unemployed – 'The Works Are Closed But The Ballot Box Is Open' – and much was expected of a government committed to alleviating such evident and worsening hardship. From the outset, MacDonald had declared Labour's intention to 'deal effectively' with unemployment, and legislation was indeed passed to amend the Unemployed Insurance Acts, to fund schemes for public works, and to ensure that the peaceful foreign relations deemed necessary to mobilising the economy were secured.[21] In this, the latter was recognised to be primary, with much of the prime minister's time in 1929 being committed to quelling naval rivalries with the United States. By January 1930, however, the number of registered unemployed had increased to 1,534,000, rising to 2,700,000 by the end of the year. Quite evidently, piecemeal reform was inadequate. To make matters worse, the detail of Bondfield's initial Unemployment Bill raised several points of contention within the party. In particular, the 'not genuinely seeking work' clause caused disquiet amongst trade unionists and socialists alike; and where the criticisms of the ILP left were expected and predictable, the anxieties of usually loyal backbenchers were a clear indicator of the problems that lay ahead. Various concerns were raised as to the limited nature of the Bill at the party conference in October, and although these were overcome temporarily following a PLP vote on the matter in November 1929, they remained none the same.

Predictably, therefore, the government's position was made worse as its various attempts to confront the economic downturn made little progress. Most immediately, Thomas's brief to assume responsibility for unemployment led to an initial burst of enthusiasm that quickly gave way to disillusionment. Although Oswald Mosley, Tom Johnston and George Lansbury were appointed to assist Thomas in a cabinet committee, the respective roles of each member remained uncertain and they rarely gathered altogether. 'A more ill-assorted team could hardly be imagined', was Johnston's own recollection, and little of substance can be said to have come from the initiative. Ultimately, Thomas himself undertook a trip to Canada and proposed a series of ill-conceived ideas, before Mosley, Johnston and Lansbury began to produce various suggestions with regard to public works, pensions and the school-leaving age, none of which found favour with either Thomas or the treasury. By the end of the year, Mosley informed MacDonald that he and his two colleagues found it 'impossible to work with Thomas', thereby bringing the committee to an effective close and paving the way for Mosley to develop his own agenda.[22] More long lasting was the fifteen-strong Economic Advisory Council of intellectuals, trade unionists and business representatives established by MacDonald in early 1930. In this instance, however, the council proved to be more discursive than decisive. Despite – or perhaps because of – the presence of Keynes, Bevin and industrialists such as Lord Weir around the same debating table, the forging of a consensus proved difficult to say the least. Similarly, Lord Macmillan was appointed to head a committee to examine the banking system and suggest means by which to develop commerce and provide employment, but again to little effect. With some understatement, the 1930 party conference was informed that 'the real substantial efforts of the government (much greater than its predecessors) have tended to be overshadowed by the grave consequences of the world economic depression'.[23]

Growing concern soon turned to criticism. Within the PLP, the ILP left wing had made their feelings clear from the outset, with Wheatley, Maxton and Jowett immediately taking issue with what they regarded as too moderate a king's speech.[24] Each government initiative, and perceived lack of initiative, was subsequently criticised by those who wanted the government to take far firmer action, before the ILP conference in April 1930 finally resolved to reassert the ILP's position as an 'independent socialist organisation' with its own 'distinctive position' in the Labour Party. This, in turn, paved the way for Maxton to reconstitute the ILP parliamentary group and insist that it no longer accepted the obligations required of it by the PLP. Instead, the conference resolved that membership of the ILP parliamentary group was to be based on 'acceptance of the policy of the ILP as laid down by the decisions of the annual conference, and as interpreted by the National Administrative Council (NAC) and to limit endorsements of future ILP candidates to nominees who accept this basis'.[25] Accordingly, tensions between the ILP group, the wider Labour Party and the government deteriorated further over 1930–1 amidst a series of acerbic *New Leader* articles, critical speeches, and parliamentary 'scenes'. Most famously, John Beckett – MP for Peckham and future fascist – removed the mace during a debate over India in 1930, while the summer of 1931 saw a fight break out in the Commons following the suspension of John McGovern for defying the speaker. More typically, the ILP group applied delaying tactics to ensure that debates such as that on the government's 1931 Anomalies Bill were drawn into bitter all-night sessions via ILP-tabled objections.

Significantly, the majority of the ILP-sponsored MPs – along with the numerous Labour MPs who were ILP cardholders – rejected the 'rebel' ILP group's open challenge to the government. Many publicly criticised the disruptive tactics of the Maxton group.[26] As Gidon Cohen has described 'the [ILP] parliamentary group was politically very diverse, covering almost the entire range of opinion within the labour movement'. Many were not active in the ILP in or out of parliament, while those such as Emanuel Shinwell, Alfred Salter, Jim Simmons and John Arnott maintained a loyalty to Labour beyond that to the ILP, despite their varied backgrounds and perspectives. Even those with reservations about government policy were not thereby prepared to organise themselves into what was effectively an internal opposition to the Labour administration. Indeed, only eighteen of the approximately 160 ILP MPs accepted the ILP conference ruling on membership to the parliamentary group.[27] As for the trade union MPs, they maintained little sympathy for the 'splitting' tactics of the 'rebels'. Subsequently, the Labour leadership was able to deflect and repel the reproaches of an ILP left. Although Henderson attempted to come to an agreement with Maxton, the PLP simultaneously reasserted its own standing orders that disallowed members to vote against a parliamentary party motion, with the party headquarters insisting further that prospective candidates declare their willingness to 'act in harmony with the standing orders of the parliamentary party'.[28] To this effect, Herbert Morrison successfully convinced the majority of the National Executive Committee (NEC) not to endorse the adoption of an ILP candidate (Tom Irwin) at the East Renfrew by-election of November 1930.[29] Conversely, however, such measures simply intensified the growing rift between the party and the ILP, provoking wider concerns with regard to freedom of action and as to the future role of the ILP inside the Labour Party. By 1931, the question of the ILP's disaffiliation from Labour was very much on the agenda.

Criticism of the government did not only come from the ILP left. As dramatic were the events surrounding the resignation of Sir Oswald Mosley from the government on 20 May 1930. Having quickly become dismayed at the apparent ineptitude of Thomas during his time in cabinet committee, Mosley soon began to prepare an alternative set of policies for dealing with the unfurling economic difficulties.[30] These had been drafted into a memorandum by January, and were presented to the cabinet (over the head of Thomas) on 3 February; a committee was then appointed to discuss Mosley's ideas and report back in due time. The details of the 'Mosley memorandum' were set into four parts, outlining proposals for the 'machinery of government', 'long-term economic reconstruction', 'short-term work plans', and 'finance and credit policy'.[31] These, in turn, proposed the formation of a powerful executive cabinet of leading ministers – headed by MacDonald and advised by appointed experts – with authority to confront the impending 'crisis'; the planned reconstruction of the British economy via tariffs, credit control and preference for the home market over exports; the establishment of loan-financed work schemes, pensions and an increased school-leaving age to offset the immediate impact of the depression; and the development of a high-wage economy and state-directed credit policy not reliant on the banks. Not surprisingly, perhaps, Mosley's distinctive fusion of state directed, Keynesian, Hobsonian and Chamberlain-influenced economics was given short shrift. MacDonald had little sympathy for its radical tenets, Snowden baulked at its economic unorthodoxy, and the treasury officials who drafted a reply deplored its potentially inflationary implications and emphasis on state intervention. Following further cabinet discussions in May, therefore, the memorandum was rejected and Mosley handed his resignation to the prime minister.[32]

Of course, the matter did not thereby come to an end. First, Mosley – a man of big ideas, big gestures and immediate action – looked for alternative outlets for his policy. On 22 May, he approached the PLP to back his proposals, only for Arthur Henderson to deflect a potential challenge to the government via an appeal for further discussion. Six days later, Mosley delivered a dramatic resignation speech to the House of Commons, outlining the objectives of his memorandum and calling on parliament to confront the economic crisis and avert Britain's continued decline. It was met with prolonged cheers, superlative press reports and, on the government's part, quiet disregard. Second, therefore, Mosley planned to appeal to the Labour Party conference.

At this time, Mosley could evidently generate some sympathy within the party. The young aristocratic war hero was a charismatic figure whose joining Labour in 1924 was a political cause célèbre. Not only had he successfully dented the Chamberlain hegemony of Birmingham politics and won a symbolic by-election victory in Smethwick in 1926, but his active and financial support for the miners throughout 1926 had earned Mosley the respect of the Miners' Federation of Great Britain (MFGB). It was with the miners' support that he had been elected to the NEC in 1927 and 1928. Of course, Mosley had his critics: Dalton, for one – with his eye on a potential rival to his own ambitions – would complain of 'how the fellow stinks of money and insincerity'.[33] More typically, Herbert Morrison would complain of the 'superiority of the aristocrat' in Mosley's attitude, a class distinction no doubt felt by many of his Labour colleagues. Within the PLP, Mosley had traditionally received few votes with regard to his election onto the parliamentary committee prior to 1930.[34] As such, Mosley was respected by some for his combative style and intellect, but was equally distrusted on the grounds of his class, ambition and independent-mindedness. Indeed, this was revealed once the conference gathered in October, where yet another powerful call for action was greeted by a grand ovation, and a resolution asking the NEC to reconsider Mosley's proposals was defeated by just 1,251,000 votes to 1,046,000. Predictably, the union block vote had guaranteed such a result, although the miners only narrowly decided to back the NEC in rejecting the resolution, ensuring simultaneously that Mosley was himself re-elected to the executive following a year's absence. Yet, Mosley had no firm basis of support within the Labour Party. As well as the aforementioned suspicions of his character – one wag was heard to shout, with some foresight, 'the English Hitler' following Mosley's conference speech – Mosley was evidently not a trade union man, he was not working class, and his socialist credentials were already in question. His committed supporters in the PLP were few and mainly middle class; his emphasis on the 'home market' and, increasingly, the empire ensured that he offended the ILP's and many a Labour member's internationalist sensibilities; and his social life brought him into closer contact with ambitious young Tories than committed Labourites. Although, following Mosley's resignation, Aneurin Bevan managed to rally 60 signatures to a petition urging the government to act decisively on unemployment, Mosley's circle of his wife, Cynthia, John Strachey, Oliver Baldwin, Dr Robert Forgan and W. J. Brown placed him on the intellectual margins of the party. Ultimately, therefore, Mosley's next move led him to burn those Labour bridges that he had established over the past half decade. In the short term, he continued to urge the party to adopt stronger relief measures for the unemployed, speaking to a special meeting of the PLP and securing the signatures of seventeen Labour MPs (and the miners' leader Arthur Cook) for his 'Mosley Manifesto' in December.[35] But his decision to form a New Party in early 1931 effectively put an end to any prevailing Labour sympathy for his ideas. Mosley had sought to split the party and thereby committed the ultimate Labour sin. Few joined him in such a venture, certainly not Bevan, paving the way for Mosley's eventual conversion to fascism.[36]

Less dramatic but potentially more damaging to the government was the growing discontent within the party's trade union base by 1930. Arthur Henderson moved to keep a lid on the mounting unease at the party conferences of 1929 and 1930, but trade union disquiet was clearly apparent. This should not be overstated. Trade union support for Labour remained solid at a general level. For the Trades Union Congress (TUC), the Labour Party and labour movement was far more than the sum of its parliamentary parts. Even so, the government's failure either to deal with unemployment or to pass legislation beneficial to the organised working class soon began to occupy the unions' attention. With regard to unemployment, the TUC accepted that the number of people out of work would rise in the adverse economic circumstances of 1929–31, but it was equally concerned that the standard of benefit should be protected against Liberal, Conservative and employer demands for cuts. This was made all the more pertinent given *Labour and the Nation*'s pledge to liberalise benefits, which was soon compromised by the limits of Bondfield's draft Unemployed Insurance Bill. In this instance, minor changes were secured following TUC and NEC pressure, although the relationship between the government, Bondfield, the unions and the wider party was undoubtedly damaged in the process.[37] At the party conference in October 1930, Bondfield's union – the National Union of General and Municipal Workers (NUGMW) – introduced a resolution asserting that 'the complete solution of the problem can only be accomplished by the application of definite socialist principles, so as to secure the reorganisation of industry and the land in the interest of the people, and a more equitable distribution of the Nation's wealth'. This loyally welcomed the efforts of the government and accepted the limits of a minority administration, but further urged MacDonald to 'facilitate schemes of nationalisation'.[38]

For the unions, the government appeared once more to be following the flawed path of 1924. In the first place, only six of MacDonald's initial cabinet were trade union-sponsored MPs, while dialogue and co-operation between the unions and the government was limited to say the least. If Henderson duly passed on to the prime minister Walter Citrine's assertion of 5 June 1929 that the TUC should meet regularly with the cabinet during the government's lifetime, then it made little notable impression. Similarly, TUC attempts in 1930 to revitalise the National Joint Council (NJC) were adopted only cautiously by the NEC and with little noticeable enthusiasm in the PLP. Although a brief meeting took place in May 1930, its first since 8 December 1928, a proposed follow up did not occur until 7 December 1931, some months after the government's fall. Not surprisingly, the unions objected to the fact that ministers – including trade unionists such as J. R. Clynes – refrained from consulting the TUC on proposed legislation. By as early as January 1930, Citrine was warning the prime minister of the unease within 'our movement'.[39] Accordingly, the TUC endeavoured to forge alternative economic strategies, presenting in 1930 a controversial economic report that proposed the formation of a Commonwealth trading bloc, the involvement of the League of Nations in economic disputes, and the opening up of the tariff question.[40]

Not dissimilarly, trade union disquiet increased as much of the legislation prepared by the government failed to live up to expectations. Ratification of the Washington Hours Convention, which called for a 48-hour week and eight-hour day for all industries, was buried in the face of logistical problems; proposed factory legislation and workmen's compensation legislation failed to find enough parliamentary time; and the government recoiled from proposing direct intervention to help the failing textile industry. With regard to the miners, the MFGB had hoped that a Labour government would offer some relief to the severe blows sustained by the industry throughout much of the 1920s, and especially in the wake of the 1926 lockout. *Labour and the Nation* had outlined the party's basic mining policy, committing the Labour government to the repeal the Eight Hours Act (1926) and the introduction of a seven-hour day. With the onset of the depression, however, the PLP again retreated into economic orthodoxy before protracted negotiations between the government, the mining unions, and the mine owners paved the way for the 1930 Coal Mines Act. This reduced the miners' day by half an hour but failed to protect miners' wage rates. The prevarication led, eventually, to a split in the MFGB – with Herbert Smith resigning the presidency – and a futile industrial action in early 1931.[41]

Hesitation and compromise also hindered Labour attempts to repeal the 1927 Trade Disputes and Trade Union Act. TUC pressure had ensured that the government brought the issue to the Commons agenda in the summer of 1930. But although fears of Liberal obstruction were initially unfulfilled, the Bill was effectively killed once it passed into the committee stages. Here, Liberal insistence on key amendments – maintaining 'contracting in' and the prohibition of sympathetic action – emasculated the Bill and ensured the wrath of the TUC. In the meantime, tensions between the TUC general council and Labour ministers mounted, before union pressure prevailed and the government removed the amended Bill from the standing committee.[42] Evidently, the TUC's patience with the government was wearing thin.

As such, problems contrived to blight the government at every turn. Even when MacDonald sought to take action, his choices often led to consternation within the wider labour movement. Too often, it seemed, MacDonald looked beyond Labour's own ranks for guidance and advice. A case in point was the government's decision to reappoint Lord Hunsdon as chairman of the Public Works Loans Committee in 1930. This was a man who had said in 1926 that the miners should be starved back to work, a comment that hardly enamoured him to Labour members. Though eventually ratified, it was this issue that prompted the largest PLP protest vote against the second Labour government (63).[43] Meanwhile, Sir Charles Trevelyan's Education Bill navigated a protracted course through parliament, met as it was with indifference from MacDonald, resistance on the part of Catholic MPs concerned as to the position of denominational schools, and the blocking tactics of the Lords. Significantly, too, Trevelyan's plans meant that many local parties encountered difficulties in Catholic areas, with serious divisions occurring in places such as Liverpool and Manchester where Catholics made up a considerable proportion of the electorate. As a result of Labour's refusal to stand up to such pressure, Trevelyan finally lost patience in February 1931 and resigned.[44]

Amidst such a catalogue of actual and impending disappointment, recognisable Labour government successes were modest between 1929 and 1931. Alongside the piecemeal reforms noted above, the Widows' and Old Age Pensions' Act was amended in 1929 to cover several thousand pensioners previously excluded by the initial 1925 legislation. Following this, Arthur Greenwood's 1930 Housing Act at least offered the government a semblance of achievement, granting state subsidies for slum clearance and housing schemes. Equally, Herbert Morrison's transport department emerged with some credibility following its successful passing of the Road Traffic Act in 1930. Certainly, Morrison's standing within the party was improved, earning a rare piece of praise from Beatrice Webb ('the only outstanding minister') and the respect of the civil servants with whom he worked.[45] In the foreign office, Henderson's diplomacy brought him admiration from within and without the party. His reputation in the Labour and Socialist International, his commitment to disarmament and the League of Nations, not to mention his by now long experience in politics and government, stood him in good stead, and he accomplished some notable achievements before the economic deluge of 1931 descended upon the government. In office, Henderson promoted the League of Nations, worked towards disarmament and the conciliatory revision of the peace settlements. In response, the Rhineland occupation was ended in August 1929, naval reductions were signed and Anglo–Soviet relations re-established. Amidst the turmoil of 1930–1, Henderson retained a respect that other Labour ministers soon lost.[46]

By the end of 1930, the financial implications of the economic depression were becoming acute. Most obviously, the £70,000,000 deficit accumulated by the unemployment insurance fund raised the question of further reform. Once again, the government looked beyond the labour movement for advice, with Bondfield establishing a royal commission to consider the problem and to suggest economies. Once again, the TUC complained that it was not being adequately consulted, before the commission's interim report recommending severe cuts in unemployment benefit reaffirmed the generally low opinion most union leaders and members now had of bankers, employers and unscrupulous politicians plotting to place the burden of Britain's financial problems on the workers. Indeed, such a conception was compounded further by mounting Liberal and Conservative calls for cuts in spending and the formation of the May Committee in February 1931 chaired by the head an insurance company (Sir George May).[47] In the meantime, Bondfield put forward a further Unemployment Insurance Bill (the Anomalies Act) to curtail supposed 'abuses' of the existing system, a move that essentially limited the rights of married women and short-time, casual and seasonal workers to claim benefit, and did yet more damage to the government's reputation among most Labour supporters.

Clearly, come the summer of 1931, the government was in trouble. Its relationship with the trade union movement was strained, the cabinet appeared indecisive and therefore unwilling to take firm action, and the PLP remained dormant beyond the constant interventions of the ILP group. In addition, MacDonald had become even more detached from his government colleagues. His cabinet reshuffle of mid-1930 had dispatched the increasingly erratic Thomas to the dominions office, with MacDonald himself taking on the responsibility of unemployment. But still the government's problems remained, with MacDonald confiding evermore gloomy thoughts to his diary. On 1 March 1931, he wrote in despair that 'We make no headway with it, & conditions get worse ... I am so overwhelmed in detail that I cannot plan policy ... I am old. My friends are dead. I feel solitary'.[48] Two months later and the collapse of the Austrian Kreditanstalt bank plunged Europe into a political-economic crisis that harboured serious implications for Britain. This became clear in July, when a run on the pound threatened Britain's position on the gold standard and the publication of the May Committee report recommended a series of economies to starve off a predicted £120,000,000 budget deficit. These included tax increases, a reduction in public-sector pay and, crucially, a twenty per cent cut in unemployment benefit accompanied by means testing. In response, a cabinet committee of MacDonald, Henderson, Snowden, Thomas and Graham was appointed, before a further run on the pound in early August prompted MacDonald to recall cabinet members for a series of emergency meetings.

The events of August 1931 are shrouded in myth, mainly as a result of PLP and cabinet members' subsequent attempts to salvage credibility from the debacle. The legend of MacDonald's 'betrayal' and the sinister pressures of a 'bankers' ramp' have long been raised to explain the government's division and subsequent disintegration. More realistically, the government had already run aground; the crisis meetings of August simply brought over a year of prevarication and uncertainty to a head. With the government squeezed between the trade unions and wider Labour Party on the one hand, and the opposition parties, employers and City financiers on the other, a consensual solution to what was a worldwide economic crisis was never likely. Tough choices had to be made; party members, trade unionists, backbenchers and cabinet ministers confronted a multitude of loyalties: to the prime minister, the cabinet, the party, the country, and the working class.

Initially, the cabinet meeting of 19 August 1931 accepted a package of economies worth £56,000,000. This was some £22,000,000 less than proposed by the cabinet sub-committee, and did not include the recommended twenty per cent cut in unemployed benefit. Instead, the cabinet sought to find other means to bridge the growing deficit. Further meetings were then held on 20 August, with members of the opposition in the morning, and then with the NEC and TUC general council in the afternoon and evening. While the opposition pushed for further economies, the trade unions registered their refusal to adhere to any cuts in working-class living standards, preferring instead the funding of unemployment benefit through a graduated levy, the suspension of the sinking fund for the national debt, a tax on fixed-interest securities, and a revenue tariff.[49] For Citrine and Bevin, at the head of the TUC delegation, the government's responsibility was to the workers. For MacDonald and Snowden, their parliamentary positions warranted broader considerations. Henderson remained more equivocal, though his sympathies appear to have now lain with 'the movement'.[50] If the TUC retained its 'contentious alliance' with the Labour Party, it was the evening of the 20 August that it relinquished support for the Labour government.[51]

On 21 August, the cabinet agreed to go ahead with the decisions taken two days earlier. Even so, MacDonald understood that such measures would inevitably be challenged in the Commons. Consequently, the cabinet met again on 23 August to discuss a proposed ten per cent cut in the rate of unemployment benefit. The issue split the cabinet, with an eventual vote in favour of the proposal being carried by just eleven to nine. Those for the cuts were MacDonald, Snowden, Thomas, Sankey, Amulree, Bondfield, Shaw, Morrison, Lees-Smith, Wedgwood Benn and Passfield (Sidney Webb). Those against comprised Henderson, Lansbury, Greenwood, Graham, Alexander, Johnston, Addison, Clynes and Adamson. For the minority, the opposition of the TUC had an undoubted influence; loyalty was declared with the wider labour movement. For the majority, the severity of the economic crisis entailed a more hard-headed response, although it should be noted that only three of the cabinet followed MacDonald out of the Labour Party. This, in effect, signalled the end of the Labour government. That evening, MacDonald sought to tender his resignation to the king, before being encouraged to stay on at the head of a 'National' government. With this, amidst recrimination and much disillusionment, MacDonald's 'great betrayal' entered into Labour folklore and the PLP returned to the opposition.

II. BREAKING DOWN THE WALLS OF HEARTACHE: LABOUR RESPONSES TO 1931

The resignation of the Labour government rocked an already dispirited party from top to bottom. Inside the Commons, ministers and parliamentary members evidently struggled to comprehend the unfurling events. According to Pethick-Lawrence, financial secretary to the treasury, the PLP at all levels appeared 'bewildered and distressed' by MacDonald's decision, with many of them 'quite unprepared for the catastrophic turn of events'. Dalton, meanwhile, recalled in his diary the prime minister's attempt to explain his actions: 'Christ crucified speaks from his cross', he noted, while simultaneously recalling a sense of relief in the party's decision to move into opposition.[52] More bitterly vivid responses came from the party's grass roots. Dan Weinbren has previously cited the experience of Vi Willis, a young Labour activist from East Ham, whose father's reaction to MacDonald's decision to form and lead the National government was telling:

> We had a beautiful picture of [MacDonald] in our passage. Dad's idol. My dad's idol. I came home from school, sitting there waiting for him to come in, and there was such a commotion. We'd heard him come in with his key and there was such a commotion ... There's dad in the passage, he's got the frame round his neck ... and he's standing like this: 'You bloody traitor, you bloody –' tearing the picture up into little pieces ... And afterwards he came in and mum said: 'What's all that about, about him being a traitor and

all that?' So he said to me: 'You saw what I did?' 'Yeah.' So he said, 'Well, I think he's killed the Labour Party.'[53]

Although Willis' father continued to campaign for Labour, others less committed to the cause turned away from the party in the immediate aftermath of August 1931. This section will explore the impact that the events of 1931 had upon the wider Labour Party.

Within the PLP, Philip Snowden, J. H. Thomas and Lord Sankey were the only cabinet members to follow MacDonald into the National government, although a further twelve 'lesser lights' – all middle-class backbenchers – also followed suit. Others, including the majority of cabinet ministers who had backed the proposed cut in unemployment benefit, remained in the party and moved into opposition. Taken generally, Labour members regrouped around a more obviously trade unionist perspective, one that was essentially defensive but united. Ambiguities remained, however. It took time before the extent of MacDonald's action was recognised in the language of betrayal that informed Labour history from here onwards. Inside the Commons, at least, the new PLP leadership appeared briefly uncertain as to its role in opposition, with Arthur Henderson's speech on the National government's abandonment of the gold standard being seen by many as too conciliatory. Indeed, Henderson was reportedly shaken for some time by MacDonald's defection. Not only was he reluctant to take up the position of party leader to which he was elected on 28 August 1931, but like some others in the party he hoped briefly for reconciliation with his former ministerial colleagues.[54] Ultimately, however, loyalty to the party eclipsed loyalty to individuals.

The equivocation of some leading Labour figures can be seen in the case of Herbert Morrison. Though he would soon go on to perpetuate the idea of the '1931 betrayal', claiming to have opposed the formation of a National government from the outset, Morrison actually remained on cordial terms with MacDonald immediately following the fateful cabinet split. Rumours that Morrison would accompany his erstwhile colleague soon began to circulate, before he reasserted his loyalty to Labour at the party conference in October. Conflicting interpretations of events persist, but Morrison's penchant for procedure, constitutionalism and MacDonald himself appear to have led to a period of soul searching.[55] Similarly, many party loyalists viewed the events of August–September 1931 with mixed emotions. Both David Howell and David Marquand have cited letters sent to MacDonald by Labour MPs (Lawson, Arnott, Bondfield, Turner, Ammon, Leach and others) asserting their primary commitment to the party in terms suggesting a continued respect for their former leader.[56] Even so, the overwhelming sentiment within the party appeared initially to be one of acute disappointment. In the words of the miners' MP Will Lunn, he felt 'let down' by those who he had previously 'loved' and 'revered'. The cutting of unemployment benefit negated a basic premise of the Labour Party; namely, its protection of the working class and those in its ranks who suffered from the inequities of capitalism rather than through any fault of their own.[57] For others, including loyal trade unionists such as Will Thorne as much as dissident ILPers, the defection of the prime minister, Snowden and Thomas affirmed their mounting distrust of the government.[58]

As this would suggest, the six weeks between the formation of the National government and the dissolution of parliament on 7 October proved difficult for Labour. Although its move into opposition allowed the PLP to adopt a critical position towards the government's proposed economies and policies, it simultaneously raised questions as to how Labour had found itself in such a situation in the first place. More to the point, Labour had neither the parliamentary numbers nor the alternative strategies to counter the government's economies. Even the popular rallying cry of free trade had lost its impact in the face of such abject economic depression. As such, Labour opposition in the Commons initially amounted to little of substance. Certainly, there was no chance of the party adopting the line of the ILP left, who many in the PLP still blamed for contributing to the Labour government's woes. Mosley, meanwhile, had by now moved way beyond Labour's limits. The suggestions proposed by the TUC general council during its meetings with the government in August certainly offered the basis for a future policy, but the PLP had little time to adopt and add detail to such measures amidst the dramas and uncertainties of the unfolding crisis. As animosities grew with each parliamentary session leading up to the election, so the PLP's class rhetoric intensified and the breach with MacDonald became entrenched. Nevertheless, Labour objections to the government remained defensive and ultimately ineffectual.

Evidently, by the time of the Labour Party conference in Scarborough on the 5–8 October, the disappointments of August had turned to anger throughout the party. Here, blame for the Labour government's failing was distributed amongst the vagaries, vanity and treachery of MacDonald, the government's minority status, and the so-called 'bankers' ramp' that had sought to bolster an ailing capitalism at the expense of the working class. Those who had been closest to MacDonald's government now quickly moved to reassert their party identity and re-establish their Labour credentials. Not only did Arthur Henderson call for a 'bold socialist programme', but J. R. Clynes and Morrison similarly insisted that socialism be placed at the forefront of the party's election programme.[59] To this effect, and despite Henderson's private reservations about such forthright pronouncements, Labour was to make much of capitalism's breakdown and the 'solution' of socialism in its appeal to the electorate in October 1931. 'We must plan or perish', the election manifesto proclaimed, thereby introducing the cornerstone of Labour's future policy. If the Labour government had been 'sacrificed to the clamour of bankers and finances', then socialist reconstruction was now 'imperative', meaning the nationalisation of the banking system, power, transport, coal, iron and steel.[60] From here on, 'planning' became the party mantra: the means by which socialism could supplant capitalism.

We shall consider the trade unions' practical response to the events of 1931 in due course. In the immediate aftermath of the August cabinet meetings, however, many union leaders and MPs took a combative stance. According to Lord Sankey, the trade unionists who attended the PLP meeting of 28 August brought with them talk of 'class war', while Bevin had already declared his desire to 'put everything in' to a situation he compared to the General Strike.[61] Clearly, the TUC general council's refusal to countenance the bulk of the cabinet committee's proposed economies had already greatly influenced the decision of the PLP (and several cabinet ministers) to move into opposition, and the subsequent mood of the party would be equally informed by the union's response to events after August 1931. Union-sponsored MPs, including Clynes and Bondfield of the NUGMW, were quizzed by their respective union executives as to their attitudes and conduct during the crisis, while Citrine informed the TUC that the unions could not simply subscribe to a Labour government policy that they believed was heading for disaster. 'The strength of the TUC lies in the fact that it can detach itself from political expediency and look economic facts in the face', he informed congress in September. Thus, in the TUC's estimation, it had been the borrowing and lending policies of the City of London that had precipitated the summer crisis.[62] 'Political and financial influences of a sinister character' had been 'working behind the scenes', Arthur Hayday claimed in his chairman's address. These had 'taken advantage of the difficulties arising from the policy pursued by private banking interests, not under subject to any public control, to dictate to the British government and people a fundamental change in national policy'. A 'financiers' revolution' was underway, he continued, and until there was public control of the banks, 'then the banks will govern us'. As we shall see, the unions would respond to such purported financial intrigue by establishing a far more 'hands-on' approach to Labour policy in the future. In the meantime, the 1931 TUC passed a resolution sponsored by Arthur Pugh and Ernest Bevin welcoming 'the current tendency towards a planned and regulated economy'.[63]

On the ground, Labour's divisional parties undoubtedly suffered over the course of 1930–1, as both membership and financial support fell away. So, to take a few examples based on the party's own figures, the Blackburn party lost nearly half its membership between 1929 and 1932 (falling from 892 to 500), the Peckham party membership fell from 900 to the minimum 240 by the end of 1931, while the Doncaster party lost some 3,000 members through a decline in its affiliated mineworkers between 1929 and 1931.[64] Not surprisingly, many smaller parties found that such losses could inflict serious damage. Thus, the Roxburgh and Selkirk Divisional Labour Party reported a severe drop in membership that led to its six local branches being 'more or less bankrupt' by the end of 1931. By late 1932, some of these branches had been unable to affiliate to the constituency party, leading eventually to its virtual dissolution. The party was run on a 'shoestring' until 1935, when it was finally reconstituted.[65] Interestingly, one of its party locals was actually meeting on 25 August 1931, when Ramsay MacDonald first spoke on the radio as prime minister of the National government. In a move that revealed much about the Labour Party's wider response to events of 1931, the Hawick local immediately passed a resolution congratulating 'those cabinet ministers who had resigned rather than reduce the benefit of the unemployed and urged upon all Labour MPs the importance of maintaining the standards of the unemployed and working class in general'.[66] In Gloucester, moreover, an already fractious party could hardly benefit from the recriminations that flew in response to the government's floundering fortunes. Amidst accusations that MacDonald had presided over a Conservative government for the past two years, the party organisation fell into disrepair, with its individual membership falling from 540 in 1930 to 475 by 1932.[67] Even more damagingly, the Wolverhampton party split over W. J. Brown's resignation from the PLP in February 1931. As a result, leading members and councillors resigned in support of Brown, the party lost significant financial support (contributing to a debt that stood at £155 in May), the party rooms were necessarily vacated, and a newly formed Independent Labour Association became a potent alternative to Labour over the 1930s.[68]

As in the parliamentary party, there was evidence of equivocation among sections of the party rank and file to MacDonald's decision. Within certain parties there appeared initially to be those who felt more saddened than hostile to the events of August 1931.[69] The esteem in which Labour members held MacDonald was not easily dismissed, although his siding with the Tories during the general election was plainly beyond the pale for the vast majority of party activists. In the prime minister's own Seaham Harbour constituency, the divisional party executive moved to replace MacDonald as the official Labour candidate only to find that some of its members continued to support their prestigious MP. Although a delegate conference later ratified the executive decision on 12 September, it did so by just 40 votes to 39.[70] MacDonald, of course, went on to retain the seat at the general election. Similarly, Jimmy Thomas's prestige within his union and the Derby Labour Party remained notable despite his poor performance in government and his subsequent defection. Thomas was himself reluctant to relinquish the endorsement of the National Union of Railwaymen (NUR), although the railwaymen's executive meeting of 31 August effectively forced him to resign his union positions. The Derby Labour Party, meanwhile, voted by 103 to 48 to withdraw support for Thomas. And yet, three Labour councillors, the largest NUR branch in Derby and Thomas's secretary-agent, John Cobb, all remained loyal to their MP. Despite an NUR candidate (William Halls) being placed in opposition to Thomas at the ensuing general election, he – like MacDonald – retained his seat.[71]

In Colne Valley (as in much of Yorkshire), the party retained its faith in Snowden well into 1931. Indeed, the chancellor's apparent ineffectiveness was often explained in relation to the government's minority status or, later, the intrigues of City financers and their political allies.[72] Even after Snowden's defection, the divisional party passed a resolution on 29 August 1931 recognising his services to the constituency.[73] By the end of the year, however, as the ramifications of Snowden's actions became apparent, the last residues of empathy with the once Labour chancellor were well and truly buried. Even so, the election result suggests that some 7,000 former Labour supports shifted their vote to the Liberal Party on the advice of Snowden, so losing the party a nominally 'safe' seat until 1935.

More generally, however, Labour activists and members rallied behind the party. Across Britain as a whole, *most* trade union branches retained their support for Labour, and *most* Labour members stayed loyal to the party. In particular, those constituency parties that had previously backed Labour backbenchers who supported MacDonald in August 1931 quickly took steps to disown their 'treacherous' representatives. We have already seen how South Nottingham's G. W. Holford Knight had fallen out with his divisional party by 1931, but the rift became permanent once he declared his intention to follow the prime minister and stand as National candidate at the subsequent election. Local Labour members gave him just ten minutes to state his case before rejecting his candidature.[74] Similarly, Craigie Aitchison's desertion of the party no doubt came as no surprise to many in the Glasgow labour movement, while Richard Denman's eventual support for the National government came amidst warnings of his Leeds Central party's 'ugly mood' towards 'defectors'. Only one delegate voted against Denman's deselection.[75]

Elsewhere, local and divisional parties ensured that clear distinctions were drawn between the Labour Party and MacDonald. In Manchester, the borough party resolved that 'the function of the Labour Party, as of a Labour government, is to work in the interests of the working class', so immediately affirming its support for a Labour opposition to the National government.[76] In Bedwellty, too, the party passed a resolution congratulating Charles Edwards on his decision not to follow MacDonald onto the National government benches.[77] Similarly, the Newport Labour MP James Walker vowed to support Arthur Henderson in opposition and was duly given a vote of confidence by his divisional party.[78] In North Lambeth, George Strauss was quick to state his loyalty to the Labour Party, accepting a vote of confidence from his divisional party and backing a resolution condemning the newly formed government.[79] The Edinburgh Trades and Labour Council, meanwhile, sent its congratulations 'to those members of the late Labour government who demitted office rather than agree to a policy of economy which had for its object the reduction of the already meagre allowance paid to unemployed workers ...' More humorously, the North Edinburgh branch of the ILP sent the local Conservative Association two pictures of Ramsay MacDonald and Philip Snowden with an attached note, 'passed to you please'.[80]

Overall, the experience of the second Labour government revealed much about the Labour Party. While the performance of MacDonald's administration had caused concern and even disillusionment among Labour members, the party fell back on its origins in the wake of the cabinet split. The traditions of 'loyalty' and 'unity' that underpinned the trade union basis of Labour bound the bulk of the party together in the face of crisis, allowing a ready alternative to the path taken by MacDonald, Snowden and Thomas. If trade union support for the Labour *government* had been conditional, then its commitment to the Labour *Party* remained far more enduring. As we shall see below, the events of 1931 brought the trade union movement even closer to the heart of the Labour Party. In the short term, however, Labour became the party of 'depression'. At the most basic level, Labour was to be defeated at the 1931 general election 'because of its recent record in office, because it lacked clear policies, because its leaders had forfeited their credibility, and because their opponents were more attractive to a country desperate for economic improvement'.[81]

As this suggests, the election was a disaster for the Labour Party. Labour candidates were rejected throughout the country, with the scale of the defeat surprising party activists and supporters alike. In a story indicative of the time, Stanley Bell would later recall seeing the Labour candidate for Kingston-upon-Thames, F. W. Fawcett, sitting in the Labour club following the election result, head in hands, saying 'this is the end of Labour'.[82] Even before the dissolution of parliament, the PLP had already been reduced via its various defections and a string of by-election defeats over the course of 1930–1. But the massacre of 27 October was something else entirely. Labour returned just 46 MPs, plus a further six associated candidates not endorsed by the NEC (five ILP and Wedgwood as an Independent).[83] Across the floor of the Commons they faced 554 National MPs, the vast majority of them Conservative (471). Cabinet members and well-known Labour leaders had been routed, with Henderson, Clynes, Morrison, Bondfield, Johnston, Adamson, Alexander, Shinwell, Shaw, Dalton and Greenwood all among those to lose their seats. Previously hard-fought gains in Liverpool, Birmingham, Cardiff, Plymouth and Edinburgh were also lost. Even the Labour strongholds appeared to suffer. In Durham, Labour lost all but its two most concentrated mining seats at Spennymoor and Chester-le-Street. In Yorkshire, the number of Labour

MPs fell from 39 (in 1929) to seven, with the West Riding Labour heartland returning just one Labour member.[84] Lancashire returned just five Labour members, three of whom were MFGB-sponsored, as cotton union branches, members and voters deserted the divisional parties.[85] In the capital, Labour retained five London constituencies, having won 36 in 1929. In Scotland, meanwhile, Labour's advance was severely checked, with only four (non-ILP) Labour MPs returned from 64 constituencies, and with serious defeats in Glasgow and among the industrial and mining divisions of Lanarkshire, Fife and South Ayrshire. Finally, the 25 Welsh constituencies represented by Labour in the House of Commons in 1929 fell to fifteen in 1931, alongside the unendorsed ILP candidate R. C. Wallhead in Merthyr Tydfil.

Clearly, Labour had been buried beneath a landslide in 1931. And yet, the peculiarities of Britain's electoral system again necessitate some qualifying remarks. First, the 'National' opposition – effectively a Conservative–Liberal coalition with the odd rogue National Labour candidate – meant that in 359 constituencies Labour faced a single opponent; a record for any post-war election.[86] This, and the subsequent Liberal absorption into the elected National government, confirmed the bi-party political arrangement that would dominate British politics for the remainder of the twentieth century. Second, Labour still recorded 6,362,561 votes, some two million less than in 1929, but still a significant number.[87] Third, as noted above, the party retained its trade union foundation and, in most cases, its active constituency membership. The party's own figures suggest that five trade unions and 63,947 affiliated union members left the party over the course of 1931.[88] Of course, none of this should distract us from the severity of Labour's defeat; the party had been devastated across much of Britain. However, it revealed that even at such a low ebb, a notable basis of Labour support remained in place.

If the immediate impact of 1931 had prompted disillusionment, anger, electoral disaster and political soul-searching across the broad ranks of Labour, then in what position did the party find itself by 1932? Most obviously, the PLP had returned to something of a miners' trade union rump, with no less than 23 of its initial 46 members being sponsored by the MFGB. But while the majority of the mining contingent was loyally committed to the party, only Aneurin Bevan could be said to offer anything in the way of political bite.[89] More generally, the PLP consisted of 32 trade union, thirteen divisional party, and one Co-operative Party members. No Labour women were returned to parliament in 1931. In such circumstances, and with Henderson's electoral defeat, the PLP chair was taken up by the 72-year-old George Lansbury, the only erstwhile cabinet minister to survive the election and, for a time, the only MP on the NEC. Although Sir Stafford Cripps was reputedly thought by some to be an alternative leadership candidate, this was probably unlikely given his recent party membership and a class background that roused suspicion in sections of the party. Inside the Commons, however, Cripps and Clement Attlee proved to be Lansbury's most capable lieutenants, combining to offer at least a semblance of opposition to the government. Indeed, Lansbury, Attlee and Cripps worked well together, rotating their parliamentary duties and ensuring that they retained their links with the Labour backbenches via regular PLP meetings.[90] Yet, the sheer paucity of Labour members inevitably made the PLP appear somewhat ineffective. Even when Greenwood and Henderson returned to parliament – in 1932 and 1933 respectively – the PLP remained weak under the shadow of the government's huge majority. As such, the PLP comprised a relatively left-wing leadership and a moderate parliamentary body, suggesting that David Howell's summation that 'the temper of the PLP was set by an articulate minority who held the dominant positions because of their parliamentary gifts, but who did not always represent accurately the conformity of many backbenchers', is an apposite one.[91]

Looked at generally, Lansbury's leadership was as much emblematic as proficient. Unusually, the PLP that elected Lansbury in November 1931 had done so as a temporary measure, simultaneously retaining Henderson as party leader in preparation for his expected return to the Commons. Unfortunately, Henderson's health was such that he would prove unable to give an effective lead to the party either inside or out of parliament, finally resigning his position in October 1932. Henderson was evidently ailing by this time; he appeared unconvinced of the party's direction and committed himself primarily to questions of disarmament from 1932, for which he eventually won the Nobel Peace Prize. Though he won the Clay Cross by-election in September 1933, Henderson would no longer be a determining Labour presence. Lansbury, meanwhile, issued the odd stinging critique of the government from the opposition benches, but his reliance on Attlee's more technical approach brought with it some criticism. He was also absent for much of 1934, having fallen and broken his thigh opening a Labour fete at Gainsborough in December 1933, during which time Attlee again proved an able deputy. Overall, Lansbury led the party competently if unspectacularly in extremely difficult circumstances; while offering little in the way of constructive political ideas, he proved able – for a time at least – to provide the party with a sense of unity and a link with its past that was untarnished by the 'betrayal' of MacDonald.[92] In truth, however, the real power in the Labour Party now lay with Bevin, Citrine, Morrison and Dalton in the reconstituted NJC and NEC.

Clement Attlee's emergence as a credible and effective 'deputy' was one of the more encouraging aspects of PLP activity over the early 1930s. If not regarded as a 'front rank' Labour politician in 1931, Attlee was a well-established Labour figure in the East End of London, and a former junior minister of some repute. By 1934, his stature had grown considerably, primarily as a result of his speeches on unemployment and India – two of the more predominant issues of the time.[93] Although he was an Oxford-educated lawyer born into a middle-class family in 1883, he had nevertheless become the Labour mayor of Stepney in 1919 and sat as the MP for Limehouse from 1922. Having given up the law to become a social worker, he joined the ILP in 1908 in response to the poverty and desperation that his chosen career revealed to him. As such, his socialism was arguably more instinctive than cerebral, informed by a sense of social injustice at the negative effects of capitalism. At the same time, Attlee's personal character was illusive; he appeared nervous and shy, he was known for his curtness, but he retained also a reputation for efficiency and reliability. Colleagues may have continued to refer to him as 'inconspicuous' and something of 'nonentity', but this was perhaps a misreading of the future prime minister's quiet determination.[94]

Cripps, meanwhile, was the son of Lord Parmoor, the former Tory MP who had served in both of MacDonald's Labour cabinets. A trained barrister, Cripps did not enter politics until he was 41, having been persuaded to join Labour and become a prospective parliamentary candidate by Herbert Morrison in 1929. Prior to this,

Cripps appears to have had some sympathy for Labour's position, although his private musings reveal his early politics to have been instinctively Tory.[95] Initially, at least, Cripps seemed to fulfil the role of a party loyalist on his election to parliament and appointment as solicitor-general in early 1931. Come the crisis of August 1931, however, and he began to move leftwards, becoming a proverbial thorn in the NEC's side throughout the 1930s. That said, his debating skills – though dry and technical – ensured that he remained a valuable presence in the Commons. To some, moreover, he was a gifted and inspirational politician, although his wealth – which he topped up by maintaining his legal work throughout the 1930s – brought him disdain from some inside and out of the party. To others, therefore, the 'red squire' was another potential 'loose cannon' on a par with Mosley; an intellectual whose militant pronouncements revealed his apparent disdain for the unity that underpinned the Labour Party.[96]

The final 'big hitter' to feature in the PLP between 1931 and 1935 was Arthur Greenwood. Greenwood returned to parliament in April 1932, following his victory in the Wakefield by-election, and was another possible alternative to Lansbury as party leader in the wake of Henderson's resignation. Born in Leeds in 1880, his working-class credentials were complemented by ministerial experience and a good relationship with the trade unions that stemmed from his position as secretary to the joint research department in the early 1920s. For the time being, however, Greenwood appeared nonplussed by any such 'promotion', preferring to maintain his important 'backroom' role in the research department developing party policy.[97] Unfortunately, too, his 'rising star' would be tainted by an affection for drink, something that arguably derailed his eventual leadership challenge in 1935.

In stark contrast to the transformed PLP, the composition of the NEC was left largely unaltered following the upheavals of 1931, although it obviously no longer contained so evident a parliamentary party presence. The trade union and women's sections changed little from 1929, with Hirst (Transport and General Workers' Union; TGWU), Clynes (NUGMW), Roberts (Typographical Association), Brothers (United Textile Factory Workers' Association; UTFWA), Robinson (National Union of Distributive and Allied Workers; NUDAW), Kaylor (Amalgamated Engineering Union; AEU), Compton (National Union of Vehicle Builders; NUVB), Smith (National Union of Boot and Shoe Operatives; NUBSO), Swan (MFGB), Walker (Iron and Steel Workers) and Dobbie (NUR) being almost ever-present members on the former in the early-to-mid 1930s, and with Gould, Lawrence, Adamson and Carlin similarly dominating the latter. In the constituency party section, too, important 'second generation' members such as Dalton and Morrison continued alongside the more experienced Lansbury and Dallas over the early 1930s. Indeed, if the executive appeared to be a mix of loyal trade unionists and ambitious politicians, then the relationships within it were largely amicable. Potential radical or left-wing critics such as Trevelyan and Cripps were irregular members and always in the minority. Thus, Trevelyan was only elected to the executive once, in 1933, while Cripps was elected to the NEC just twice in the 1930s, in 1934 and 1937. Generally, the dominant trade unionists continued to lend their support to the initiatives of the politicians, who in turn began to work closely with representatives of the TUC. As such, the policy committee established on 16 December 1931 comprised three out-and-out trade unionists, one trade union politician, one co-operator, two constituency politicians (and former MPs), and the

PLP leader; namely, in order, Lathan, Hirst, Compton, Clynes, Williams, Dalton, Morrison and Lansbury. As we shall see, although left-wing criticism and alternatives continued to circulate within the Labour Party over the 1930s, they proved vocal but largely ineffective.

The moderate, continuous and generally harmonious character of the NEC would prove integral to Labour's recovery from the debacle of 1931. In particular, it served to balance and complement the party's relationship with the TUC and the NJC. Although the parliamentary head had been effectively decapitated in 1931, the political and organisational body of the Labour Party remained intact. This enabled the party to close ranks and both re-establish and realign its political identity, reinterpreting its socialism in a practical sense distinct from the verbally alluring if politically vague hypotheses associated with MacDonald's party. To this effect, Dalton and Morrison were perhaps the two most influential members on the party executive from 1931. Despite losing his seat at Hackney South, Morrison's importance remained on account of his position at the head of the London Labour Party (LLP) and his almost compulsive political appetite. He was, as Dalton noted, 'important in the EC, intellectually able but aggressive, and a pedantic stickler for procedural precision and party discipline'.[98] Throughout the 1930s, these qualities ensured that Morrison was to the fore in the development of Labour's organisation and future policy direction. Dalton, meanwhile, who had schooled at Eton, Cambridge and the LSE, where he lectured after the Great War, used his economic expertise and connections to help shape Labour's future fiscal policies. As such, his contribution to Labour's political development over the 1930s was extensive, pushing the party towards a more assertive response to fascism and helping put detailed flesh on the bones of Labour's evolving political programme. Even so, Dalton's generally warm and outgoing character was seen by some to be insensitive and ultimately careerist. It was in this context that his fellow NEC member Susan Lawrence would accuse him of manipulating the executive's trade union members for his own ends. Certainly, Dalton worked amicably with Citrine, Bevin and the trade unionists on the NEC. But this was largely because Dalton's basic outlook of 'practical socialism' more closely resembled that of his working-class colleagues than those on the intellectual left of the party who mistrusted his motives. Throughout the 1930s, Dalton would work in tandem with those who sought to protect Labour from what he called the 'adolescent Marxist miasma' articulated by Cripps and his comrades.[99]

At a constituency level, the impact of August 1931 appeared to be more devastating on Labour's vote than its core membership support. Officially, the party's individual membership continued to grow throughout the crises of 1930–2, from 227,897 in 1929 to 277,211 in 1930, to 297,003 in 1931, and 371,607 in 1932.[100] However, we should be wary of reading too much into this. As Neil Riddell has demonstrated, the 1930 figure appears to have been falsified, with the official figure not corresponding with the membership returns of the various parties, which totalled 319,715 for the same year. It seems, therefore, that the official 1930 figure published in 1931 was reduced to disguise a significant fall in numbers over the course of 1929–31.[101] As the published breakdown of constituency party memberships clearly shows, many divisional parties registered losses in membership, while affiliation fees to head office fell from £4,363 to £3,160 between 1930 and 1931.[102] Moreover, the loss of members and subsequent loss in finance led some parties to relinquish the service of agents (Darlington), to sell party cars (Roxburgh and Selkirk), and to close down party newspapers (York). Even so, Labour's divisional organisation appeared relatively resilient to the crises that engulfed the party nationally and at the polls.

The loss of wider support for Labour had been discernible before the crises of August 1931 and the subsequent general election. Not only had by-election results begun to turn against the party from February 1930 (in terms of defeats and shrinking majorities), but the municipal election returns of 1930–1 suggested, in large part at least, discontent with regard to the Labour government's record. Although the triennial character of municipal elections means that year-to-year shifts in electoral support are difficult to gauge, such data can point to general trends in political attitudes and responses. Thus, in the twelve Yorkshire county boroughs examined by Sam Davies and Bob Morley, Labour support fell from 50 per cent of the vote cast in November 1929, to 41 per cent in 1930, to 39 per cent in 1931. From this, Davies and Morley suggest that unemployment and the Labour government's failure adequately to respond to the problem lay at the heart of the party's diminishing support, particularly in the Yorkshire woollen industry centres plagued by industrial unrest at this time. In 1930, the party lost control of four county borough councils (Barnsley, Hull, Leeds and Wakefield), and uniformly lost support and seats elsewhere. The following year, soon after the government's collapse, such a trend continued, with Labour losing Bradford and registering a net loss of 34 council seats over the twelve county boroughs as a whole.[103] Of course, the downward trend was evident elsewhere. In London, for example, Labour's performance in the metropolitan borough elections of 1931 compared unfavourably with the party's 1928 result. The Labour vote fell from 253,700 to 198,100, with the number of Labour council seats won falling from 459 to 257.[104] Clearly, Labour support at both a national and local level was damaged by the experience of 1929–31, ensuring that the divisional organisations were faced in 1932 with the considerable task of re-establishing the party's reputation and a sense of trust with their constituents.

For many on the ILP left, however, the election defeat merely confirmed their belief that the Labour Party had run its course. With capitalism in the midst of crisis, so radical – even revolutionary – solutions were now raised. In such circumstances, Maxton and his comrades moved further to the left, with many, particularly Brockway, predicting imminent capitalist collapse. This, in turn, complemented the outlook of ILP left wingers in the mainly London-based Revolutionary Policy Committee (RPC). Yet, it was primarily the 1931 Labour Party conference decision to ratify the NEC's enforcement of party standing orders on recalcitrant members that eventually precipitated the final separation of the ILP from Labour.[105] This, as Cohen has demonstrated, widened the debate from one of policy to one centred squarely on the basic relationship between the ILP and the Labour Party.[106] Thus, the veteran ILP leader Fred Jowett insisted that the ILP maintained the right of its MPs to vote 'in accordance with the principles and the policies of socialism'. 'That is why', he insisted, 'it cannot agree to obey the present standing orders of the Labour Party. The answer to those who demand that it must surrender the freedom of MPs to fulfil their pledges, honestly made in accordance with the principles of policy advocated officially by the Labour Party for election purposes, is – NO – NO – NEVER'.[107] For this reason, nineteen ILP candidates remained unendorsed at the 1931 general election, before a special conference of the ILP in July 1932 ended almost a year's discussion with its vote to disaffiliate from Labour by 241 votes to 142.

This decision cast the ILP into the political wilderness. Nevertheless, the original situation was complex, with a variety of moods, perspectives and strategies revealed across the nine ILP divisions during the various conferences held to discuss the issue in 1931–2. Many members agreed with the need for a more assertive socialist policy, many agreed that Labour discipline hampered the advance of socialism as propagated by the ILP; but the majority continued to envisage their future within the larger party. Ultimately, however, the question of party standing orders brought ILP–Labour relations to an impasse. Following further unconstructive negotiations between the two parties in spring 1932, Maxton put it to the July conference that the 'Labour Party were not prepared to allow the ILP to abide by its principles', suggesting that to remain inside the party was to become the 'docile' supporter of 'whatever the wider movement desired'.[108] It now come down, in the words of Jennie Lee, to a choice between 'either the Labour Party or the ILP. It could not be both'.[109]

Following the decision to disaffiliate, many ILP members returned to the Labour fold, although the situation varied from place to place. Certainly, the ILP reportedly lost the support of 203 of its 653 branches between July and November 1932, while official ILP membership dropped from 16,773 to 7,166 between 1932 and 1934.[110] Although there were instances of local ILP's maintaining notable local support, as in Norwich, there were also occasions where members simply left en masse, as in Leicester and Bermondsey. In Glasgow, the ILP's electoral base remained in parts of the city, although the wider consequences of disaffiliation were soon apparent. Only seven of the 40 ILP councillors on the Glasgow corporation disaffiliated, while many other erstwhile ILPers (including Kirkwood) agreed with Patrick Dollan that a socialist left could only have an impact *inside* the Labour Party. Accordingly, Dollan immediately formed the Scottish Socialist Party (SSP) to pursue the distinctive role that the ILP had previously played in Scotland and the labour movement more generally.[111] Indeed, the disparity between the ILP left and the bulk of its Scottish members had been clear even as the Labour government flailed in 1930–1, with the war of words that flew between Wheatley's *Glasgow Eastern Standard* and Tom Johnston's *Forward!* effectively challenging Maxton's claim to speak for Scottish Labour. The ILP retained a presence in Glasgow throughout the 1930s, but not to the extent of its 1920s heyday. That said, the loss of the ILP in Scotland as a whole undoubtedly provided Labour with an organisational headache, as premises, activists and finance disappeared. In the words of Arthur Woodburn, appointed secretary of the Scottish Labour Party in 1932, the party in Scotland had been 'a federated body and the real drive was in the ILP ... my job was practically to build from scratch'.[112] This proved to be no easy task. In Bradford, meanwhile, only one of the 32 Labour council group was prepared to leave the Labour Party in 1932, with the rest issuing a statement defending their socialist credentials and their record in municipal government. Concurrently, the Bradford ILP lost more than half of its 750 members in the wake of disaffiliation.[113] Even so, we should note that the ILP retained a presence in the east of the city (forcing Labour to compete against it in the 1935 general election), while other branches maintained an ambiguous relationship with both Labour and the ILP though until 1934, when they finally decided to go with the larger party.[114]

Given such developments, the mantle of the Labour left was taken up by the Socialist League at the end of 1932. Formed on 2 October of that year, the Socialist League was a product of ILP disaffiliation and G. D. H. Cole's attempts to invigorate Labour policy and propaganda. Cole had already begun to reconsider the practical application of Labour policy in his 1929 book *The Next Ten Years in British Social and Economic Policy*, and he continued to develop his ideas in response to the MacDonald government's evident limitations.[115] In 1931, therefore, Cole organised a series of weekend meetings to mobilise interest in his initiative, from which the New Fabian Research Bureau (NFRB) and the Society for Socialist Inquiry and Propaganda (SSIP) were instigated. It was the latter of these that later fed into the Socialist League.

In time, the Labour hierarchy would see the Socialist League as a liability akin to the former ILP left wing. Initially, however, its intention was to push for a more socialist Labour policy within the bounds of the party constitution. Both the NFRB and SSIP had received support from notable Labour members across the party's ideological spectrum, including Henderson, Bevin, Pugh, Cripps, Attlee, Kirkwood, Lansbury, Wilkinson, Pritt and Lord Ponsonby, with Bevin actually taking the chair of the SSIP in 1931.[116] By 1932, moreover, amidst the uncertain political climate and bitterness engendered by the 1931 general election, both the NFRB and SSIP appeared to form part of Labour's necessary realignment. This changed following the ILP's disaffiliation. As ex-ILPers returned to the Labour fold, so they absorbed the SSIP and sought to rekindle their former party's distinctive role within the wider Labour Party. Not surprisingly, such a move roused the suspicion of Bevin, who refused Cole's attempt to involve him in the new body. The influx of former ILPers convinced Bevin that the Socialist League would quickly become a home for 'careerists'; such an organisation would 'always have a bias against trade unionism', he informed Cole during negotiations in September, predicting that the Socialist League would not 'change very much from the old ILP attitude, whoever is in the executive'.[117] In many ways, Bevin was proven right, with Cole, Kirkwood and Pugh similarly withdrawing from its ranks, or at least its national council, over the course of 1932–3. Just five weeks after the formation of the Socialist League, moreover, a special meeting of the SSIP rejected the October decision and opted for dissolution.

Very quickly, the Socialist League established itself as a distinctive organisation within the Labour Party. Its first chairman was the former civil servant Frank Wise, who had headed the ex-ILPers' return to Labour in 1932. He was assisted by a range of intellectuals, including Sir Stafford Cripps, William Mellor, H. N. Brailsford and Frank Horrabin, all of whom could be regarded as situated on the left of the party and articulate critics of Labour moderation. Subsequently, and despite the reservations of certain founder members (not to mention a section of the NEC), the Socialist League established itself as an affiliated Labour society.[118] Membership was open to all socialist members of the Labour Party, co-op and trade unions, an annual conference was constituted, a national council elected, and local branches established in seven regional committees. The branch sections reputedly numbered 74 by March 1934, with approximately 3,000 members based primarily – though not exclusively – in London and the Home Counties.[119] Politically, the

Socialist League focused initially on education and research; lectures, study programmes and conferences were instigated, policy proposals drafted, and memorandums issued to the NEC (which consistently ignored or rejected them). From such activity, however, and as an increasingly coherent political position became more discernible, so the Socialist League began to mirror the old ILP in its endeavour to forge a 'definite and clearly understood programme of real socialism' that was, ultimately, in opposition to that of 'official' Labour Party policy.[120]

Following the death of Wise in November 1933, Cripps emerged as the preeminent figure within the Socialist League. He had already replaced Wise as chairman in June, from which position he began to articulate the League's policies in a language imbued with references to the class struggle and economic planning.[121] Essentially, the events of 1931–2 had convinced Cripps that capital was willing to overthrow democracy in order to safeguard its interests: only socialism could protect and/or proceed towards a properly moral, just and democratic society. To this effect, the Socialist League advocated an explicitly socialist Labour programme, meaning immediate wholesale nationalisation, self-government in industry and, if necessary, the implementation of emergency powers to safeguard democracy from the protests of capital. Ostensibly, therefore, the Socialist League's 'road to socialism' remained a parliamentary road, with any resort to coercive measures being implemented constitutionally. So:

> From the moment when the Labour Government takes control, rapid and effective action must be possible in every sphere of the national life. It will not be easy to detect the machinations of the capitalists and, when discovered, there must be means ready to hand by which they can be dealt with promptly The greatest danger point will be the financial and credit structure of the country and the foreign exchange position … The Government's first step will be to call parliament together at the earliest possible date and place before it an Emergency Powers Bill to be passed through all its stages in one day. This Bill would be wide enough in its terms to allow all that will be immediately necessarily to be done by ministerial orders. These orders must be incapable of challenge in the courts or in any way except in the House of Commons.[122]

But the violent and ultimately revolutionary ramifications of such a perspective were clearly apparent. Indeed, Cripps' rhetoric was soon renowned for its insurgent overtones and evidently began to embarrass the Labour leadership, particularly as his prominent place within the PLP assured him a very public profile. Most famously, in 1934, Cripps made reference to overcoming 'opposition from Buckingham Palace', a piece of purple prose that confounded both the NEC and the TUC. At the very least, such confrontational pronouncements jarred with the more cautious approach of Labour's official policy, and the subsequent furore in the press necessitated a hasty Labour disclaimer.[123] As Morrison, who remained on good terms with Cripps, later wrote him, such speeches appeared more 'calculated to help the enemy than the party', though he appreciated that Cripps 'never intended it so'.[124] Accordingly, stand-offs between Cripps and Dalton, Bevin, Clynes and others became a characteristic of the Labour conference in the 1930s.

Ultimately, the Socialist League made little direct impact on party policy between 1932 and 1935. True, the 1932 Labour conference that met the day after the Socialist League's formation passed a Wise-sponsored amendment committing Labour to the nationalisation of joint stock banks against the wishes of the NEC, but such successes proved rare.[125] While many Labour leaders and members recognised the untrustworthiness of capital, they retained a commitment to more moderate and conventional solutions. Similarly, if Cripps remained personally close to Lansbury, Attlee and Morrison, then he did not have the wider support of either the NEC or the TUC; Dalton and Bevin, respectively, loathed and distrusted him. As such, the Socialist League may have boasted charismatic speakers, but its actual membership was small, and its composition unrepresentative of the wider Labour Party. Of the 23 people who served on the League's national council between 1932 and 1937, Ben Pimlott has estimated that two were Etonians, two were Wykehamists, one was a Harrovian, at least nine had an Oxbridge education, and four were students of London University.[126] From such lofty heights, talk of class struggle and Marxism had, for many, a rather hollow ring. Headlines, it would appear, were easier to make than 'real' socialists.

Clearly, the events of 1931 ensured that the balance of power within the Labour Party shifted to its extra-parliamentary sections, and towards the trade unions in particular. In the severe circumstances of 1931–5, Labour parliamentarians and politicians recognised the need to work closely with the unions to forge a practical socialism centred on a realistic but distinct party programme. Despite Henderson's concern to avoid too drastic a departure from the moderation of the 1920s and *Labour and the Nation*, the presumptions of Webb, MacDonald and Snowden had been shown to be fallacious amid the circumstances of 1929–31.[127] New and distinct policies were now needed, a more assertive party approach was necessary, and a period of rebuilding was evidently required. In such a way, the heady optimism that had often sustained the Labour Party over the 1920s gave way to more protracted but hard-headed struggle during the 1930s. Labour, itself, now had to plan or perish.

III. RECLAIMING LABOUR:
PLANNING FOR THE FUTURE

On Monday 3 October 1932, Arthur Henderson spoke to the thirty-second Labour Party conference on the aims of 'organised Labour'. He used the term deliberately, he said, '[for] I would remind you that the constitution set up by the annual party conferences laid down in explicit terms years ago that the Labour Party, in seeking to give effect to the principles and policies approved by the conference, was to co-operate with the Trades Union Congress and kindred organisations'. Such co-operation must be as close as possible, Henderson continued, and he insisted that the party be 'determined' that it 'become even more intimate in the future, in order that the power of the workers as citizens, as producers, and as consumers may be effectively organised for the triumph of democratic principles and ideas'.[128] Although Henderson would show some misgivings as to the political direction in which Labour moved over the early 1930s, the recognition of the need for closer party–union relations proved integral to the party's realignment following the events of 1931. Consequently, the links that bound the PLP, NEC and TUC were reaffirmed in the aftermath of the Labour Party's return to opposition. The TUC exerted greater authority on the NEC and, with the reconstitution of the NJC, henceforth contributed greatly to the development of party policy on a wide range of issues. In particular, a preoccupation with economic planning and nationalisation became evident, as Labour sought to establish a set of explicitly socialist policies that distinguished it from a capitalism that seemed – in the context of the early 1930s – to be moribund. This section will look first, therefore, at the party–union rapprochement of the early 1930s, before examining a shift in Labour policy and perspective towards the 'practical socialism' that formed the basis of the 1945 Attlee government.

The failings of the second Labour government, not to mention the subsequent electoral disaster of 1931, brought to a head tensions evident in the historic relationship between the Labour Party and the trade union movement. Crucially, the TUC retained its commitment to Labour and, further, moved – partly out of necessity – to reassert its role in the party's electoral and political development.[129] This had become immediately apparent. The so-called 'counsel of war' that met in Arthur Henderson's office following Labour's return to opposition on 24 August 1931 comprised Henderson, Lansbury, Middleton and Dalton, alongside Walter Citrine, Ernest Bevin and Stanley Hirst (a member of both the NEC and TGWU). Consequently, contact between the two wings of the labour movement was put on a firmer footing in an attempt to recover the Labour Party's primary purpose. This, in turn, was reiterated by Citrine in November 1931, when he reminded the NEC that the party had been 'created by the trade union movement to do those things in parliament which the trade unions found ineffectively performed by the two party system'.[130] To this effect, the revival the NJC in the following month ensured that the TUC had the right and the means by which 'to initiate and participate in political matters which it deems to be of direct concern to its constituents'.[131] The NJC was charged with securing 'a common policy and joint action, whether by legislation or otherwise, on all questions affecting the workers as producers, consumers and citizens'. This was accepted by the NEC in January, affirmed at the 1932 party conference, and helped to define party–union relations over the ensuing decade.[132]

From late 1931, therefore, regular and extensive discussion was undertaken between the departmental officers of the TUC and the NEC. Joint meetings and cross-representations were established between the NEC policy committee and the TUC economic committee; the TUC general council was consulted on related legislative proposals drawn up by the NEC. In effect, the NJC – renamed the National Council of Labour (NCL) in 1934 – became the means by which the wider labour movement consulted with the PLP, whether in or out of government.[133] Indeed, the shifting balance of power within the labour movement and Labour Party was embodied in the composition of the NJC. Where previously the joint council had comprised equal representation of the TUC, PLP and NEC, its reconstitution ensured that seven trade union representatives sat with three each from the NEC and PLP. From here on, moreover, the NJC/NCL met monthly and issued a series of public statements on Labour policy that ranged from foreign affairs to unemployment, public ownership, local government and fiscal policy. In such a way, directives from the NJC/NCL often appeared to supplant directives from the NEC over the early 1930s, as the Labour executive concerned itself primarily with organisational responsibilities. In the meantime, as Lewis Minkin has noted, the PLP's meagre numbers ensured that its leadership was effectively 'circumscribed in its initiatives by powerful extra-parliamentary forces shaping both immediate and future policy', a fact that even extended to the decision as to whether Labour should once again form a government.[134] Thus, the NEC constitutional committee's report on 'Labour and Government' (1933) insisted that the NJC would pass opinion on the 'advisability or otherwise' of the Labour Party taking office should the occasion arise.[135] Evidently, the lessons of MacDonald's minority government were not to be forgotten.

It is difficult to overestimate the influence that Citrine, Bevin and the trade union representatives on the NEC and NJC had on the Labour Party's development over the 1930s. From their powerful positions in the TUC, Citrine and Bevin worked effectively together despite the fact that relations between the two were not especially close. In particular, they contributed much to the style and character of Labour's unfolding political programme, helping to reassert Labour's identity as a party of practical politics beneficial to the broad ranks of the British working class. Both were keen to develop the policy ideas emerging from within the TUC during the MacDonald government, and both sought to add substance to the initially vague concepts of 'planning' and 'public ownership' that began to pepper Labour statements from late 1931.[136] Simultaneously, they helped form a bulwark against those on the left of the party who wished to pursue more radical socialist objectives. Within a year of the Labour government's collapse, Bevin could insist that 'the statement that capitalism was doomed to collapse was misleading', suggesting instead that 'trade union people' now recognised that capitalism was simply 'adjusting itself'.[137] In effect, therefore, the TUC harnessed the apparent 'left turn' in Labour attitudes post-1931 – epitomised in the 1932 conference resolution that a Labour government would 'stand or fall' on a definite socialist programme[138] – and channelled such energies toward the construction of a practical political programme that amounted to a fundamental reorganisation of Britain's economic basis.

As this suggests, trade union influence could be discerned with regard to Labour's political priorities throughout the 1930s. The NEC's concentration on plans for nationalisation post-1931 were, in part, informed by the apparent failure of capitalism in the context of the depression; but they were also a reflection of trade union demands for basic industrial-economic change. The fact that such policies were formed distinctively – industry by industry and often on the initiative of the respective union – only confirmed the trade unions' integral role in such a development. Within this process, the unions tended to play a consultative role, stressing their right to decide on wages and conditions of employment whilst leaving the political means by which these would be achieved to the party politicians. As David Howell has noted, TUC adoption of a proposal for nationalisation typically preceded its subsequent acceptance at the party conference, as was the case with iron and steel in 1934 and the cotton industry in 1935.[139] Conversely, such procedure highlighted deficiencies within the Labour Party's own organisation. The flow of policy documents that emerged from the party research department was not quite as gushing as hoped, leading eventually to its overhaul in 1938. Most obviously, if the respective union did not take the initiative on a policy proposal, then Labour's plans with regard to that particular industry could remain vague. So, for example, although a staple feature of the party programme, there was no detailed statement regarding the public ownership of gas supply issued in the 1930s. Finally, at a national level, the party's emphasis on industrial policy served somewhat to overshadow the social-welfare concerns of Labour. As *Labour's Immediate Programme* (1937) made clear, the reconstruction of finance, land, transport and power would *lead* to benefits in food, wages, leisure and security.[140] Beyond industrial policy, of course, the unions' influence would become important in realigning Labour's foreign policy in the face of fascism (see below).

Yet, such a shift in the balance of power within the Labour Party was conducted in accord with the 'unwritten rules' that had evolved over the course the party's history. If a more assertive trade union presence was evident from 1931, then there continued to be recognition of the distinct industrial and political spheres in which the TUC and the Labour Party functioned. Thus, within the NJC, the responsibilities of the NEC, PLP and TUC were clearly defined so as to prevent overlapping activities. Moreover, the standing orders asserting a Labour candidate's and MP's loyalty to the PLP remained in place. The NJC enabled the TUC to be involved in the development of Labour's changing political initiatives, but no constitutional modifications were considered to guarantee trade union control over the party; TUC general council members were still excluded from sitting on the NEC, and the number of union representatives on the executive was not increased.[141] Indeed, the TUC had no desire to ensure total domination of the Labour Party. To do so would have limited, or compromised, the distinctive role that Citrine and Bevin had been carving out for the trade union movement since approximately late 1926. True, the events of 1931 had convinced the TUC that its pursuit of collective bargaining and cordial relations with the employers was dependent on wider political action on the part of the government, but the basic premise of establishing the unions as a functioning part of Britain's political-economic structure remained. The TUC maintained a dialogue with the National government from the outset, enabling what Robert Taylor has called 'a limited *modus vivendi*' to exist between the state and the trade union movement. Equally, therefore, there was no desire to return to a policy of direct action.[142] For Citrine, the labour movement continued to consist of 'two broad divisions', each complementing the other, and which worked closely and consulted together on matters of policy.[143]

Simultaneously, of course, the unions did not constitute a homogeneous bloc within the Labour Party. Priorities and objectives varied across the organised working class over the 1930s. As Charlie Dukes of the NUGMW reputedly commented later in the decade, 'the unions have never fought the employers half as tenaciously as they fought each other'.[144] That said, the five largest trade unions – miners, transport workers, railwaymen, municipal workers, and textile workers – each boasted memberships of over 100,000 in 1931, and generally remained loyal to the Labour leadership. As such, their substantial block votes ensured that they could effectively direct the party conference, while their representatives had often been involved in drawing up those policies put before the annual gathering. At the same time, the position of the trade union movement in general was far from healthy in a period of economic depression. Many trade unions, including the miners' and textile workers' unions, had suffered declining memberships over the 1920s, and continued to do so into the 1930s.[145] The impact of the trade depression had exerted a toll on both union morale and funds, thereby giving the politicians in the NEC, NJC and PLP an importance to rival that of Bevin, Citrine and the TUC general council. It was, after all, the party and its political leaders who gave Labour policy its coherence and presented it to the all-important electorate.

Clearly, the trade union influence reasserted within the Labour Party from August 1931 did not overwhelm it. Certainly, opposition to – or at least criticism of – Labour policy was mobilised by some unions. The South Wales Miners' Federation (SWMF), for instance, raised regular concern at what it perceived to be the NEC's moderate politics, particularly with regard to unemployment, the means test and, later, the Spanish civil war. The NUDAW, too, was a consistent critic of the party leadership. Typically, however, trade union concerns were raised on specific issues, with the combined vote of the larger unions continuing to form a solid and loyal bedrock of support for the NEC.

Politically, the ramifications of the worldwide economic depression added credence to Labour's socialist tendencies, prompting a notable shift in party language and priorities. Had not capitalism been seen to falter with dire consequences, and had not the piecemeal reformism and economic orthodoxy of MacDonald and Snowden been discredited by the events of 1929–31? Accordingly, from late 1931 onwards, the term 'socialism' became more boldly a feature of Labour rhetoric and propaganda; the label 'socialist' was from here on more likely to be displayed than downplayed. 'I say we are no longer frightened of the term socialism', Clynes insisted at the 1931 party conference, 'we must affirm it more than ever ... as an alternative to the crushing burdens of the vicious and foolish system of capitalism ...'[146] Thus, the party's 1931 general election manifesto asserted that 'socialism provides the only solution for the evils resulting from unregulated competition and domination of vested interests'; three years later, *For Socialism and Peace* became the first major party programme to include the term in its title.[147] Although clause four had ostensibly committed Labour to a socialist objective, although most Labour leaders and members would have described themselves as 'socialist', and although socialism remained a visionary future to be raised at party conferences, local meetings and even during parliamentary debate, party propaganda had often refrained from using the 'S' word. So, for example, Reverend Richard Lee could complain in 1924 that Ramsay MacDonald visited Glasgow to make 'uplifting speeches with not a word of Socialism and not a word to satisfy reasonable enquiry ... My daughter says that any Tory could have made Mac's speech.'[148] Indeed, the term was not used in any of Labour's general election manifestos between 1918 and 1923, and was used just once in 1924 (in the final paragraph) and twice in 1929 (including a negative reference to Tory 'misrepresentations' of the word).[149]

The point is worth dwelling on, as it reveals much about Labour in the early 1930s. At a local level, the Labour stronghold of Durham provides an interesting case in point. The vast majority of Labour Party election material kept in the Durham record office contains very few references to socialism pre-1931, despite the socialist beliefs of many Durham Labour leaders. As such, promises of 'public ownership' were couched in language that highlighted 'efficiency [as] the key note of economy' rather than in ideological terms. In the same way, the 'public interest' and 'the unity of the working classes' were more commonly referred to than 'socialism'.[150] Only after 1931 does party election literature in the county begin to refer to the Labour 'plan' for a 'new socialistic order of society'.[151] Similarly, divisional annual reports – such as those of the party in Houghton-le-Spring – refrain from mentioning 'socialism' until 1931, from which point the term becomes a staple feature of the party literature.[152]

Labour's reticence to label itself 'socialist' was, perhaps, understandable in places with a history of Liberal trade union support. Thus, the *Newport Labour Party Manifesto* for 1919 concentrated on social issues under the premise that the council's affairs would be better conducted 'by persons whose sole desire is that of public welfare'. No mention was made of socialism, although the issue of water supply was deemed a 'national' one. Similarly, the party's 1920 manifesto emphasised Labour's 'efficiency', 'economy', and proper management rather than its ideological basis.[153] In the wake of the Labour government's collapse in 1931, however, the party's general committee readopted James Walker as its parliamentary candidate with a specific commitment to fighting the election 'as socialists'.[154]

Such examples should not be overstated. Labour downplayed rather than disavowed its socialism in the 1920s, and many party candidates openly stood throughout the interwar period as socialists, particularly those who had cut their political teeth in the ILP.[155] Often, however, divisional parties and candidates adapted their message to suit local circumstances; appeals to civic pride, efficiency and community were regarded as a potentially more effective means of widening Labour's vote, especially given that the 'socialist bogey' had been utilised as a Tory–Liberal weapon to stigmatise Labour candidates from the party's conception.[156] However, as capitalism continued to struggle in Britain and beyond, as Labour sought to re-identify itself as a party distinct from that of MacDonald and the National coalition, and as Labour-controlled councils began to put their policies into practice, so the party was able to proclaim more boldly its socialist creed. For example, the Norwich Labour Party in the mid-1930s would boast proudly that it was 'the socialist majority' on the council that brought improvements to the city.[157] Whatever the reasoning, it was far more common to read Labour literature calling for a 'broad comprehensive socialist policy' after 1931 than before.[158]

Of course, Labour still had to articulate just what its socialism meant in practice. If the first Labour government had given rise to concern that the party lacked a practical policy, then this was confirmed by the experience of 1929–31. Subsequently, in the wake of Labour's election defeat, the NEC established an eight-man policy committee to put flesh on the bones of the party's future vision. This, in turn, set up four sub-committees responsible for the development of Labour policy on finance and trade, on the reorganisation of industry, on local government and social services, and on constitutional matters. These included a mixture of trade unionists, NEC members and various co-opted experts and party intellectuals such as Harold Laski, C. W. Key, H. B. Lees-Smith and F. W. Pethick-Lawrence. On Dalton's initiative, too, contacts were made with sympathetic City experts (the XYZ club) and young economists (Durbin, Gaitskell) to advise on fiscal policy, while G. D. H. Cole continued to develop the NFRB. Indeed, this was to become increasingly prolific over the course of the 1930s, producing some 42 pamphlets, seven books, and various memoranda by 1938.[159] Finally, Arthur Greenwood headed Labour's own research department, compiling data 'of value to the movement', issuing memoranda to the PLP, and reports for the policy committees.[160] Within the party hierarchy, Dalton and Morrison were particularly influential, working closely to give expression to the party's socialist principles. Morrison was especially involved with the sub-committees on local government and the reorganisation of industry, preparing documents on transport and electricity, and publishing his *Socialisation and Transport* in 1933. Dalton, meanwhile, chaired the sub-committee on finance and trade, drafting most of Labour's economic policy statements over the course of the decade.

The results of such activity would emerge gradually, although a commitment to economic planning immediately formed the basis of Labour policy. In such a way, Labour accepted that its vision of a socialist commonwealth depended on a far-reaching overhaul of the economic functions of the state, and not simply 'gradualist' policies of piecemeal legislation, administration and taxation. Of course, Labour had long advocated the nationalisation of key industries; but the party had not previously articulated the concept of a co-ordinated economic plan in any detailed sense. Throughout the 1920s, Labour had broadly conceived of socialism emerging out of a vibrant capitalism, with improved social services, education and international peace paving the way for common ownership. True, the ILP's *Socialist Programme* (1923) and 'Socialism in our Time' (1926), along with Mosley and Strachey's *Revolution by Reason* (1925), had included references to planning, but these either lacked thorough explanation or, in Mosley's case, emphasised control of finance rather than industry.[161] As Richard Toye has demonstrated, 'there was little connection between the ILP's economic ideas and the form of economic planning taken up by the Labour Party in and after 1931'.[162] It was, therefore, from 1931, in the context of capitalist 'crisis', and in qualified recognition of the achievements of the Soviet five-year-plan, that Labour began to think about the logistics of a planned socialist economy based upon nationalised industry.

By the time of the 1932 party conference, both Dalton's finance and trade sub-committee and Morrison's sub-committee on the reorganisation of industry had produced a series of proposals. To this effect, the former's 'Currency, Banking and Finance' advocated the nationalisation of the Bank of England and the establishment of a National Investment Board (NIB) to regulate industrial development. Largely in response to the experience of 1931 and the associated conception of a 'bankers' ramp', the control of currency, finance and investment had moved to the centre of Labour's economic policy. For many in the party, the intrigues of the City financiers – with their evident self-interest and false 'orthodoxies' – now rivalled employer recalcitrance as the principal block on socialist development, paving the way for a wide-ranging debate throughout the movement.[163] Notably, however, the sub-committee's eventual report made no reference to the public ownership of joint-stock banks, hence the 1932 party conference vote to include these and other financial institutions in the party's plans for nationalisation against the wishes of the NEC.

As for sub-committee on the reorganisation of industry, this focused initially on transport and power in 1932–3, recommending that the existing transport and electricity undertakings be brought under the auspices of 'national boards' appointed by the relevant government minister. As always, the devil was to be found in the detail, with Morrison's resolution giving rise to a prolonged debate as to the scope and composition of the proposed boards. In particular, the concept of 'workers' control' – often evident in the myriad currents of Labour's political thought – had by the 1930s come to inform discussion over the relationship between the trade unions and any nationalised industry.[164] For Morrison, the state provided the key to introducing an efficient, fair and socialist economy, a view reinforced by Labour's economic 'experts' who remained sceptical of too overt trade union or worker involvement. Thus, Labour's official vision of common ownership encompassed the amalgamation and co-ordination of private and municipal enterprises into public corporations, administered by boards appointed by the respective ministry 'on grounds of ability' rather than their representation of a 'particular interest'. 'The party must be clear in its mind as to whether it is syndicalist or socialist', Morrison argued (rather disingenuously) at the party conference, having ventured that 'socialists above all must insist that persons of ability and competence must be in charge of our socialised industries'.[165] Against this, Bevin and Harold Clay of the TGWU argued for the trade unions' right both to nominate members to and be represented on the proposed national boards. Otherwise, Clay insisted, the workers would be doomed to 'remain hewers of wood and drawers of water under the perpetual control of their bosses': in other words, Morrison's proposal did not encompass a recognisable transfer of power to the working class. 'You have a public corporation now in the BBC', Clay went on, recalling the recent general election, 'what effective control do you have there?'[166] Consequently, Morrison – speaking on behalf of the NEC – agreed to the party conference's recommendation that further negotiations take place over the course of 1932–3. In the event, the NEC's policy sub-committee and TUC economic committee brokered a compromise whereby the national boards would encompass appointed members, 'normally' including trade unionists. In addition, trade unions would be allowed to nominate representatives, although the final decision would reside with the respective government minister; there was to be no 'statutory' trade union representation.[167] This time, and despite TUC support for the compromise resolution, the NUGMW moved against the NEC proposals, leading the 1933 Labour conference to vote in favour of workers' statutory inclusion.[168]

Inevitably, the work of the NEC sub-committees soon necessitated the formation of a general policy statement. Already, at the Labour conference of October 1933, the party had endorsed a report on 'Socialism and the Condition of the People' that broadly set out Labour's 'socialist objective'.[169] This was then followed in 1934 by the publication of *For Socialism and Peace: The Labour Party's Programme of Action*, a more detailed programme that revealed the extent to which Labour priorities had changed since the 1920s. Most obviously, the application of 'full and rapid socialist planning' was placed at the top of the party's domestic agenda, with a commitment to the common ownership of banking and credit, transport, water, coal, electricity, gas, agriculture, iron and steel, shipping, shipbuilding, engineering, textiles, chemicals, insurance, and land. Moreover, detailed policy statements outlining the nature and scope of the proposed nationalisation supplemented many of the programme sections, while the party promised that wages and conditions would become 'for the first time a paramount consideration in the conduct of industry'. In this, trade unions were to be actively involved, and the establishment of a government-appointed National Investment Board was charged with facilitating economic expansion in accord with a nationalised Bank of England. As such, the NIB would license and direct investment for the national interest rather than in the interests of capital, substituting 'socialist planning for the present anarchy' of capitalism.[170]

Significantly, extensive social provisions were envisaged to complement Labour's 'national reconstruction'. To this effect, a programme of house building was detailed in tandem with the 'final destruction of the slums'; measures to secure 'fair rents' were posited; extensive health provisions were promised towards the ultimate objective of a state health service; and free secondary education and improved facilities were outlined. Again, more detailed accounts of such measures were supplied in NEC policy sub-committee publications, including *Up With The Houses! Down With the Slums!* and *Labour and Education.* With regard to the unemployed, the abolition of the means test and the guarantee of 'adequate maintenance' were promised alongside extensive plans for electrification, road building, drainage and work associated with the socialisation of industry. In addition, Labour planned to raise the school-leaving age, introduce a 40-hour week, improve pensions, and redistribute tax burdens. Constitutionally, *For Socialism and Peace* pledged to implement reforms to speed up parliamentary procedure and to prevent the House of Lords from intervening to block government policy.[171] Nevertheless, Labour's objectives were still to be achieved via parliament and with the democratic mandate of the British people. Taken generally, therefore, the Labour Party committed itself in 1934 to a fundamental overhaul of Britain's economic – and, by extension, social – basis. This was to be implemented rather than simply administered, as the party had appeared to envisage in the 1920s, and was to be applied immediately to ensure socialism rather than 'mere social reform'.[172] Gone were the flowery phrases of MacDonald, replaced by an often dry, technical language geared more towards action than intellect.

Such a programme revealed much about Labour's character in the mid-1930s. First, the experience of 1931 had not dented Labour's belief in parliamentary democracy, although it had hardened many a party member's commitment to promoting and introducing a more rigorous set of policy proposals. There was certainly a recognition that socialism would not simply emerge from the continued advance of capitalism. There appeared, too, to be recognition that the beneficiaries of capitalism would not peaceably allow their wealth and privilege to be redistributed along socialism's egalitarian and meritocratic guidelines. Fascism was seen by many to be evidence of this, and Labour's programme asserted a far more active and practical method of introducing socialist policy than hitherto. Even so, while Labour's distrust of capital had been affirmed by the events of 1931, and did much to shape the party's understanding of and relationship to the National government, the party remained committed to a peaceful and, ultimately, reformist means of action and change.[173]

This, certainly, had become apparent during the meetings of the party's sub-committee on constitutional matters. Here, Cripps' recommendations of compulsory voting, emergency powers, tighter laws on election spending and the abolition of the House of Lords were countered by Dalton, Dallas, Lees-Smith and Citrine's focus on reforming the existing parliamentary procedure.[174] As such, proposals were drafted by the NFRB, leading to recommendations for tighter cabinet control, departmental committees, and measures to speed up parliamentary procedure. True, as a sop to the left, Cripps' resort to 'emergency powers' was accepted in 'extraordinary circumstances', but the vague phraseology of the resolution is telling.[175]

Second, the national solutions proffered by *For Socialism and Peace* tended to overshadow Labour's previous focus on 'enabling' local authorities to administer essential and social services. Arguably, Labour's rise to government, its increasingly centralised and nationwide organisation, its adoption of socialist planning, not to mention the concern raised by the party's municipal election losses of 1930–1, combined to supplant previous commitments to 'municipal socialism'.

National, rather than local, solutions were now entrenched at the top of the party's agenda, as demonstrated by Morrison's proposals for national boards to oversee the socialised industries. Where previously the LLP secretary's concept of a 'public corporation' had suggested an increased role for local government, as evidenced by his earlier plans for London transport, he now clearly envisaged control to be located and administered at central-state level. Significantly, too, 'planning' could be applied to social policy, adding credence to and encouraging Labour demands for extensive state intervention into health care and social services. As such, the local government and social services sub-committee's initial concerns were directed towards the 'expenses of public representatives on local authorities' and the administration of unemployed relief.[176]

Third, Labour saw economic planning as the bedrock of a future socialist society. In this, the party was obviously influenced by the advances made by the Soviet five-year plan, which had brought rapid dividends in contrast to capitalism's continued ills. A number of Labour leaders and intellectuals visited the Soviet Union in the early 1930s, including Dalton, Cole, Pethick-Lawrence, Pritt, Johnston, Bevan and the Webbs, many of whom comprised the NFRB and the policy committee that looked specifically at the question of economic planning from 1931. Yet, Labour did not thereby seek simply to imitate the Soviet example. Rather, the party sought to take its premise – a co-ordinated economy – and apply it to British circumstances. 'If the Russians can do it and make much remarkable progress in so short a time', Dalton wrote on his return, 'how much more effectively could we in England do it'.[177] At the same time, Dalton and the party generally remained hostile to Soviet policy and communism in general. Moreover, Labour's economic policy was further informed by wider economic debate, albeit refracted through Labour priorities. Certainly, Keynes' views influenced Labour figures such as Cole, Bevin and many of the young economists recruited to advise the party's policy committees. As Foote has suggested, Labour could concur with Keynes' belief in the state management of credit and currency markets, and if the state was dominant 'in the sphere of production, rather than distribution', then it was possible for 'the Labour Keynesians' to link this with 'the necessity of replacing an unplanned market economy with a planned socialist economy'.[178] At the same time, Labour economists (particularly Dalton) and the wider party membership less readily accepted Keynes' commitment to the market and private ownership.

The policies that would comprise *For Socialism and Peace* were presented to the 1934 Labour Party conference, where they were ratified emphatically. There was criticism from sections of the party, not least the Socialist League, which tabled 75 amendments to the draft document. These were reduced to twelve by the standing orders committee and focused largely on the perceived moderation of the document, with Cripps demanding that Labour commit itself to using emergency powers to ensure a 'decisive advance within five years towards a socialist Britain'.[179] Certainly, Labour's new programme bore the mark of the more considered approach of the NEC, TUC and NCL, suggesting that although the conferences of 1931–3 had been capable of pushing Labour to the left, the moderating influence of Bevin, Dalton, Citrine and Morrison remained dominant. Given the weak position of the PLP, even Lansbury and Attlee's sympathy for some of Cripps' more radical policies was of little consequence. Accordingly, the

Socialist League's position was dismissed as one of bombast, with Morrison's speech reiterating in detail the logistics of implementing public ownership reflecting more accurately the mood of the conference and the NEC.[180]

But *For Socialism and Peace* was not concerned solely with domestic policy. As its title suggests, a section of the programme dealt with international affairs, reflecting the party's growing alarm in response to capitalism's apparent 'drift towards another world war'.[181] Not surprisingly, Japanese expansionism, Italian Fascism and, from January 1933, German Nazism, had each begun to challenge Labour's position as a party of peace. Consequently, a somewhat protracted period of debate and realignment took place over the 1930s, as Labour sought to develop a coherent policy in response to the unfolding international situation

Initially, in 1931–2, Labour had continued to present itself as a party committed to collective security through the League of Nations, the Geneva Protocol and world disarmament, with the 1932 party conference declaring its 'unqualified hostility to the rearming of any country in any circumstances'.[182] Certainly, Labour registered its opposition to Japanese aggression in Manchuria, and the party similarly expressed its revulsion at Nazism from 1933. Herbert Morrison's *London News* included regular articles documenting the brutality of Hitler's regime, publishing extracts from *Mein Kampf* to demonstrate Nazi anti-Semitism, and urging a boycott of German goods and services.[183] On 12 April 1933, a mass meeting in opposition to German Nazism was held at the Royal Albert Hall under the auspices of the NJC to raise funds for those persecuted in the Nazi terror, while local parties throughout the country began to organise events responding to the 'fascist threat'. In Edinburgh, for example, the party's May Day events of 1933 included a talk by Dr Salis Daiches, a Jewish rabbi, on the persecution of Jews in Germany.[184] Nevertheless, the subsequent Labour conference endorsed a resolution moved by Sir Charles Trevelyan pledging the party 'to take no part in war and to resist it with the whole force of the labour movement', meaning recourse to a general strike if necessary.[185] In the immediate wake of Hitler's rise to power, it seemed that Labour was retreating towards a more overtly pacifist position.

Evidently, Labour's parallel commitments – to collective security and opposition to war – were becoming untenable. In Pethick-Lawrence's words:

> Up to then, it had seemed possible to ride at once the two horses of pure pacifism and loyalty to the League. But now it had become apparent that the time might come when they would take us in opposite directions. Loyalty to the League meant support of collective security and a willingness, if need arose, to co-operate in the application of sanctions. If there was actual aggression, that might involve us in war. It was therefore necessary for members of the Labour Party, individually and collectively, to choose which horse, in that event, they would continue to ride.[186]

Accordingly, as Hitler further revealed his militarist objectives, as Japan and Germany withdrew from the League of Nations, and as Mussolini began to cultivate his imperialist ambitions, so a variety of responses emerged across the Labour Party. Lansbury, as party leader, had long recognised the inherent contradiction of his pacifism and Labour's official foreign policy. But while this had been manageable in the relatively peaceful climate of the 1920s, it became increasingly unsustainable thereafter. For a man who believed Britain should 'stand unarmed before the world', the events of the early 1930s brought much soul-searching and, eventually, his resignation.[187]

Clement Attlee, who led the PLP for much of 1934 in Lansbury's enforced absence, had similar concerns as to Labour's official position. Writing to his brother in that year, Attlee complained that the party did not know whether it was 'to take up an extreme disarmament and isolationist attitude or whether it will take the risks of standing for the enforcement of the decisions of a world organisation against individual aggressor states'.[188] Certainly, Attlee led the way in opposing the government's plans for rearmament, and evidently took some time to reconcile himself to the changing international situation. However, his distrust of MacDonald's National government did not lead him to a pacifist position or the quasi-Marxist conclusions of Cripps. Indeed, Attlee stoutly defended the party's reaffirmed commitment to collective security at the 1934 conference, insisting the 'we cannot wash our hands of responsibility for [the fate of] socialist workers and comrades in other countries'.[189] Cripps, meanwhile, began to assert an increasingly 'pure' if impractical left-wing position. His basic premise was that capitalism led inevitably to war and, further, had paved the way for fascism. As such, fascism could only be fought in tandem with the class struggle against capitalism and imperialism. 'Whether the imperialism is British, French, German, Italian or Japanese, it is equally wrong', Cripps told the Socialist League conference in 1935.[190] From such a perspective, the League of Nations was dismissed as an 'international burglar's union' of capitalist states representing the imperialist interests of one group of countries over another. Simultaneously, the British National government could not be trusted with the deployment of sanctions; and nor could it be trusted with armaments that were likely to be used against the interests of the working class.[191] What was needed, Cripps and party left wingers such as Bevan and Wilkinson believed, was a 'united front' of working-class organisations opposed to fascism and war.[192] Accordingly, Labour was implored to advocate withdrawal from the League of Nations, to initiate an alliance with the Soviet Union abroad and with the Communist Party of Great Britain (CPGB) at home, and to oppose all measures proposed by the National government, including rearmament and sanctions.

Aspects of the Socialist League argument could rouse Labour sympathies. Relations between the party and the government were bitter, and Labour's obligation to the League of Nations was linked to its distrust of the British government's wider imperialist motives. Not surprisingly, however, the NEC rejected any suggestion of Labour joining a 'united front against fascism' with the CPGB. Not only was any link to the Communist Party seen to be electorally damaging, but most Labour leaders, including Morrison, Bevin and Dalton, retained a deep-seated distrust of the CPGB's motives and methods. In the same year that the communists had tried once again to build bridges with the Labour Party, the NJC produced *Democracy versus Dictatorship* (1933), a pamphlet that stated explicitly Labour's opposition to dictatorship in all its forms. In the words of Attlee, speaking to parliament in June 1934, 'we of the Labour Party are opposed to both communists and fascists. They are both out to destroy democracy, and they say so. They are both out to destroy free speech'.[193] Labour, by contrast, was committed to democracy and showing 'the world the peaceful path to socialism'.[194]

Eventually, therefore, Labour policy came to reflect the practical approach of the NEC and NJC/NCL. Already, by 1933, concern at the Nazi suppression of the powerful German trade union movement had brought unequivocal condemnation from the TUC. Moreover, Citrine and the TUC general council recognised that collective security necessitated the credible threat of military action. 'Moral resolutions are no good', Citrine told the TUC in 1935 in the midst of the Abyssinian crisis, '[There] is no real alternative now left to us but the applying of sanctions involving, in all possibility, war'.[195] Bevin, in particular, had remained nonplussed by the 1933 Labour conference's commitment to direct action, refusing 'to go on talking glibly, misleading the people and ourselves as to what we could do with the general strike weapon in the event of a world war'.[196] Significantly, too, such a perspective was shared by Dalton in the NEC. Consequently, the meeting of the 'three executives' (TUC, NEC, PLP) held on 28 February 1934 to formulate Labour policy trod a path midway between Lansbury's pacifism and the theoretical class analysis of Cripps. To this end, a draft memorandum, 'War and Peace', was presented to a further joint meeting on 28 June, removing Labour's commitment to a general strike, reasserting the party's belief in collective security and, crucially, conceiving of situations whereby Britain may have to use force to resist an aggressive power.[197] This – as Henderson noted and Attlee made clear during his conference speech – was effectively a reaffirmation of Labour's original policy: support for the League of Nations and a dedication to socialism, peace and disarmament. In the context of the mid-1930s, however, the potential ramifications of collective security in the face of fascist aggression were soon brought into sharp relief.[198]

Ultimately, Pethick-Lawrence's 'two horses' finally parted company at the 1935 party conference, as Mussolini's belligerence towards Abyssinia raised the immediate possibility of sanctions and military action. Pethick-Lawrence himself made a decision after 'great searchings of heart', finally accepting the need to take part in a 'common effort' to defend liberty and 'public right'.[199] And while some, including Thomas Johnston, tried to disentangle economic sanctions from potential military action, the Labour Party generally came to similar a conclusion.[200] Thus, in July, the NCL condemned Italian aggression, before the three executives met in September to draft a resolution to the TUC that approved the implementation of economic sanctions against Italy should it invade Abyssinia.[201] Come the Labour conference at the end of the month, and the TUC's endorsement of such a resolution paved the way for Lansbury's resignation. Following an unusually acrimonious meeting of the NEC on 19 September, after which Cripps resigned and Lord Ponsonby stood down as party leader in the House of Lords, Lansbury prepared to present his case to the party conference in the knowledge that the TUC decision would almost certainly be ratified. Famously, amidst a series of speeches that included a particularly blunt reply by Bevin, Lansbury's appeal was lost, and he subsequently tended his resignation as party leader.[202] In the meantime, the conference endorsed the NEC's resolution to support 'necessary measures provided by the covenant [of the League of Nations] to prevent Italy's unjust and rapacious attack upon the territory of a fellow member of the League'.[203] Peace, the Labour Party recognised, may now be dependent on war.

As the above account suggests, the evolution of Labour's foreign and domestic policy was informed to a notable extent by the outlook of the TUC. In the context of the early 1930s, Labour socialism prioritised the industrial over the social, thereby reflecting the more 'hands-on' role played by the TUC general council in the party from 1931. At the same time, evidence of greater trade union influence should by no means suggest that Labour became subordinate to the TUC, as the debate over 'national boards' demonstrated. If trade union leaders helped set the agenda and direction of the party in the 1930s, then the politicians – particularly Dalton and Morrison – informed the party's strategy and political detail. As such, Labour's realignment from late 1931 was less a turn 'to the left', as seemed briefly the case in the immediate aftermath of MacDonald's departure, and more an affirmation of its political independence and distinctiveness. Most obviously, the party moved to establish a clearly stated political programme from 1931, so forging a 'practical socialism' that showed as great a disdain for variations to the 'intellectual left' as it did compromise to the 'Liberal right'. In this, 'planning' and nationalisation were brought to the fore, with 'socialism' being presented boldly as an alternative to the uncertainties, inefficiencies and moral reprehensibility of capitalism. This, in turn, remained moderate, constitutional and cautious, but it was a socialism that married Labour's ideology to its industrial roots.[204] By 1933, it was possible for the NUR's Charlie Cramp to write:

> In the main the trade unionist today is a socialist. He does not quibble about academic points. He knows precious little about Karl Marx, but after listening to propaganda for many years he does believe that until the land, capital, resources, and skill of the people of this country are utilised for the people he will never obtain decent conditions.[205]

At last, socialism had become a word indistinguishable from the interests of labour.

IV. TENDING THE ROOTS

The political realignments notable in the higher echelons of the Labour Party from 1931 were complemented by a 'grass roots' drive towards recruitment, canvassing and the bold assertion of the party's socialist message. 'Our immediate task is clear', the NEC reported to conference in 1932, 'affiliated societies, divisional and local parties, and individual members must direct their energies and activities to the work of creating, by education and organisation, a mighty force of socialist faith that will carry Labour to victory ...'[206] Initially at least, given the circumstances of 1931–3, Labour had much to rally its members around. As the political temperature increased with a rate of unemployment that reached 2,979,000 in January 1933, so Labour dusted off its calls for 'work or maintenance' and condemned the various economies introduced by the National government.[207] In particular, the means test set up to assess rates of unemployment benefit payable to claimants became a major stick with which Labour could beat the government, its unpopularity allowing Labour to appear as the champion of the jobless even when the overall rate of unemployment began to fall steadily through 1933–5. Significantly, however, Labour's emphasis in the early 1930s was concentrated not so much on organising the unemployed as on presenting a planned (socialist) alternative to the National government's 'false economy'. This was controversial in that Labour continued to proscribe the communist-led National Unemployed Workers' Movement (NUWM), but it simultaneously allowed Labour to offer a constructive, as opposed to defensive, response to the problem. As Walter Citrine put it in 1936, referring to that year's hunger march of unemployed workers, after 'you have brought thousands of men at very considerable expense down to London ... at the end of it what is there? ... We decided as citizens, as politicians, as trade unionists, we would raise our voice wherever we could against the regulations and try to convert the general public to our point of view. That, in the long run, will be the soundest course'.[208] Of course, Labour members and supporters did take part in unemployed demonstrations, but the party's official emphasis was clearly based on mobilising for votes and members rather than mass protest.

To this effect, Labour moved quickly to limit the damage caused by the 1931 general election, launching a 'million members' campaign in January 1932 amidst a series of regional conferences featuring 'star speakers' and *Daily Herald* 'special reports'. According to figures published by the party conference later in the year, this met with some success, as 428,399 (gross) membership cards were supplied to the divisional parties prior to 31 August, compared to 297,003 (net) over the whole of 1931.[209] It certainly acted as a fillip to local party branches, and the following year saw the NEC announce the commencement of a 'Victory for Socialism' campaign. This sought to mobilise the party towards the next general election, to raise £50,000, to co-ordinate party and trade union activity in the constituencies, to issue monthly literature into 'every home', and to launch a nationwide 'platform campaign' to increase membership and support. The objective was parliamentary power, with the NEC targeting a return of 400 MPs.[210] Such a grand ideal would not be attained ('Victory for Socialism' raised £8,600[211]), but such initiatives arguably helped focus and mobilise Labour members following the morale-sapping experience of 1931. Although, come September 1935 on the eve of the general election, there were calls to 'ginger up' the campaign, individual membership had risen to a stated 419,311 – almost double the figure of 1929.[212]

The attempts to forge a more uniform and efficient party organisation referred to in the previous chapter were also continued into the 1930s, underlying Labour's belief that progress would come with co-ordination, a strong apparatus, and a mass membership. As well as the continued publication of *Labour Organiser*, an aptly titled pamphlet – *Party Organisation* – was regularly issued from 1932, offering guidelines for party officers and outlining model rules, account procedures, report forms, and suggesting various wider-party activities. '[Every] party should each year take stock of its general condition', the pamphlet instructed, with the objective of 'spreading the socialist idea' and mobilising 'an immense electorate for Labour'.[213] For Mary Agnes Hamilton, writing in 1938, the local parties were the 'training schools of service and of ideas', from where 'elections were won by the work done in the intervening period' via meetings and sustained members' activity.[214]

With regard to electioneering, 1932 saw moves to reorganise the party by-election fund in recognition of the 'difficulties' experienced by many constituency parties. Thus, the NEC recommended that the fund become compulsory to all affiliated organisations, with the objective being both to guarantee income and ensure more even contributions toward such activity. Discussion continued over 1932–3, with the NEC proposing in 1933 a scheme to regulate election expenditure. It was agreed, therefore, that trade unions were to contribute a maximum of 80 per cent to a candidate's election expenses, with the remaining percentage being found by the constituency party. A limit was also placed on the annual grant a union could pay to a respective constituency. This, of course, ensured trade union finance without overly dictating or centralising it, whilst simultaneously compelling divisional parties to bolster their own income via increased membership.[215]

Significantly, however, the party's emphasis on member recruitment and organisation led to something of a paradox. While, at a national level, the influence of the trade unions could be more readily discerned from 1931, then the membership campaigns at a local level helped augment expanding constituency parties that served to counter diminishing trade union finance and affiliates (not to mention the loss of the ILP). So, as the number of trade unionists affiliated to Labour fell from 2,044,279 to 1,912,924 between 1929 and 1935, the party's individual membership grew from 227,897 to 419,311.[216] Such figures are general and relative – affiliated trade union members continued to dwarf the number of individual party cardholders. However, they are indicative of Labour's shifting organisational base, revealing the extent to which constituency parties had developed since their official inauguration in 1918. In particular, the party's focus on the divisional apparatus helped facilitate Labour's gradual extension into non-union, less industrial areas, particularly in the South East. This, in turn, gave rise to demands in the constituencies for greater representation on the party executive and at the party conference. The ramifications of this will be discussed in the next chapter. Let us here, however, examine the social-cultural branch life that had developed within the Labour Party by the 1930s.

We have already considered the political activities expected of and undertaken by constituency party members throughout the 1920s, and such work obviously carried on into the 1930s. Indeed, meetings, door-to-door canvassing and electioneering would continue to take up the bulk of a party member's time. As noted above, membership campaigns were instigated by the NEC, while the annual round of municipal elections ensured Labour minds never strayed too far from the ballot box. Simultaneously, however, local parties became sites for a variety of social and cultural pursuits. These often had their origins in the pre-war labour movement, but local Labour members and parties evidently sought to maintain, complement and extend pre-existing trade union, ILP and Socialist Sunday School initiatives throughout the interwar years.[217] In Durham, for example, the annual miners' gala was a pivotal event for the local labour movement, at which county Labour MPs, candidates and leaders such as Dalton, Shinwell, Swan and Lawther were regular speakers.[218] From its inception, the Durham Labour Women's Advisory Committee concentrated much of its time on preparation for the gala.[219] Similarly, the party in Rhondda inherited a wide range of social and cultural activities synonymous with the South Wales mining community.[220] More widely, May Day was increasingly recognised again as an event through which Labour men and women could put on their best suits and frocks to display the party's message and unity of purpose. Although the weather could sometimes dampen the best intentions, many local parties put considerable effort into May Day events. To take a typical example, the Islington Borough Labour Party each year established a May Day committee to organise a band, decide what propaganda to disseminate, appoint marshals and determine the procession route (Manor House to Highbury, down Seven Sisters Road, Islington Road, Hornsey Road etc.).[221] The Nottingham party, meanwhile, was extolled for its May Day organisation in 1925. On this occasion, competitions (best decorated car, fancy dress, May queen) were arranged, publicity and photography organised, speakers secured, and the wearing of red flowers planned so as to 'flood the city' in Labour colours.[222]

But Labour's social-cultural activity was not necessarily so public or ceremonial. In practical terms, the socials, bazaars and whist drives organised in party or trade union rooms and clubs throughout the interwar period gave members an extra-political meeting place to develop friendships, identities and purpose. Of course, such activity made for busy people. May Banks, a member of the ILP in

Salford in the 1920s and Labour in the 1930s, later recalled her weekly diary comprising 'a proper kind of meeting on Monday evening, choir practice on Tuesday, events committee on Wednesday, dramatic society on Thursday, League of Youth on Friday, social and dancing on Saturday, and Sunday afternoons we had a Socialist Sunday School'.[223] As such, the holding of party socials became an integral part of Labour membership, providing a point of focus between election contests that helped sustain activity and members' interest. In particular, party social events were important in marginal Labour constituencies, where they no doubt gave succour to members who must often have felt that they were struggling against adversity. Over time, therefore, the social activities of local Labour parties merged into the political to form a distinct cultural space: an enjoyable evening or Sunday was also a means of raising funds for and championing 'the cause'. 'We must not only work our way to socialism', Herbert Morrison stated in 1934, but 'with joy in our hearts, we must sing in the course of the journey'. To this effect, he had in the 1920s helped instigate Labour choirs, a drama federation, and even a London Labour Symphony Orchestra. Indeed, the London party's annual reunion was a highlight of the yearly calendar, with members meeting every January to play whist, dance and sing.[224]

The range of activities organised by local Labour activists was extensive, and most parties included a social committee as part of their apparatus by the 1930s. In Ealing, for instance, a party that numbered 3,000 by the mid-1930s offered its members dances, sports clubs, a choir, an orchestra and a burgeoning Socialist Sunday School.[225] Party outings were also popular. Thus, the North Lambeth party toyed in 1927 between a 'circular motor coach tour' of 120 miles with tea on Saturday and Sunday, or a trip to Hampden Court followed by a boat trip to Windsor with tea and sandwiches on board.[226] In 1937, the Halifax, Huddersfield and Colne Valley parties organised a joint excursion to North Wales; the Caerphilly party even planned trips to Europe in conjunction with the Workers' Travel Association.[227] A number of parties organised children's outings to places such as Kew gardens, while annual picnics, Christmas bazaars and harvest festivals became typical features of local party life. Such events were usually diverse affairs, with an assortment of bands, competitions, stalls and sideshows. Accordingly, the Leeds party's annual gathering in 1937 included gymnastics, a magic show and fancy dress competition; in 1929, the Swindon party May Day festival included a balloon competition, beauty contest and firework display.[228]

Not surprisingly, sports were popular among Labour members, often taking the form of sports days and competitions, but also in conjunction with May Day or some other outdoor party gathering. Nationally, the party had supported the formation of the British Workers' Sports Federation in 1923, only to disown it once communists had risen to dominate the federation leadership by 1928.[229] In 1930, therefore, the NEC and TUC general council helped form a National Workers' Sports Association (NWSA), with G. H. Elvin as secretary. This remained a relatively small, if active, organisation, with 250 sections and 9,000 affiliated members recorded in 1935. A variety of sports came under the NWSA's remit, including football, tennis, athletics, cycling and swimming, with teams regularly travelling abroad to compete in international competitions such as the workers' olympiad.[230] Similarly, local initiatives were widespread if on a small scale. The Norwich Labour Party had, by the 1930s, a football team and a bowls section, while the Colne Valley Divisional Labour Party developed a billiards tournament in the mid-1930s to 'create opportunities for social intercourse between the members of the various [Labour] clubs'.[231] Similarly, the Edinburgh and District Trades and Labour Council established a football league in 1934, to which thirteen clubs affiliated and competed throughout the decade, while the Reading Trades Council and Labour Party was singled out for praise due to its 'most advanced centre', with football, cricket, tennis, swimming, netball and rowing sections.[232]

More experimentally, some Labour members began to embrace film technology. Certainly, the NEC was being pestered by Labour activists keen to utilise film propaganda by as early as 1917, although the party never fully embraced the idea prior to the Second World War.[233] True, the NEC recommended in 1919 that its literature, publicity and research sub-committee consider Charles Kendall's suggestion that the party form a production company to make Labour films, leading to a Labour committee on film propaganda (chaired by Sidney Webb). But little of substance came from the initiative.[234] Later, in 1929, the ILP launched the Masses Stage and Film Guild, though this was wound up in 1932 for financial and political reasons. In 1933, moreover, the Socialist Film Council was established by Labour intellectuals such as Raymond Postgate and Rudolph Messel, producing three films in 1933–4. Again, however, the project appears to have quickly subsided, leaving local parties in Cambridge, Sheffield and sympathetic film-makers (Paul Rotha) to take up the notion of Labour film.[235] As such, Labour was in this instance clearly playing catch-up with the Conservative Party. Just as Stanley Baldwin had mastered the use of radio broadcasts for issuing 'common sense' broadcasts to 'middle England', so the Conservative leader also took well to film. By as early as 1925, the Conservatives had deployed a daylight cinema van to fascinate and woo voters in the localities. And although Labour duly followed suit, owning two such vans by 1935, the Tories had by this time a fleet of ten.[236]

In addition to such leisure pursuits, Labour sought to maintain the educational traditions of the British labour movement. Alongside already-existing Labour colleges, therefore, divisional parties sought to encourage self-education and political discussion. In Manchester, for example, the borough party held lectures in the Clarion café, with a syllabus that included talks on banking, socialism, education and sex.[237] Typically, the LLP was very active in this area, arranging study circles, reading groups, and weekend schools at which Herbert Morrison would often speak on local government or other political issues. In the 1930s, Morrison organised an annual series of lectures on such subjects as 'Planning London for Socialism', many of which were delivered by esteemed and sympathetic London academics.[238] Certainly, those Labour activists included in Daniel Weinbren's *Generating Socialism* often referred to the educational role of the Labour Party, both intellectually and practically. Along with May Banks' recollection of members being encouraged to attend further education classes and gain degrees, Stanley Bell – later a Labour councillor in Kingston-upon-Thames – remembered how the party trained him 'in the procedures of civic activity'. Not dissimilarly, Scott Garnett described his time in the Beeston Labour Party in the 1930s as his 'political apprenticeship', recalling lively party meetings, running errands for the secretary, and taking responsibility for party literature. It was there that he had 'training in [public] speaking' and learnt to 'argue his corner'.[239] Nevertheless, evidence suggests that such cerebral activity was not to the taste of all

Labour members. Although the North Islington party insisted that it had done much to improve the educational facilities available to its members, it was forced to report that 'little advantage has been taken' of such opportunities. Attendance at lectures had been 'fair' but insufficient.[240] Similarly, low attendances at propaganda meetings prompted the Merton and Morden Labour Party to call for a 'socialist week' and campaign to follow May Day in 1937.[241] Ultimately, whist and tea remained the most common extra-electoral activity: parties such as that in North Islington could order draughts and chess sets for their party rooms, and lectures could be organised, but whist remained *the* pursuit of choice.[242]

The role of local Labour clubs in furthering Labour's cause and forging party identity is a subject that needs further investigation, although Savage has made a strong case for their relevance in Preston. Clearly, the establishment of a Labour club gave a party the means by which it could hold events, fund activity, and attract members and potential members into the Labour fold. Thus, the Labour club in Newport formed the basis of the party's superficially large individual male membership, with club members automatically being 'conscripted' into the party.[243] In the scattered division of Colne Valley, too, Labour clubs helped compensate for the absence of a concentrated trade union base, contributing to the constituency's committed Labour support and ethical socialist roots.[244] In Romsey, meanwhile, the Labour club opened by the party in 1928 became its headquarters and provided a meeting place for several unions and the local Women's Co-operative Guild.[245] Similarly, the monthly calendar of Colchester's two Labour clubs in 1925 revealed an almost daily round of dances, discussion classes, whist drives, music and party meetings.[246] As Stephen Jones has suggested, such clubs existed as 'social adjuncts of the labour movement', and though not always centres of political activism, were 'pioneers of new kinds of commodity production and distribution, and associational forms designed to encourage participation and mutual self-help'.[247] But in spite of this, the national Labour Party remained equivocal with regard to certain aspects of Labour club life. In 1927, the *Labour Organiser* replied to a query on the setting up of 'licensed clubs' that 'we do know licensed clubs that have been established by enthusiasts with the best motives that have degenerated into mere drinking dens, and proved a real obstacle to the promotion of socialist ideas'. Teetotal clubs were deemed to be 'more in harmony with the general ideas of our movement', but were obviously 'less paying'. As such, the journal advised caution and, if a club was established and a licence sought, suggested that 'rigid restrictions' be implemented so 'abuses do not creep in'.[248] Looked at more generally, however, we may conclude that by locating Labour physically and socially in the heart of their constituencies, Labour and workingmen's clubs helped broaden the party's social-political basis. Given that there were 2,692 clubs affiliated to the Working Men's Club and Institute Union by 1933, they remained an important part of (male) working-class life and thus an important site of potential Labour support.[249]

Much of the extra-political and educational activity outlined above was bound up together in Labour attempts to recruit young people to the party. To this effect, Labour Leagues of Youth (LLY) catering for individual members aged between fourteen and twenty-one were formed over the mid-to-late 1920s. The impetus for this co-ordinated approach to young Labour members appears to have emerged at the 1922 women's conference, although local youth sections, such as the London-based Young Labour League and the Rhondda Labour League of Youth, had already been established by 1920.[250] These, however, took a variety of forms and an NEC sub-committee was formed in 1923 to assess party youth work and recommend a scheme on which to base the party's subsequent youth organisation.[251] After some debate, the 1924 party conference endorsed the formation of Young People's Sections under the auspices of the divisional parties, with their own management committees, with two representatives on the divisional party general committee, but without consent to make political decisions or resolutions. The youth organisation was to be a 'training ground' for party members, yet it was not intended to 'over-emphasise their political side', prioritising instead 'recreational' activity, education, and 'participation in election work'.[252] By June 1926, some 185 sections existed, and it was decided to change the organisation name to Labour League of Youth, to establish a national advisory committee, and to provide for joint LLY–Labour Party membership up to the age of twenty-five ('Young men and young women are only just acquiring experience and becoming fit for leadership at twenty-one').[253] An annual conference was further held from 1929, and a monthly newspaper was produced, first as a *Bulletin*, then as *New Nation*. Come 1935, following an NEC-initiated campaign encouraging local parties to recruit young members – to which the party propaganda officer Maurice Webb was dedicated from 1933 – and it was reported that 526 LLY branches were functioning across the country.[254]

Unfortunately, the LLY had a troubled existence, with many branches forming only to disintegrate and reform ad infinitum. The reasons for their lack of success were numerous, although the party elders' attempts to keep politics off the LLY agenda was one major bone of contention. Some LLY members evidently felt restricted in their party membership: wheeled out to help in election battles but surplus to requirements in between times.[255] As noted above, the LLY was conceived primarily as a social or recreational organisation, with dances, rambles and sports activities supposedly to the fore. In such a way, the adult party sought to nurture the younger members, but not necessarily in ways that LLY recruits wished. Generational differences were often apparent, and older heads did not always appreciate the 'high spirits' of young Labour members. An understanding that 'without youth there will be no socialist majority' did not necessarily lead to concerted or sympathetic responses from the various divisional Labour parties.[256] Similarly, the NEC regularly blocked appeals by the LLY to exert a more significant influence within the party, although a youth representative was briefly included on the national executive in the mid-1930s.

Examples of local LLY problems are numerous. In Newport, the first step towards forming a young people's organisation was to buy four racquets and some tennis balls, before the inaugural conference of a Young People's League suggested its remit include a mixture of sport, dances and education. Politically related topics of discussion were allowed, such as 'is it imperative for a Christian to be a socialist?', but the results were not particularly impressive. Throughout the late 1920s and 1930s, the Newport party received complaints about the 'conduct' of League members, with the discovery of surreptitious liquor being smuggled on a Labour Party outing being one of the more serious offences. Nevertheless, the party persevered, forming a Labour League of Youth in 1933, setting up 'mock trials', and holding debates whereat the secretary Mr Chaplin talked in favour of fascism in the hope that the LLY would demolish his argument and 'squash him'. Still, an essay competition brought just one entry – 'Why I joined the League of Youth', written by the aforementioned secretary under the pseudonym of Osley Moswald. Clearly, the organisation of Labour youth was no easy task, even in a relatively large divisional party.[257]

In similar fashion, a North Lambeth Labour League of Youth was regularly established and disbanded by the 'adult' party over the 1920s and 1930s. After complaints about the behaviour of the then named Young People's Section in July 1926, Ernest Allen reported to the party secretary Sidney Harford that 'it was apparent to any stranger that there was strong antagonism to the parent body, both on the part of the [LLY] chairman and some of the male members, which created a sort of mild antagonism among the female members, or some of them'. Allen went on to say that he had to 'step in' to stop the section's discussion giving the wrong impression of Labour policy, an intervention that led to him, along with the party leadership in general, being 'attacked and abused'. Allen was then 'grossly insulted by [a] loud mouthed lad', with only one 'able and permissible girl' (Miss Gates) coming to his defence. Not surprisingly, he recommended that the party disband the section and reform the LLY.[258] Similar problems continued into the 1930s. At the end of 1932, following the temporary shutting of the party social club due to 'noise and trouble', the executive reported that the LLY was so 'difficult to control' that it had had to be closed down, suggesting it only be reorganised once the party had found a way to keep the 'high spirits in check'.[259]

Of course, there were sections that proved successful, and many members enjoyed the social activities and political discussions initiated by the LLY.[260] Branches of the LLY provided facilities and encouraged camaraderie among young Labour supporters; some met future husbands and wives there. In London, LLY members were even able to open a hostel in Hoddesdon (Hertfordshire) by 1933, providing young party recruits with pavilions for dancing, a camping field, library, tennis courts and other sports facilities.[261] Elsewhere, summer camps were organised, drama groups and bands established, and – inevitably – whist drives held by young members. In particular, rambling and cycling appear to have been popular pastimes: and ones that could often be combined with propaganda purposes. Finally, the educational role of the LLY prioritised by the NEC was given substance by its affiliation to the National Council of Labour Colleges. To this effect, at least one LLY member has suggested that he owed 'a lot to the League of Youth', gaining a 'better education in the [LLY] than at school'.[262] Ultimately, however, tensions remained, as we shall see in chapter four.

The impulses behind Labour's social-cultural activity were threefold: first, to develop the party's collective, ethical values, its sense of fellowship; second, to raise finance and membership in order to sustain the party's political activity; and third, to offer an alternative to capitalist or paternal-employer forms of leisure deemed detrimental to, or a distraction from, the workers' interests. In the main, the first two impulses outweighed the last, and such initiatives could not claim to rival the development and popularity of professional or non-associated sports and leisure cultures during the interwar period, most obviously association football, the pub, and the cinema. By the 1920s, commercialised leisure had become well established in Britain, and Labour succeeded mainly in supplementing, imitating or building on already existing working-class organisations and interests. In so doing, moreover, the party sometimes revealed the disparity that could exist between its own ideals and the lives of many workers, as the question of licensed clubs demonstrated. Additionally, for all Labour's encouragement of education and extra-political activity, the party was unwilling to commit the bulk of its (limited) resources to such ends; electioneering was prioritised and the pursuit of direct political ends evidently overshadowed the social-cultural objective of 'making socialists' by the 1930s. Finally, and linked to this, the party's objectives appeared better served via the implementation of municipal policies – extending funding to libraries, education, health and sports facilities – than setting up party equivalents, a perspective that was reinforced as Labour made local governmental progress over the period as a whole. Accordingly, the bulk of Labour members and, particularly, supporters, remained outside the immediate remit of the party and the wider labour movement. Alongside the glowing testimonies of contemporary members, the minute books of many a local party reveal the limited returns of Labour-sponsored initiatives, with 'poor attendances' and 'poor support' often being recorded.[263]

For all Labour's renewed emphasis on grass-roots activity, therefore, party progress was evident but limited. Taken generally, many divisional parties continued to face familiar problems throughout the 1930s. Membership in 'safe' or trade union-dominated parties remained low and often inactive, and although union representatives and members could help maintain a party organisation and provide both officials and voters for Labour, they did not always lend themselves to extending the party's appeal. Reports of union members' inactivity are legion.[264] Elsewhere, in contrast to some of the enthusiastic remembrances listed above, Owen Heather could recall party life in Withington (Manchester) in 1934–6 as being largely confined to the November municipal elections and the general election of 1935.[265] Similarly, the Storer Local Labour Party (affiliated to the Loughborough Labour Party) functioned with a registered membership of around fifty in the 1930s, with meetings sometimes attracting as few as four people. By 1937, the party was complaining that its work could not be done properly with so small an active membership.[266] More practically, a number of parties continued to experience financial problems in the 1930s, as the impact of the Trade Disputes and Trade Union Act combined with falling trade union membership to cause a loss in party income. Equally, a well-worn refrain continued to be heard: thus, from the Norwich party this time, 'it is noticeable that in every effort connected with our movement, we are apt to leave the bulk of the work to our women folk'.[267]

Even so, Labour's constituency parties survived the trauma of 1931, and were in many instances noticeably reinvigorated by the membership campaigns of the early 1930s. Politically, too, there was much for local Labour members to get their teeth into, especially given the rise of fascism abroad and the widely barren economic circumstances at home. The bitter general election contest, epitomised by the (false) National coalition claim that a Labour government would use post office savings to fund unemployment relief, was followed by a year of intense and often violent demonstrations organised by the communist-led NUWM. And even when the economy began to show signs of recovery from late 1932, its uneven nature meant that many areas – often Labour heartlands – remained in severe depression. Most obviously, South Wales, Scotland, the North East and Lancashire continued to suffer throughout the 1930s. As such, the introduction of the means test and its application by usually non-Labour public-assistance committees gave the party much political ammunition amongst suffering working-class communities, with unemployment remaining perhaps the central issue for Labour in such constituencies. Thus, Jack Braddock focused four of his six manifesto points on unemployment when canvassing for his re-election as Labour member for the Everton ward in Liverpool in 1932; several municipal election contests in Yorkshire were fought under anti-means test slogans in 1932–4; and campaigns to attract new industries were instigated, particularly following the introduction of the Distressed Areas Act in 1934.[268] On local councils, meanwhile, Labour representatives could simultaneously criticise opponents for not doing enough to alleviate the plight of the jobless while pointing to the shortcomings of the government to explain their own inability to do more. Only a Labour administration, armed with a socialist policy, could ultimately solve the problem of unemployment and, at the same time, raise the standard of living for the British people as a whole.

Given this, Labour soon showed signs of revival at a municipal level in the early 1930s. Despite the setbacks of 1930–1, the party made significant electoral gains from 1932, recovering much lost ground in its heartlands and showing signs of making inroads elsewhere. Come 1934, and Labour held majorities on three county councils, 21 county borough councils, eighteen non-county borough councils, fifteen metropolitan borough councils, and eleven Scottish burgh councils. So, where Labour had recorded a net loss of 238 provincial borough seats in 1931, the party recorded a net gain of 250 in 1933 and 305 in 1934.[269] Promisingly, too, Glasgow was won for Labour for the first time in 1933 (with ILP support), with a majority of nine rising to 28 in 1935; Norwich was finally won for Labour in 1933, as was Lincoln; Burnley was won in 1934. Places such as Sheffield, Swansea and Leeds were quickly regained and, notably, Labour took control of the London County Council for the first time in 1934, following a well-planned campaign that ran under such slogans as 'Let Labour Rule And London Flourish' and 'A Healthy London: Up With The Houses, Down With The Slums'. With its 69 councillors and eleven aldermen, Labour had a majority of sixteen and the mandate of 51 per cent of the electorate.[270] Although Labour remained a minority in local government over Britain as a whole, it was evidently a growing minority by the mid-1930s.

On the eve of the 1935 general election, the Labour Party appeared to have made up at least some of the ground lost amidst the traumatic events of 1930–1. The party organisation had retained both its trade union basis and its divisional party apparatus, while the overhaul of Labour policy initiated immediately following the defection of MacDonald had, by 1934, given rise to a practically applicable and relatively detailed political programme. As the economic situation continued to be bleak in many parts of the country, and as the threat of fascism increased over the 1930s, so Labour launched ever more critical attacks on what it regarded as a government complicit in the rise of reaction. Yet, Labour itself was in the process of coming to terms with its response to fascist aggression, losing its leader in the process of a major realignment in party foreign policy. Such change had, in turn, led to internal squabbles, most obviously with Sir Stafford Cripps' Socialist League. Moreover, Labour's new policies could not totally eclipse the memory of the previous Labour government. If Labour had made evident progress by 1935, therefore, its future development was by no means assured.

Chapter Four

Socialism, Peace and Democracy:
Labour on the Brink of War, 1935–9

The aim of socialism will be to see that every family in the country has a house with electric light and power for cooking, central heating, refrigerator and plenty of floor space, one in fact that is well-furnished with everything that a modern housewife needs.[1]

Clement Attlee, 1937

Twenty years after the close of the World War the dark cloud of an even more catastrophic world war casts its evil shadow over the assembly of representatives of the British Labour and Socialist Movement.[2]

George Dallas, 1939

The Labour Party entered into the 1935 general election with a new and 'temporary' leader in Clement Attlee, with no realistic expectation of victory, and with the record of the previous Labour administration still fresh in the minds of the electorate.[3] Labour was, unquestionably, the principal opposition to the dominant Conservative Party, but this eclipse of the Liberals meant that in many instances the party took part in a two-horse race with Tory National candidates who could point to a steady (if qualified) economic recovery over the preceding four years. Evidently, too, Labour's own recovery had been due in large part to the resilience of its trade union foundations, something that arguably reaffirmed the party's perceived identity as a sectional, class-based organisation in the minds of many. This, of course, was of less consequence in the old Labour heartlands, but continued to prove problematical in less-industrial, rural and middle-class constituencies, and was not yet a plausible (or effective) identity for the party in many developing 'new' industrial areas.[4] As such, this chapter will begin with a brief overview of the changing social-economic and political context in which the Labour Party existed in the 1930s, before assessing the development of Labour organisation and support over the decade.

In terms of policy, Labour continued to refine its programme for a planned transition to a socialist commonwealth. Most obviously, the party published an 'immediate programme' in 1937, outlining those measures that an elected Labour government would seek to enact during a full term in office. Much of this would prove relevant to the Attlee government of 1945, though recast via the subsequent upheavals of the Second World War. More central to our period, perhaps, were the measures introduced by Labour where it was already in a position of power: that is, in municipal government. Labour conceptions of 'municipal socialism' changed over the 1920s and 1930s, but the assumption of council responsibility was part of Labour's transition from a party of protest to one of authority. Given that the interwar period as a whole saw an increase in municipal activity, particularly in areas of health, education and housing, so Labour endeavoured to present itself as a party of local services and amenities. This, in turn, raised questions as to the responsibilities of Labour's council representatives, but it also allowed the party to exert potential influence over Britain's social-cultural development in certain localities. By the 1930s, therefore, there was evidence of the party establishing new bases of support in working-class neighbourhoods and on the housing estates synonymous with municipal authority.

Inevitably, Labour's history in the 1930s was entangled with the growing threat of fascism. As shown in the previous chapter, Hitler's rise to power and Italian aggression in Abyssinia had already led to a reinterpretation of Labour's traditional foreign policy by 1935, and such a process continued up to the eventual outbreak of the Second World War in September 1939. In particular, the Spanish civil war and Hitler's increasingly belligerent disregard for international agreement gave Labour causes to champion and a means by which to criticise the National government. As usual, different approaches and responses were apparent throughout the party. Ultimately, however, Labour's critique of appeasement helped undermine the Chamberlain government and allowed for Labour's eventual return to office as part of a wartime coalition in 1940. Five years later, of course, and the war's end would allow Labour to form its first majority administration.

I. LABOUR IN CONTEXT: BRITAIN IN THE 1930s

The trade union basis of the Labour Party ensured that its priorities and perspectives were shaped to a considerable extent by industrial-economic developments. In particular, union representatives of Britain's staple industries informed a significant proportion of Labour's (affiliated) membership, the Parliamentary Labour Party (PLP) and National Executive Committee (NEC) throughout the interwar period; Labour strongholds had emerged in and around localities based on the mining, textile, engineering, shipyard and transport industries. Consequently, the condition of these industries and the plight of those who worked in them were of obvious relevance to Labour, while the party's conception of Britain's economic well-being was largely informed by the experiences of such economic sectors. As noted previously, the British economy had performed sluggishly through the 1920s, as increased competition, the high value of the pound, and a lack of adequate (private and public) investment combined to ensure falling export orders, wage cuts and unemployment in many key industries. This, of course, was compounded by the onset of depression at the decade's end and the unprecedented growth in the number of those out of work. Come the 1930s, therefore, and the myth of returning to some pre-war 'normality' had been blatantly exposed. The following section will look at the social-economic context in which the Labour Party existed in the 1930s. This, inevitably, concentrates primarily on working-class employment and society, the principal 'spaces' in which Labour members functioned between the wars.

The British economy recovered over the 1930s, but it did so slowly, incompletely and inconsistently. While the staple industries generally continued to suffer, the emergence of more concentrated and technologically advanced 'new industries' took place gradually and in specific geographical areas, mainly the Midlands, London and surrounding Home Counties. As such, the effects of Britain's industrial-economic realignment varied from region to region, from place to place, and from industry to industry. Accordingly, unemployment remained a problem throughout the 1930s, only falling below 2,000,000 in 1936, and fluctuating between 1,400,000 and 2,000,000 thereafter.[5] Predictably, too, it remained highest in the old staple industries: in coalmining (where it averaged 19.6 per cent between 1923 and 1939), shipbuilding (36.8 per cent), and cotton textiles (20.7 per cent). Although there were signs of improvement in the mid-to-late 1930s, these were limited – staple exports remained someway short of their 1920s level – and partly undone by a further economic downturn in late 1937.[6] Thus, from a 'traditional' Labour perspective in South Wales, the North East, Lancashire, Yorkshire and parts of Scotland, economic recovery was a chimera: poverty, insecurity and unemployment remained very much a part of everyday reality for a great many people. Simultaneously, however, in other parts of Britain, there was clear evidence of economic growth. For example, industries such as those based on electrical engineering, chemicals, vehicle construction, silk and rayon, building and electricity supply 'increased their percentage of total employment from just above 20 per cent to more than a third' between 1923 and 1939, thereby accounting for 21 per cent of Britain's total net output value by 1935, compared to 14.1 per cent in 1924.[7] Indeed, low interest rates helped sustain a boom in the construction industry in the early-to-mid 1930s, providing both jobs and homes whilst also stimulating associated consumer activity. Employment in the service industries increased by 1,200,000 between 1931 and 1939.[8] Despite the existence of severely 'distressed areas', therefore, Britain's economy continued to grow by an average of 3.4 per cent between 1929 and 1937, primarily via the emergence of 'new', domestic and consumer-driven industries.[9]

Given such economic and technological developments, the composition of the British workforce changed over the interwar period. Certainly, Britain remained an overwhelmingly working-class nation, with manual workers comprising upwards of 75 per cent of the population throughout the 1930s.[10] However, there were shifts within the broad ranks of the working class as employment in the old staple industries declined. So, for example, the number of cotton workers fell from 621,000 to 288,00 between 1912 and 1938.[11] Mining, too, was especially hard hit, with its workforce falling from 1,162,800 in 1922 to 766,300 by 1939.[12] In South Wales alone, the coalfields that dominated the region were decimated between 1921 and 1936, as 241 mines closed down and a workforce that had numbered 271,161 fell to 126,233.[13] By contrast, there was a large increase in the employment of metal and light industry workers, with the number of machine-tool setters alone increasing from 12,000 to 112,000 between 1912 and 1951.[14] As for unskilled workers, those displaced by a decline in, say, dock work, could in some instances find ready employment in the building, engineering and metal trades over the 1930s.

Amidst such change, skill and associated wage differentials remained evident, although these had narrowed in the 1920s and persisted to do so over the 1930s. Unlike in the late nineteenth century, the wages of a skilled worker were generally 'closer to those of a semi or unskilled worker than to those of other social groups' between the wars.[15] That said, real wages continued to rise, especially among skilled and semi-skilled workers in continuous employment, before falling back slightly in the late 1930s in response to inflation.[16] Wage rates were also determined by the condition of a particular industry, suggesting that national trends should not lead us to forget the plight of those jobless workers – both short-term and, increasingly, long-term – caught in Britain's structural adjustment.

Furthermore, most unskilled workers saw their average earnings change little from the mid-1920s.[17] For working-class women, meanwhile, there were initially few opportunities for skilled employment occasioned by the development of new industries; the decline in textiles actually led to a loss of work in specific areas. Even so, there was a significant increase in female clerical and retail work; the number of women clerical workers grew from 180,000 before the Great War to nearly 650,000 in 1931 and to well over 1,000,000 by 1951.[18] For many young unmarried women, domestic service was often the principal option, while teaching and nursing allowed access to the lower professions.[19] Lastly, in geographical terms, structural changes in the economy led to a migration of labour. By the end of the 1930s, the proportion of industrial working-class families living in the Midlands and the South East had evidently increased.

Beyond the workplace, the interwar years witnessed various changes to people's living and social environment. By the turn of the century, the withdrawal of the middle classes from the old Victorian industrial cities had ensured that urban spaces increasingly became the preserve of the working class. Simultaneously, as the urban working population became more stable and settled, so distinct working-class communities developed, a process arguably consolidated by the introduction of rate controls in 1915.[20] Within these, complex networks of social contact and interaction formed alongside a rich associational culture to which the labour movement (party, union and co-op) generally had a connection. Of course, such development varied from place to place in terms of extent, substance and chronology. Nevertheless, as McKibbin has made clear, the working-class neighbourhood was a 'physical entity', replete with shops, cinemas, pubs, baths and libraries, to which people were deeply attached.[21] Underpinning it all, moreover, was the family unit, in which the working-class woman's role as mother and wife was pivotal.[22]

Such urban environments continued to evolve over the 1920s and 1930s. Most obviously, slums were torn down and replaced by better quality municipal and private housing. Although 58 per cent of all housing continued to be rented privately in 1938 (compared to 90 per cent in 1914), and much municipal housing remained beyond the wage packet of many working-class families, over 1,000,000 council houses were built between the wars, and over 4,000,000 people lived in them.[23] In many cases, municipal housing and a considerable proportion of private construction was built in suburban locations, something encouraged by the migration of workers from the declining staple industrial areas to the emerging 'new' industrial towns. Indeed, places such as Coventry, Slough, Oxford and Greater London grew dramatically over the 1930s.[24] This, in turn, allowed for an increase in the number of people who owned their own homes, primarily among the middle class but also among many working-class families in the expanding industrial centres. Moreover, changes within the urban environment were facilitated by the extension of municipal authority power over the early twentieth century, particularly during and after the Great War. This, of course, contributed to an improved standard of living for many, and simultaneously helped change conceptions regarding the benefits of public intervention.

Given such economic and social change, patterns of leisure were similarly transformed over the 1920s and 1930s. Alongside the aforementioned domestic improvements, the general increase in real income, the shorter working week from 1919, the gradual provision of paid holidays (extended to include eleven million workers from 1938), and the development of both private- and public-sponsored cultural initiatives all contributed to an expanding recreational environment. Of course, pubs, clubs, the bookies, doorstep and church remained an integral part of British life, but they faced increased competition from sports events, the cinema, wireless, hobbies, and a diversifying national press. The cinema, in particular, became a popular pastime; by 1935, there were 4,448 cinemas in Britain, with weekly attendances averaging over 18,000,000 in 1934. Radio, too, began to play an integral part in people's everyday lives, with 75 per cent of all households claiming a wireless by 1939.[25] Similarly, spectator sports such as football and dog-racing were attracting ever-larger crowds, while public dances gained in popularity and, less commonly, the motorcar allowed travel opportunities for those who could afford it. In effect, cultural and leisure activities became more accessible and diverse; in some ways, too, they became more domesticated (or private) in the form of the radio, reading (newspaper and magazine circulation and titles increased over the 1930s, more books were read), the football pools, and the various family-based pursuits facilitated by improved living conditions. Even so, such activity continued to take place primarily in a local context and was therefore rooted in the immediate community. Family ties remained strong, as did workplace connections for men, while supporting your local football, rugby, or cricket team could even strengthen a sense of local pride and identity.

The developments outlined above could not help but have an impact on the history of the Labour Party. In particular, they would help inform a gradual change in the composition of Labour membership, as we shall see in the following section. Measuring the extent to which social-economic trends impacted on Labour's support and identity is more difficult. There are, certainly, a number of factors suggesting a degree of working-class homogenisation over the interwar period as a whole, and these may well have proven beneficial to Labour. Not only were workers increasingly concentrated in sectors of manufacturing, trade and transport, but wage differentials narrowed across the working class, and the possibility and actuality of unemployment was a visible and widespread concern.[26] Trade union membership increased, and while the number of Labour-affiliated unions fell, affiliated union members to the Labour Party rose from 1,857,524 to 2,226,575 between 1934 and 1940, suggesting both concentration and expansion.[27] In addition, cultural activities became more universal over the 1930s, with 'people travelling more, and watching the same films and, increasingly, reading the same newspapers'.[28] By the late 1930s, the Labour-supporting *Daily Mirror* and *Daily Herald* were challenging the *Daily Express* and *Daily Mail* as the most popular newspapers, while regional press circulation continued to decline in contrast to the London-based 'nationals'. Perhaps, then, Labour's status as a workers' (or people's) party was consolidated by such developments, giving it a common identity within Britain's primarily working-class electorate. Indeed, the party's increasing individual membership and the growing importance of local constituency and ward organisation suggest Labour had been, and was continuing to be, successful in broadening its appeal across local communities. In other words, the party was becoming synonymous with the urban working class rather than simply the trade unionist or active socialist.

As always, we must be wary of such social-economic determinism. Labour leaders and members had to recognise and construct links between their politics and the experiences of the electorate in order for the party to tap into potential support. This the party did to a certain, if ultimately limited, extent. Nationally, the party's growing concern with the 'international situation' in the 1930s was complemented by its continued focus on unemployment, economic reconstruction and social welfare. This, in turn, reflected Labour's on-going local campaigns for improved social services and amenities, allowing the party to maintain its emphasis on improving the everyday lives of working people; something that gained credence as Labour won control of local councils and as municipal employment, housing and services more positively connected people with their local authority. Labour was undoubtedly the party most closely associated with the extension of local governmental power, endorsing public ownership of amenities, house building, municipal employment and social reform. In such a way, Labour evidently gained support on many of the new council estates built between the wars, where the party's affinity with the inhabitants would lead to regular reference (positive and negative) to estates being 'as "red" as the brick of which the houses were built'.[29]

Yet, the extent to which such contentious developments necessarily benefited the Labour Party must be qualified. Within any broad social-economic and political observation, ambiguities, fluctuations and inconsistencies abound. Most obviously, the extent to which urban areas became the preserve of the working class varied considerably, with places such as Birmingham retaining strong links to its Unionist elites into the 1930s. Structural changes often destabilised traditionally working-class areas, either in the form of unemployment and migration, or as a result of housing development. Equally, of course, local, religious and workplace differentials continued to exist, even if to less divisive effect. In particular, the experience of working-class women differed greatly from men, both in the home context and the workplace. For all its growing constituency apparatus and increased female membership, Labour generally remained a party associated with male trade unionism and employment, a masculine bias ingrained in the party's constitution. Similarly, if the party did relate – and speak a language recognisable – to large sections of the electorate in the 1930s, then approximately half the working-class population consistently declined to vote Labour. Labour support continued to be very region-specific over the 1930s.

Clearly, certain wider factors conspired against Labour in the 1930s. Primarily, the 'failings' of the second Labour government remained fresh in the minds of many and helped blunt the party's criticism of a National administration that – for all its faults and inadequacies – oversaw a moderate economic recovery. True, Labour's reassertion of its socialism and development of a more precise political programme established the party as a distinctive alternative to the Tory-dominated coalition. However, the radical overhaul of Britain's infrastructure proposed by Labour arguably rubbed against the grain of many people who sought stability rather than wholesale change. Second, at a local level, Labour's emphasis on intervention perhaps alienated as many people as it attracted; it certainly did not fit seamlessly into the generally self-reliant and contained working-class communities that existed in many parts of Britain. Local authority provision could mean intrusion as well as social support. Concurrently, Labour councils were often associated (rightly or wrongly) with higher rates, something that did not necessarily appeal to cash-strapped working-class families, however well the party underlined the long-term benefits of its collective approach. Third, if Labour's identity as an urban, trade unionist and working-class party was consolidated in the 1930s, then such a source of strength simultaneously made it difficult to appeal to other sections of society. This, as noted above, was conceivable with regard to women, but Labour's identity also sat uncomfortably with rural workers, the middle and upper classes, and – perhaps still – those workers who were not trade union cardholders. Many other people, of course, simply continued to have little interest (or trust) in politics. Fourth, as we saw in the previous chapter, Labour attempts to develop extra-political social activities generally failed to compete with the burgeoning 'commercial' culture of the 1920s and 1930s. For the Norwich Labour Party, it seems, emerging cultural trends were regarded as an impediment on the party's effectiveness, with the small attendances at the regular Sunday meetings in the Labour club being blamed on members' penchant for the radio. 'Can this class of entertainment take the place of lectures such as those given by John Morgan, Lady Noel Buxton, alderman Fred Henderson, H. E. Witard and others?', the party's annual report asked rhetorically.[30] Fifth, whatever the reality of Britain's economic and social development over the 1930s, it was possible to construct a variety of political interpretations. For Labour, its origins and basis of support ensured that the party campaigned on and highlighted the plight of those sections of society adversely affected by Britain's structural social-economic change. Such an emphasis was encapsulated in Hugh Dalton's address to the 1937 conference:

> [At] the height of a so-called trade boom, a million-and-a-half workers are still unemployed – hundreds and thousands for years on end. Millions are underfed, ill-housed and living in poverty. Millions are overworked and underpaid, with never even a week's holiday with pay. The cost of living is rising. This is what is called 'prosperity' today. And what of tomorrow? It is the natural law of capitalism that slump follows boom, as surely as night follows day. The government is making no preparation against the coming slump, when the whole country will become one great Distressed Area, unless, indeed, war comes before the slump. And then the whole country will become one great target for enemy bombs.[31]

But although this was a recognisable analysis of the time, it did not necessarily conform to the experience of many British people. While it may have struck a chord with Labour supporters in Rhondda, Rochdale or Jarrow, it did not necessarily reflect the worldview of someone living and working in Oxford or parts of Essex, let alone the still extensive rural areas of Britain.[32] As Savage and Miles have suggested, Labour could sometimes appear 'the party of old and decaying places, rather than the new and dynamic ones'.[33]

Ultimately, therefore, the Conservative Party remained politically dominant throughout the 1930s. Despite MacDonald's continuing as prime minister following the Labour government's demise, the Tories effectively determined the outlook of the National coalition government both before and after the 1931 general election. The Liberals, predictably, soon split amongst themselves and with the government over the question of tariffs, leaving the cabinet and the Commons benches largely in the hands of the Tories. But even before the Liberal division, the Conservatives had boasted 470 of the coalition's 554 seats. Come June 1935, at which point Baldwin replaced MacDonald as premier, and the cabinet comprised fifteen Conservatives, four Liberal Nationals and three National Labour representatives.

Significantly, too, Conservative political hegemony was not simply the product of Labour inadequacy. Arguably, support for the Conservative Party was consolidated by a recognisable shift in the social-political perspective of the middle classes between the wars. In Ross McKibbin's estimation, economic, cultural and political changes had contrived to bring together formerly distinct social networks of Liberals and Tories under one ostensibly non-political, but essentially Conservative, banner by the 1930s. This, in turn, enabled the middle class to forge a far more consistent political allegiance than the working class in the years up to the outbreak of the Second World War.[34] In this, the insecurities occasioned by the economic instability and industrial unrest of 1919–23 were informative, and were no doubt confirmed by the crises that consumed the second Labour government.[35] Given such circumstances, former Liberal shibboleths and the credibility of Labour socialism were both undermined. Of course, there remained clear distinctions within the middle classes, between the business sector and professional, the urban and provincial, men and women, and in terms of income, status and stability. There was also evidence of a growing sympathy for Labour and socialism among sections of the middle class, within both the intellectual milieu and among members of the growing lower middle class affected by the uncertainties and insecurities of the time. But this should not be exaggerated, as the 1935 general election result makes clear.[36]

Equally, large sections of the working class continued to vote Conservative. This again was not due simply to Labour's failings; the Tories were evidently successful in presenting themselves as the defender of the national interest and purveyors of 'conventional wisdom' in many constituencies.[37] Baldwin, especially, proved adept at portraying Conservatism as synonymous with British values and interests, famously utilising radio and film to do so.[38] As David Jarvis has demonstrated, initial Tory fears of the enlarged electorate led the party to concentrate on honing its message clearly and in a way designed specifically to present itself as a reliable response to Labour's dangerous socialist 'other'. Conservative associations sought to integrate working-class women and trade unionists into their ranks, simultaneously extending their influence (albeit with some uncertainty) into 'non-party' organisations such as women's institutes, ratepayers' associations and businessmen's leagues.[39] Even on issues closely related to Labour, the Conservatives could often present an effective counter. On housing, for example, the Tory image of 'the home' – as a private, safe place – could, for some, exert greater appeal than Labour's more communal representation. Labour depictions of the home often alluded to a woman's workplace rather than a site of cosy domesticity. Indeed, the Conservative emphasis on home ownership arguably had more aspirational appeal than Labour's municipal schemes. Finally, Tory housing programmes had sometimes proven successful, as in Birmingham and Newport. Tory paternalism could easily reconcile itself to the problem of city slums, and such an emphasis became clear once the National government economies of 1932 cut all general subsidies bar those for slum clearance, with low interest rates providing for private construction. By the early-to-mid 1930s, the housing boom was a key part of Britain's limited economic recovery, although issues such as rents, building priorities, and public or private initiative remained contentious political topics.[40]

But whatever the broad social-economic changes occurring in Britain over the 1930s – and whatever influence these had on Labour's wider historical development – the party would have had to stage a quite dramatic recovery to overturn the National government's majority in 1935. True, on the eve of the general election, the party had made some progress since the nadir of 1931. The PLP had increased in size, to 59, following a steady stream of by-election victories that had begun in Wakefield on 21 April 1932, and included further gains at Wednesbury, Twickenham (with a 17.8 per cent swing), Rotherham, Fulham East, Hammersmith North, Swindon, and Liverpool Toxteth (with an 18.9 per cent swing). The parliamentary party had also acquired three members as a result of returnees from the Independent Labour Party (ILP) and one disaffected Liberal (Major H. Nathan). But this was scant reward indeed; Labour would have needed to secure a massive 20 per cent swing in order to defeat the government in 1935.[41] More to the point, the timing of the election did nothing to help Labour's challenge, coming just weeks after Lansbury's very public resignation as party leader. Not surprisingly, therefore, a National government was once again returned, with 429 seats to Labour's 154.

Interwar Britain was characterised by notable structural social-economic change and a major realignment in its political configuration. The extent to which these two developments were linked is open to debate, although the history of the Labour Party reflected and informed both. This was not inevitable; it involved Labour adapting its organisational and political approach in order to establish the party within Britain's shifting and diverse social environment. It further relied on Labour members constructing and articulating an identity that related and responded to the communities from which they emerged and to whom they appealed. Such a process was invariably discontinuous, uneven and contingent. By 1939, Labour had won the support of well over a third of the British population, yet its transition from established opposition to majority government was evidently still in process.

II. SOLID FOUNDATIONS?
LABOUR ORGANISATION IN THE LATE 1930s

Organisationally, the Labour Party encompassed both continuity and change over the late 1930s. In purely electoral terms, the party appeared to remain on an all-too-familiar footing. As noted above, Labour was never realistically in a position to win the 1935 general election, although the eventual result was rather less favourable than certain leading party figures had predicted. Dalton, for one, expected to win at least 200 seats, and would have hoped for more (275) had the party been able to drop the so-called 'Red Indian bomb' – a government-associated document on conscription that Dalton and Morrison wished to leak to the press immediately prior to the election.[42] In the event, caution prevailed, the 'bomb' was not dropped, and Labour's 552 candidates won just 154 seats. In so doing, however, the party secured 8,325,491 votes – 38 per cent of the electorate and Labour's highest to date, with the anomaly between seats and votes being due primarily to the relatively small number of three-cornered contests in 1935. Clearly, in terms of seats, Labour had made up much lost ground but won little new. The party's parliamentary representatives remained concentrated in the same industrial localities and urban centres that they had done in the 1920s; in no British county other than Inverness, moreover, did the party match or better its 1929 general election performance (see Table 4.1). As this suggests, Durham, Yorkshire, South Wales, Lancashire, Staffordshire, London, Glasgow and the Scots mining regions continued to form Labour's bedrock. Even then, there were obvious disparities. Over Scotland as a whole, Labour's twenty seats came from a total of 63, with a further four going to the ILP in Glasgow and one to Willie Gallacher of the Communist Party of Great Britain (CPGB) in West Fife. Similarly, the results in Lancashire suggested that Labour had much to do if it was to make up the ground lost in 1931, with the party winning less than half the total seats recorded in 1929. In the Midlands, where Labour had made notable gains in 1929, the party took just nineteen of a possible 83 seats, none of which were in Birmingham.[43] Beyond Greater London, meanwhile, Labour's three Gloucestershire MPs were the only dashes of red throughout the whole of southern England.

	May 1929	*October 1931*	*November 1935*
Berkshire	1	0	0
Cheshire	4	0	0
Cumberland	3	1	2
Derbyshire	8	1	4
Devon	1	0	0
Durham	17	2	12
Essex	12	4	8
Gloucester	5	1	3
Hampshire	3	0	0
Kent	2	0	0
Lancashire	41	5	18
Leicestershire	3	0	0
Lincoln	2	0	1
London	35	5	22
Middlesex	6	0	4
Norfolk	3	0	0
Northants	4	0	0
Northumberland	5	0	1
Nottinghamshire	5	2	4
Salop	1	0	0
Staffordshire	14	0	9
Warwickshire	8	0	1
Wiltshire	1	0	0
Worcester	2	0	0
Yorkshire	39	7	27
Brecon and Radnor	1	0	0
Carmarthen	2	1	2
Denbigh	1	0	1
Glamorgan	16	10	11

	May 1929	*October 1931*	*November 1935*
Monmouth	5	4	4
Aberdeen	1	0	1
Ayrshire	2	0	1
Berwick and	1	0	0
Dumbarton	2	1	1
Dundee	1	0	0
Dunfermline	1	0	0
Fife	2	0	2
Inverness	0	0	1
Lanark	17	3	9
Linlithgow	1	0	1
Midlothian-Peebles	4	0	1
Renfrew	2	0	0
Stirling and	3	0	3
Total	287	46	154

Table 4.1 Distribution of Labour Party Parliamentary Seats, 1929–35

Despite this, the increase in the Labour vote was significant, suggesting that the party was beginning to spread its appeal more widely. Most importantly, perhaps, Labour was able to pick up votes in areas where it had barely made an impression in the 1920s. For example, the Labour vote in Chelmsford increased from 4,060 (22.8 per cent) in 1929, to 11,690 (29.2 per cent) in 1935. During the same period, the Labour vote in West Lewisham grew from 10,958 (25.9 per cent), to 14,803 (35.3 per cent); in Bedford from 9,147 (25.1 per cent), to 13,604 (37.7 per cent); in Ilford from 11,952 (20.7 per cent), to 25,241 (36. 9 per cent); and there were similar increases in places such as Oxford and Luton.[44] Labour still fell short of winning these seats of course, but such constituencies appeared far more attainable in 1935 than at any time previously. Ultimately, however, it would need the deteriorating international situation and the complex social-political changes affected by the Second World War finally to undermine Tory support and translate Labour minorities into majorities. Of the seats listed above, Labour won all except Oxford in 1945.

Once elected, the PLP comprised 79 trade union-sponsored members, 66 divisional party members, and nine co-operators in November 1935. Of the trade union MPs, 34 were miners, seven were sponsored by the Transport and General Workers' Union (TGWU), six were railways clerks and four supported by the National Union of Railwaymen (NUR); the National Union of General and Municipal Workers (NUGMW) backed six successful parliamentary candidates, the National Union of Distributive and Allied Workers (NUDAW) five, and the Amalgamated Engineering Union (AEU) three. Most significantly, perhaps, all six candidates sponsored by the United Textile Factory Workers' Association

(UTFWA) failed to win their respective seats.[45] Generally, however, changes in PLP composition over the 1920s and 1930s were relatively minor with regard to the number and sponsorship of trade union MPs, as demonstrated if we compare the 1935 PLP with the similarly sized parliamentary party elected in October 1924. Then, 88 trade union MPs sat with 25 divisional party members, 29 ILPers, one Fabian, three SDF members, and five co-operators (see Table 4.2).

Sponsor	1924	1935
Trade Union	88	79
Divisional Party	25	66
Co-operative Party	5	9
ILP	29	0
Fabian Society	1	0
SDF	3	0

Table 4.2 Composition of the PLP in 1924 and 1935

Thus, trade union-sponsored MPs continued to form the highest percentage of members within the PLP. Nevertheless, the number of unions backing MPs had become more concentrated, and there was a small increase in the number of general and clerical union sponsored members. The mining contingent remained predominant, if slightly reduced.[46] More striking, therefore, was the growing importance of the divisional Labour parties. True, there was no repeat of 1929, when divisional party-sponsored MPs outnumbered their trade union colleagues, but this belied the fact that 395 of Labour's 552 candidates were financed by their constituency organisation in 1935.[47] Clearly, the divisional organisations had stepped into the breach left by the ILP's departure, and there were further signs that the constituency parties would form the basis of Labour growth in other parts of the country (see below). Finally, the figures show evidence of the on-going attempts by Labour to harmonise its relationship with the co-operative movement. A series of meetings between representatives of the NEC and Co-operative Party had taken place following the establishment of a national joint committee in 1927–28, with the objective of formalising an effective *modus operandi* between the two organisations, particularly during election time. Partly as a result of this, ten co-op sponsored MPs had been elected in 1929, and nine were returned to parliament in 1935. While the Co-operative Party continued to decline Labour invitations to affiliate and join the National Council of Labour (NCL), there were further moves from 1935 to overcome remaining local obstacles to electoral collaboration.[48]

Whatever its limitations and ambiguities, the election result at least ensured a more prominent and assertive Labour opposition in parliament. In this, the return of 'known' Labour politicians such as Morrison, Dalton, Alexander, Clynes, Johnston and Shinwell was obviously significant, both in terms of public profile and in taking the burden off Attlee, Cripps, Greenwood and, to a now lesser extent, Lansbury. Similarly, a number of experienced PLP and NEC members returned to give solidity and competence to the parliamentary party, among them Roberts, Compton, Robinson, Lathan and Walker. As this suggests, the long-standing trade union members of the PLP executive (Williams, Morgan Jones, Grenfell) were from 1935 accompanied by those more closely associated with the formation of Labour policy (Morrison, Dalton, Lees-Smith, Pethick-Lawrence). Less positively, just one of the party's 26 women candidates was elected: Ellen Wilkinson as the MP for Jarrow. Although not especially youthful – only ten of the PLP were under forty – the parliamentary party post-1935 undoubtedly displayed a more vibrant character than its predecessor.[49]

As for the leadership, the 'temporary' position of Attlee was soon made permanent. Nevertheless, the leadership contest of November 1935 was keenly fought, with Herbert Morrison and Arthur Greenwood standing as alternatives to Lansbury's former deputy. Morrison's already bright star had risen further in accord with his growing stature on the NEC, and this was confirmed with the success of the London Labour Party (LLP) in winning the London County Council (LCC) in 1934. As such, Morrison had some notable support, most obviously from Dalton, Wilkinson, and amongst party intellectuals such as Pethick-Lawrence, Laski, Pritt and Cripps, the latter of whom regarded Morrison as the 'ablest and soundest man in the labour movement'.[50] Greenwood, too, could boast significant support within the party apparatus, having proven an effective minister for health, and having worked closely with the trade unions as secretary of both the research department and the policy sub-committee. Accordingly, he initially secured the backing of Bevin's Transport House and a number of northern trade unionist MPs.[51]

Despite such a challenge, Attlee held the day come the PLP vote on 26 November 1935, winning the first ballot with 58 votes to Morrison's 44 and Greenwood's 33. In the second ballot, Attlee polled 88 votes to Morrison's 48. With hindsight, such an outcome was not overly surprising. Greenwood was a well-respected and potentially gifted politician; but his penchant for alcohol undoubtedly lost him much support. As a man about whose drinking even Winston Churchill made jovial reference, Greenwood was not trusted to be a reliable party leader.[52] Morrison, meanwhile, had talents that were not necessarily recognised by MPs beyond the capital. His closeness to MacDonald, his distance from Ernest Bevin, his opposition to mandatory trade union representation on the boards of Labour's proposed nationalised industries, and his relative lack of parliamentary experience all seem to have worked against him. The support of the party intelligentsia, too, was something of a poisoned chalice so far as many trade unionists were concerned. Evidently, therefore, a number of union-backed MPs switched their vote from Greenwood to Attlee on the second ballot. This is not to suggest that Attlee became Labour leader by default. He had proven an effective parliamentarian, famously taking up more column inches in *Hansard* than any other Commons member in 1932, while his ostensibly quiet but committed persona was a prefect antithesis to the still potent spectre of MacDonald. In short, he was trusted, liked, competent, and more party 'chairman' than party 'leader' – representative rather than individualist. He also had the backing of the miners' MPs, to whom he had shown regular support; David Grenfell (MP for Gower) and Tom Williams (Don Valley) proposed Attlee's candidacy, Jack Lawson was among his closest parliamentary friends, and his initial appointment as temporary leader had rested on the bedrock of miners' MPs elected in 1931.[53] Subsequently, Greenwood was adopted as deputy leader following Morrison's rather bitter rejection of the post, while rumours of a further Morrison challenge to Attlee surfaced sporadically in 1937 and 1939.

Beyond the Commons, the NEC maintained its relatively stable and continuous membership, giving the wider party an important semblance of solidity and consistency. Among its 24 members (26 from 1937), nine served continuously between 1931 and 1940; namely three trade unionists, Hirst (TGWU), Roberts (Typographical Association) and Robinson (NUDAW); three constituency party representatives, Dallas, Morrison and Dalton; and three women's representatives, Gould, Lawrence and Adamson. These and other long-serving members such as Clynes, Lathan and Dobbs further continued to comprise and oversee the policy sub-committees, while each of the principal unions – miners, textile workers, transport workers, general and municipal workers, railwaymen, engineers, distributive workers, and ironworkers – were habitually represented on the executive. Simultaneously, the NCL continued to exert its influence under the constant joint secretariatship of Citrine, Middleton and H. Scott Lindsay; so much so, that a delegate of the Eastbourne divisional party moved a resolution at the 1939 party conference complaining that the NCL was exceeding its advisory functions and usurping the authority of the NEC.[54] The resolution was easily defeated, and the NCL and NEC retained firm control over the party organisation, policy and conference. Indeed, the NCL was named as 'the authority for the labour movement' in August 1939.[55] Although the executive registered seven defeats at conference during the relatively tumultuous period of 1932–3, it was rarely defeated thereafter.[56] Moreover, none of the defeats prompted a major realignment of party policy or strategy; where conference decisions went beyond the desired remit of the NEC, they were simply ignored or buried in subsequent policy procedure. For example, the commitment to nationalise the joint stock banks was quietly dropped from the party's agenda over the 1930s.[57] While potential 'loose cannons' could still be elected onto the NEC, usually meaning intellectuals such as Cripps or Pritt, they were assuredly outnumbered. As we shall see, the NEC even felt confident enough to accept a change in its constitution from 1937, approving local party demands for an increase in the number of constituency party members represented on the executive and a change in voting procedure.

Crucially, perhaps, such stability was similarly apparent in the cadres staffing Labour's head office. Even where changes were made – usually out of necessity rather the expediency – there remained evident continuity. This was certainly true with regard to three principal appointments. First, George Shepherd became national agent following the death Egerton Wake in March 1929. Shepherd, a former shop worker from Spalding, had worked closely with Henderson and Wake throughout the 1920s and quickly gained credit for the maintenance of the party organisation during the 'dark days' of 1931–2. He would eventually retire in 1946. Second, James Middleton became acting party secretary following Arthur Henderson's resignation in May 1934, finally taking up the position permanently on 28 November. Middleton had served as assistant party secretary since 1903, assuming Henderson's responsibilities when the latter travelled abroad, which was often in the early 1930s. Third, Mary Sutherland replaced Marion Phillips as chief women's officer in 1932. Having gained considerable experience as the party women's organiser in Scotland, Sutherland essentially took up where Phillips left off, overseeing the women's department in loyal deference to the party executive. She retained the position through until 1960.[58] As this suggests, changing faces did not necessarily lead to changing methods or relations within the party hierarchy. In terms of the centrally appointed party organisers, all nine female district organisers employed by the party 1939 had held their positions since at least 1932, with seven having been appointed organisers following the adoption of Labour's 'general scheme of organisation' in 1920 (Anderson, Fenn, Tavener, Somers, Townley, Francis and Andrews).[59] The turnover of male district organisers had been more notable. Even so, six men retained their position as district organiser between 1932 and 1939 (Lewcock, Atkinson, Kneeshaw, Jones, Morris and Woodburn).[60] Such consistent contact between the party centre and the divisional parties (and vice versa) can only have benefited Labour, allowing the party to sustain and cultivate its organisation throughout the 1930s. Equally, contact was maintained via the steady stream of leaflets and posters produced by the policy committees and Will Henderson's press and publicity department.

Changes in the party's composition were arguably more notable at the grass roots, certainly in terms of Labour affiliation. The party's interwar 'high-point' in terms of membership was reached back in 1920, when Labour boasted 4,359,807 members. Of these, 4,317,537 were affiliated trade unionists from 122 trade unions. By 1930, following the general decline in union membership and the 1927 Trade Disputes and Trade Union Act, the party registered 2,069,697 members, 2,011,484 of whom were affiliated via 89 trade unions. In addition, the party included 277,211 individual members, with a further 58,213 affiliated through their socialist society or the Royal Arsenal Co-operative Society (RACS). Come 1937, and the affiliated trade unions continued to provide the bulk of the party's 2,257,672 members. However, just 70 unions now contributed 2,037,071 members, with individual party cardholders accounting for 447,150. A further 43,451 members affiliated through their socialist society, professional association, or the RACS.[61] Thus, while trade union levels began to recover from the mid-1930s, the number of individual party members provided an equally significant source of party growth.

Certain other trends were evident amidst the party figures. As trade union membership recovered from 1933, there was a notable increase in the number of organised service and consumer industry workers, particularly in sectors such as food and drink, clothing, and distribution. This, in turn, was reflected in the composition of the party conference. So, for example, the NUDAW affiliated 150,000 members to the Labour Party in 1938, compared to 93,712 in 1927. Even more impressively, the size and influence of Bevin's TGWU grew significantly over the 1930s, affiliating to Labour with 337,000 members in 1938, compared to 250,000 in 1927. And while there was a recovery in the health of the miners' union (union density was up to 81.1 per cent by 1939) and on the railways (67.2 per cent), both the Miners' Federation of Great Britain (MFGB) and NUR recorded membership levels lower in the late 1930s than in 1920s. Where the MFGB had affiliated with 800,000 members in 1927, it did so with 442,875 in 1938; the respective figures for the NUR were 340,108 and 224,809. As for the textile workers' union, industrial decline ensured that its Labour-affiliated membership fell from 289,866 members to 129,890 between 1927 and 1938.[62] Of course, these remained large and important trade unions, and their domination of the party conference continued. As noted above, structural change in Britain occurred gradually and unevenly, and this was reflected in the ranks of the Labour Party. Nevertheless, degrees of influence at conference were slowly shifting; a development encapsulated in Bevin's growing authority.

With regard to individual party members, Labour claimed an interwar peak of 447,159 in 1937, compared to 214,970 in 1928. Measured in percentages, this meant that individual party cardholders accounted for 17.7 per cent of the overall Labour membership in 1937, compared to 9.4 per cent in 1928.[63] Within this, there were approximately four individual men for every three individual women members, a differentiation that remained broadly consistent amidst the rise and fall of general individual membership over the 1930s. Thus, there were 222,777 individual men and 158,482 individual women members in 1934, 258,761 and 189,090 in 1937, and 175,606 and 128,518 in 1940.[64]

Interestingly, the extent to which women continued to join the party primarily through the established women's sections appears to have declined over the 1930s. Accurate figures are difficult to ascertain, as women's sections constantly formed and reformed over time, and as the party did not differentiate between its individual male and female membership until 1933. Even so, the party claimed 1,601 women's sections in 1938, compared to 1,969 in 1930, while attendance to the Labour women's conference fell notably over the decade. Thus, the 1937 women's conference attracted just 489 delegates, compared to 1,184 in 1930. At the same time, individual female membership continued to increase, from 154,790 in 1933, to a peak of 189,090 in 1937.[65] For Pamela Graves, such figures are suggestive of women becoming more integrated into the Labour Party, relinquishing those campaigns that sought to advance women's status within the party, or that focused on specifically gendered issues, favouring instead broader social-political issues that ranged from housing to unemployment to the threat of fascism and war. These, Graves argues, were increasingly expressed from a class (or community-based) perspective, rather than in overtly gendered terms.[66] Certainly, the proposed constitutional changes of the 1930s did not excite any significant campaign from the party women, nor was there any protest once the adjustments of 1937 failed to address the relatively marginalised position of women within the overall party structure (see below). Indeed, the extent to which men and women shared responsibility and power within the party remained grossly disproportionate. The changes to the party constitution in 1929, whereby local parties could only send a second delegate if they had over 2,500 female members, made women an even rarer sight at the Labour conference in the 1930s. Equally, fewer women were selected to stand in the 1935 general election (26) than in 1929 (37), while women remained a minority on the executive committees of their constituency and local level parties, as they did within the Labour groups elected to municipal government.

Despite such obvious inequality, certain factors lend credence to Graves' view. Certainly, the organisational sub-committee report to the NEC following the death of Marion Phillips in 1932 suggested that younger Labour women were less 'swayed' by the 'sex antagonisms or sex interests' of the suffrage generation, noting that men and women were 'joining together in all phases of common party work'.[67] This was often the case. Not only did the expanding branch life of local Labour parties bring men and women together, but the social-political issues predominant in many local party programmes, such as housing, health and unemployment, had indeed begun to blur the distinction between male and female political 'spheres'. Even so, the NEC was not sufficiently convinced to dissolve the women's sections, as the report proposed. Second, party membership figures do suggest that divisional women's sections became less significant over the 1930s, even in those divisions which maintained a sizeable number of female party cardholders. In York, for instance, where over 100 members had informed the party's women's section in the 1920s, approximately ten did so in the early 1930s. Even so, the party could still claim 379 individual female members by 1935.[68] Third, it is possible to discern a greater recognition, or acceptance, of female participation within sections of the Labour Party in the 1930s. In London, for instance, Herbert Morrison actively encouraged women to seek election to the LCC; a quarter of those Labour councillors elected in 1934 were women.[69] In the same year, Labour's 729 London borough councillors included 150 women, with sixteen in Southwark, fifteen in Hackney and Bermondsey, twelve in Stepney, and eight in Poplar.[70] Such a trend was made possible by Labour's municipal advance, which enabled women to be co-opted onto local authority committees over the interwar period.[71] Thus, as female Labour candidates began to be elected onto municipal councils, so the scope for women's intervention into the political arena widened. Of course, obstacles and prejudices continued to hamper progress; female councillors were often marginalised, ignored or belittled by their male 'colleagues' on their election. However, the extension of accepted (or expected) municipal responsibility brought politics into areas to which women were the acknowledged experts. As Hannah Mitchell recalled, when she sat on relief committees she 'knew just how much food could be bought out of the allowance, knew the cost of children's clothes and footwear, could tell at a glance if an applicant was in ill health'.[72] From such positions, women contributed to the enactment of important practical reforms beneficial to their constituents: building health clinics, maternity centres, wash houses, parks and play grounds, all of which helped to extend Labour's appeal and to provide women with a distinctive and important role within Labour and municipal politics.

Yet, it would not do to overstate the extent to which a woman's experience in the Labour Party changed during the 1930s. As Graves makes clear, women's sections remained an essential and established component of many a divisional party, with female members continuing to meet together and engage in distinct types of activity – organising bazaars and jumbles, canvassing, arranging party socials. Although Margaret Gibb could bemoan the lack of new faces in certain Yorkshire women's sections in the 1930s, the party organiser for the North East would later recall that women's organisation continued to develop over the decade via regular conferences, meetings and party schools.[73] To this effect, the Durham Labour Women's Advisory Council in the 1930s, as in the 1920s, maintained its focus on educational initiatives, including the provision of scholarships for the annual summer school at Barrow House, along with its regular contribution to the annual miners' gala.[74] Furthermore, we have already seen that women's sections had from their inception discussed a wide range of topics, and such variety was maintained into the 1930s. Certainly, the topics discussed by the party women's section in Bishop Auckland ranged from health matters and issues raised in *Labour Woman* to lectures on capitalism and 'surprise items' – which could mean the reading of a Tennyson poem or a song performed by local children.[75] In Seaham, too, discussion of Manny Shinwell's articles for *The Socialist* and events in Spain complemented rather than replaced the lectures given on children's health and the usual round of party socials and outings.[76] A focus on 'traditional' women's issues evidently remained. Thus, Mrs Lambeth's lecture to the Crook women's section on 'the adaptation of the home to modern conditions' demonstrated how 'women need to stay in their homes, but now the house was a sort of café, a place where we eat and sleep. Cinemas and all sorts of attractions took women out of the house, and the fact that we were meeting together ... proved that.' The labour-saving devices of modern housing meant that women must 'educate ourselves for the leisure that was coming', she continued, offering a roll call of the box mattresses, hoovers, electric irons, sewing machines, mops and scales that would be of 'great help' to women.[77]

In Manchester, Karen Hunt has argued that women's campaigns and discussion continued to 'galvanise' Labour Party women in the 1930s.[78] To this effect, the Manchester Labour Women's Advisory Council (MLWAC) organised conferences on maternal mortality in 1933 and 1934, before the very public death of Molly Taylor – a 19-year-old who died after being turned away from St Mary's Hospital and giving birth on the hospital steps – made the issue a prominent one in Manchester politics. Notably, too, the MLWAC called for the 'cessation' of free voting on issues such as housing, education and maternity services within the Labour group on the Manchester city council, thereby endeavouring to ensure that such concerns were treated as party (rather than personal) political issues. As this would suggest, topics such as family allowances, maternity and birth control continued to be discussed by Labour women alongside reports of general party activity and political education. This was certainly true with regard the Gorton Labour Party women's section, and was also the case in Loughborough, where Labour women keen to emphasise the need for female municipal candidates got involved in raising aid for Spain alongside campaigns for new maternity homes and improvements in local child welfare.[79] Nationally, of course, Labour's policy review of the 1930s meant that social welfare issues relevant to women (and men) were not forgotten amidst the more prominent plans for nationalisation, with close attention paid to maternity care, education and wider social provision integral to the party's 'practical socialism'.[80] Equally, the topics that informed the annual women's conference did not see a dramatic shift in emphasis over the interwar period. In 1924, the conference discussion included education, maternity care, women's wages, housing, rents, pensions, and disarmament; in 1928, it included birth control, nursery schools, pensions, maternal mortality, disarmament, and the mining situation; in 1933, it included housing, disarmament, unemployment, school meals, and fascism; in 1937, it included a children's charter, pensions, maternity care, housing, Spain, and unemployment.[81]

Finally, many women's sections continued to function in a more introspective and primarily social manner. Although the Sedgefield Federation of Women's Sections did occasionally hold lectures on topics such as 'socialism under a socialist government', the bulk of its time was dedicated to fund-raising, socials, and the evidently popular annual egg-dyeing competition.[82] Likewise, the minutes of the small Merton women's group in the 1930s record an organisation concerned mainly with its social evenings and whist drives. The section was called upon to address envelopes at election time, but discussions with regard to jumble sales and the formation of a tennis club appear to have prompted greater urgency. Thus, the minutes for the section meeting of 21 March 1933 recounting a recent whist evening read:

> A very enjoyable evening was had. There were five-and-a-half tables, being 22 players, ten
> hands were played, then a short interval for refreshments. Coffee, tea, cakes etc being

handed round to the players. We had a raffle, there being a very nice cake made and given [by] Mrs Webb, a Guild member. Mrs E. Greedus won this. We then resumed for the other ten hands ... Mrs Welsh kindly came along and helped considerably with the refreshments.[83]

As such, women members and women's sections remained very much a part of the Labour Party organisation over the 1930s. Again, what this entailed, and the extent to which women were welcomed or able to exert an influence within their respective parties, could depend on local circumstances, traditions, and wider national political priorities. No doubt, closer research would reveal significant regional variations in the experience of female party members. While the trend towards integration noted by Graves was evident, women continued to contest their place within the party and continued to discuss gender-related issues. In many instances, there continued to be an ambivalence as to the exact role of the party women's sections. Male activists could still conspire both to alienate and quash the input of actual and potential women members, as Savage has demonstrated with regard to Preston.[84] In 1935, moreover, Betty Fraser of the London University Labour Party spoke to conference about the 'considerable difference' in approach among local parties. Where some continued to expect their female members to 'make tea and do the washing up', she reported, others encouraged their women members to discuss politics and assume an effective role within the party organisation.[85] Equally, ageing membership, indifference and poverty conspired to hamper activity in a number of places.[86] At the same time, women were undoubtedly becoming a more ingrained presence within the party apparatus across the interwar period, an interactive process that gradually and unevenly helped inform the politics of the Labour Party and those men and women who comprised it.

Taken from a broader perspective, the general increase in both male and female individual membership reflected the growing importance given by the party to divisional organisation throughout the interwar period. While the trade unions continued to provide the bulk of Labour's affiliated membership and financial support, it was the network of constituency and local parties that increasingly co-ordinated, articulated and personified Labour's political outlook at a grass-roots level. Indeed, constituency parties had from the mid-1920s begun to organise themselves into regional or county federations better to co-ordinate their activity and offer 'mutual help' to each other. This, in turn, had been encouraged by head office, primarily in recognition of the potential electoral benefits of such co-operation. Accordingly, much of a divisional party's time remained committed to canvassing support, distributing party literature, and raising party funds. Approaches still varied, although some divisional parties developed relatively complex methods of maintaining a local Labour presence. Ray Roberts, for instance, followed Herbert Morrison's example and introduced a regimented programme of dues collecting on his appointment as party agent in North Lambeth in the early 1930s. This was based on the electoral register, involved wall charts and street indexes, and necessitated weekly collectors' meetings. In addition, he established a four-point plan to broaden and sustain local party membership, allocating 'routine work' to members of the division's general council, initiating regular reports on membership, distribution of propaganda and political training, allotting an hour of each general council meeting to social policy, and forming discussion circles in all ward party groups. Though the executive vetoed the first suggestion, the rest were adopted and implemented from the summer of 1935. As such, a 'special appeal for membership' leaflet was printed, posted to all houses, and then followed up with a personal call two days later. Membership was then maintained by the habitual checking of party cards to ensure regular subscription, while a fortnightly 'open forum' was planned for Wednesday evenings in an attempt to arouse local interest.[87]

Not all parties went to the lengths of North Lambeth, of course. Most Labour members continued to be 'passive', paying subscriptions but not necessarily taking part in the wider political activity of party. Labour activists typically remained a minority within both the party and the wider community. Furthermore, the nature and character of Labour organisation continued to differ throughout Britain. As in the 1920s, trade unions formed the basis of the party in most mining and heavily industrial areas, and union members and interests obviously remained at the heart of Labour politics. Many parties – Barnsley, Newcastle-under-Lyme, Cardiff, Wigan, and several Liverpool divisions among them – continued to affiliate to Labour with little more than the 'party minimum' membership in 1939. This could prove both positive and negative. In most mining localities, the unions continued to maintain Labour support within the wider community. In Lancashire, however, the sectional politics of the still dominant cotton unions sometimes served to hamper Labour progress, either in terms of alienating potential Labour voters due to cotton-union domination of a local party, or by cotton worker resistance to Labour as a party deemed unrepresentative of their interests.[88] Elsewhere, certain divisional party organisations had evidently come to rely on religious or racial loyalties, as in Liverpool and parts of London. Thus, approximately a third of Stepney's Labour-dominated council were Jewish and a third Irish between the wars, while the 'Catholic caucus' was central to the development of the Liverpool Labour Party.[89] Increasingly, however, Labour did endeavour to develop community- or neighbourhood-based constituency organisations to complement the party's initial trade union base. This had long been the case in much of London, and was increasingly so in places such as Preston, Oldham, Nelson, Aberdeen, Rotherham, Halifax, and even parts of the South Wales and Durham coalfield.[90] Such a process did not always run smoothly; divisional party memberships ebbed and flowed over the interwar period, and sometimes appeared to fail in spite of concerted effort. In Edinburgh, where the number of Labour councillors had stalled at between fifteen and seventeen by the mid-1930s – on a council of 71 – the trades council formed an Edinburgh and South East Federation of Labour Parties in 1933 to 'augment' the propaganda of the affiliated constituency parties. Frank Smithies, previously the Edinburgh party's well-known political officer, undertook the co-ordination of 'day-to-day propaganda work' in and around the city, organising meetings, demonstrations and targeting Labour policy at the rural population.[91] Yet, the Labour group saw no significant change, and party membership remained low. In Scotland more generally, the formation of the Scottish Socialist Party (SSP) and the departure of the ILP meant that constituency organisation developed only slowly over the 1930s. Not only did the ILP retain a presence in certain places, but the SSP continued to organise and function distinct from the wider Labour Party. As a result, individual Labour membership remained low in Scotland, and the constituency organisations relatively weak.[92] Over Britain as a whole, moreover, the advent of neighbourhood organisation did not necessarily lead to a dilution of trade union power within a particular party.[93] At the same time, the 1930s did see the eventual flourishing of neighbourhood-based parties in less industrial localities, particularly in the south of England (Twickenham, St Albans, Hendon, Harrow). Indeed, the growing importance of individual membership and constituency organisation can be gleaned from the fact that some 32 divisional parties boasted individual memberships of over 2,000 by 1938, compared to just eight in 1930.[94] Of these, 26 were in the south of England (27 if we include Norwich).

In such instances, Labour had necessarily forged its local identity via its ward organisation. In Lewisham, Labour appeared to benefit from the construction of three working-class housing estates over the 1920s and 1930s, the associational culture of which was tapped into by the constituency parties. Thus, drama groups and choral associations were formed, and an efficient party organisation maintained regular contact with members and supporters alike. Here as elsewhere, housing issues formed a dominant theme in local Labour politics, and this provided the party with a means by which to become synonymous with the well-being of large sections of the local community.[95] By 1938, the party had 4,774 members in the east of the borough, and 2,295 in the west.[96] Similar developments were discernible elsewhere. As Dan Weinbren has shown, LCC housing projects helped redistribute potential and actual Labour voters.[97] Certainly, the Wimbledon, Merton and Morden Labour Party benefited from the building of the Ravensbury Park and St Helier estates, providing the party with a focus for its canvassing and the injection of a working-class electorate into the Surrey constituency. As this suggests, Labour support could shift with an area's topography. In Hendon, the building of the Watling estate caused much alarm among middle-class inhabitants, but helped simultaneously to provide Labour with a sizeable local party within a traditionally Conservative constituency. In Norwich, too, where the Labour council carried out extensive slum clearance in the mid-to-late 1930s, the party noted how its ward organisation and municipal vote changed in tandem with such development.[98]

Not surprisingly, such a change in Labour Party composition led to questions being raised as to the relative influence of individual members and their respective constituency organisations. This had long been a point of issue. In the early 1920s, Herbert Morrison had regularly addressed conference (as the LLP delegate) in an attempt to gain better representation for those constituency party members endeavouring to extend Labour's organisation at a grass-roots level.[99] Similarly, during the debate over the party constitution at the 1929 conference, constituency party delegates bemoaned the trade unions' block vote and the apparent impotency of the constituency organisations with regard to decision-making. Ultimately, however, such disquiet from the conference floor had made little impact on the NEC.[100]

Despite this, the early 1930s saw the emergence of a national constituency parties' movement campaigning for greater divisional party representation on the NEC. The initiative was undertaken by Ben Greene, an Oxford-educated factory manager and previously unsuccessful Labour candidate for Gravesend. Writing in *The Labour Candidate* in September 1932, Greene argued that constituency parties needed to organise and co-ordinate their activities, proposing the formation of a national movement to give more coherent expression to individual members' concerns. To this end, a circular was sent to the divisional parties in June 1933 and an Association of Labour Parties established in July, with Greene appointed secretary and the former communist MP, Lieutenant Colonel L'Estrange Malone, taking the chair.[101]

Predictably, such an enterprise provoked anxiety inside the party headquarters (Transport House). Although Greene had made clear that his association posed no 'opposition' to either the party leadership or the trade unions – it simply endeavoured to give constituency parties 'a greater voice within the councils of the party' – the NEC remained suspicious of such independent action. Consequently, and despite a meeting between Shepherd, Middleton, Greene and Malone, the NEC interceded to offset the association's planned inaugural conference, further censuring Greene for his circumventing official party procedure. Accordingly, neither the Hastings conference of 1933, nor the Stockport conference of 1934, discussed the issues raised by the association, despite protests from the conference floor.[102]

And yet, the points made by Greene were deep-rooted. As such, his response to the NEC comprised the formation of yet another association of constituency parties, this time within the party's Home and Southern Counties district. This, of course, was where many of the larger individual party memberships were located, and an initial conference organised by Greene through the Surrey Labour Federation on 16 February 1935 attracted 315 delegates representing 49 divisional and 40 local Labour parties. At this, and in the face of further NEC disapproval, resolutions against the Labour Party's existing constitutional arrangements were passed, before a second conference in June officially constituted the Home Counties Labour Association (HCLA) with the objective of securing 'alterations' to the party constitution. By so doing, the HCLA endeavoured to provide 'satisfactory representation of local constituency organisations' on the NEC, and 'a medium for the preliminary consideration of resolutions' on the national party conference agenda.[103]

Little progress was made in 1935, as the NEC deferred and deflected the constituency parties' demands. Nevertheless, Greene continued to gather support, organising for over a hundred constituency parties to petition the NEC.[104] Assistance was also forthcoming from Sir Stafford Cripps, something that Ben Pimlott has suggested was perhaps more hindrance than help to the wider constituency movement. Certainly, association with the Socialist League gave both the NEC and the trade unions reason to remain suspicious of constituency party intentions, particularly during the heightened political climate of 1935–6. Not surprisingly, therefore, the NEC report to the 1936 party conference rejected all of the constituency parties' demands, further recommending that constitutional questions should not be discussed at conference for a further three years.[105] This time, however, the constituency party delegates' response was immediate and assertive. Midway through the conference week, over 200 delegates attended a meeting called by Greene to discuss divisional party reaction to the NEC report. A provisional committee of constituency Labour parties was subsequently established, with Greene again occupying the secretarial chair, resolving to take steps to mobilise nationwide divisional party support for constitutional change. Fearing open rebellion, the NEC refused any immediate discussion for the remainder of the conference but promised to consult and consider the parties' concerns over the coming year.[106]

Attitudes toward the provisional committee's nationwide campaign varied within the party. On the one hand, grass-roots support for constitutional change was widespread. Throughout the country – 'from Aberdeen in the north to Bristol in the south' – regional meetings were held to discuss the constituency party movement's proposals, while divisional party minute books reveal that party executives received regular correspondence from Greene's provisional committee. More to the point, as George Dallas reported to the party conference in 1937, 'every one of the regional consultations' brought unanimous support for the right of the constituency parties to elect their own representatives to the NEC.[107] As such, many on the party executive came to accept the need to respond to the members' demands, including the then chairman Hugh Dalton.[108] From such a position, Dalton was able to ensure that cordial relations with the constituency parties were maintained over 1937, arranging party delegate meetings held under the auspices of the NEC, and backing the NEC organisation sub-committee's proposal that constituency party representation on the executive be increased from five to seven, and that they be directly elected by the parties themselves.[109] In addition, Dalton sought to bring the trade unions round to such an idea, securing from Ernest Bevin an 'open mind' with regard to changes on the composition and election of the NEC, and ultimately attaining the backing of the MFGB.[110]

On the other hand, there was much uncertainty within sections of the trade union movement, and this was sometimes brought to bear on local party organisations. Thus, in early 1937, the Halifax Labour Party secretary-agent Sara Barker (a member of the provisional committee) had convinced her party executive of the need to revise the constitution and attend an area committee meeting organised in Leeds in February. But although a permanent regional committee was established in Yorkshire with the specific objective of mobilising rank-and-file support for the constituency party movement, the large trade union membership of the region's parties appear to have quickly dampened this initial bout of enthusiasm. Pressure from Arthur Greenwood (MP for Wakefield) and leading Labour members such as Leeds councillor and full-time organiser for the NUDAW Arthur Godfrey, who insisted that 'trade unionists in the party were not distinct from the rank-and-file', and that they were 'often the most active members', soon offered a potent counter-argument. Within a month of her appointment to the regional committee, Barker was arguing *against* tampering with the block vote, and took her executive with her.[111]

More generally, important unions, including the NUR, the textile workers and the NUGMW, were opposed to reform, and often for the same reasons as Godfrey. Equally, many trade unionists retained a suspicion of Greene's personal and political intentions. In this, Greene's relationship with Cripps was important. Clearly, trade union support would not be forthcoming if the unions feared constitutional change would allow the Socialist League greater influence. To this effect, Greene quickly detached himself from the League's newly launched *Tribune* newspaper and associated 'unity campaign' in early 1937. At the same time, Greene's evident sympathy for German National Socialism and accusations of misdoings in his Gravesend constituency no doubt did as much to undermine his personal and political reputation. Suspicion of his 'jiggery-pokery' was certainly raised during the eventual conference discussion. 'We cannot dismiss from our minds', Charlie Dukes of the NUGMW asserted, 'the attitude of the people who have been mainly responsible for promoting this change and their attitude towards Labour Party policy, particularly in the last two or three years'.[112]

In the event, the 1937 party conference agreed to the NEC's main proposals, defeating only a resolution on the right of 'proxy delegates' to represent central Labour parties or federations of constituency parties unable to attend conference in their own right. The voting was close, and Dalton had been forced to enter into some lunchtime persuasion finally to gain Bevin's backing for increased constituency party representation.[113] Ultimately, of course, the trade union majority remained intact, but greater scope for non-union participation was facilitated. In typical Labour style, change had occurred within clearly defined boundaries.

Such *quid pro quo* was not necessary with regard to other challenges to central party authority. As we shall see, the party successfully blunted and contained the Socialist League's attempts to push Labour towards a united front with the CPGB and ILP, despite notable rank-and-file – and some trade union – support. Indeed, renewed attempts by the communists to affiliate to Labour were rejected in 1936, and the party maintained its list of proscribed organisations that it deemed formed part of the 'communist solar system'.[114] By January 1937, moreover, the NEC had discussed the problem of communist activity within certain local parties in relation to the proposed 'united front', and issued an appeal for loyalty 'to the movement' that was overwhelmingly ratified by the party conference.[115] Similarly, although there continued to be some sympathy for the communist-led National Unemployed Workers' Movement (NUWM) within the divisional parties, the NEC refused to countenance any official co-operation between Labour and Communist Party members. Even firebrands such as Jack Braddock had to sit out the unemployed demonstrations of the early 1930s for fear of 'compromising the Labour Party'. As the Liverpool unemployed mobilised, so Jack, a former communist and unemployed leader in the 1920s, 'sat in the Kardomah café and drank tea'.[116] This did not mean that local co-operation did not happen, but that it was limited and resisted by the wider Labour Party apparatus. Thus, Jarrow's Labour town council was careful to avoid overt association with the NUWM during its organisation of the 'Jarrow crusade' in October 1936, despite Ellen Wilkinson (the town's MP) asking Wal Hannington for advice.[117] Even then, the NEC looked disparagingly on such extra-political initiative.

Of course, communist influence could still find its way into the party, and such realisation helped inform Labour's relationship with the Labour League of Youth (LLY) in the 1930s. The LLY had long endeavoured to acquire a greater say within the party, and the party conference continued to hear regular appeals urging the NEC to show more urgency in its organisation of young members.[118] Such demands had been met, in part, in 1933, with the launch of a LLY development campaign and, in 1934, the co-option of an LLY representative onto the NEC. Come 1935, however, with the number of LLY branches exceeding 500, the youth conference resolved to ask the NEC for the power to consider policy matters and pass associated resolutions. Initially, the NEC offered succour. George Shepherd, as national agent, reminded the LLY that 'all young men and young women of sixteen years of age and over who have joined the party have the same rights and privileges as men and women over 60 years of age', meaning they could join their local party and discuss and vote on policy as they pleased. Nevertheless, the NEC insisted that the LLY 'was not established to make policy but to recruit and educate young people for the party' – as such, it rejected any attempt to extend the remit of the youth organisation.[119] A year later, moreover, and the LLY was in disarray. An NEC report detailed the problem, focusing primarily on the supposed influence of young communists within the LLY's ranks – the 1936 youth conference had supported the formation of a united front with the CPGB – and youth members' penchant for criticising the party instead of organising their own affairs within the League. The solution was draconian: the *New Nation* was suspended, the League's advisory committee was dissolved, and the 1937 youth conference cancelled. Instead, proposals to reconstitute the League as a 'youth section of the party' were endorsed by the party conference, along with a reassertion of the LLY's social, educational and electoral role; the LLY representative was also removed from the NEC.[120] The League was subsequently reconstituted, with a new paper (*Advance!*) and national organiser in John Huddleston. Nevertheless, tensions remained, as Labour continued to find it difficult to reconcile its desire to harness youthful exuberance with a steadfast loyalty to the party.

The Labour Party was resting on solid foundations by the end of the 1930s. Although tensions were evident within the party, and personal animosity existed between some of its leading members, both the NEC and the NCL comprised a relatively continuous and firmly established membership. The leaders of the Trades Union Congress (TUC) and the party politicians generally worked harmoniously, committing Labour to a moderate and practical socialism that contrasted with the more militant and theoretical approach of those on the left within and without the party. More importantly, the basis of Labour's support was extending in the late 1930s. On the one hand, trade union membership was increasing; on the other, the party's constituency organisations were for the most part expanding and diversifying over the country as a whole. There were clear limits to this, but the trend was towards the dissemination rather than concentration of Labour support. Within the PLP, moreover, the flexible and astute leadership of Clement Attlee complemented the pragmatic and administrative approach of his NEC and NCL colleagues. This did not mean that Labour had, by 1939, recovered enough to offer a decisive challenge to the Conservatives at any forthcoming election. But, as the 'dark cloud' of war began to form, so the credibility of Chamberlain's Tory-dominated National government was being slowly undermined.[121] As such, two important components of Labour's dramatic 1945 victory were evident by 1939. First, a distinctive political programme was in place and continuing to develop. This worked on two levels: nationally, with regard to plans of common ownership and, more locally, in terms of extending social-welfare provision such as housing, health and education. Second, the events leading up to the outbreak of war gave Attlee's parliamentary party a means by which to challenge and help undermine the authority of the Chamberlain government.

III. IMPROVING THE CONDITION OF THE PEOPLE: POLICY AND PRACTICE IN THE LATE 1930s

We shall consider the evolution of Labour's foreign policy in due course. Simultaneously, the Labour executive continued to refine the party's domestic programme from 1935, setting priorities and defining its objectives in an increasingly realisable and electable form. The 1935 general election had been fought on a manifesto entitled *The Labour Party's Call to Power*, which offered a relatively concise synopsis of *For Socialism and Peace*. Drafted by Greenwood, it was 'improved' by the NEC on 22 October 1935, with Dalton further preparing a section on foreign policy to be ratified the following day – an executive process deemed by Dalton as being 'much better than farming it out to the likes of little Laski'.[122] As such, the manifesto concentrated on immediate and practical policies rather than theoretical precepts and long-term objectives – the proposed nationalised industries were listed (coal, transport, banking, land, electricity, cotton, iron and steel), and the party pledged to uphold the collective security of the League of Nations. In addition, work schemes and planned development were promised to offset unemployment, while the party again distanced itself from the militant rhetoric of the Socialist League by reasserting its commitment to 'constitutional and democratic means'.[123]

Such a process of political fine-tuning continued thereafter. A range of policy and 'campaign' documents emerged from the party sub-committees, NEC and NCL, amongst which the most important was *Labour's Immediate Programme*, published in March 1937. This, as its title suggests, outlined those 'measures of socialism and social amelioration, which a Labour government would carry out during a full term of office when returned to power by the electors'.[124] Presented by the policy committee to the NEC in February, the programme was primarily the work of Dalton, Attlee and Greenwood, and provided an effective summation of Labour's political progression from 1931–2.[125] Its format was simple, outlining the four 'vital measures of reconstruction' – finance, land, transport, coal and power – needed to provide the 'four great benefits' of society: food, wages, leisure, and security. To this effect, the programme committed Labour to the nationalisation of the Bank of England, coal, gas, electricity, the land and transport; to economic planning via the National Investment Board (NIB), including the redistribution of wealth through taxation, investment in 'public development', and the promotion of new industry 'if the national interest demands it'; and to regional policies designed to alleviate the 'distressed areas'. Such structural change, Labour envisaged, would then be complemented by a series of social reforms, including the 40-hour week, paid holidays, the raising of the school-leaving age to fifteen (and later sixteen), the abolition of the means test, and improved health services and pensions. Finally, the party once more reaffirmed its support for the League of Nations.[126]

Taken generally, *Labour's Immediate Programme* offered a realistic and practical outline of what could be achieved by a future Labour government. As Attlee made clear in his speech to the party conference in October 1937, the programme 'was made up of decisions that you [the conference] have already taken', but it was also a deliberately short programme with a 'definite aim'. 'The attitude of a Labour government coming in with power is entirely different from that of a capitalist government', he continued. Where a 'capitalist government comes in and accepts the existing structure, proposes to put a patch here and a patch there, a socialist government comes in and proposes to change the fundamental conception of government in this country'. The proposals included in *Labour's Immediate Programme*, therefore, were 'a table of priorities showing what will be done first' – measures to take Britain but part of the way towards a socialist commonwealth.[127]

At the same time, the programme raised questions as the extent of Labour's socialist vision.[128] First, Labour's plans for national ownership were evidently scaled down, and although this could be explained by the limited remit of the programme, it also provided a means by which the leadership could trim party policy of its more controversial aspects, such as the nationalisation of the joint stock banks.[129] Second, much of the detail of *Labour's Immediate Programme* was contained in previously published documents drawn up by the TUC and party research departments. Nevertheless, gaps remained. So, for example, where plans for the nationalisation of coal, transport and electricity had been outlined over the early-to-mid 1930s, there had yet to be a similar policy publication with regard to gas. As this suggests, and for all its talk of planning, management boards and co-operation with the trade unions, Labour remained vague as to the wider mechanics of a fully co-ordinated economy.[130] Finally, Attlee's reference to changing 'the fundamental conception of government' remained within the parameters of Britain's existing political structure, with socialism emerging via parliament, government appointment, and state direction.[131] Accordingly, as David Howell has suggested, *Labour's Immediate Programme* could just as readily be interpreted as a means to increase efficiency and reduce the inequalities of the existing capitalist system as it could a step towards socialism.[132] This, certainly, was the view of many on and to the left of the party.

Whatever its potential shortcomings, *Labour's Immediate Programme* served as a rallying point for the party in the late 1930s, providing Labour with a clear and distinctive political agenda. In many ways, it offered a summation of the practical socialism espoused by the party from 1931; it was both constitutional and gradualist, yet simultaneously radical in its promises of common ownership and a more equitable society. True, there continued to be a sense of inevitability about Labour's conception of socialism, which led some on the left to suggest that the party underestimated the potential for capitalist resistance to its socialist legislation.[133] But *Labour's Immediate Programme* proposed a series of realisable measures to precede the social, educational and moral changes that the party further recognised as necessary in the transition to socialism. More significantly, perhaps, its policies would later help form the basis for Attlee's first post-war Labour government in 1945.

In the meantime, Labour continued to be more likely to enact its proposed reforms at a local, rather than national, level. The gradual increase in Labour councillors throughout much of Britain, along with the formation of Labour councils in certain towns and cities, allowed party members to propose a range of policies offering a collective response to problems relating to housing, health and education. Although Labour generally recognised such reform as being but a partial response to the inequities of capitalism, local election successes meant that more attention was given to municipal policy over the 1920s. Local government conferences were held, the party campaigned for the extension of local governmental powers (and had helped legislate for such in 1924), and the NEC took measures to develop closer links between head office and the growing number of Labour council groups. The objective, as stated in a manifesto drafted by the PLP, TUC and NEC in 1925, was to improve 'the condition of the people' by taking the 'maximum advantage from the legislation now on the statute book … [to] develop local public services for the benefit of the public.[134] Thus:

> The more strongly Labour is represented on local governing authorities, the more attention will be given to social conditions, to the care of the poor and the sick, to better housing for the people, and to more generous educational facilities for the children of the workers.[135]

Come the 1930s, and the growth of Labour representation on municipal bodies led the party to organise a further series of 'educational conferences' on local government. 'Practical problems' were discussed, while the research department endeavoured to ensure that party representatives were fully aware of the extent of municipal authority.[136] Equally, a set of model standing orders was adopted in 1930 to formalise relations between council groups and their respective constituency parties. These, not surprisingly given Herbert Morrison's place on the NEC sub-committee, related closely to the practice of the LLP, where Morrison's party machine had endeavoured to offer guidance to Labour groups on the capital's borough councils from 1919. For Morrison, it was essential that each Labour group act as a unified block, meeting before council sessions to decide on a common approach. As such, the party standing orders authorised for groups to elect their own officers and hold meetings in preparation for council meetings. The Labour group was, of course, committed to carrying out the policies determined by the central, divisional and local Labour parties; unity was expected, with abstention only allowed for matters of conscience.[137] However, in an echo of the PLP's relationship with the wider party, the Labour group itself determined policy once elected onto the council. In other words, 'while it is the function of the appropriate local section of the party to determine election policy, it is the definite responsibility of the Labour group to decide group policy and action on the council'.[138] That said, regular contact with the divisional and national party was encouraged, leading eventually to the establishment of a local government policy committee and, in 1936, a local government department.

But to what extent could Labour make a difference? By April 1939, Labour's position with regard to England and Wales' municipal authorities was as follows:

	Total	*Labour controlled*
counties	62	4
county boroughs	83	18
metropolitan boroughs	28	17
other boroughs	289	24

Table 4.3 Labour's position with regard to England and Wales' municipal authorities

In addition, Labour controlled 76 urban district councils, 26 of which were in Wales. In Scotland, Labour controlled 14 Scottish burgh councils at the outbreak of war.[139] As this suggests, Labour remained a minority on most local authorities, with anti-socialist alliances continuing to block the party's progress in many places. Traditionally, too, Labour had had to compete with a hostile local press, while it was not uncommon for organisational manoeuvres to be utilised to limit Labour influence in areas where the party appeared close to gaining power. Thus, the appointment of aldermen – senior councillors elected by the council to serve a six-year term – was supposed to correspond to the balance of power within the council.

Nonetheless, Labour's opponents sometimes refused to conform to such 'tradition'; in Sheffield, for example, it had taken a Labour boycott of council committee work to ensure the appointment of a proportionate share of aldermen in 1921.[140]

Despite this, the party's approach to local election contests – alongside the policies pursued and implemented by Labour councillors – was integral to the construction of a Labour identity at a local and, by extension, national level. It was in such a context that 'labour' candidates had first made an impact in the late nineteenth and early twentieth century, on school boards, boards of guardians, and councils. The yearly elections provided a regular rallying point for the party; it was during the April and November contests that local Labour activists and members were most visible and most able to present their policies and ideas to the wider public. Where general elections enabled Labour to focus on 'national' policies of peace, unemployment and (increasingly) nationalisation, local election campaigns saw the divisional and ward parties concentrate primarily on issues of housing, health and education. These, of course, were the areas in which the scope of local government action had extended most by the 1920s, and although centralisation was characteristic of the interwar period, particularly in the realm of poverty relief, municipal authorities retained a notable influence with regard to the provision of social welfare. Similarly, while Labour gradually endeavoured to co-ordinate its policy and organisation over the interwar period, there remained much scope for local parties to develop campaigns and agendas, putting their own stamp – for good or bad – on the party's development.

As the interwar period progressed, so local Labour parties developed more focused and applicable political programmes. These could vary in their range and method, but common concerns clearly emerged across the party. Thus, in Rhondda, the dominant Labour council had been elected on a detailed party programme that promised free education, house building, rate reform, mothers' pensions, and the employment of direct labour to offset unemployment. Ultimately, the deleterious economic circumstances of the time meant that Labour's progress towards such ends were notable but limited. Even so, measures such as the provision of free milk to children of low-income families helped alleviate some of the worst effects of the depression.[141] In Swansea, the party's municipal programme included plans for 'a large housing initiative, slum clearance, ward clinics to improve maternity and child welfare, and the provision of a central municipal hospital'.[142] A nursery school was also opened, the means test was relatively humanely exercised, and a government grant was further procured to finance a variety of civic building projects.[143] For Labour in Glasgow, as in many places, the question of housing predominated. Accordingly, Patrick Dollan's Glasgow corporation persevered with a slum-clearance programme that led to the building of some 20,000 houses between 1934 and 1939.[144] Similarly, in Leeds, Labour Party pressure was integral to the implementation of wide-ranging housing schemes in the 1930s. On winning a council majority in 1933, following a campaign largely centred on the question of slum clearance and a simultaneous house-building programme, the Labour group finally got to work. By late 1935, some 6,000 slum houses had been demolished and a similar number of homes constructed, often by direct labour.[145] In Barnsley, meanwhile, the Labour council aspired to educational reform, increasing the school-leaving age by six months so as to promote education and keep some 500 teenagers off the unemployment figure. Typically, slum clearance and house building were also prioritised.[146]

As should now be clear, the Labour Party's municipal campaigns prioritised issues of health, education, and housing, and Labour councils endeavoured to act on such a basis. In Sheffield, the Labour borough council instigated a series of health-care reforms from 1926, including the building of public abattoirs and a hospital for suffers of tuberculosis. Led by Ernest Rowlinson, the Sheffield Labour group initiated slum clearances, built improved municipal housing, extended the city's transport network, and widened educational opportunities and standards. By offering a range of municipal services, moreover, including markets and a very profitable printing department, Labour increased the number of people who were employed by, reliant on, and thereby responsive to a sympathetic Labour council.[147] Reform in Norwich was equally impressive. Labour had taken control of the city council in 1933, from which point Herbert Palmer's housing committee ensured that 5,000 houses were built over the first two years of Labour administration; 'fair rents' were set for council tenants. Health care and unemployed relief also improved, with councillors proudly defending the party's efforts to cure the 'ills of poverty and unemployment'. The council emphasised its provision of nutritious school meals, building hygienic schools and nurseries designed to provide an 'equal opportunity to every child, however poor their parents may be'.[148] In Lincoln, the council's maternity and child welfare centre was the jewel in Labour's municipal crown.[149]

London, of course, was a site of much municipal Labour activity between the wars. The LLP had continued to expand over the 1930s, boasting 63,225 individual members by 1939 (compared to 29,227 in 1926), and such growth was accompanied by increased municipal success.[150] Most obviously, Labour secured control of LCC in 1934, an authority that encompassed a population of some 4,500,000. Led by Morrison and his 'presidium' of Lewis Silkin, Isaac Hayward and Charles Latham, the LCC in the mid-to-late 1930s was the site of a progressive and notably successful Labour administration. As Donoughue and Jones have argued, Morrison's objective was to make the LCC an example of Labour's ability to govern. This entailed highlighting Labour efficiency in decision-making, its principled method of office holding, and its fairness in all aspects of council work. In terms of policy, the Labour LCC led an offensive against the capital's slums, building houses, enforcing repairs, and reducing rents for those moving from slum areas to new municipal accommodation. Expenditure on health, education and welfare services increased from 1934, with more staff employed in hospitals on better salaries and in superior conditions. Patient care similarly improved, new schools were built, amenities provided (more milk, playing fields and health visits were initiated), and more free places in secondary education were offered. The LCC also endeavoured to ensure that reforms to alleviate the harshness of public assistance were implemented. Even more distinctively, the LCC introduced Morrison's dream of a 'green belt' surrounding London, providing the relevant local authorities with funds to buy and maintain land.[151] Despite press and Conservative criticism, Morrison's LLP was rewarded at the 1937 LCC elections, winning 446,100 votes (compared with 341,400 in 1934), gaining a further six seats, and establishing a working majority of 30. Following the relative disappointment of the 1935 general election, Labour's control of the English capital was comfort indeed.

At a municipal level, London Labour councils displayed priorities similar to their provincial equivalents, with social welfare policies predominating. As Naomi Wolff recalled on remembering her time as a Labour councillor in Hammersmith from 1934, 'the domestic political thing – that was the basis of the Labour Party … housing and health I think dominated the politics of the Labour Party at that time'. As such, piecemeal but important reforms, such as letting working-class families without bathrooms use the public baths for free, formed an integral part of the party's council agenda.[152] In Islington, too, where Labour held the majority on the council, the borough party's 1937 local election campaign for a 'Healthier, Brighter Islington' involved campaigns for improved maternity and child welfare, a convalescence home, and a gynaecological clinic.[153] Elsewhere, the Labour council in Fulham set up a municipal laundry service on its gaining overall control in 1919, while the Walthamstow Labour council established a municipal savings bank in 1932.[154] In Hackney, council employees soon replaced contractors in collecting the borough's refuse, a municipal insurance scheme was adopted, council houses were built, and the municipality profitably administrated the borough's electricity supply.[155] Most impressive, perhaps, was Bermondsey, where Alfred and Ada Salter led the Labour council in the introduction of municipal health centres, baths and clinics. Alongside an extensive house-building scheme (2,700 between 1929 and 1938), it also established a 'beautification committee' to brighten up the borough, planting over 9,000 trees and initiating gardening competitions to elicit public participation. Local rates were relatively high, but Bermondsey council retained its Labour majority from 1922, with the Salters even going so far to convert their country house at Fairby Grange into a convalescence home for mothers. Although their own daughter died of scarlet fever, the Salters strived to raise the health of the borough in which they lived via health propaganda campaigns, the opening of a solarium to fight off tuberculosis, and the distribution of free milk, insulin and food to those in need.[156]

For all their best intentions, party representatives were generally quick to recognise the administrative limits of local authority power in the 1930s, necessarily working within defined legal guidelines. True, some Labour councils – such as Bedwellty and West Ham – had continued to offer levels of poor relief above the government recommendation into the mid-to-late 1920s, but they tended to be the exception rather than the rule. On the 1920s boards of guardians and the early 1930s public assistance committees, Labour representatives typically endeavoured to offset the ravages of poverty and unemployment as best they could within existing structures.[157] This often amounted to piecemeal (but nevertheless important) intervention, including the provision of free school meals or ensuring that benefit claimants got the relief owed to them. In administering the means test, Labour councils overwhelmingly sought to do so in the most favourable terms possible, often providing the maximum rate of relief available and accepting a greater percentage of applications for transitional benefit than in non-Labour localities.[158] Conversely, of course, expenditure on unemployed relief often meant cuts in other services or relatively high rates. Ultimately, however, Labour priorities ensured that the party became associated with providing social welfare, affordable housing, and local amenities. In so doing, Labour councillors could acquire a reputation as both the representatives and servants of their communities. Thus, to take a telling if admittedly apocryphal story, an opponent of Labour's A. E. Killip claimed to overhear two voters discussing the local elections in West Ham in 1921. 'Who's Killip?', one asked. 'The man who gives you [unemployed] relief at Cumberland Road', was the reply.[159] As this suggests, George Lansbury's 39 Bow Road was perhaps just the most famous address of a Labour councillor (and MP) on whom constituents were welcome to call. In Dorothy Deeming's words, Labour councillors in Poplar 'weren't isolated. They lived amongst you, they worked amongst you, and they came round and took your subs'.[160]

Linked to this, Labour councils sought to present themselves as 'model employers'. Most had established municipal works departments by the 1930s, carrying out construction and repair work without resort to a private contractor. Moreover, Labour council employees tended to be paid at or above union wage rates and were subject to union-recognised conditions. In Poplar, for example, the Labour council elected in 1919 immediately agreed to (and raised) a minimum wage for all employees.[161] Typically, therefore, Labour councils endeavoured to employ direct labour to embark on their municipal building schemes. This was certainly the case in Wigan, where those employed to build the town's municipal houses were subject to trade union pay, conditions and holidays.[162] Consequently, Labour councils not only brought relief to the poorest sections of the community, they provided opportunities for employment and, through the funding of education and library facilities, self-improvement.

More often than not, Labour groups remained in the minority on their respective council. Nevertheless, they and their supporters mounted campaigns to defend and extend people's standard of living. Minority Labour groups could, for example, seek to block council initiatives deemed to be antithetical to the interests of their constituents. In Liverpool, the group regularly used delaying tactics to offset 'repressive measures'. Council time was used to the maximum to ensure that policy decisions were held over to a later session. This could get out of hand; Bessie Braddock often resorted to hurling insults at her Tory counterparts, a 'tactic' that once led to her being forcibly removed from the council chamber by police after calling the chairman of the housing committee a liar. 'If you didn't do something outrageous', she reasoned, 'nobody would take any notice of you and no one would know what was going on in the city council, except the few dozen Liverpool citizens who were sufficiently interested to turn up for its monthly meetings.'[163] Alternatively, more concerted protests were instigated. In Kingston during the 1930s, Labour members campaigned to ensure that housing regulations were enforced, organising tenants' rallies of some 2,000 people.[164]

Despite such achievement, the acquirement of council office could lead to tensions developing between the constituency parties and their group representatives. Most commonly, Labour groups had to reconcile their relationship with the party on the one hand, and with their constituents on the other. In the words of Joseph Parton, on becoming a Labour councillor in Wrexham in 1934, 'I represent the Labour Party, but I recognise that I am not there to represent one class but to look after the interests of all'.[165] For this reason, there were frequent complaints that Labour councillors were losing contact with party members. To take a typical example, the North Lambeth Divisional Labour Party discussed such concern in the summer of 1927, following complaints that there was 'a lack of co-operation between the party and the group'. Suggestions that 'borough councillors are not doing their duty' were countered by complaints that local parties were adopting local candidates to exclude sitting councillors, holding ward meetings without councillors being present, or in such a way that councillors could not 'give account' of themselves prior to nomination. The general committee considered the problem and concurred that 'co-operation' was lacking, reaffirming the failure of Labour group representatives to attend party meetings, but drawing up plans for closer contact. Even so, the problem re-emerged nine years later, when a special joint meeting of councillors and the party management committee was held in September 1936 to discuss 'attacks' made against the Labour group. The case against was supplied by the party agent, Ray Roberts, who gave details of councillors not paying their membership fees, obstructing the formation of a women's section, and failing to attend party meetings or contribute to socials. In defence, the party councillors complained of over work, although the meeting resolved in favour of Roberts and recommended greater discipline and dedication within the Labour group.[166] Similarly, the fractious Wolverhampton party suffered a series of internal rows over Labour group policy in the 1920s, with councillors being censured over accusations of mismanagement and, in 1928, for voting in favour of providing a £400 grant to the local Catholic college.[167]

Pressure could also come from local trade unions keen to ensure that Labour councillors campaigned for and protected their interests. Thus, in December 1936, the Electrical Trades Union (ETU) complained to the Islington Borough Labour Party over the council's employment of non-union and non-local labour. Similarly, in Colne Valley, the NUR proposed a resolution to the divisional party's 1932 annual meeting stating that 'we deprecate the action of certain members of our local Labour Party and local authorities in lending their support to private transport undertakings which do not observe trade union conditions, or debar their employees the right to trade union organisation'.[168] In Loughborough, the question of direct labour provoked a dispute between and within the borough party and the minority Labour group. While a section of the party wished the group to push for the employment of direct labour, councillor Dean spoke for others who felt such a policy was 'mistaken' in the context of Labour's position within the council.[169] More unusually, the TGWU in Darlington complained to the party about the behaviour of councillor Griffiths following an argument with a bus conductor.[170]

Most commonly, tensions emerged in relation to Labour councillors 'going native', acquainting themselves with the benefits of office and straying from their supposed Labour principles. On becoming mayor of Hackney in 1920, Herbert Morrison had initially followed George Lansbury's example in not wearing the mayoral robes and disregarding formal ceremony. Very soon, however, having visited a children's Christmas party and seen 'disappointment and disillusion' at his brown tweed suit, Morrison adopted the full office regalia for himself and his council officers.[171] This stood in contrast to the attitude of party members elsewhere. In Bermondsey, for instance, the red flag was flown over the town hall, and London's first woman mayor – Ada Salter – eschewed such traditions as appointing a council chaplin.[172] Not dissimilarly, Edward Sheerien's tenure as mayor of Barnsley saw him reject the concept of mayoral neutrality (he remained head of the council Labour group) and appoint his nine-year-old daughter Sara as mayoress.[173] More seriously, Labour group members were sometimes chastised for displaying sympathy for their opponents in the council chamber. In Edinburgh, councillors Paris and Rhind both had the 'whip withdrawn' in 1932 for refusing to leave office in protest against 'the lack of fair play on the part of the other side [the Tory-dominated Moderate Party] in refusing to allow Labour at least two Bailieships'. In Birmingham, the Labour alderman Sir Percival Bower was expelled for his supporting a council motion to award Neville Chamberlain the freedom of the city.[174] In South Shields, the constituency party expelled alderman Curbison and the then Labour mayor, Charles Henderson, for not adequately consulting with the party over the appointment of local magistrates.[175]

As this suggests, Labour ire was often raised by the inequitable conduct of local council representation, and Labour prided itself on its integrity and service to the wider community. This entailed a respect for established rules and traditions, but with an equal emphasis on parity and justice. Any sign, therefore, that Labour's own representatives were somehow profiting from their position was frowned upon. In Newport, for example, the general committee resolved in December 1920 'that this meeting strongly resents the action taken by certain Labour councillors and other members of the party in attending the mayor's banquet ...' Not only did the 'spending of public money on mayoral banquets and similar functions' challenge Labour scruples, but it also raised questions as to Labour's identity. An amendment to the committee's resolution stating that party representatives' 'personal or social relationship towards elected representatives of other parties is entirely a matter for the decision of the Labour councillors themselves' was defeated by ten votes to seven.[176] Even so, the problem re-emerged in 1935, this time in the context of the 'unemployment and distress' being experienced by many Labour voters. Consequently, in February 1936, the party discussed whether all municipal candidates should be able to prove they had given three years' service to the party – careerists were evidently not welcome.[177] Indeed, the Wrexham party drew up a 'code of honour' for its public representatives that barred receipt of 'favours or hospitality' and the appointment of 'near relatives' to council positions.[178] Even so, there were obvious examples of places where Labour members soon adopted the 'bad habits' of their predecessors, as in West Ham, Stepney and Swansea, where council employment was allegedly prioritised for Labour Party members, relatives and associates.[179]

Finally, the specifics of Labour policy could raise problems within and without the party. While most Labour councils had similar priorities, there remained a variety of different approaches to policy across the country. Thus, where certain Labour councils sought to build public housing for low rent, as in Sheffield, Norwich and Glasgow, others placed greater priority on the *quality* of working-class housing, as in Swindon. Because of this, some Labour schemes ensured that municipal housing remained beyond the reach of many workers and their families, or were deemed unfair. This was arguably the case in Leeds, where the Labour council's introduction of a differential rent system perhaps contributed to Labour's losing municipal control in 1935.[180] Not dissimilarly, in Sheffield, where the council had sought to keep rents at a reasonable level, there were complaints about the lack of amenities provided for the new housing estates. It was only after the holding of a referendum in 1936 that the council agreed to provide land and leases for the building of local pubs, and money was set aside in 1939 for the provision of recreational facilities.[181] In Islington, meanwhile, Labour attempts to convert houses into flats met with only limited success.[182] As this also suggests, Labour policy with regard to the setting of rates could vary considerably.

Throughout the interwar period, Labour endeavoured to utilise municipal authority power to improve the living and working environments of its primarily working-class constituents. In this, party representatives were limited by an array of political, legal and governmental factors. Simultaneously, the party generally began to shift its focus towards more central, as opposed to local, 'solutions' from at least 1931. Thus, the second Labour government had failed to persevere with the Local Authorities (Enabling) Bill that it had propagated throughout the 1920s, while Clement Attlee made clear his penchant for local administrations 'energized and controlled by central government' in the context of the mid-1930s.[183] Even so, those Labour councils that did form in the 1920s and 1930s did much to embody the priorities projected by the party. True, the transition from protest politics to responsibility did not always come easily, and the extent to which Labour was able to effect notable social-political change varied across the country. But local politics remained integral to the wider development of the Labour Party between the wars, providing a context in which members could be active, and in which political identities could be forged.

IV. CONFRONTING FASCISM

The growing menace of fascism and authoritarianism was a defining characteristic of the 1930s. Following Mussolini's earlier triumph in Italy, the rise of Hitler and the eventual victory of Franco in Spain were but the most renowned examples of democratic collapse throughout much of Europe. Despite the spectre of communism gaining substance following the Russian revolutions of 1917, reaction became the dominant political creed of the interwar period. Not surprisingly, therefore, with the possibility of war once again on the political agenda, much of the Labour Party's energy in the 1930s was put towards forging an alternative response to the political-economic crises of the time. But although the party went some way towards developing its social democratic credentials 'at home', it often appeared uncertain as to the best approach to the threat of fascism abroad. As we have seen, the party encompassed a variety of opinions: pacifist, pragmatic, and progressive. Appropriately, then, a definite Labour policy appeared slowly, hesitantly, and amidst much dispute.

At the same time, the conflict in Spain and the need to confront fascism in Europe and in the form of Sir Oswald Mosley's British Union of Fascists (BUF) excited the passions of many within (and without of) the labour and socialist movement. Spain, in particular, became symbolic of the struggle between 'left and right': the forces of democracy and progress versus those of tyranny and reaction. Consequently, the three-year civil war (1936–9) became a point of focus for much local Labour Party activity, as aid was collected and the 'imperialist' intentions of the National government were apparently revealed in its refusal to assist a democratically elected government fighting for survival. This section will look at four aspects of Labour's attempt to confront fascism: its attitude towards the BUF; its reaction to the Spanish civil war; its rejection of the Socialist League's call for unity with the CPGB; and its hardening policy towards Nazi Germany and preparation for war.

Although some on the left of the party recognised the roots of a peculiarly British form of fascism in the policies and attitudes of the National government, official Labour policy tended to concentrate on the threat of fascism abroad.[184] More unusual, if rather more combative, was the threat posed by the BUF. Formed in October 1932, the BUF remained a relatively small organisation on the margins of British politics. Nevertheless, it initially recorded a brisk recruitment of members between 1932 and 1934, peaking at an estimated 50,000 in mid-1934, at which time Mosley was able to call on the support of Lord Rothermere's *Daily Mail*. Although membership (and Rothermere's support) collapsed following the notorious Olympia meeting of 7 June 1934, at which violence erupted as hecklers were forcibly removed by Mosley's blackshirted stewards, the BUF recovered thereafter on the back of its more overtly anti-Semitic stance. By late 1936, the party registered some 15,500 members, growing erratically to approximately 20,000 by the outbreak of war. Its principal bases of support were located in London's East End and parts of Lancashire, although BUF branches also existed in places such as Reading, Aberdeen, Leeds and Bristol.[185]

Labour's response to the activity of Mosley and his blackshirts was evident if sometimes tentative. In June 1934, the party sent a circular to each of its divisional organisations in an attempt to gauge the extent of fascist influence, with the mainly non-committal replies generally confirming the party's arms-length approach.[186] Moreover, the political realm of the BUF was primarily the street, while the Labour Party by the 1930s was far more focused on the legislative levers of power inside parliament and the city hall. As such, Labour tended to disavow Mosley's policies and the violence which became synonymous with his actions, but generally sought to work around the BUF, favouring reasoned argument and constitutional procedure to demonstration. In 1934, for example, Attlee led a Labour delegation to the home secretary to demand action be taken to curb the apparently growing problem of fascist violence. More specific to London, meanwhile, Herbert Morrison organised a conference in September 1934 that brought together 1,200 delegates to work towards 'constructive propaganda and education' to stifle the fascist threat.[187] At a national level, Labour – and the PLP in particular – were more likely to ignore the BUF than engage with it.[188]

Such an approach appeared justified as BUF support fell away in late 1934, before the notoriety occasioned by fascist and anti-fascist violence – culminating in the 'Battle of Cable Street' on 4 October 1936 – necessitated a further Labour response. Once again, however, the party executive favoured an administrative, rather than physical, solution. While many Labour and trade union members joined with communists, Jews and non-party workers to do battle with the blackshirts – in Cable Street, Bermondsey and elsewhere – the official Labour line was to demand government action to prevent fascist parades and incitement to violence.[189] Thus, Herbert Morrison led yet another deputation to the home secretary on 20 October 1936, recommending the outlawing of military uniforms and military training for political parties, in addition to stronger police measures to deal with marches designed to stir up civic or racial conflict, and legal proceedings against fascist speeches that contravened the law – much of which informed the subsequent Public Order Act (1936). At the same time, the LLP established an East London advisory committee to disseminate and co-ordinate anti-fascist propaganda in the capital, suggesting that educational campaigns, (indoor) public meetings and leaflets were to be Labour's principal weapons against fascism.[190] In the estimation of both the Labour Party and TUC leadership, fascism flourished where constitutional democracy was weak; to countenance extra-parliamentary action against the BUF would therefore fan – rather than douse – the flames of reaction.[191]

Despite the party's official approach, many active local party members were nevertheless forced to deal with the fascist presence on a day-to-day level. Tom Riley, who joined the LLY in the early 1930s, later recalled 'narrow escapes from being caught by the police over scraps with the fascists up on Spouters Corner opposite Wood Green station', where the BUF used to meet on Saturdays.[192] In Bermondsey, too, attempts by the BUF to speak and, in 1937, to march through the borough were prevented by Labour, trade union and Communist Party members, despite the pacifist appeals of the local MP Alfred Salter.[193] Across the East End, confrontation with the BUF became a part of political life in the 1930s. Beyond the capital, Labour activists' reaction to the BUF varied in accordance with the perceived extent of the fascist threat. In Yorkshire, where the BUF was generally a marginal presence, the party tended to follow the official party line, issuing anti-fascist propaganda but refraining from overt confrontation. That said, members of the LLY reputedly engaged physically with fascists in Leeds and Huddersfield.[194] Elsewhere, such as Manchester and Liverpool, Labour members undoubtedly took part in more concerted protest.[195] More unusually, there were some reported instances of party members being sympathetic to the BUF. In Newport, the party executive wrote to the NEC asking for guidance in response to members 'connected' to fascism.[196]

In contrast to the variegated Labour reaction to the BUF, the outbreak of the Spanish civil war in 1936 caught the imaginations of Labour members across the country.[197] Indeed, the campaigns in support of the Spanish republic arguably helped breathe life into many a local party following the disappointing general election result of 1935. Nevertheless, the party's official reaction to Franco's offensive was conditional. While the vast majority of Labour MPs, officers, activists and members felt sympathy with the republican cause, the PLP agreed to support the National government policy of non-intervention.[198] This, in turn, was ratified by the NEC at a meeting with the PLP executive and TUC general council, and presented to the TUC and Labour Party conferences under the jurisdiction of the NCL. In effect, Labour offered humanitarian support to the Spanish people, but simultaneously endorsed an arms embargo for so long as all sides observed it.[199]

The reasons behind this were varied. First, Labour's position was based on pragmatic political thinking. On the one hand, it was hoped – erroneously as it turned out – that a policy of non-intervention would contain the war and allow the republic to defeat Franco's rebel forces.[200] On the other, Leon Blum, the leader of the French Socialist Party and head of a popular front government, had agreed to the policy, thereby making it difficult for Labour to contradict.[201] Second, electoral fears of alienating the Catholic vote evidently impinged on Labour thinking. Such reasoning was apparent in the NCL, and appears to have informed the outlook of Labour leaders such as Citrine and Bevin.[202] Similarly, local parties with large Catholic constituencies were often divided over their position on the civil war.[203] Third, the 'emotive' side to the Spanish civil war gave much concern for Dalton, Bevin and other Labour leaders. While Spain provided a just crusade for many, neither the NCL nor the NEC saw it as an immediate priority for the majority of

British workers. Indeed, local parties could sometimes complain that their Spain committees received a 'lack of support' from the wider labour movement, suggesting a cause for the activist was not necessarily a cause for the wider membership.[204] Equally, the trades council in Birmingham complained about the Borough Labour Party's apparent preoccupation with Spain.[205] For Dalton, Bevin and Citrine, Britain's defence (and the threat of Nazism) was a more pressing issue, while support for the Spanish republic raised the question of why guns for the Spanish were acceptable, but guns for 'ourselves' were still at this time beyond the Labour pale – a reference to the party's reluctance to support British rearmament.[206] Finally, a fear of appearing too close to the CPGB no doubt prompted caution on the part of the NEC and NCL, and would continue to do so once the party had dropped its adherence to non-intervention. The communists supported active intervention in Spain, organised the international brigades of volunteers who travelled to partake in the civil war, and eulogised a Soviet Union that similarly sent material and manual aid to the republic. Moreover, the issue of Spain was inevitably bound up with the campaign for a united front. As always, Labour sought to avoid any suggestion that it was somehow working in tandem with communism.

At the same time, the leadership decision was by no means unanimous, and the issue of Spain was certainly not a simple case of the party left versus the party right. Within the NEC, for example, Herbert Morrison took a consistently pro-republican line. Shinwell, too, harboured reservations over the party's original position, while Greenwood's speech to conference endorsing the NCL report was far from convincing.[207] For many in the party, government inaction over Spain was tantamount to being 'pro-fascist'; its refusal to act collectively through the League of Nations had undermined both the League and the moves towards disarmament pioneered by Arthur Henderson and others. In the words of the Blaydon Divisional Labour Party, neutrality was 'black crime' tantamount to writing a 'blank cheque to Hitler to attack France'.[208] Accordingly, the party's initial position was soon challenged, particularly once it became clear that both Germany and Italy were providing extensive material support for Franco. Although the NCL report was endorsed by the party conference, the evident ill-feeling towards such a line – along with the impassioned speeches of two invited Spanish delegates – prompted the NEC to propose an immediate investigation into alleged breaches of the non-intervention agreement, and to commit support for the Spanish republic's right to buy arms should any such violation be proven.[209]

From here on, the party maintained a consistently critical approach to government policy. In the Commons, Attlee led the way in condemning the government's refusal to respond to German and Italian contravention of the non-intervention policy, demanding that the republic be allowed to buy arms, and later going to visit the British international brigades stationed in Spain.[210] The NCL, meanwhile, called a meeting of the Second International and the International Federation of Trade Unions (IFTU) that adopted a resolution declaring it 'the common duty of the working class of all countries' to campaign for the 'complete commercial liberty' of Spain. A similar resolution was then passed by the NEC, PLP and TUC general council on 28 October 1936, paving the way for a series of conferences, demonstrations and deputations to Anthony Eden's foreign office over the course of 1937. By July, the NCL was declaring that the war in Spain was 'indissolubly bound up with the external policy of the fascist powers', and called on the League of Nations to 'assist the Spanish people to recover their independence'.[211] More practically, campaigns for aid, milk and relief for the Basque children were launched, with the NCL claiming to have raised £53,000 for the international solidarity fund by May 1939.[212]

Beyond the party hierarchy, Spain quickly found its way to the top of many a local party's agenda in the late 1930s. Most divisional parties established campaigns to collect money and aid for the republic. So, for example, the Edinburgh Trades and Labour Council raised £117/18/4 over the latter part of 1936 and early 1937; the Swansea party raised nearly £300 in a door-to-door collection in 1938; the Bradford Trades Council opened a home for Basque children; and the Leeds party reported in 1937 that it had collected some £300 for its Spanish fund through a series of indoor and cinema meetings.[213] The same was true in London. 'We had two garages full of collected goods at one time', John Platts-Mills – then a Finsbury party member – later remembered; 'we must have had 300 tins of something which could be shipped abroad and endless woolly coats and woolly jackets and thick singlets and shirts and so on'.[214] In Islington, a 'Spain week' in May 1937 involved a public meeting at the Co-op Hall on Monday, a collection with a barrel organ and poster parade on Tuesday, an indoor exhibition on Wednesday, a ward party social on Thursday, a public meeting on Friday, and a Unity Theatre showing of 'Waiting for Lefty' and 'Where's that Bomb' on Saturday. In addition, local ward parties organised film shows, raised money, knitted jumpers and made Spanish ribbons. By 1939, the borough party had resolved that:

> [Believing] that the government of Spain is receiving the most unjust treatment by the British and other governments adhering to the non-intervention pact, and believing also that the government does not truly represent public opinion on the question of the purchase in this country of arms for the defence of Spain by its legal government, [the party] hereby declares its intention to purchase at the earliest possible date, a rifle or other armament for transmission to the republican government of Spain, in defiance of the ban on arms, and as an attempt to break the ban openly and thus render it ineffective.[215]

Clearly, the Spanish civil war made a notable impact on the Labour Party. Not only did it contribute to a shift in party thinking on the need actively to intervene against fascism, but it gave party members an honourable cause to rally round. That said, the various campaigns inspired by the conflict made little impression on the British government. Similarly, while Spain acted as fillip to the party rank-and-file and the left inside and out of the Labour Party, providing a platform for a wave of extra-parliamentary activity, it remained one of many issues preoccupying the party leadership in the late 1930s. While the NEC, NCL and TUC lent their support to the republican cause, they continued to do so within limits. The TUC was certainly not going to take industrial action over the issue, and the Labour Party repeatedly rejected rank-and-file calls for emergency conferences and more concerted action.[216] As this suggests, the Labour Spain Committee set up to persuade the Labour leadership to exert greater pressure on the government made little real progress.[217] The pragmatic political concerns that had informed Labour's initial response to the war remained in place throughout its course.

At the same time, the campaigns surrounding the Spanish civil war ensured that questions of wider labour movement unity again came to the fore. In particular, extra-parliamentary activity brought Labour members into regular contact with the

Communist Party. Put simply, such interaction passed through three phases in the mid-to-late 1930s. From 1933, the CPGB had begun to make overtures towards the Labour Party, trade unions and ILP as to the possibility of a 'united front against fascism'. In the CPGB's estimation, the National government was more likely to align *with* fascism in opposition to the Soviet Union and the working class than fight against it. For this reason, support for the League of Nations, sanctions and rearmament could not be given whilst the National government remained in place. What was needed, therefore, was an alliance with the Soviet Union and a quarantine of the fascist powers, a policy only achievable if the British labour movement united in opposition to both fascism and the National government.[218] Such an approach was given short shrift by the Labour and trade union leadership, although some local party members did indeed begin to co-operate with communists, while many on the left of the party welcomed the possibility of united action, if with evident reservations.[219] CPGB policy was then overhauled in 1935 to endorse a popular front of all progressive forces – working class, middle class, socialist, Liberal, radical etc – against fascism. In Britain, this entailed seeking affiliation to the Labour Party, a move that was welcomed and supported by the Socialist League as a step towards genuine working-class unity. The League already concurred with much of the CPGB's political-economic analysis of the 1930s, although its conception of unity continued to remain more class-based than the CPGB. If socialism was the only answer to fascism, as the Socialist League maintained, then there could be no co-operation with the representatives of capital, whether they be democrat, Liberal or otherwise. Thus, the Socialist League officially remained committed to a united – as opposed to popular (or people's) – front in 1935–7. Nevertheless, the CPGB's change of line paved the way for greater collaboration; the League supported resolutions for communist affiliation and the establishment of a united front at the 1936 Labour conference – both of which were rejected – and entered into negotiations with the CPGB and ILP on the possibility of united action.

As this suggests, the 'unity campaign' launched by the Socialist League, CPGB and ILP in January 1937 was not based on particularly firm strategic foundations.[220] Its stated objective, as outlined in a 'unity manifesto' propagated in the *Tribune* newspaper, was for the 'unity of all sections of the working class' in the struggle for the return of a Labour government. This, the manifesto continued, was 'the next stage in the advance to working-class power', and was committed to 'oppose fascism in all its forms, to oppose the National government as the agent of British capitalism and imperialism, to oppose all restrictions upon civil and trade union liberty, [and] to oppose the militarisation of Great Britain'. Accordingly, a 'fighting programme of mass struggle' was adopted, urging the working class to 'mobilise for the maintenance of peace, for the defence of the Soviet Union', and for a series of immediate demands such as the abolition of the means test and the establishment of a 40-hour week.[221] In truth, the broad demands of the campaign masked deep divisions. The Socialist League had itself adopted the unity manifesto by just 56 votes to 38, with 23 abstentions, suggesting that many Labour activists who sympathised with the Socialist League's perspective were not enamoured by its strategy. Indeed, the League suffered from a falling membership in 1937.[222] Moreover, the likelihood of the CPGB, ILP and Socialist Left agreeing on anything beyond the most general policy was extremely unlikely. Each had come to the unity campaign from vastly different positions, in terms of political strategies, objectives and values. The negotiations that led to the manifesto were reputedly 'long and difficult', with the bitter recriminations exchanged between the ILP and CPGB reflecting the two parties' conflicting past histories.[223] Consequently, Pimlott's assertion that the campaign was something of a 'private game based on long traditions and complicated rules which had no relevance to the shaping of major events, or to the factors which influenced real electors as opposed to an idealised image of the working class', has much to recommend it.[224]

Certainly, the Labour leadership's response to the unity campaign was swift. An appeal to party loyalty had already been issued by the NEC on 12 January 1937, reaffirming the Labour Party's own socialist credentials and insisting that association with either the united or popular front should be 'withheld' in the interests of party unity.[225] This was followed, on 27 January, by a further NEC resolution condemning the Socialist League's adoption of the unity campaign, declaring the League ineligible for continued affiliation to the Labour Party. On 24 March, the NEC resolved that any members still aligned with the Socialist League by 1 June 1937 would be expelled from the party.[226] In reply, the Socialist League voted to dissolve itself in May 1937, thereby allowing its members to campaign individually for 'unity' from inside the party.

The third general phase of co-operation between Labour members and the CPGB therefore followed the dissolution of the Socialist League. By this time, with the international situation evidently deteriorating, many erstwhile League members had converted to the idea of a popular front, with Cripps following suit in early 1938. Within the Labour Party, a committee of party members sympathetic to unity was established and outlawed by the NEC in mid-1937, and resolutions in support of united action continued to be sent by local parties to the executive.[227] An emergency conference on Spain was then held in April 1938 under the auspices of ten cross-party MPs, to which Cripps invited 'all those to the left of Neville Chamberlain'.[228] One month later, and Cripps, Laski, Pritt and Wilkinson formally proposed to the NEC that a popular front be established with non-Labour socialist organisations and anti-government Liberals. This, not surprisingly, was rejected by all but its four proponents.[229] More generally, a number of cross-party campaigns were launched, ranging from the specifically local to Victor Gollancz's eminently successful Left Book Club, which registered some 58,000 members by 1938. Most impressively, perhaps, supporters for the popular front achieved a by-election victory in Bridgwater in November 1938, where an independent progressive candidate (Vernon Bartlett) overturned a Conservative majority of 10,000 with the joint support of the local Labour and Liberal parties.

Such success brought the question of the popular front to a head, leading eventually to the expulsion of Sir Stafford Cripps from the Labour Party. With war appearing ever more imminent, Cripps launched a final appeal for unity on 9 January 1939, sending a memorandum to the NEC urging Labour to join forces with all opponents of the National government on the basis of a twelve-point programme of immediate reform. Once again, the NEC rejected his proposition, prompting Cripps to circulate his memorandum to the press and the party's various constituency organisations.[230] After some consultation, therefore, the NEC insisted that Cripps withdraw his memorandum and reaffirm his allegiance to the Labour Party. Failure to do so would mean expulsion.[231] As a result, Cripps was duly expelled, along with Aneurin Bevan, Robert Bruce, George Strauss and E. P.

Young – all of whom refused to disassociate themselves from the popular front.[232] Soon after, of course, the campaign was fractured by the CPGB's change of line in response to the Nazi–Soviet pact and the eventual outbreak of war.

Two aspects of this drawn out debate are particularly worth noting. First, the apparently unsympathetic response of the NEC masked certain differences within the party leadership. The initial decision to disaffiliate the Socialist League had been passed by just fourteen votes to nine, while both Attlee and Morrison argued in favour of allowing Cripps to remain in the party so as to put his case to the party conference later in 1937. Evidently, the talent and political standing of Cripps and certain other League members was recognised by many in the party. That said, toleration should not be mistaken for empathy. Morrison, in particular, believed the united front 'would split the Labour Party from top to bottom', and he was to the fore in maintaining both the LLP's and the national party's distance from the CPGB.[233] As such, the debates over the united and popular front were in many ways a clash between conceptions of loyalty – to the party as an organisation, or to a particular set of policies and perspectives. They also related as much to methods of procedure as to the arguments involved. This, in turn, was perhaps a clash between Labour's trade union and radical traditions. Even so, we should note that the campaign for united action had its supporters on the industrial side of the party. The MFGB backed the CPGB's campaign for affiliation to the Labour Party (though not the united front), while the AEU tabled the 1936 conference resolution in favour of a united front, to which the NUDAW gave its support.[234]

Second, the 'high' political debates surrounding the united front should not obscure the fact that party members and voters 'on the ground' responded to the possibilities of united action in a variety of ways. In South Wales, for instance, communists had long been a staple part of the labour movement, and such a presence partly helps explain the dedicated support for republican Spain in the region.[235] Consequently, calls for the united and popular fronts were evident in certain Welsh mining lodges (and so the South Wales Miners' Federation; SWMF), as well as within constituency parties such as Cardiff, Swansea and Pontypool. Over in Bedwellty, it took an appeal from Charles Edwards to curtail his constituency party members' engagement with the unity campaign. In Pontypridd, too, Labour members co-operated with the CPGB on local council of action committees organised in the struggle against fascism and war.[236] Here and elsewhere, a number of Labour members held joint membership with the CPGB over the 1930s, thereby blurring the distinction between the Labour and Communist Party in the minds of many. In Manchester, Owen Heather recalled joining the Young Communist League while still a member of his local Labour Party. But while his and others' joint affiliation 'must have been suspected', he later remembered, the local organiser 'took no action'.[237] Indeed, the Manchester Borough Labour Party gave its support to the popular front, and parties such as that in Stockport were ravaged by disputes relating to the CPGB, Spain and co-ordinated Labour–Communist activity.[238]

Support for the united and popular front was certainly evident in and around London, as well as in places where Labour was weak and an alliance with other parties (CPGB, ILP or Liberal) offered a means of gaining greater influence.[239] We have already noted how Labour members in the East End joined with communists and the local community to repel the BUF. Elsewhere, Greater London seems to have supplied the main bases of support for the Socialist League, although actual League branches experienced a rapid turnover of affiliates, averaging just 35 members per branch in 1935, and 29 in 1936.[240] It was, obviously, in London that those George Ridley called 'Bloomsbury revolutionaries' – meaning middle-class intellectuals politicised by the events of the 1930s – continued to agitate in favour of the united and popular fronts in the face of the leadership's protestations.[241] Thus, as Hugh Chaplin – a librarian from Bloomsbury who joined the Labour Party in the late 1930s – later remembered, 'Labour Party people and the Communist Party people locally were working together, co-operating on local problems, local issues. In fact, very often one didn't know which of the two parties the people one knew belonged to ... People weren't deterred by rules ... we worked together'.[242] Elsewhere, middle-class areas such as Highgate combined a small membership with militant and vociferous activity. As part of the Hornsey Labour Party, Highgate (along with Mill Hill) campaigned vigorously to provide aid for Spain, pushed for communist affiliation to the Labour Party and, in 1938, defended the divisional party president – the former communist and Socialist League general secretary Jack Murphy – from local trade union criticism. Where Highgate ward party meetings had had to be cancelled due to lack of attendance in 1935, Labour activity grew notably in conjunction with the rising political tension during the late 1930s.[243]

More generally, however, sympathy for Cripps, the Socialist League and the united front was contained within the Labour Party. At head office, Hugh Dalton and Arthur Greenwood, along with the party organising staff and the vast majority of the executive's trade union members, had little patience for the aspirations and methods of those on the left of the party. To this effect, J. R. Clynes endeavoured to express the prevailing mood within the party leadership at the Labour conference in 1937, pointing to the apparent contradiction of a campaign for unity that appeared more disruptive than unifying. 'You cannot have unity unless you have something of a kindred spirit', Clynes insisted, a sentiment that was echoed by the MFGB's J. McGurk when he called the erstwhile League members 'the biggest assets the Tory Party has got'. 'Sir Stafford Cripps is a rich man with rich pals', he continued, 'and they are the biggest danger to the Labour Party in this country'.[244] As this suggests, there was an element of class tension in the party and trade unions' distrust of the Socialist League. 'I saw Mosley come into the labour movement', Bevin recalled, 'and I see no difference between the tactics of Mosley and Cripps'.[245] Bevin, indeed, was instrumental in pushing the NEC to take its decisive stand against those campaigning for a popular front in 1938–9.[246]

At a local level, too, the Labour leadership's line against both the Socialist League and co-operation with the CPGB was broadly – if often contentiously – accepted. This did not mean that local members, supporters or voters necessarily took notice, but divisional party officers generally ensured recognition of party guidelines. Even in places where support for united action with communists and others was deep-rooted, local party officials sought to replicate the national party position. Thus, George Strauss' North Lambeth party was suspended from the borough party and trades council in 1937 for its support of Cripps' unity manifesto.[247] Similarly, the Newcastle-under-Lyme party involved itself in campaigns against unemployment and fascism, but nevertheless rejected overtures from the CPGB and refused to countenance an 'official' united front.[248] The Nottingham party, too, resolved in 1935 to prohibit all united front activity, thereby upsetting the local Broxtowe party, but simultaneously allowing a way back in for the NUR branch that had disaffiliated from the trades council in protest against the party's previous support for the proscribed Anti-War Movement.[249] In South Wales, divisional parties such as that in Rhondda sought to limit the extent of co-operation between its members and the CPGB. Here, party representatives came to view the united front as a communist manoeuvre designed to undermine the Labour Party, and measures were taken to ensure that communist influence within the party was circumscribed.[250] More widely, the formation of a South Wales Regional Council of Labour in 1937 was designed partly to co-ordinate party activity and thereby negate communist influence. Certainly, the NEC was quick to advise party officers of the official Labour 'line'. Thus, when the Newport Labour Party voted by 55 votes to six to refuse CPGB affiliation to the Labour Party but simultaneously agreed to accept local communist assistance during its 1936 municipal election campaign, the NEC immediately condemned such a compromise and, in 1937, the divisional party president and vice-president were forced to agree not to attend the 'unity meetings' organised in the town. By July, the Newport party resolved 'to have nothing to do with such futility', and even a visit by the Left Book Club was later deemed 'inconsistent' with party objectives.[251] In Scotland, SSP support for the united front led to the expulsion of several party members (including the SSP secretary Arthur Brady) and, in 1938, the separation of Trades and Labour councils in an attempt to prevent communist trade union delegates voting on Labour matters.[252]

In many other areas, the issue of the united or popular front was less problematic. According to Reynolds and Laybourn, the Socialist League and unity manifesto made very little impact in West Yorkshire, with parties in the region seeing no real purpose in such a campaign and generally endorsing Dalton's criticism of the League as a 'rich man's toy' that made much noise but engendered little actual support. Some recognition for a united front was apparent in the region during the early 1930s, but this was not transferred into support for the later popular front.[253] In places such as Peterborough, Darlington, Wolverhampton, Houghton-le-Spring and Nottingham, too, resolutions or activities favouring unity and/or supporting the Socialist League were easily defeated.[254] Ultimately, therefore, Labour members often took part in joint campaigns with communists – either in relation to unemployment or the struggle against fascism, particularly Spain – but this was typically carried out 'unofficially', with the local Labour apparatus maintaining its independence and loyalty to the directives of head office.

Throughout the debate over the united and popular front, the Labour Party repeatedly asserted its independence and poured scorn on the possibility of working harmoniously with the CPGB. The NEC reaffirmed Labour's commitment to socialism, to its broad basis of support, and to its formulation of a socialist programme 'wide enough ... to have enabled, and to still enable, hundreds and thousands of men and women to express their socialist faith clearly and without reservation'.[255] In so doing, it further underlined the importance of loyalty and unity within the party's own ranks. The sanctity of – and loyalty to – the majority decision lay at the basis of Labour democracy. As tellingly, perhaps, the party remained convinced that an alliance with the relatively small (and notoriously disruptive) CPGB would serve only to 'bring a few thousand votes to the alliance; but it may well drive millions into Mr Chamberlain's camp'.[256] Equally, the idea of co-operating with a weak and divided Liberal Party made little political sense.

Although the national press portrayed the NEC's quarrels with Cripps as damaging and divisive, depicting a 'grave internal crisis' (*Daily Mail*) that eventually led 'the Labour Party to blow its brains out' with the expulsion of Cripps in 1939 (*Daily Express*), the party's position was informed by long-term electoral considerations.[257] Ultimately, as David Blaazer has suggested, Labour saw no need for a popular front when it already existed – in the party's estimate – within the organisational structure and policies of the Labour Party.[258]

But what was the Labour Party's policy with regard to the worsening international situation in 1935–9? As we have seen, Labour's approach modified over the early 1930s, and it continued to do so from 1935 as each international 'crisis' necessitated that the party leadership provide a distinctive and effective response to events abroad and the policies of the National government at home. This proved difficult. Many in the party retained a deep aversion to war of any sort, while distrust of Baldwin's, and later Chamberlain's, National government was deep-rooted. As such, the debate over whether to support rearmament and other national defence measures must be seen in relation to Labour's belief that the National government would use force not to uphold the collective security of the League of Nations, but to defend and pursue its own national and imperialist interests. Indeed, such a position was given credence by the government's readiness to appease Mussolini over Abyssinia and to conclude an Anglo-German Naval pact with Hitler. At each turn, the government seemed more willing to negotiate with the fascist powers than to work through the League of Nations in the interests of peace and democracy. And although such a position appeared to change in the build up to the general election and in response to the results of the Peace Ballot, the notorious Hoare-Laval pact – by which Britain and France contrived to appease Mussolini's Abyssinian ambition – suggested that little had really changed following the National government's election victory. True, Sir Samuel Hoare was forced to resign amidst the furore, but the government's non-intervention policy in Spain suggested that it was in general more sympathetic than antagonistic towards fascism.

Labour's official policy continued to reflect these ambiguities. While often providing stinging critiques of the National government's intent and apparent impotence, Labour simultaneously presented a rather woolly alternative. On the one hand, Bevin and Citrine continued to push for a more robust response. Although they sympathised with Labour distrust of the National government, the threat of fascism was of more pressing concern. Thus, in regard to Hitler's reintroduction of conscription and planned rearmament in early 1935, the TUC general council, along with Hugh Dalton, recommended that Labour support the government's arms estimates in May 1935.[259] From the other perspective, those on the left of the party continued to argue against any form of compliance with the government. So, for instance, Cripps and Bevan could regularly portray the government as an effectively 'proto-fascist' force dedicated to the interests of the British Empire and the subjugation of the British working class.[260] 'We are not', Bevan famously said to the party conference in 1937, 'going to put a sword in the hands of our enemies that may be used to cut off our own heads'.[261] In between, the majority of the PLP – most obviously Attlee and Morrison – accepted the need to countenance the use of force through the League of Nations, but continued to vote against the government's arms estimates as a protest against wider government international policy.[262]

The emphasis within such an approach shifted over time, particularly following Hitler's occupation of the Rhineland and the outbreak of the Spanish civil war. In mid-1936, the NCL published *Labour and the Defence of Peace*, in which Labour openly asserted that it would 'be prepared to accept the consequences' of its commitments to collective security. In a section that aptly reflected the NCL *modus operandi*, the manifesto stated that:

> A man who joins a trade union accepts the obligation of collective action in defence of its principles. A man who enjoys the collective security of a trade union must be prepared to take the risks of loyalty to his principles when a strike or lockout is threatened. Similarly, a movement which supports the League system cannot desert it in a crisis.[263]

This, in turn, was followed by a special resolution endorsed by the Labour conference in October 1936, committing Labour to the retention of enough armaments to carry out its obligations to the League of Nations, but simultaneously criticising the government's 'competitive armament policy'. Again, however, ambiguity served to cover – albeit tenuously – differing priorities within the party leadership. In response to Dalton's speech in favour of rearmament, Morrison concurred only if such a policy formed part of the collective rearmament of the 'peaceful powers'. In so doing, he – along with Attlee, who wound up the debate by refusing to give the government a 'blank cheque' – continued to focus on the inadequacies of the Baldwin administration rather than the wider connotations of Labour's critical position.[264] Even so, the ground was now set for a 'full examination' of Labour policy to be prepared in readiness for the 1937 party conference in Bournemouth.

Over the ensuing year, the international situation proceeded to deteriorate, tipping the political balance ever more in the favour of Dalton and his trade union colleagues on the NCL. Alongside W. Gillies of the NEC's international department, Dalton set about more firmly realigning party policy. Within the PLP, moreover, the argument that to vote against the government's proposed arms estimates would suggest to the British public that the party was indifferent to the country's defence now began to carry some weight. In July, the PLP voted by 45 to 39 to abstain – rather than oppose – the government's defence estimates, with only eleven Labour MPs refusing to comply.[265] Subsequently, Dalton's address from the chair to the 1937 party conference argued that Britain must be 'powerfully armed', otherwise 'a British Labour government, coming into power tomorrow, would be in danger of humiliations, intimidations and acts of foreign intervention in our national affairs', before the NEC report on 'International Policy and Defence' committed the party to the return of a Labour government 'strongly equipped to defend this country, to play its full part in collective security, and to meet any intimidation by the fascist powers'. Still, however, there was no specific reference to Labour giving open support to government plans for rearmament.[266]

The Anschluss in March and the Munich crisis of August–September 1938 completed Labour's transition. In particular, the fact that German claims upon the Sudetenland of Czechoslovakia led only to British-backed concessions that effectively facilitated Hitler's plans for German expansion was enough for the NEC to conclude that such agreement amounted to a 'complete and abject surrender imposed' upon the Czechoslovakian people.[267] In the Commons, Attlee condemned

Chamberlain's appeasement of Hitler and decried the 'humiliating position' that the government had placed the country in. 'The day ... when we left the path of collective security in the League of Nations, when we abandoned the attempt to make peace through the League ... that day we took a step towards war'.[268] Meanwhile, the TUC adopted in September an NEC-backed declaration 'Labour and the International Situation: On the Brink of War', condemning the government's policy and calling on Britain to take the lead in collective action to 'unite with the French and Soviet governments to resist any attack on Czechoslovakia'. 'Whatever risks are involved', the report stated, 'Great Britain must make its stand against aggression'.[269] At last, Labour's strategy of standing up to fascism while condemning the pusillanimity of the government's policy of appeasement had found a coherent balance.

With the government's policy becoming less credible by the day, and with war becoming ever more probable, so political tensions mounted and the possibility of Labour co-operating with Liberals and anti-Munich Conservatives to bring down Chamberlain was floated within the higher echelons of the PLP. This proved premature; when the NCL heard of such scheming in November, its angry response was wholly predictable and consistent with Labour's determination to maintain its independence.[270] Similarly, while Labour accepted the need for voluntary national service in the circumstances of 1938–9, it continually rejected the government's plans for conscription. Recognition that the party must support the war effort did not mean a complete reversal of Labour principles. Even so, the party had agreed from as early as 1935 to participate in air-raid precautions (ARP), although such a position was criticised by many in the party as contributing to the creation of a 'war mentality'.[271] For others, including Herbert Morrison as leader of the LCC, such precautions were essential. While Morrison retained his opposition to wider government policy, he nevertheless instigated wide-ranging ARP measures across the capital. Following the Munich crisis, plans to evacuate some 500,000 school children were drawn up and work teams established to tend to the injured and repair the inevitable damage.[272] Similarly, while parties in Halifax, Bradford, Nelson and elsewhere refused to involve themselves in activities that they believed encouraged the likelihood of war, others – such as those in Leeds, Sheffield and Newport – immediately got involved in the provision of ARP.[273]

Clearly, therefore, the rise of fascism and the evident threat that it posed to international peace and stability facilitated a fundamental change in Labour's approach to foreign policy. Though the party retained its devotion to peace and collective security, and refused publicly to accept the 'inevitability of war' until at least mid-1939, Labour nevertheless came to recognise the need for national defence in resistance to fascist intimidation. The party's old pacifist tradition was nearly wholly expunged, while the left's more overtly theoretical approach was marginalised, if still able retain a claim on the party conscience. The failure of the League of Nations had been central to the party's change of emphasis, but so too was the appeasement policy of the National government, which Labour insisted had been 'a major disaster to the peace of the world'.[274] As this suggests, a commitment to war and rearmament cut across much of Labour's 'traditional' thinking on international affairs. While the circumstances of 1939 meant that Labour support for a war against fascism found favour amongst the majority of its members and supporters, this was accepted only with a distinctively heavy heart. In the words of the Colne Valley Labour Party:

> The war we have dreaded for months back has now come to pass and we are again at war. Our young men are being trained in the use of weapons of destruction with which to maim and kill their fellow workers in other lands. Apparently, no useful lesson was learnt by our rulers from the last war.[275]

Ultimately, only a socialist Labour government could save the world from further economic and social disaster.

The Labour Party that entered the Second World War in September 1939 was very different to that which had confronted war in August 1914. Opposition was limited within the party; once war had been declared, Labour appeared committed to the task whilst retaining a critical approach towards the beleaguered Chamberlain administration. Come May 1940, and the disastrous Norwegian campaign finally split the Conservative ranks and paved the way for Churchill's wartime coalition government, so Attlee and Greenwood joined the five-man cabinet. Paradoxically, therefore, after nine years of reasserting Labour's independence and the distinctiveness of its socialist ideal, Labour returned to government in coalition with someone who had claim to be the party's political nemesis. This, in many ways, was a remarkable turn of events. Although Labour had made much of Chamberlain's evident shortcomings, the party's electoral fortunes had shown little real progress from 1935. Thirteen by-election victories had been complemented by moderate local government gains and, from 1938, a falling party membership. Had war not arrived and an election been held in 1940, Labour would have stood little chance of victory. Once war did come, however, Labour was the principal beneficiary of a conflict that it had struggled so hard to prevent. But whatever the permutations of Labour's return to office, the party that had dreamt of becoming the principal opposition following the First World War, was now on course to become the party of government at the end of the Second.

Conclusion

I sometimes think of the Labour Party as a tree, sprung from a seed planted by a dreamer long ago; today a strong, fast-growing, fruit-bearing tree native to this little pocket of British soil, from which it draws many of its most characteristic and best qualities … But without the trade unions our British tree would have no roots and no stability; without the constituency parties it could bear no crop of political fruit.[1]

Hugh Dalton, 1937

[The] difference between intellectuals and the trade unions is this: You have no responsibility of leadership. We, however, must be consistent and we have a great amount of responsibility. We cannot wake up in the morning and get a brain wave, when father says 'turn' and half a million people turn automatically. That does not work.[2]

Ernest Bevin, 31 December 1935

The truth about the relationship between the political and industrial sides is really very simple. There is no attempt by either side to 'boss' the other. There is a recognition of their partnership in action on behalf of the workers, and of their freedom of action in their respective spheres.[3]

Clement Attlee, 1937

The history of the Labour Party between the wars contains a good deal of progress, several disappointments and frustrations, and regular bouts of internal dispute. On the one hand, the party broadly continued to advance over the interwar years; its position in 1939 was certainly far more entrenched than in 1918, its basis of support was wider, its organisation more consistent and stable, and its political programme more clearly defined. On the other hand, the party's apparent rise to power was checked by the disasters that beset the second minority Labour government in 1929–31. Claims that Labour had become the 'natural' party of the working class sat uncomfortably with electoral statistics in certain localities, while there continued to be stark divisions within (and to the left of) the party with regard to both the nature of socialism and the means by which the party should achieve its stated aim. In short, the Labour Party remained an organisation that encompassed a wide range of traditions, outlooks, objectives and expectations. If the trade union movement provided the party with a solid foundation on which to build its political base, then Labour's development was refracted through a variety of structural, ideological and political determinants that impacted on the party in a number of different ways, and at number of different levels within the party apparatus.

In terms of organisation, Labour became more centralised and disciplined in the years prior to the Second World War. The restructuring of the party in 1918 obviously facilitated such a development, but Labour's organisational strictures, along with its appeals for internal party unity, became more resolute as the interwar period progressed. Communist, Independent Labour Party (ILP) and Socialist League attempts to alter the party's political and strategic direction were met with an ever-firmer response; a penchant for procedure became a characteristic of Labour's *modus operandi*. Where the Labour Party before the Great War could be described as a coalition of trade unionists and socialists encompassing a variety of political perspectives but committed first and foremost to the representation of the 'labour interest', then the party by 1939 was a far more assured organisation with a practical programme geared towards a fundamental realignment of Britain's social-economic base. Yet, this should not suggest that Labour had become a monolithic, or one-dimensional, party. Labour continued to comprise a series of linked but distinct sections – the Parliamentary Labour Party (PLP), the affiliated trade unions, the National Executive Committee (NEC) and central party apparatus, the affiliated socialist and professional societies, and the constituency parties that themselves comprised union affiliates, ward organisations, women's sections and Labour council groups. Power relations, perspectives and approaches varied in each of these, and authority within and between each section of the party was liable to shift over time. Of course, Labour's relationship with the trade union movement was integral to the party's constitution and identity. Trade unions continued to provide the bulk of Labour's support, finance and membership throughout the 1920s and 1930s, and both the Trades Union Congress (TUC) and the larger trade union leaderships could exert a notable influence on the party. But such pressure was never all consuming. The 'political' wing of the labour movement retained a significant degree of autonomy, while the growing importance attached to Labour's constituency organisations ensured that parties began to develop in non-union or non-industrial areas, thereby broadening the party's composition. Equally, the formulation of a detailed political programme should not suggest that the party precluded a variety of practical and theoretical perspectives.

As this implies, Labour's objective – from 1918, its socialism – was necessarily open to broad interpretation. Indeed, the party's conception of socialism remained contentious; what it meant could differ from person to person, and leftist critics have consistently insisted that Labour's notion of a 'socialist commonwealth' fell someway short of the imagined ideal.[4] Consequently, Labour socialism continued to encompass aspects from all sections of the party – the moral, visionary and self-improving outlook of the ILP remained a key component of Labour's imagined future, even after its disaffiliation in 1932. Likewise, the practical and immediate social and economic reforms envisaged by Labour members could be traced to either the progressive milieu from which the Fabians imagined their higher form of administration, or to the more practical trade union objective of better wages, living conditions and equitable status for the worker. Crucially, however, the trade unions further helped instil the values of collectivism, loyalty, pragmatism and submission to majority decision that maintained the party in those moments of crisis that periodically confronted it. To this end, Labour socialism remained a fluid concept, as did Labour's means of enacting it. If Labour policy in the 1920s foresaw a socialist future emerging from a buoyant and more efficiently regulated capitalism, then the experience of 1931 demonstrated the need for a programme of practical and applicable policies that could transform fundamentally existing social-economic structures. What this entailed aroused much discussion, although the legacy of MacDonald provoked many to insist in the 1930s that '[we] must preach incessantly this new philosophy of life [socialism]. The inevitability of gradualness must be expunged from our vocabulary'.[5] Similarly, the religious precepts that had informed the beliefs of many a Labour pioneer gave way to a more secular, assertive and ultimately pragmatic interpretation of Labour socialism over the interwar years – a shift encapsulated in the confrontation between Lansbury and Bevin at the 1935 party conference.

Of course, Labour's outlook retained a number of unifying factors that helped bind the party together and enabled it to gather support. In practical terms, Labour maintained a commitment to parliamentary democracy – something that was as true for a left-winger like Nye Bevan as it was for Dalton, MacDonald or Morrison. Ideologically, Labour consistently held to collectivist principles; it retained an aversion to the inequities of capitalism, to the apparent injustices of Britain's class society, and to the imperialist rivalries that divided nation against nation. Labour claimed to speak on behalf of the majority, rather than in defence of a wealthy minority, promoting social welfare and empowerment for those traditionally emasculated. Simultaneously, Labour looked for order amidst the chaos of capitalist relations and development, a notion that gradually transformed from a belief in more efficient administration and common ownership to a system of economic planning. More broadly, Labour encompassed a set of core values based on notions of equality, co-operation and social improvement. These were not necessarily class-based, and the overlapping of certain Labour and Liberal perspectives was clear. But Labour's composition – along with its principal focus on industrial relations and urban environments – ensured that it would be regarded as a party that related most closely to the interests of the industrial and/or urban working class. It was from the organised working class that the party emerged, and it was on such a foundation that the overriding identities and ethos of the Labour Party were based.

Accordingly, Labour's electoral support was consistently strongest in areas characterised by traditions of trade unionism and heavy industry, with its strongholds developing around the pits, factories and mills of industrial Britain, before extending unevenly and gradually into most – but not all – urban centres over the course of the 1920s. By the 1930s, the development of suburban and neighbourhood parties ensured that progress was made into the emerging 'new' industrial areas. Middle-class and rural voters proved more difficult to come by, although the party was able to absorb erstwhile Liberal support in those areas that had previously boasted a nonconformist or radical tradition. In the 1930s, too, the political-economic climate occasioned by the depression and the rise of fascism began to attract more intellectuals and middle-class radicals to socialism and, in many cases, the Labour Party.

Ultimately, the uneven and fractured nature of Labour support – even in largely urban and working-class areas – serves against too determinist an account of Labour's political progress. As recent research has tended to demonstrate, the party's development was informed by a variety of social, economic, cultural and political factors. These, moreover, were experienced, expressed and understood at a national, local, institutional and personal level, suggesting that any broadly defining characteristics must be complemented by a range of local, cultural, gendered and structural considerations. Once inside the gate, however, either in parliament or municipal government, then Labour members throughout Britain endeavoured to work for a fairer and more just society. This, of course, would prove difficult in the varied and often adverse conditions affecting Britain between the wars. Nevertheless, those who represented, worked, campaigned and voted for Labour combined to realign fundamentally Britain's political configuration, providing the potential for change in a world of inequality and uncertainty.

Notes

Introduction

1.   Cited in G. Foote, *The Labour Party's Political Thought: A History* (Basingstoke, 1997 edition), p. 47.

2.   Clement Attlee, speaking on a 1940 BBC radio broadcast, quoted in S. Fielding, 'Labourism in the 1940s', *Twentieth Century British History*, 3, 2 (1992), p. 145.

3.   The post-1945 party has been examined in far greater detail, primarily due to the efforts of those associated with the Labour Movements Group of the Political Studies Association. For more on this and associated texts, see S. Fielding, *The Labour Party: Continuity and Change in the Making of 'New' Labour* (Basingstoke, 2003); S. Fielding, '"New" Labour and the "New" Labour History', *Mitteilungsblatt des Instituts für soziale Bewegungen*, 27 (2002); L. Black, *Old Labour, New Britain? The Political Culture of the Left in 'Affluent' Britain, 1951–64* (London, 2002); L. Black, 'Still at the Penny-Farthing Stage in a Jet-Propelled Era: Branch Life in 1950s Socialism', *Labour History Review*, 65, 2 (2000), pp. 202–23; S. Fielding, P. Thompson and N. Tiratsoo, *'England Arise!' The Labour Party and Popular Politics in 1940s Britain* (Manchester, 1995).

4.   See the bibliography for a detailed list of publications. For just some of the most important examples, see G. D. H. Cole, *A History of the Labour Party from 1914* (London, 1948); H. Pelling, *A Short History of the Labour Party* (London, 1961); A. Thorpe, *A History of the British Labour Party* (Basingstoke, 1997); R. McKibbin, *The Evolution of the Labour Party, 1900–24* (Oxford, 1974); D. Tanner, *Political Change and the Labour Party, 1900–18* (Cambridge, 1990); D. Howell, *MacDonald's Party: Labour Identities and Crisis, 1922–31* (Oxford, 2002); B. Pimlott, *Labour and the Left in the 1930s* (Cambridge, 1977); D. Marquand, *Ramsay MacDonald* (London, 1977); K. Harris, *Attlee* (London, 1985); B. Pimlott, *Hugh Dalton* (London, 1995); P. Graves, *Labour Women: Women in British Working-Class Politics, 1918–39* (Cambridge, 1994); L. Minkin, *The Contentious Alliance: Trade Unions and the Labour Party* (Edinburgh, 1991); M. Savage, *The Dynamics of Working-Class Politics: The Labour Movement in Preston, 1880–1940* (Cambridge, 1987); C. Williams, *Democratic Rhondda: Politics and Society, 1885–1951* (Cardiff, 1996).

5.   M. Pugh, 'The Rise of Labour and the Political Culture of Conservatism, 1890–1945', *History*, 87, 288 (2002), especially p. 529. Thus, in relation to Labour in London, Pugh points to the radical–socialist traditions of George Lansbury in Bow and Bromley, and to the populist–patriotism of Will Thorne and Jack Jones in West Ham.

6.   Tanner, *Political Change and the Labour Party*; McKibbin, *The Evolution of the Labour Party*; D. Howell, *British Workers and the Independent Labour Party, 1888–1906* (Manchester, 1983); Howell, *MacDonald's Party*.

7.   Thorpe, *A History of the British Labour Party*; A. Thorpe, *The British General Election of 1931* (Oxford, 1991); A. Thorpe, 'J. H. Thomas and the Rise of Labour in Derby, 1880–1945', *Midland History*, 15 (1990); A. Thorpe, 'The Consolidation of a Labour Stronghold, 1926–51', in C. Bindfield et al. (eds.), *The History of the City of Sheffield, 1843–1993* (Sheffield, 1993); N. Riddell, *Labour in Crisis: The Second Labour Government, 1929–31* (Manchester, 1999); D. Tanner, C. Williams and D. Hopkin (eds.), *The Labour Party in Wales, 1900–2000* (Cardiff, 2000); D. Tanner, P. Thane and N. Tiratsoo (eds.), *Labour's First Century* (Cambridge, 2000).

8.   For example, Graves, *Labour Women*; Savage, *The Dynamics of Working-Class Politics*; J. Hannam and K. Hunt, *Socialist Women: Britain, 1880s to 1920s* (London, 2002); P. Thane, 'The Women of the British Labour Party and Feminism, 1906–45', in H. L. Smith (ed.), *British Feminism and the Twentieth Century* (Aldershot, 1990).

9.   Savage, *The Dynamics of Working-Class Politics*; Williams, *Democratic Rhondda*; Tanner, *Political Change and the Labour Party*; S. Davies, *Liverpool Labour: Social and Political Influences on the Development of the Labour Party in Liverpool, 1900–39* (Keele, 1996); J. Marriott, *The Culture of Labourism: The East End Between the Wars* (Edinburgh, 1991); C. Macdonald, *The Radical Thread: Political Change in Scotland: Paisley Politics, 1885–1924* (East Lothian, 2000).

10.   See M. Worley (ed.), *Labour's Grass Roots: Essays on the Activities of Local Labour Parties and Members, 1918–45* (Aldershot, 2005); C. Howard, 'Expectations Born to Death: Local

Labour Party Expansion in the 1920s', in J. Winter (ed.), *The Working Class in Modern British History: Essays in Honour of Henry Pelling* (Cambridge, 1983); D. Tanner, 'Labour and its Membership', in Tanner, Thane and Tiratsoo (eds.), *Labour's First Century*; D. Tanner, 'The Pattern of Labour Politics, 1918–39', in Tanner, Williams and Hopkin (eds.), *The Labour Party in Wales*, pp. 113–39.

11. M. Savage, 'The Rise of the Labour Party in Local Perspective', *The Journal of Regional and Local Studies*, 10, 1 (1990), pp. 1–15. The current writer concurs with Savage's view that the local context did not necessarily decline in significance with the growing import of the nation state. Rather, a relationship – or a 'continued dialectic of tension' (p. 2) – was maintained between local and national government between the wars.

12. Ibid. See also Stefan Berger's comments in his 'The Decline of Liberalism and the Rise of Labour – The Regional Approach', *Parliamentary History*, 12, 1 (1993).

13. Labour Party, *Labour Party Foundation Conference and Annual Reports* (reprinted, London, 1967), pp. 1–2.

14. Although exact figures detailing the extent to which Labour members served in local government have yet to be compiled, Dan Weinbren has estimated that there were over 250 Labour councillors by 1914. See D. Weinbren, *Generating Socialism: Recollections of Life in the Labour Party* (Stroud, 1997), p. 14. It has also been estimated that 196 Labour councillors were elected to councils in England and Wales in 1913, compared to 113 in 1910. See McKibbin, *The Evolution of the Labour Party*, p. 85; M. G. Sheppard and J. Halstead, 'Labour's Municipal Election Performance in Provincial England and Wales, 1901–13', *Bulletin of the Society for the Study of Labour History*, 39 (1979). For important qualifications with regard to such figures, see D. Tanner, 'Elections, Statistics, and the Rise of the Labour Party, 1906–31', *The Historical Journal*, 34, 4 (1991), pp. 898–908. Sam Davies and Bob Morley are currently undertaking a massive research project to compile and analyse county borough election results between the wars. See S. Davies and B. Morley, *County Borough Elections in England, 1918–38* (eight volumes, Aldershot, 1999 onwards).

15. M. Kinnear, *The British Voter: An Atlas and Survey since 1885* (London, 1981).

16. C. Harvie, 'Before the Breakthrough, 1886–1922', in I. Donnachie, C. Harvie and I. S. Wood (eds.), *Forward! Labour Politics in Scotland, 1888–1988* (Edinburgh, 1989), p. 7.

17. Labour Party, *Report of the Annual Conference of the Labour Party, 1935* (London, 1935), p. 180.

18. As well as 361 Labour candidates, there were eighteen Coalition Labour candidates and ten Co-operative candidates.

19. Although Sinn Fein gained more seats than Labour, its members refused to take their places in the House of Commons.

20. McKibbin, *The Evolution of the Labour Party*, pp. 236–47. McKibbin's work was partly a response to P. F. Clarke, *Lancashire and the New Liberalism* (Cambridge, 1971). In this, simply put, Clarke pointed not to 'class' reasons to explain the rise of Labour, but to the divisions that ravaged the Liberal Party during the war. But see also H. Pelling, 'Labour and the Downfall of Liberalism', in his *Popular Politics and Society in Late Victorian Britain* (Basingstoke, 1968); K. Laybourn and J. Reynolds, *Liberalism and the Rise of Labour, 1890–1918* (London, 1984).

21. McKibbin, *The Evolution of the Labour Party*, p. 7. Individuals joined via ward committees organised for election purposes, as in Edinburgh.

22. Thorpe, *A History of the British Labour Party*, pp. 24–7.

23. Tanner, *Political Change*, pp. 1–16; J. Lawrence, *Speaking for the People: Party, Language and Popular Politics in England, 1867–1914* (Cambridge, 1990); J. Lawrence and M. Taylor (eds.), *Party, State and Society: Electoral Behaviour in Britain since 1829* (Aldershot, 1997). For a recent overview of the debate, see Macdonald, *The Radical Thread*, pp. 13–21. For earlier criticism, arguing for the continued relevance of Liberalism, see R. Douglas, 'Labour in Decline, 1910–14', in K. Brown (ed.), *Essays in Anti-Labour History: Responses to the Rise of Labour in Britain* (London, 1974).

24. D. Tanner, 'Class Voting and Radical Politics: The Liberal and Labour Party', in Lawrence and Taylor, *Party, State and Society*, p. 106.

25. L. Black, 'Labour at 100', *Mitteilungsblatt des Instituts für soziale Bewegungen*, 27 (2002), pp. 19–34.

26.   Tanner, 'Class Voting and Radical Politics', pp. 112–3.

27.   Ibid.

28.   Again, Tanner's analysis is more complex than this, but interpretations of his work, particularly critical analyses, tend to simplify his conclusions. Essentially, therefore, the debate surrounding Tanner's work has contrived a dualism.

29.   Class attitudes certainly influenced Liberal attitudes to Labour. See D. Blaazer, *The Popular Front and the Progressive Tradition: Socialists, Liberals, and the Quest for Unity, 1884–1939* (Cambridge, 1992), ch. 4.

30.   Quoted in A. Bullock, *Ernest Bevin: A Biography* (London, 2002), p. 20. Consider, too, this quote from George Hodgkinson, a Coventry socialist: 'The social and class anomalies were obvious and the seeds of resentment took root in the soil of bitter experience. Poverty and disease had taken a heavy toll in our household ... To see my mother stricken down and condemned to a slow and painful death, to witness the daily deterioration in her health, culminating in the deathbed scene, seared my heart and mind. What kind of society were we living in which condemned the mother of a working-class family to go in such circumstances? ... Was this the price to pay for an accident of birth, of being in the wrong social class?'. G. Hodgkinson, *Sent to Coventry* (London, 1970), p. 9.

31.   E. Biagini and A. Reid (eds.), *Currents of Radicalism: Popular Radicalism, Organised Labour and Party Politics in Britain, 1850–1914* (Cambridge, 1991).

32.   Macdonald, *The Radical Thread*, pp. 207–66; Blaazer, *The Popular Front*, pp. 25–97.

33.   Williams, *Democratic Rhondda*, pp. 29–82.

34.   N. Kirk, *Change, Continuity and Class: Labour in British Society, 1850–1920* (Manchester, 1998), pp. 182–207. For the early development of labour representation and the ILP, see Howell, *British Workers and the Independent Labour Party*.

35.   Declan McHugh makes this point in relation to Manchester. See S. Fielding and D. McHugh, 'The *Progressive Dilemma* and the Social Democratic Perspective', in J. Callaghan, S. Fielding and S. Ludlam (eds.), *Interpreting the Labour Party: Approaches to Labour Politics and History* (Manchester, 2003), pp. 142–3.

36.   Berger, 'The Decline of Liberalism and the Rise of Labour', p. 89.

37.   For the period covered in the current book, see R. McKibbin, *Classes and Cultures: England, 1918–1951* (Oxford, 1998). Also, G. Stedman Jones, *Languages of Class: Studies in English Working-Class History, 1832–1982* (Cambridge, 1983); E. Hobsbawm, *Worlds of Labour: Further Studies in the History of Labour* (London, 1984); R. McKibbin, *The Ideologies of Class: Social Relations in Britain, 1890–1950* (Oxford, 1990). Tanner, certainly, does not discount the importance of class, but suggests that any connection that it forged between social-economic circumstances and politics had to be created and maintained. See Tanner, 'Class Voting', p. 112.

38.   The formation and development of the War Emergency Workers' National Committee has been seen as integral to this. See R. Harrison, 'The War Emergency Workers' National Committee', in A. Briggs and J. Saville (eds.), *Essays in Labour History, 1886–1923* (London, 1971), pp. 212–59.

39.   For an overview of how the war influenced Labour's economic thinking, see J. Tomlinson, 'Labour and the Economy', in Tanner, Thane and Tiratsoo (eds.), *Labour's First Century* (Cambridge, 2000), pp. 46–55.

40.   For an excellent overview, see C. Wrigley, 'The State and the Challenge of Labour in Britain, 1917–20', in C. Wrigley (ed.), *Challenges of Labour: Central and Western Europe, 1917–20* (London, 1993), pp. 262–89. Also, B. Waites, *A Class Society at War, 1914–18* (Leamington Spa, 1987); J. M. Winter, *Socialism and the Challenge of War: Ideas and Politics in Britain, 1912–28* (London, 1974); J. N. Horne, *Labour at War: Britain and France, 1914–18* (Oxford, 1991); T. Adams, 'Labour and the First World War: Economy, Politics and the Erosion of Local Peculiarity?', *The Journal of Regional and Local Studies*, 10, 1 (1990). The co-operative movement was another 'beneficiary' of such developments. Membership increased, and the movement became politicised via the formation of the Co-operative Party in 1917.

41.   S. Ball and I. Holliday, 'Mass Conservatism: An Introduction', in S. Ball and I. Holliday (eds.), *Mass Conservatism: The Conservatives and the Public since the 1880s* (London, 2002), pp. 1–15.

42.   Howell, *MacDonald's Party*, p. 54.

43.   Labour Party, *Labour Party Conference Report, 1907* (London, 1907).

44.   Labour Party, *Labour Party Conference Report, January 1918* (London, 1918).
45.   Howell, *MacDonald's Party*, p. 55. See also L. Minkin, *The Labour Party Conference: A Study in the Politics of Intra-Party Democracy* (London, 1978).
46.   McKibbin, *The Evolution of the Labour Party*, pp. 164–7.
47.   E. Wertheimer, *Portrait of the Labour Party* (London, 1929), pp. 1–9.
48.   Minkin, *The Contentious Alliance*, p. xiii, pp. 3–9. For a good overview of Labour–trade union relations before 1918, see R. Taylor, 'Out of the Bowels of the Movement: The Trade Unions and the Origins of the Labour Party, 1900–18', in B. Brivati and R. Heffernan (eds.), *The Labour Party: A Centenary History* (Basingstoke, 2000), pp. 8–49.
49.   T. Jones, 'Labour's Constitution and Public Ownership: From Old Clause IV to New Clause IV', in Brivati and Heffernan (eds.), *The Labour Party*, pp. 294–8.
50.   Winter, *Socialism and the Challenge of War*, p. 272.
51.   Foote, *The Labour Party's Political Thought*; D. Tanner, 'The Development of British Socialism, 1900–18', *Parliamentary History*, 16 (1997).
52.   The classic account remains S. Yeo, 'The New Life: The Religion of Socialism in Britain, 1883–96', *History Workshop*, 4 (1977), pp. 5–56. See also L. Barrow and I. Bullock (eds.), *Democratic Ideas and the British Labour Movement, 1880–1914* (Cambridge, 1996).
53.   P. Catterall, 'Morality and Politics: The Free Churches and the Labour Party between the Wars', *The Historical Journal*, 36, 3 (1993), p. 681.
54.   H. Beynon and T. Austrin, *Masters and Servants: Class and Patronage in the Making of a Labour Organisation* (London, 1994), p. 271.
55.   *Minutes of the Newport Labour Party*, 20 November 1925 (Wakefield, 1999).
56.   Quoted in Weinbren, *Generating Socialism*, pp. 35–6. Hodgkinson's autobiography – *Sent to Coventry –* makes countless reference to the religious basis of his socialism.
57.   Quoted in Catterall, 'Morality and Politics', p. 679.
58.   J. Shepherd, *George Lansbury: At the Heart of Old Labour* (Oxford, 2002); P. Clarke, *The Cripps Version: The Life of Sir Stafford Cripps, 1889–1952* (London, 2002); I. Wood, *John Wheatley* (Manchester, 1989).
59.   Quoted in Harvie, 'Before the Breakthrough', p. 18.
60.   R. MacDonald, *Socialism* (London, 1907), p. 84.
61.   Quoted in Howell, *MacDonald's Party*, p. 227.
62.   See Foote, *The Labour Party's Political Thought*, for a more detailed examination of Labour socialist ideas.
63.   J. Harris, 'Labour's Political and Social Thought', in Tanner, Thane and Tiratsoo (eds.), *Labour's First Century* (Cambridge, 2000), pp. 14–23.
64.   R. McKibbin, 'Why was there no Marxism in Great Britain?', in McKibbin, *The Ideologies of Class*, pp. 1–41. See also S. Macintyre, *A Proletarian Science: Marxism in Britain, 1917–33* (London, 1980).
65.   See Harris, 'Labour's Political and Social Thought', pp. 14–23, for the tensions inherent in Labour socialism.
66.   J. E. Cronin, *Labour and Society in Britain, 1918–79* (London, 1984), pp. 38–9.
67.   Lew Smith, a Stepney communist and later Labour supporter, in Weinbren, *Generating Socialism*, p. 16.
68.   By as late as 1937, Bevin was still warning the party that it had to take into account 'thousands of our people paying the political levy who are not conscious socialists'. Labour Party, *Report of the Annual Conference of the Labour Party, 1937* (London, 1937), p. 146.
69.   Quoted in Savage, *The Dynamics of Working-Class Politics*, p. 1.
70.   Bullock, *Ernest Bevin*, p. 183.
71.   For a discussion of the terms 'labourism' and 'Labourism', see S. Fielding, '"Labourism" and Locating the British Labour Party within the British Left', *Working Papers in Contemporary History and Politics*, Working Paper No. 11 (Salford, undated). The classic critique remains R. Miliband, *Parliamentary Socialism: A Study in the Politics of Labour* (London, 1961).
72.   Savage, 'The Rise of the Labour Party in Local Perspective', pp. 1–15.
73.   *Bermondsey Labour Magazine*, January 1924, quoted in S. Goss, *Local Labour and Local Government: A Study of Changing Interests, Politics and Policy in Southwark from 1919 to 1982* (Edinburgh, 1988), p. 146.
74.   *Workers! Vote for Witard* (Norwich, 1909).

75. Howell, *British Workers*, pp. 373–88.

76. Quoted in Marriott, *The Culture of Labourism*, p. 33.

77. D. Butler and J. Freeman, *British Political Facts, 1900–69* (London, 1969), p. 141.

78. For overviews of the debate, see Tanner, 'Class Voting and Radical Politics', pp. 106–11. See also D. Tanner, 'The Parliamentary Electoral System, the "Fourth" Reform Act and the Rise of Labour in England and Wales', *Bulletin of the Institute of Historical Research*, 3 (1993); H. C. G. Matthews, R. I. McKibbin and J. Kay, 'The Franchise Factor in the Rise of the Labour Party', *English Historical Review*, 91 (1976), pp. 723–52.

79. See B. R. Mitchell and P. Deane, *Abstract of British Historical Statistics* (Cambridge, 1962), p. 105, for a breakdown of occupational groups in Britain in 1911, 1921 and 1931. At least 70 per cent of the working (and unemployed) population in Britain could be designated 'working class' between the wars.

80. J. J. Smyth, *Labour in Glasgow, 1896–1936* (East Lothian, 2000).

81. 'Letter from P. A. Harris to J. W. Black', 28 January 1919, in Minutes of the Harborough Division Liberal Association (Leicestershire Record Office).

Chapter One

1. H. Beynon and T. Austrin, *Masters and Servants: Class and Patronage in the Making of a Labour Organisation* (London, 1994), p. 274. The quote is taken from a speech to the Sunderland Rotary Club in April 1925. Peter Lee was chairman of the Labour-controlled Durham county council elected in April 1919 and 1925, and later general secretary of the Durham Miners' Association.

2. Edinburgh and District Trades and Labour Council, *Annual Report for year ending 31 March 1921* (Edinburgh, 1921). The annual reports form part of the 'The Origins and Development of the Labour Party in Britain at a Local Level' series (Wakefield, 1986 and 1999).

3. These include Irish parties, the Communist Party, Co-operative Party, independent MPs and, in 1918, uncouponed Tories.

4. Labour Party, *Report of the Annual Conference of the Labour Party, 1923* (London, 1923), p. 178.

5. 'Analysis of the Constituencies fought at the General Election, December 1919' (undated), *Minutes of the National Executive Committee* (Woodbridge, undated) (hereafter *NEC Mins*); A. Thorpe, *A History of the British Labour Party* (Basingstoke, 1997), p. 47.

6. Quoted in C. Wrigley, *Arthur Henderson* (Cardiff, 1990), p. 127.

7. D. Howell, *MacDonald's Party: Labour Identities and Crisis, 1922–31* (Oxford, 2002), p. 23.

8. H. Tracey (ed.), *The British Labour Party: Its History, Growth, Policy and Leaders* (London, 1948).

9. Quoted in C. Wrigley, *Lloyd George and the Challenge of Labour: The Post War Coalition, 1918–22* (Hemel Hempstead, 1990), pp. 182 and 303.

10. T. Johnston, *Memories* (London, 1952), pp. 100–9.

11. A. Thorpe, 'J. H. Thomas and the Rise of Labour in Derby, 1880–1945', *Midland History*, 15 (1990), pp. 120–4; D. Howell, '"I Loved My Union and My Country": Jimmy Thomas and the Politics of Railway Trade Unionism', *Twentieth Century British History*, 6, 2 (1995), pp. 145–73; G. Blaxland, *J. H. Thomas: A Life for Unity* (London, 1964); J. H. Thomas, *My Story* (London, 1937).

12. For biographies of Henderson, see Wrigley, *Arthur Henderson*; F. Leventhal, *Arthur Henderson* (Manchester, 1989); M. A. Hamilton, *Arthur Henderson* (London, 1938).

13. *NEC Mins*, 9 April 1919.

14. Sir Eric Geddes headed a government committee established on 16 August 1921 to examine government spending. From February 1922, the committee's reports recommended, among other things, large cuts in government spending on education, housing, health, pensions and the military. See K. O. Morgan, *Consensus and Disunity: The Lloyd George Coalition Government, 1918–22* (Oxford, 1979).

15. I. S. Wood, 'Hope Deferred: Labour in Scotland in the 1920s', in I. Donnachie, C. Harvie and I. S. Wood (eds.), *Forward! Labour Politics in Scotland, 1888–1988* (Edinburgh, 1989), pp. 32–4.

16. S. Davies, *Liverpool Labour: Social and Political Influences on the Development of the Labour Party in Liverpool, 1900–39* (Keele, 1996), pp. 69–73.

17. M. Childs, 'Labour Grows Up: The Electoral System, Political Generations, and British Politics, 1890–1929', *Twentieth Century British History*, 6, 2 (1995).

18. For an example, see Jennie Lee's autobiography, which refers to the shifting attitudes – to politics and religion – of her grandfather, father and herself. J. Lee, *This Great Journey* (London, 1963).

19. The classic biography remains D. Marquand, *Ramsay MacDonald* (London, 1977).

20. Quoted in R. Toye, *The Labour Party and the Planned Economy, 1931–51* (Woodbridge, 2003), p. 17.

21. K. Laybourn, *Philip Snowden: A Biography, 1864–1937* (Aldershot, 1988).

22. J. Shepherd, *George Lansbury: At the Heart of Old Labour* (Oxford, 2002), pp. 1–250; A. Thorpe, 'George Lansbury 1932–35', in K. Jefferys (ed.), *Leading Labour: From Keir Hardie to Tony Blair* (London, 1999), p. 63.

23. W. Knox, '"Ours is Not an Ordinary Parliamentary Movement": 1922–26', in A. McKinlay and R. J. Morris (eds.), *The ILP on Clydeside, 1893–1932: From Foundation to Disintegration* (Manchester, 1991), p. 157.

24. W. Knox, *James Maxton* (Manchester, 1987).

25. Howell, *MacDonald's Party*, p. 28. Although Emmanuel Shinwell and Rhys Davies had trade union backgrounds, they were by this time more closely associated with their political careers. For Shinwell, see E. Shinwell, *Conflict Without Malice* (London, 1955).

26. Quoted in Howell, *MacDonald's Party*, p. 29. The article was published in *Forward!*, 23 December 1922.

27. N. Mansfield, 'Farmworkers and Local Conservatism in South West Shropshire, 1916–23', in S. Ball and I. Holliday (eds.), *Mass Conservatism: The Conservatives and the Public since the 1880s* (London, 2002), pp. 36–57; *Labour Organiser*, October 1923; C. Howard, 'Expectations Born to Death: Local Labour Party Expansion in the 1920s', in J. Winter (ed.), *The Working Class in Modern British History: Essays in Honour of Henry Pelling* (Cambridge, 1983), pp. 69–71. See also C. Wrigley, 'Explaining Why So Many as well as So Few: Some Aspects of the Development of the Labour Party in Small Towns and Rural Areas', *Journal of Regional and Local Studies*, 10, 1 (1990).

28. Minutes of the Harborough Conservative and Unionist Association Women's Branch (Leicestershire Record Office).

29. Quoted in D. Tanner, 'The Pattern of Labour Politics, 1918–39', in D. Tanner, C. Williams and D. Hopkin (eds.), *The Labour Party in Wales, 1900–2000* (Cardiff, 2000), p. 126.

30. Thorpe, *A History of the British Labour Party*, p. 55.

31. J. Reynolds and K. Laybourn, *Labour Heartland: A History of the Labour Party in West Yorkshire during the Interwar Years, 1918–39* (Bradford, 1987), p. 58.

32. Wrigley, *Lloyd George and the Challenge of Labour*, p. 245.

33. D. McHugh, 'The Labour Party in Manchester and Salford Before the First World War: A Case of Unequal Development', *Manchester Region History Review*, 14 (2000), pp. 13–24; L. Baston, 'Labour Local Government, 1900–99', in B. Brivati and R. Heffernan (eds.), *The Labour Party: A Centenary History* (Basingstoke, 2000), p. 451.

34. C. Williams, 'Labour and the Challenge of Local Government', in Tanner, Williams and Hopkin (eds.), *The Labour Party in Wales*, p. 142.

35. B. Donoughue and G. W. Jones, *Herbert Morrison: Portrait of a Politician* (London, 2001 edition), p. 655.

36. Marquand, *Ramsay MacDonald*, pp. 291–2.

37. Wrigley, *Lloyd George and the Challenge of Labour*, pp. 1–21.

38. Wrigley, *Arthur Henderson*, pp. 112–24.

39. *NEC Mins*, 7 November 1918.

40. R. McKibbin, *The Evolution of the Labour Party, 1900–24* (Oxford, 1974), pp. 102–3; *NEC Mins*, 9 April 1918.

41. See R. Skidelsky, *Oswald Mosley* (London, 1975), pp. 77–83.

42. Quoted in P. Catterall, 'Morality and Politics: The Free Churches and the Labour Party between the Wars', *The Historical Journal*, 36, 3 (1993), p. 676.

43.   'Letter from Sir William Robertson to Mr Anderson', 14 December 1920, in Minutes of the Scottish Liberal Federation (National Library of Scotland).

44.   *Edinburgh Evening News*, 20, 23 and 24 November 1923.

45.   Minutes of the Harborough Division Liberal Association, 14 June 1919 and 21 May 1921; Minutes of the Leicestershire Liberal Association, 1918–24 (Leicestershire Record Office).

46.   *Constitution of the Durham Municipal and County Federation* (Durham Record Office, undated). For Headlam, see S. Ball (ed.), *Parliament and Politics in the Age of Churchill and Attlee: The Headlam Diaries, 1935–51* (Cambridge, 2000).

47.   H. A. Clegg, *A History of British Trade Unions Since 1889: Volume II, 1911–33* (Oxford, 1985), p. 570.

48.   McKibbin, *The Evolution of the Labour Party*, pp. 156–61.

49.   *NEC Mins*, 12 June and 10 July 1918.

50.   'Memorandum on Party Staff and its Work', undated [1919], *NEC Mins*, 1919.

51.   C. Wrigley, 'The Trade Unions between the Wars', in C. Wrigley (ed.), *A History of British Industrial Relations, 1914–45* (Brighton, 1987), pp. 73–83.

52.   Clegg, *A History of British Trade Unions*, p. 568.

53.   I. McLean, *The Legend of Red Clydeside* (Edinburgh, 1983); J. Marriott, *The Culture of Labourism: The East End Between the Wars* (Edinburgh, 1991), pp. 35–9.

54.   Quoted in Marquand, *Ramsay MacDonald*, p. 270.

55.   *NEC Mins*, 9 August 1920.

56.   *Minutes of the Newport Labour Party*, 11 March 1920.

57.   N. Branson, *Poplarism, 1919–25: George Lansbury and the Councillors' Revolt* (London, 1985), p. 21.

58.   Clegg, *A History of British Trade Unions*, p. 568.

59.   Thorpe, *A History of the British Labour Party*, p. 49.

60.   Wrigley, *Lloyd George and the Challenge of Labour*, p. 305.

61.   Edinburgh Trades and Labour Council, *Annual Report for year ending 31 March 1921*, p. 5. Also quoted in J. Holford, *Reshaping Labour: Organisation, Work and Politics – Edinburgh in the Great War and After* (London, 1988), p. 201.

62.   Quoted in Wrigley, *Arthur Henderson*, p. 124. Henderson was speaking to the Labour Party conference in January 1918.

63.   *NEC Mins*, 20 October 1920.

64.   Clegg, *A History of British Trade Unions*, pp. 308–11.

65.   McKibbin, *The Evolution of the Labour Party*, pp. 206–21.

66.   Quoted in Howell, *MacDonald's Party*, p. 186.

67.   See, for example, *NEC Mins*, 12 June 1918.

68.   Howell, *MacDonald's Party*, pp. 93–221.

69.   Minutes of the Hornsey Divisional Labour Party, 23 March 1922 (Wood Green and Hornsey Labour Party Office).

70.   Norwich Labour Party and Industrial Council, *Executive Report and Balance Sheet, 1924* (Norwich, 1924); Houghton-le-Spring Labour Party, *Annual Report and Balance Sheet*, 1918 and 1925 (Durham, 1919 and 1926); Holford, *Reshaping Labour*, p. 246.

71.   For just one example, see 'Annual Meeting 12 November 1921', in Minutes of the Bedwellty Divisional Labour Party (Gwent Record Office).

72.   Clegg, *A History of British Trade Unions*, p. 570.

73.   F. Pethick-Lawrence, *Fate Has Been Kind* (London, 1943), p. 139.

74.   Howell, *MacDonald's Party*, pp. 312–4.

75.   D. Blaazar, *The Popular Front and the Progressive Tradition: Socialists, Liberals, and the Quest for Unity, 1884–1939* (Cambridge, 1992), pp. 72–122; C. A. Cline, *Recruits to Labour: The British Labour Party, 1914–31* (New York, 1963), pp. 8–23.

76.   Wrigley, *Arthur Henderson*, pp. 21–39.

77.   *Labour Candidate's Record*, Widnes by-election flyer 1919, in *NEC Mins*, 1919.

78.   *NEC Mins*, 3 January 1919.

79.   McKibbin, *The Evolution of the Labour Party*, pp. 114–15. Debates on party 'independence' were raised at the 1920, 1921 and 1922 national conferences.

80.   M. Pugh, 'The Rise of Labour and the Political Culture of Conservatism, 1890–1945', *History*, 87, 288 (2002), pp. 526 and 532; M. Pugh, '"Class Traitors": Conservative Recruits to

Labour, 1900–30', *English Historical Review*, 113 (1998). The Conservative MP for South Nottingham, Henry Cavendish Bentinck, declared himself a Labour sympathiser in 1918–22, supporting the miners' strike and later voting against the Baldwin government's Trades Disputes Bill. Labour managed to win the seat in 1929 by nominating the London barrister G. W. Holford-Knight. Ironically, however, Holford-Knight went on to support MacDonald and severely criticised the trade union movement that, as the local party recognised, had 'helped him to his present position'. See P. Wyncoll, *The Nottingham Labour Movement, 1880–1939* (London, 1985).

81.   This is made extremely clear in Jack Jones's autobiography. Having railed against 'prohibition fanatics', he urges his readers to vote. Otherwise, '[the] liberty-snatchers and the water-drinkers and the non-smokers succeed only because you are too lazy to go to the ballot box'. J. Jones, *My Lively Life* (London, 1928), p. 64.

82.   Pugh, 'The Rise of Labour', pp. 515–37; D. Tanner, *Political Change and the Labour Party, 1900–18* (Cambridge, 1990), pp. 130–96; D. Howell, *British Workers and the Independent Labour Party, 1888–1906* (Manchester, 1983), pp. 204–82.

83.   J. Boughton, 'Working Class Conservatism and the Rise of Labour: A Case Study of Birmingham in the 1920s', *The Historian* (Autumn, 1998), pp. 17–20.

84.   Pugh, 'The Rise of Labour', pp. 515–37.

85.   Marriott, *The Culture of Labourism*, pp. 27–67.

86.   M. Pugh, *Women and the Women's Movement in Britain, 1914–59* (Basingstoke, 1992), pp. 64–6.

87.   Labour Party, *Labour and the Nation* (London, 1928), p. 29.

88.   Labour Party, *Labour and the New Social Order* (London, 1918); M. Phillips, *Women and the Labour Party* (London, 1918).

89.   P. Graves, *Labour Women: Women in British Working-Class Politics, 1918–39* (Cambridge, 1994), p. 25; C. Collette, 'Questions of Gender Labour and Women', in Brivati and Heffernan (eds.), *The Labour Party'*, pp. 406–7.

90.   *NEC Mins*, 30 May and 7 November 1918.

91.   *NEC Mins*, 20 September 1918.

92.   Collette, 'Questions of Gender', pp. 406–7; 'Report of the Standing Joint Committee of Women's Industrial Organisations, October 1920–21', *NEC Mins*, 1921.

93.   'By-Election Address to Woolwich, 1921', *NEC Mins*, 1921; Labour Party, *Labour's Call to the People* (London, 1918).

94.   Labour Party, *Why Women Should Vote Labour* (undated [1929]).

95.   J. J. Smyth, *Labour in Glasgow, 1896–1936* (East Lothian, 2000), p. 183.

96.   MacDonald is quoted in J. E. Cronin, *Labour and Society in Britain, 1918–79* (London, 1984), p. 38.

97.   Quoted in L. Black, '"What Kind of People are You?" Labour, the People, and the "New Political History"', in J. Callaghan, S. Fielding and S. Ludlum (eds.), *Interpreting the Labour Party: Approaches to Labour Politics and History* (Manchester, 2003), p. 27.

98.   D. Tanner, 'Labour and its Membership', in D. Tanner, P. Thane and N. Tiratsoo (eds.), *Labour's First Century* (Cambridge, 2000), p. 270. Latimer was writing to H. N. Brailsford in 1926.

99.   M. Philips Price, *My Three Revolutions* (London, 1969), p. 247; S. Macintyre, *A Proletarian Science: Marxism in Britain, 1917–33* (London, 1980), p. 204.

100.   Quoted in B. Pimlott, *Hugh Dalton* (London, 1995), p. 221. Beatrice Webb recorded Lawrence's comments in a diary entry in the mid-1930s.

101.   'Leith Trades Council Annual Report', in Edinburgh and District Trades and Labour Council, *Annual Report for year ending 31 March 1921*.

102.   Smyth, *Labour in Glasgow*, pp. 17–18, 31 and 70–94.

103.   T. Adams, 'Labour Vanguard, Tory Bastion, or the Triumph of New Liberalism? Manchester Politics 1900 to 1914 in Comparative Perspective', *Manchester Region History Review*, 14 (2000), pp. 29–30.

104.   Wyncoll, *The Nottingham Labour Movement*, pp. 181–96; A. Flinn, 'Labour's Family: Local Labour Parties, Trade Unions and Trades Councils in Cotton Lancashire, 1931–39', in M. Worley (ed.), *Labour's Grass Roots: Essays on the Activities of Local Labour Parties and Members, 1918–45* (Aldershot, 2005), pp. 103–24.

105.   R. C. Whiting, *The View from Cowley: The Impact of Industrialization upon Oxford, 1918–39* (Oxford, 1983), pp. 130–50.

106.   J. Henry, 'Salford Labour: A Party in Waiting, 1919–32', *Manchester Region History Review*, 14 (2000), pp. 49–59.

107.   Macintyre, *A Proletarian Science*, p. 206.

108.   H. Morrison, 'Can Labour Win London without the Middle Classes?', *Labour Organiser*, October 1923.

109.   Pimlott, *Hugh Dalton*, p. 112.

110.   Quoted in Wood, 'Hope Deferred', p. 44.

111.   Quoted in Tanner, *Political Change and the Labour Party*, p. 399.

112.   R. Mansfield, quoted in Marriott, *The Culture of Labourism*, p. 35.

113.   Labour Party, *Labour and the Nation*, pp. 5–46.

114.   N. Robertson, 'The Political Dividend: Co-operative Parties in the Midlands, 1917–39', in Worley (ed.), *Labour's Grass Roots*, pp. 148–70; McKibbin, *The Evolution of the Labour Party*, pp. 178–91.

115.   G. D. H. Cole, *A History of the Labour Party from 1914* (London, 1948), p. 10. Labour organisation took a variety of forms, being based on trades councils, Trades and Labour Councils, Trades Council and Labour Representation Committees, Labour Councils, Local Labour parties, Labour Representation Committees and Labour Associations.

116.   C. Harvie, 'Before the Breakthrough, 1886–1922', in Donnachie, Harvie and Wood (eds.), *Forward! Labour Politics in Scotland, 1888–1988* (Edinburgh, 1989), pp. 7–14; W. W. Knox and A. MacKinlay, 'The Re-Making of Scottish Labour in the 1930s', *Twentieth Century British History*, 6, 2 (1995), p. 174.

117.   E. May, 'The Mosaic of Labour Politics, 1900–18', in Tanner, Williams, Hopkin (eds.), *The Labour Party in Wales, 1900–2000* (Cardiff, 2000), pp. 61–85.

118.   C. Williams, *Democratic Rhondda: Politics and Society, 1885–1951* (Cardiff, 1996), pp. 29–82.

119.   McKibbin, *The Evolution of the Labour Party*, p. 5.

120.   See D. McHugh, 'Labour, the Liberals and the Progressive Alliance in Manchester, 1900–14', *Northern History*, 39, 1 (2002).

121.   Tanner, *Political Change and the Labour Party*, p. 160.

122.   M. Savage, *The Dynamics of Working-Class Politics: The Labour Movement in Preston, 1880–1940* (Cambridge, 1987), pp. 134–7; A. Olechnowicz, 'Union First, Politics After: Oldham Cotton Unions and the Labour Party Before 1914', *Manchester Region History Review*, 14 (2000), pp. 1–10.

123.   Tanner, *Political Change and the Labour Party*, pp. 130–61 and 317–48.

124.   Ibid., pp. 228–48.

125.   Cole, *A History of the Labour Party*, pp. 9–15.

126.   Tanner, *Political Change and the Labour Party*, pp. 183–9.

127.   D. Howell-Thomas, *Socialism in West Sussex: A History of the Chichester Constituency Labour Party* (Chichester, undated), p. 2.

128.   P. Thompson, *Socialists, Liberals and Labour: The Struggle for Labour, 1885–1914* (London, 1967); Donoughue and Jones, *Herbert Morrison*, pp. 15–35. Morrison was appointed London Labour Party secretary on 27 April 1915.

129.   D. Tanner, 'Class Voting and Radical Politics: The Liberal and Labour Party', in J. Lawrence and M. Taylor (eds.), *Party, State and Society: Electoral Behaviour in Britain since 1829* (Aldershot, 1997), pp. 112–13. See Tanner, *Political Change and the Labour Party*, pp. 317–48, for a more extensive overview of the progressive alliance in 1914.

130.   Cole, *A History of the Labour Party*, p. 140.

131.   *NEC Mins*, 9 November 1919 and 31 August 1920; McKibbin, *The Evolution of the Labour Party*, pp. 174–8.

132.   *NEC Mins*, 25 June 1918 and 7 October 1919.

133.   Labour Party, *Report of the Annual Conference of the Labour Party, 1920* (London, 1920); Wrigley, *Lloyd George and the Challenge of Labour*, p. 246.

134. C. Williams, 'Britain', in S. Berger and D. Broughton (eds.), *The Force of Labour: The Western European Labour Movement and the Working Class in the Twentieth Century* (Oxford, 1995), p. 123.

135. See Beynon and Austrin, *Masters and Servants*, pp. 100–7; W. R. Garside, *The Durham Miners, 1919–60* (London, 1971). See also, J. Lawson, *A Man's Life* (London, 1944).

136. M. Callcott, 'The Nature and Extent of Political Change in the Interwar Years: The Example of County Durham', *Northern History*, 16 (1980), p. 218.

137. Such a trend continued; Seaham was later won by Ramsay MacDonald in 1929 and Emanuel Shinwell in 1935. See ibid., pp. 215–37; Beynon and Austrin, *Masters and Servants*, pp. 285–305.

138. Beynon and Austrin, *Masters and Servants*, pp. 285–305.

139. Ibid.

140. D. Clark, *We Do Not Want the Earth: The History of South Shields Labour Party* (Whitley Bay, 1992).

141. Callcott, 'The Nature and Extent of Political Change', pp. 215–37.

142. K. Laybourn, *The Rise of Labour: The British Labour Party, 1890–1979* (London, 1988), pp. 54–5.

143. Reynolds and Laybourn, *Labour Heartland*, pp. 33–62.

144. H. Mathers, 'The City of Sheffield 1893–1926', in C. Bindfield et al. (eds.), *The History of the City of Sheffield, 1843–1993* (Sheffield, 1993), pp. 53–84.

145. S. Davies and B. Morley, 'The Reactions of Municipal Voters in Yorkshire to the Second Labour Government, 1929–32', in Worley (ed.), *Labour's Grass Roots*, pp. 125–47.

146. Williams, *Democratic Rhondda*, pp. 83–118; Tanner, 'The Pattern of Labour Politics', pp. 113–39.

147. W. Paynter, *My Generation* (London, 1972), pp, 110–11.

148. Williams, 'Labour and the Challenge of Local Government', p. 143.

149. *Newport Trades Council Annual Report, 1923*. The annual reports form part of the 'The Origins and Development of the Labour Party in Britain at a Local Level' series (Wakefield, 1986 and 1999).

150. T. Graham, *Willie Graham* (London, 1948).

151. So, for example, national trade union memberships fell by 32.6 per cent between December 1919 and December 1922. In Edinburgh, the NUR No. 1 branch membership fell by 32.3 per cent. See Holford, *Reshaping Labour*, p.125.

152. Edinburgh and District Trades and Labour Council, *Annual Report for year ending 31 March 1921*.

153. I. McLean, *The Legend of Read Clydeside*; J. Foster, 'Working Class Mobilisation on the Clyde, 1917–20', in C. Wrigley (ed.), *Challenges of Labour: Central and Western Europe, 1917–20* (London, 1993), pp. 149–75.

154. Smyth, *Labour in Glasgow*, pp. 98–100.

155. R. J. Morris, 'The ILP, 1893–1932: Introduction', in McKinlay and Morris, *The ILP on Clydeside*, p. 6.

156. Smyth, *Labour in Glasgow*, pp. 90–124.

157. Thorpe, 'J. H. Thomas', pp. 111–28.

158. Tanner, *Political Change and the Labour Party*, pp. 398–400.

159. Wyncoll, *The Nottingham Labour Movement*, pp. 91–178.

160. R. P. Hastings, 'The Birmingham Labour Movement, 1918–45', *Midland History*, 5 (1979–80).

161. J. and B. Braddock, *The Braddocks* (London, 1963), p. 81.

162. Davies, *Liverpool Labour*, pp. 233–5. See also P. J. Waller, *Democracy and Sectarianism: A Political and Social History of Liverpool, 1868–1939* (Liverpool, 1939).

163. S. Davies and B. Morley, 'The Politics of Place: A Comparative Analysis of Electoral Politics in Four Lancashire Cotton Textile Towns, 1919–39', *Manchester Region History Review*, 14 (2000).

164. Norwich Labour Party and Industrial Council, *Executive Report and Balance Sheet* (Norwich, 1924 and 1925).

165. *Minutes of the Peterborough Divisional Labour Party* (Wakefield, 1986), 1918–29 passim. Similar concerns were raised, but this time overruled, in 1925.
166. Minutes of the East Grinstead Labour Party, 1918–20 (LSE).
167. London Labour Party, *Labour Party Organisation in London* (London, 1930).
168. Branson, *Poplarism*, pp. 32–101.
169. Ibid., pp. 166–70.
170. J. Gillespie, 'Poplarism and Proletarianism: Unemployment and Labour Politics in London, 1918–34', in D. Feldman and G. Stedman Jones (eds.), *Metropolis–London: Histories and Representations since 1800* (London, 1989), pp. 163–88.
171. The description comes from Dr E. Rickards, a former member of the London Labour Party executive, quoted in Donoughue and Jones, *Herbert Morrison*, p. 63.
172. Ibid.
173. D. E. McHenry, *The Labour Party in Transition, 1931–38* (London, 1938), pp. 125–9.
174. Quoted in Donoughue and Jones, *Herbert Morrison*, p. 71.
175. S. Goss, *Local Labour and Local Government: A Study of Changing Interests, Politics and Policy in Southwark from 1919 to 1982* (Edinburgh, 1988), pp. 9–23; F. Brockway, *Bermondsey Story: The Life of Alfred Salter* (London, 1949).
176. These included Edinburgh South (1920), Hereford (1921) and Dover (1921).
177. Howell-Thomas, *Socialism in West Sussex*, pp. 1–13.
178. Minutes of the Bedwellty Divisional Labour Party, 29 September 1918.
179. 'Report on Organisation of Women, 1 July–31 October', *NEC Mins*, 7 November 1918.
180. Graves, *Labour Women*, p. 231; McKibbin, *The Evolution of the Labour Party*, p. 141.
181. 'Report on the Formation of Women's Advisory Councils', *NEC Mins*, 5 February 1920. The report said the councils were to: (a) co-ordinate the work of the women's sections and Labour women generally; (b) co-operate with the Labour Party in relation to women's interests; (c) call conferences; and (d) provide speakers.
182. 'Report on Organisation of Women in Scotland', *NEC Mins*, June 1922.
183. E. Andrews, *A Woman's Work is Never Done* (Rhondda, 1948).
184. See N. Evans and D. Jones, '"To Help Forward the Great Work of Humanity": Women in the Labour Party in Wales', in Tanner, Williams and Hopkin (eds.), *The Labour Party in Wales*, pp. 215–40.
185. M. Callcott, 'Labour Women in North East England', in *North East Labour History*, 17 (1983).
186. Minutes of the Durham Labour Women's Advisory Council, 1920–37 (Durham Record Office).
187. Quoted in D. Weinbren, *Generating Socialism: Recollections of Life in the Labour Party* (Stroud, 1997), p. 157.
188. P. Thane, 'The Women of the British Labour Party and Feminism, 1906–45', in H. L. Smith (ed.), *British Feminism and the Twentieth Century* (Aldershot, 1990), p. 127–9.
189. South Shields Labour Party, *Annual Report and Balance Sheet, 1927* (South Shields, 1927).
190. Pugh, *Women and the Women's Movement*, pp. 43–71.
191. Minutes of the Hawick Local Labour Party Women's Section, 28 January, 18 February, 22 September 1924 and 26 January 1925 (NLS).
192. *Minutes of the Newport Labour Party*, 17 May, 19 September, 20 October 1918; *Minutes of the Newport Labour Party Individual Members' Meeting*, 24 September 1918.
193. *Minutes of the Newport Labour Party*, 20 November 1919, 11 March and 15 July 1920.
194. *Newport Labour Party Manifesto* (Newport, 1919).
195. *Minutes of the Newport Labour Party*, 31 July, 14 August and 1 September 1933; D. Tanner, 'Gender, Civic Culture and Politics in South Wales: Explaining Labour Municipal Policy, 1918–39', in Worley (ed.), *Labour's Grass Roots*, p. 179.
196. Quoted in Weinbren, *Generating Socialism*, p. 158.
197. Minutes of the Crook Labour Party Women's Section, 1927–34 (Durham Record Office).
198. For an overview of women in local politics prior to 1914, see P. Hollis, *Ladies Elect: Women in English Local Government, 1865–1914* (London, 1987).

199. Wood, 'Hope Deferred', pp. 30–1.

200. Quoted in Weinbren, *Generating Socialism*, p. 184.

201. Quoted in Graves, *Labour Women*, p. 165.

202. *Minutes of the Peterborough Divisional Labour Party*, 8 February 1925.

203. P. Thane, 'Labour and Welfare', in Tanner, Thane and Tiratsoo (eds.), *Labour's First Century*, pp. 80–9.

204. 'Conference of Labour Organisations in the Bedwellty Division', in Minutes of the Bedwellty Divisional Labour Party, 7 September 1918; Colne Valley Divisional Labour Party, *Annual Report and Balance Sheet, 1920*. The annual reports form part of the 'The Origins and Development of the Labour Party in Britain at a Local Level' series (Wakefield, 1986 and 1999).

205. Labour Party, *Labour and the New Social Order* (London, 1918).

206. *NEC Mins*, 13 March and 16 April 1918.

207. McKibbin, *The Evolution of the Labour Party*, pp. 217–19. The eleven advisory committees from 1920 were centred on agriculture, army, navy and pensions, education, finance and commerce, home office and mines, industrial affairs, international questions, legal, local government, machinery of government, and public health. The advisory committee on temperance was shelved.

208. Labour Party, *Labour's Call to the People* (London, 1918); *Labour's Call to the People* (London, 1922).

209. Wrigley, *Arthur Henderson*, p. 123.

210. D. Roberts, 'Labour in Office: 1924–31', in C. Cook and I. Taylor (eds.), *The Labour Party: An Introduction to its History, Structure and Politics* (London, 1980), p. 108. The Duke of Northumberland predicted the 'free love'.

211. Tiverton Conservative Association, *Electors, Which Will You Have?* (undated); *The North Norfolk Elector* (13 November 1922).

212. P. S. Gupta, *Imperialism and the British Labour Movement, 1914–64* (London, 1975).

213. Wrigley, *Arthur Henderson*, pp. 135–7.

214. Labour Party, 'The Constitution and Standing Orders of the Labour Party', *Report of the Annual Conference of the Labour Party, 1919* (London, 1919).

215. Savage, *The Dynamics of Working-Class Politics*, pp. 36–63 and pp. 134–87.

216. The following section draws largely from B. Lancaster and T. Mason (eds.), *Life and Labour in a Twentieth Century City: The Experience of Coventry* (Coventry, undated).

217. Williams, *Democratic Rhondda*, p. 96.

218. Norwich Labour Party, *To The Electors of Thorpe Ward* (Norwich, 1933); *To the Electors of Fye Bridge Ward* (Norwich, 1923).

219. Williams, 'Labour and the Challenge of Local Government', pp. 147–50.

220. Edinburgh and District Trades and Labour Council, *Annual Report for year ending 31 March 1923*.

221. Quoted in Wrigley, *Lloyd George and the Challenge of Labour*, p. 248.

222. D. Weinbren, 'Sociable Capital: London's Labour Parties, 1918–45', in Worley (ed.), *Labour's Grass Roots*, pp. 195–216.

223. Wood, 'Hope Deferred', pp. 30–1.

224. Goss, *Local Labour and Local Government*, p. 28.

225. Branson, *Poplarism*, pp. 20–1.

226. Savage, *The Dynamics of Working-Class Politics*, pp. 28–33.

227. Branson, *Poplarism*, pp. 20–1.

228. Holford, *Reshaping Labour*, p. 88.

229. Edinburgh and District Trades and Labour Council, *Annual Report for year ending 31 March 1922*.

230. Wrigley, *Arthur Henderson*, p. 139.

231. Newport Labour Party, *The Tolybont Water Scheme* (Newport, 1920); *Minutes of the Gloucester Trades Council and Labour Party, 1899–1951* (Wakefield, 1986).

Chapter Two

1. Quoted in L. Minkin, *The Contentious Alliance: Trade Unions and the Labour Party* (Edinburgh, 1991), p. 5.

2.   Quoted in D. Howell, *MacDonald's Party: Labour Identities and Crisis, 1922–31* (Oxford, 2002), p. 143.

3.   C. L. Mowat, *Britain Between the Wars, 1918–40* (London, 1968); K. Laybourn, *Britain on the Breadline: A Social and Political History of Britain, 1918–39* (Gloucestershire, 1990).

4.   There are several books on the General Strike. For a good overview, see K. Laybourn, *The General Strike of 1926* (Manchester, 1993).

5.   Labour Party, *Labour and the Nation* (London, 1928), pp. 5 and 46.

6.   The most detailed account remains R. W. Lyman, *The First Labour Government, 1924* (London, 1958).

7.   J. R. Clynes, *Memoirs, 1869–1924* (London, 1937), p. 345.

8.   J. Lawson, *A Man's Life* (London, 1944), pp. 165–70.

9.   E. Shinwell, *Conflict Without Malice* (London, 1955), p. 119. Shinwell refers to Walsh's predicament at a ceremonial dinner. See also A. J. Davies, *To Build a New Jerusalem: The British Labour Party from Keir Hardie to Tony Blair* (London, 1992), p. 125.

10.   G. Lansbury, *My Life* (London, 1928), p. 268. Also, J. Shepherd, *George Lansbury: At the Heart of Old Labour* (Oxford, 2002), p. 215.

11.   F. Brockway, *Socialism Over Sixty Years: The Life of Jowett of Bradford* (London, 1946), pp. 208–9.

12.   *Minutes of the National Executive Committee* (Woodbridge, undated) (hereafter *NEC Mins*), 12 and 13 December 1923.

13.   D. Marquand, *Ramsay MacDonald* (London, 1977), p. 298.

14.   Ibid.

15.   Ibid., pp. 298–304.

16.   Alongside MacDonald and Snowden were the seven trade unionists, Henderson, Thomas, Clynes, Adamson, Shaw, Walsh and Hartshorn; the two Fabians, Webb and Lord Olivier; the four former Liberals, Trevelyan, Viscount Haldane, Wedgwood and Buxton; and the former Conservative Lord Parmoor. Wheatley and Jowett represented the Independent Labour Party (ILP), and Lord Chelmsford remained a Conservative. Lord Thomson does not appear to have been active in politics prior to 1918, but he became a close friend to MacDonald thereafter.

17.   Shepherd, *George Lansbury*, pp. 209–11.

18.   Marquand, *Ramsay MacDonald*, p. 305.

19.   A. Thorpe, *A History of the British Labour Party* (Basingstoke, 1997), p. 58.

20.   *NEC Mins*, 23 April and 25 June 1924; Howell, *MacDonald's Party*, pp. 30–3.

21.   See I. Wood, *John Wheatley* (Manchester, 1989), pp. 131–45.

22.   Howell, *MacDonald's Party*, p. 31.

23.   Labour Party, *Report of the Annual Conference of the Labour Party, 1924* (London, 1924), p. 104; Howell, *MacDonald's Party*, p. 143.

24.   C. Wrigley, *Arthur Henderson* (Cardiff, 1990), pp. 144–7.

25.   B. Donoughue and G. W. Jones, *Herbert Morrison: Portrait of a Politician* (London, 2001), pp. 116–23. The final quote is from a report to the London Labour Party executive, 1928–29.

26.   Thorpe, *A History of the British Labour Party*, p. 60.

27.   C. Wrigley, 'James Ramsay MacDonald, 1922–31', in K. Jefferys (ed.), *Leading Labour: From Keir Hardie to Tony Blair* (London, 1999), pp. 28–32.

28.   Marquand, *Ramsay MacDonald*, pp. 297–389.

29.   A. Thorpe, *The British Communist Party and Moscow, 1920–43* (Manchester, 2000), pp. 76–9.

30.   Quoted in D. Roberts, 'Labour in Office: 1924–31', in C. Cook and I. Taylor (eds.), *The Labour Party: An Introduction to its History, Structure and Politics* (London, 1980), p. 110.

31.   Labour Party, *Report of the Annual Conference of the Labour Party, 1924*, p. 3 and pp. 113–15.

32.   M. Bondfield, *A Life's Work* (London, 1948), p. 256.

33.   Edinburgh and District Trades and Labour Council, *Annual Report for year ending 31 March 1925*; K. Laybourn, *The Rise of Labour: The British Labour Party, 1890–1979* (London, 1988), p. 60.

34.   For a detailed examination of Labour's industrial policy, see A. Thorpe, 'The Industrial Meaning of "Gradualism": The Labour Party and Industry, 1918–31', *Journal of British Studies*, 35 (1996).

35.   Labour Party, *Labour's Appeal to the People* (London, 1924).

36.   *NEC Mins*, 7 November 1924; Thorpe, *A History of the British Labour Party*, p. 56.

37.   The party constitution stated that no NEC member could be simultaneously a member of the TUC general council.

38.   For more on this, see Howell, *MacDonald's Party*, pp. 60–5.

39.   Ibid., pp. 35–41.

40.   Ibid., p. 38. The PLP executive of 1928–9 comprised MacDonald (chair), Clynes (vice-chair), Kennedy (chief whip), Henderson, Snowden, Johnston, Graham, Lees-Smith, Lansbury, Dalton, Thomas, Shaw, Adamson, Trevelyan and Webb. Dalton and Trevelyan were not in the August 1931 cabinet.

41.   In May 1929, there were 41 MFGB-sponsored MPs in a PLP of 287.

42.   Labour Party, *Report of the Annual Conference of the Labour Party, 1929* (London, 1929).

43.   Minutes of the Bedwellty Divisional Labour Party, 10 November 1928.

44.   L. Minkin, *The Labour Party Conference: A Study in the Politics of Intra-Party Democracy* (London, 1978), p. 7.

45.   D. Howell, *British Social Democracy: A Study in Development and Decay* (London, 1980), p. 13.

46.   *NEC Mins*, 27 September 1925; Minkin, *The Labour Party Conference*, p. 15.

47.   Quoted in D. Tanner, 'Labour and its Membership', in D. Tanner, P. Thane and N. Tiratsoo (eds.), *Labour's First Century* (Cambridge, 2000), p. 267.

48.   Quoted in Minkin, *The Labour Party Conference*, p. 14. MacDonald was talking in relation to India.

49.   Howell, *MacDonald's Party*, pp. 93–8.

50.   'Head Office Special Report', *NEC Mins*, 21 January 1925.

51.   *NEC Mins,* 9 November 1919 and 31 August 1920; R. McKibbin, *The Evolution of the Labour Party, 1900–24* (Oxford, 1974), pp. 74–8.

52.   Labour Party, *Party Organisation* (London, 1936).

53.   McKibbin, *The Evolution of the Labour Party*, p. 144.

54.   N. Tiratsoo, 'Labour and the Electorate', in Tanner, Thane and Tiratsoo (eds.), *Labour's First Century*, pp. 297–8; D. Matthew, *From Two Boys and a Dog to Political Power: The Labour Party in the Lowestoft Constituency, 1918–45* (Lowestoft, 1979).

55.   See D. Clark, *We Do Not Want the Earth: The History of South Shields Labour Party* (Whitley Bay, 1992), p. 30.

56.   Quoted in N. Riddell, *Labour in Crisis: The Second Labour Government, 1929–31* (Manchester, 1999), p. 17.

57.   T. Lindley, 'The Barnsley Labour Party 1918 to 1945', *Bulletin of the Society for the Study of Labour History*, 39 (1978), pp. 10–11.

58.   *Minutes of The Penistone Labour Party, 1909–51* (Wakefield, 1986).

59.   C. Howard, 'Expectations Born to Death: Local Labour Party Expansion in the 1920s', in J. Winter (ed.), *The Working Class in Modern British History: Essays in Honour of Henry Pelling* (Cambridge, 1983), pp. 78–81.

60.   Minutes of the North Lambeth Divisional Labour Party, 17 and 23 March, 22 April and 11 August 1932. The dispute with Harford was still cropping up in the minutes of meetings in 1934. A similar row broke out after the 1935 election, with Strauss and Roberts criticising the party chairman, Albert Deady, for his lack of support during the election campaign.

61.   McKibbin, *The Evolution of the Labour Party*, p. 146.

62.   Quoted in J. Holford, *Reshaping Labour: Organisation, Work and Politics – Edinburgh in the Great War and After* (London, 1988), p. 168.

63.   Ibid., p. 245.

64.   Norwich Labour Party and Industrial Council, *Executive Report and Balance Sheet, 1934* (Norwich, 1934).

65.   Minutes of the Bedwellty Divisional Labour Party, 27 April and 27 July 1929.

66.   Minutes of the Peebles and South Midlothian Divisional Labour Party, 7 June 1919, 25 September 1920 and 26 February 1921.

67.   A. Campbell, *The Scottish Miners, 1874–1938, Volume II: Trade Unions and Politics* (Aldershot, 2000), pp. 370–83.

68.   B. Pimlott, *Hugh Dalton* (London, 1995), pp. 175–81.

69.   *NEC Mins*, 10 April 1918.

70.   P. Wyncoll, *The Nottingham Labour Movement, 1880–1939* (London, 1985), p. 183.

71.   A. Flinn, 'Labour's Family: Local Labour Parties, Trade Unions and Trades Councils in Cotton Lancashire, 1931–39', in M. Worley (ed.), *Labour's Grass Roots: Essays on the Activities of Local Labour Parties and Members, 1918–45* (Aldershot, 2005), p. 109.

72.   Minutes of the East Grinstead Labour Party, 1918–20 (LSE); D. G. Pole, *War Letters and Autobiography* (London, 1961); Tanner, 'Labour and its Membership', p. 254. More widely, Pole's finances helped maintain the *Daily Herald* and launch *Lansbury's Labour Weekly* in 1925.

73.   R. Skidelsky, *Oswald Mosley* (London, 1975), p. 158; Howell, *MacDonald's Party*, pp. 321, 326.

74.   Minutes of the Nottingham South Divisional Labour Party, July 1930 and September 1931 (Nottingham Record Office).

75.   L. Manning, *A Life for Education: An Autobiography* (London, 1970), pp. 76–81.

76.   B. Pimlott, *Labour and the Left in the 1930s* (Cambridge, 1977), p. 31.

77.   Shepherd, *George Lansbury*, pp. 351–2.

78.   See, for example, Minutes of the Bedwellty Divisional Labour Party, 23 February 1924.

79.   *Minutes of the South Shields Labour Party*, 14 January, 12 August and 28 December 1930 (Wakefield, 1986); Minutes of the Darlington Labour Party General Council, 17 December 1930 (Durham Record Office).

80.   Howell, *MacDonald's Party*, p. 27.

81.   D. Tanner, 'The Pattern of Labour Politics, 1918–39', in D. Tanner, C. Williams and D. Hopkin (eds.), *The Labour Party in Wales, 1900–2000* (Cardiff, 2000), p. 137.

82.   *Minutes of Penistone and Holmfirth Divisional Labour Party*, 18 April 1931.

83.   C. Williams, 'Labour and the Challenge of Local Government', in Tanner, Williams and Hopkin (eds.), *The Labour Party in Wales*, p. 140.

84.   Municipal responsibility for electricity ended with the creation of the Central Electricity Board in 1926.

85.   N. Branson, *Poplarism, 1919–25: George Lansbury and the Councillors' Revolt* (London, 1985), pp. 17–18.

86.   *Labour Organiser*, August 1923.

87.   *Labour Press Service*, 16 June 1937.

88.   J. Reynolds and K. Laybourn, *Labour Heartland: A History of the Labour Party in West Yorkshire during the Interwar Years, 1918–39* (Bradford, 1987), p. 40.

89.   *Minutes of the Peterborough Divisional Labour Party*, 1918–30.

90.   Norwich Labour Party and Industrial Council, *Executive Reports and Balance Sheets* (Norwich, 1924, 1932 and 1933).

91.   McKibbin, *The Evolution of the Labour Party*, p. 143.

92.   Minutes of the Roxburgh and Selkirk Divisional Labour Party, 18 July and 26 December 1925 (NLS).

93.   Ibid., 3 December 1927, 9 March and 7 July 1930, and 28 March 1931. The party was also forced to pay £5 to Scott's former landlady after the rogue organiser had left without paying!

94.   *Minutes of the Newport Labour Party*, 7 November 1924, 17 June 1926 and 18 January 1929.

95.   Quoted in McKibbin, *The Evolution of the Labour Party*, p. 145. McKibbin gives other similar examples.

96.   Minutes of the Loughborough Borough Labour Party, 28 March 1930 (Leicestershire Record Office).

97.   *Labour Organiser*, April 1921; also quoted in McKibbin, *The Evolution of the Labour Party*, p. 129.

98.   D. Weinbren, 'Sociable Capital: London's Labour Parties, 1918–45', in Worley (ed.), *Labour's Grass Roots*, p. 197.

99.   Norwich Labour Club Revenue Account and Balance Sheet for year ending 31 December 1940 (Norfolk Record Office); Minutes of the North Islington Divisional Labour Party, 18 September 1928 (Wood Green and Hornsey Labour Party Office).

100.   See, for example, Minutes of the Darlington Labour Party, 28 May 1923.

101.   Minutes of the Merton and Morden Labour Party, 4 October 1928, 19 September 1929 and 27 May 1937 (LSE).

102.   *Minutes of the Newport Labour Party*, 1918–39 passim.

103.   Colne Valley Divisional Labour Party, *Annual Report*, 24 April 1920.

104.   Quoted in D. Weinbren, *Generating Socialism: Recollections of Life in the Labour Party* (Stroud, 1997), p. 12.

105.   G. D. H. Cole, *A History of the Labour Party from 1914* (London, 1948), pp. 174–5.

106.   Minutes of the Darlington Labour Party, 30 March 1928.

107.   Minutes of the Hebburn Labour Party, 18 November 1924 (Durham Record Office).

108.   *Forward!*, 18 March 1922, quoted in Weinbren, *Generating Socialism*, p. 57.

109.   Howard, 'Expectations Born to Death', p. 75.

110.   Edinburgh and District Trades and Labour Council, *Annual Reports*, 1927–31.

111.   Tanner, 'The Pattern of Labour Politics', p. 137.

112.   Tanner, 'Labour and its Membership', p. 252.

113.   *Labour Organiser*, March 1925 and June 1927; *NEC Mins*, 15 January 1925.

114.   Labour Party, *Report of the Annual Conference of the Labour Party, 1929* (London, 1929). The minimum affiliated membership was originally 180, but was raised to 240 at the 1929 conference.

115.   Tanner, 'Labour and its Membership', p. 250.

116.   Holford, *Reshaping Labour*, p. 244.

117.   Ibid., pp. 213–15.

118.   Labour Party, *Report of the Annual Conference of the Labour Party, 1929* (London, 1929).

119.   Pimlott, *Hugh Dalton*, pp. 176–7.

120.   H. Beynon and T. Austrin, *Masters and Servants: Class and Patronage in the Making of a Labour Organisation* (London, 1994), p. 311; Pimlott, *Hugh Dalton*, p. 177.

121.   Ibid., pp. 164–70.

122.   K. Teanby, 'Leftism in the Doncaster Labour Party, 1921–26', *Bulletin of the Society for the Study of Labour History*, 39 (1978), p. 11.

123.   J. and B. Braddock, *The Braddocks* (London, 1963), p. 93.

124.   Labour Party, *Report of the Annual Conference of the Labour Party, 1929* (London, 1929).

125.   G. Cohen, 'The Independent Labour Party, Disaffiliation, Revolution and Standing Orders', *History*, 86, 282 (2001), p. 204. Following Labour's adoption of clause four, there was a debate within the ILP as to the possibility of dissolving the party.

126.   Labour Party, *Report of the Annual Conference of the Labour Party, 1921* (London, 1921); Labour Party, *Report of the Annual Conference of the Labour Party, 1925* (London, 1925).

127.   For a good overview of relations within the Clydeside group on arriving at parliament, see Shinwell, *Conflict Without Malice*, pp. 76–86.

128.   Howell, *MacDonald's Party*, pp. 247–63; A. Marwick, *Clifford Allen: The Open Conspirator* (Edinburgh, 1964).

129.   A. McKinlay, '"Doubtful Wisdom and Uncertain Promise": Strategy, Ideology and Organisation, 1918–1922', in A. McKinlay and R. J. Morris, *The ILP on Clydeside, 1893–1932: From Foundation to Disintegration* (Manchester, 1991), p. 145; W. Knox, *James Maxton* (Manchester, 1987); Wood, *John Wheatley*.

130.   Quoted in A. McKinlay and J. J. Smyth, 'The End of "the Agitator Workman": 1926–1932', in McKinlay and Morris, *The ILP on Clydeside, 1893–1932*, pp. 179–80.

131.   Howell, *MacDonald's Party*, pp. 234–6 and 256.

132.   McKinlay, "Doubtful Wisdom and Uncertain Promise"', pp. 158–64.

133.   Howell, *MacDonald's Party*, p. 33.

134.   See J. Scanlon, *Decline and Fall of the Labour Party* (London, 1932). Also, McKinlay, '"Doubtful Wisdom and Uncertain Promise"', p. 164.

135.   Knox, *James Maxton*, p. 79.

136. For the executive, see Howell, *MacDonald's Party*, pp. 35–7.

137. Shepherd, *George Lansbury*, pp. 248–52.

138. Brockway, *Socialism Over Sixty Years*, p. 225.

139. Thorpe, *A History of the British Labour Party*, p. 66.

140. Howell, *MacDonald's Party*, pp. 265–6.

141. Marquand, *Ramsay MacDonald*, pp. 450–5.

142. Howell, *MacDonald's Party*, p. 273.

143. 'The Cook–Maxton Manifesto, 1928', reproduced in A. Reekes, *The Rise of Labour, 1899–1951* (Basingstoke, 1991), pp. 68–9.

144. *Minutes of the Newport Labour Party*, 23 and 30 March, 16 and 28 April 1923.

145. Sunderland Labour Party, *Adventure into the Past* (Sunderland, 1954); A. Potts, 'Forty Years On: The Labour Party in Sunderland', *North East Labour History*, 24 (1980), pp. 12–18.

146. A. McKinlay and J. J. Smyth, 'The End of "the Agitator Workman"', p. 181.

147. F. Bealey, J. Blondel and W. P. McCann, *Constituency Politics: A Study of Newcastle-under-Lyme* (London, 1965), p. 81; *NEC Mins*, 4 June 1919.

148. Skidelsky, *Oswald Mosley*, pp. 155–78; M. Newman, *John Strachey* (Manchester, 1989), pp. 7–18.

149. Shepherd, *George Lansbury*, p. 254.

150. V. I. Lenin, *Left Wing Communism* (London, 1942), p. 70. (Lenin's tract was originally published in 1920.)

151. For two good overviews of the discussions between Labour and the CPGB, see L. J. Macfarlane, *The British Communist Party: Its Origins and Development until 1929* (London, 1966); Thorpe, *The British Communist Party and Moscow*, pp. 19–20, pp. 35–111 passim.

152. The quote is from MacDonald. See Labour Party, *Report of the Annual Conference of the Labour Party, 1922* (London, 1922), p. 199.

153. 'Letter from the NEC to the CPGB', 21 October 1921, in Labour Party, *Report of the Annual Conference of the Labour Party, 1921*, p. 20.

154. See Labour Party, *Report of the Annual Conference of the Labour Party*, various years 1920–9.

155. CPGB membership in the 1920s peaked following the 1926 General Strike at some 12,000. It soon fell, however, and generally averaged around 5,000 throughout the 120s. A. Thorpe, 'The Membership of the Communist Party of Great Britain, 1920–45', *The Historical Journal*, 43, 3 (2000).

156. *Minutes of the Edinburgh and District Trades and Labour Council*, 13 September 1921; Clark, *We Do Not Want the Earth*, p. 56.

157. *Minutes of the Colne Valley Divisional Labour Party*, 8 April 1922.

158. Minutes of the North Lambeth Divisional Labour Party, 14 July and 30 September 1926.

159. Minutes of the Merton and Morden Labour Party, 11 April 1927. See also Minutes of the Bedwellty Divisional Labour Party, 17 October 1925.

160. Howell, *MacDonald's Party*, pp. 390–4.

161. Labour Party, *Report of the Annual Labour Party Conference, 1928* (London, 1928).

162. P. Graves, *Labour Women: Women in British Working-Class Politics, 1918–39* (Cambridge, 1994), pp. 126–38.

163. M. Francis, 'Labour and Gender', in Tanner, Thane and Tiratsoo (eds.), *Labour's First Century*, p. 215.

164. Quoted in S. Rowbotham, *A New World for Women: Stella Brown – Socialist Feminist* (London, 1977), pp. 35–6.

165. I. S. McLean, *The Legend of Red Clydeside* (Edinburgh, 1983), pp. 223–4.

166. Rowbotham, *A New World for Women*, p. 36.

167. Howell, *MacDonald's Party*, pp. 356–69.

168. Francis, 'Labour and Gender', pp. 202–3.

169. 'Special Report on Organisation', *NEC Mins*, 25 March 1924. Men received between £410 and £450 per annum, women between £310 and £370.

170. Arthur Henderson quoted in Francis, 'Labour and Gender', p. 195.

171. Graves, *Labour Women*, p. 160.

172.   Labour Party, *Parliamentary General Election, South Edinburgh Division* (Edinburgh, 1929).

173.   Quoted in B. D. Vernon, *Ellen Wilkinson* (London, 1982), pp. 79–80. Wilkinson did champion women's causes in the Commons throughout her time as an MP. Generally, however, her outlook was primarily class-, rather than gender-based.

174.   Quotes from Graves, *Labour Women*, pp. 29 and 112; Branson, *Poplarism*, p. 65.

175.   Graves, *Labour Women*, pp. 29 and 156.

176.   Labour Party, *Report of the Annual Conference of the Labour Party, 1921*, p. 157.

177.   Labour Party, *Report of the Annual Conference of the Labour Party, 1928*, pp. 27–8.

178.   Labour Party, *Report of the Annual Conference of the Labour Party, 1929* (London, 1929).

179.   Minkin, *The Contentious Alliance*, pp. 9–16.

180.   Labour Party, *Labour Party Foundation Conference*, pp. 11–12.

181.   H. Dalton, *Call Back Yesterday: Memoirs, 1887–1931* (London, 1953), p. 148.

182.   Quoted in A. Bullock, *Ernest Bevin: A Biography* (London, 2002), p. 65.

183.   Quoted in A. Fenley, 'Labour and the Trade Unions', in Cook and Taylor (eds.), *The Labour Party: An Introduction to its History, Structure and Politics*, p. 59.

184.   Labour Party, *Report of the Annual Conference of the Labour Party, 1933* (London, 1933), p. 161. Also cited in Howell, *MacDonald's Party*, p. 217.

185.   Labour Party, *Report of the Annual Conference of the Labour Party, 1925*, p. 244.

186.   H. A. Clegg, *A History of British Trade Unions Since 1889: Volume II, 1911–33* (Oxford, 1985), pp. 369–77.

187.   Ibid., p. 381.

188.   Quoted in Howell, *MacDonald's Party*, p. 20.

189.   Clegg, *A History of British Trade Unions*, p. 381.

190.   R. Taylor, *The TUC: From the General Strike to New Unionism* (Basingstoke, 2000), pp. 20–50. The quote is from Citrine's *Democracy or Disruption?* (London, 1928); N. Riddell, 'Walter Citrine and the British Labour Movement, 1925–35, *History*, 85, 278 (2000), pp. 285–306.

191.   Minkin, *The Contentious Alliance*, p. 28.

192.   Ibid., p. 22.

193.   Marquand, *Ramsay MacDonald*, pp. 422–36.

194.   J. R. Clynes, *Memoirs, 1924–37* (London, 1938), p. 76.

195.   Howell, *MacDonald's Party*, p. 137.

196.   Clegg, *A History of British Trade Unions*, p. 568.

197.   Quoted in Beynon and Austrin, *Masters and Servants*, p. 361.

198.   Cole, *A History of the Labour Party*, p. 480.

199.   Labour Party, *Report of the Annual Conference of the Labour Party, 1929* (London, 1929).

200.   D. E. McHenry, *The Labour Party in Transition, 1931–38* (London, 1938), pp. 47–50.

201.   Labour Party, *Labour Party Annual Report, 1929* (London, 1929), p. 196.

202.   For the trade unions' relatively successful response to the Trades Dispute Act, see M. M. Pinto-Duschinsky, *British Political Parties, 1800–1980* (AEI Studies, 1981), pp. 74–7.

203.   Clegg, *A History of British Trade Unions*, pp. 419–21.

204.   M. Worley, *Class Against Class: The Communist Party of Great Britain between the Wars* (London, 2002), pp. 62–4.

205.   Edinburgh and District Trades and Labour Council, *Annual Report for year ending 31 March 1927*; *Minutes of the Newport Labour Party*, 5 November 1926.

206.   J. Boughton, 'Working Class Conservatism and the Rise of Labour: A Case Study of Birmingham in the 1920s', *The Historian* (Autumn, 1998), pp. 17–20.

207.   C. Cook, 'Liberals, Labour and Local Elections', in G. Peele and C. Cook (eds.), *The Politics of Reappraisal, 1918–39* (Oxford, 1975), p. 171.

208.   In 1928, Nottingham city council comprised 22 Labour members, eighteen Conservatives and seven Liberals.

209.   Donoughue and Jones, *Herbert Morrison*, p. 655. It should be noted that Labour's vote actually fell, although it did so in the context of a lower electoral turnout. Moreover, the Municipal Reform (Conservative) vote similarly fell, with only the Liberal and CPGB vote increasing.

210.   Cole, *A History of the Labour Party*, p. 458.

211. Thorpe, 'The Industrial Meaning of "Gradualism"', pp. 84–113.

212. *NEC Mins*, 7 April 1925.

213. Labour Party, *Report of the Annual Conference of the Labour Party, 1925*, p. 352.

214. Labour Party, *Report of the Annual Conference of the Labour Party, 1927* (London, 1927), p. 332.

215. *NEC Mins,* 26 October 1927.

216. *NEC Mins*, 28 March 1928.

217. Quoted in Howell, *MacDonald's Party*, p. 72.

218. Marquand, *Ramsay MacDonald*, p. 478.

219. *NEC Mins*, 2 May 1928 and 25 March 1929.

220. *NEC Mins*, 2 May 1928.

221. Quoted in Thorpe, *A History of the British Labour Party*, p. 65. In less favourable language, Thomas Johnston called it 'a sort of dog's breakfast in which there are scraps for every palate'. See G. Walker, *Thomas Johnston* (Manchester, 1988), p. 88.

222. Labour Party, *Labour and the Nation*, pp. 1–50.

223. Labour Party, *Report of the Annual Conference of the Labour Party, 1928* (London, 1928), pp. 228–41 and 347; Labour Party, *Labour and the Nation*, p. 47.

224. M. Taylor, 'Labour and the Constitution', in Tanner, Thane and Tiratsoo (eds.), *Labour's First Century*, pp. 156–61.

225. Labour Party, *Labour and the Nation*, pp. 1–50.

226. *NEC Mins*, 26 June 1928; Labour Party, *Report of the Annual Conference of the Labour Party, 1928*, pp. 196–222.

227. Labour Party, *Labour's Appeal to the Nation* (London, 1929).

228. C. Cook, 'Labour's Electoral Base' in Cook and Taylor (eds.), *The Labour Party*, p. 89.

229. Riddell, *Labour in Crisis*, p. 23; Tanner, 'Labour and its Membership', pp. 251–2.

230. R. McKibbin, 'Class and Conventional Wisdom: The Conservative Party and the "Public" in Interwar Britain', in his *The Ideologies of Class: Social Relations in Britain, 1890–1950* (Oxford, 1990), pp. 259–93.

231. D. Jarvis, 'The Shaping of Conservative Electoral Hegemony, 1918–39', in J. Lawrence and M. Taylor (eds.), *Party, State and Society: Electoral Behaviour in Britain since 1829* (Aldershot, 1997), pp. 131–51; S. Ball 'Local Conservatism and the Evolution of the Party Organization', in S. Ball and A. Seldon (eds.), *Conservative Century: The Conservative Party since 1900* (Oxford, 1994), pp. 261–311.

Chapter Three

1. Labour Party, *Report of the Annual Conference of the Labour Party, 1930* (London, 1930), p. 180.

2. Quoted in G. Foote, *The Labour Party's Political Thought: A History*, (Basingstoke, 1997 third edition), p. 174.

3. 'Victory for Socialism', in Labour Party, *Report of the Annual Conference of the Labour Party, 1933* (London, 1933), pp. 290–1.

4. For a more detailed overview of these events, see A. Thorpe, *The British General Election of 1931* (Oxford, 1991); P. Williamson, *National Crisis and National Government: British Politics, the Economy and Empire, 1926–32* (Cambridge, 1992); C. Cook and J. Stevenson, *The Slump: Society and Politics in the Depression* (London, 1989); R. Skidelsky, *Politicians and the Slump: The Labour Government of 1929–31* (London, 1967); S. Pollard, *The Development of the British Economy, 1919–90* (London, 1992).

5. *Ministry of Labour Gazette*, December 1930 and 1931.

6. A. Thorpe, 'The Industrial Meaning of "Gradualism": The Labour Party and Industry, 1918–31', *Journal of British Studies*, 35 (1996), pp. 98–104.

7. N. Riddell, *Labour in Crisis: The Second Labour Government, 1929–31* (Manchester, 1999), p. 24. The quote is from the *Nelson Gazette*, 4 June 1929.

8. J. Beadle, *A Glorious Century: One Hundred Years of the Derby Labour Party* (Derby, 2000), p. 38; D. Clark, *We Do Not Want the Earth: The History of South Shields Labour Party* (Whitley Bay, 1992), p. 71.

9. D. Marquand, *Ramsay MacDonald* (London, 1977), p. 489.

10.   Minutes of the Darlington Labour Party Annual Meeting, 12 June 1929; Riddell, *Labour in Crisis*, p. 115.

11.   D. Howell, *MacDonald's Party: Labour Identities and Crisis, 1922–31* (Oxford, 2002), pp. 8–13.

12.   The chancellor of the duchy of Lancaster was a ministerial position free of departmental responsibility, but designed to help the government in an advisory capacity.

13.   Marquand, *Ramsay MacDonald*, pp. 489–93.

14.   Thorpe, *The British General Election*, pp. 27–8.

15.   Howell, *MacDonald's Party*, p. 40.

16.   See, for example, Dalton's diary entry for 22 May 1930, in B. Pimlott (ed.), *The Political Diary of Hugh Dalton, 1918–40, 1945–60* (London, 1986), p. 112; J. Lee, *This Great Journey* (London, 1963), p. 18.

17.   Pimlott (ed.), *The Political Diary of Hugh Dalton*, pp. 95–6; H. Beynon and T. Austrin, *Masters and Servants: Class and Patronage in the Making of a Labour Organisation* (London, 1994), p. 339. Will Davis had taken over as secretary by 1932.

18.   Quoted in Howell, *MacDonald's Party*, p. 45.

19.   Minutes of the Bedwellty Divisional Labour Party, 15 April and 8 November 1930.

20.   L. Manning, *A Life for Education: An Autobiography* (London, 1970), p. 87. Also quoted in Riddell, *Labour in Crisis*, p. 162.

21.   G. D. H. Cole, *A History of the Labour Party from 1914* (London, 1948), p. 230.

22.   For Thomas and his attempts to 'solve' the unemployment problem, see Marquand, *Ramsay MacDonald*, pp. 521–2 and 534; J. Shepherd, *George Lansbury: At the Heart of Old Labour* (Oxford, 2002), pp. 258–60; R. Skidelsky, *Oswald Mosley* (London, 1975), pp. 179–92; T. Johnston, *Memories* (London, 1952), pp. 100–9. According to Dalton, Johnston told him in May 1930 that the unemployment committee had met just once that year. It should be dissolved on paper, he said, 'as it had long been dissolved in fact'. See Pimlott (ed.), *The Political Diary of Hugh Dalton*, entry for 13 May 1930, p. 107.

23.   Labour Party, *Report of the Annual Conference of the Labour Party, 1930*, p. 81.

24.   F. Brockway, *Socialism Over Sixty Years: The Life of Jowett of Bradford* (London, 1946), p. 259.

25.   Howell, *MacDonald's Party*, p. 292.

26.   Ibid., pp. 290–4.

27.   G. Cohen, 'The Independent Labour Party, Disaffiliation, Revolution and Standing Orders', *History*, 86, 282 (2001), pp. 208–9. The group were Maxton (chair), Beckett, Brockway, Brown, Forgan, Hirst, Horrabin, Jowett, Kirkwood, Lee, Lees, McGovern, Sandham, Stephen, Strachey, Wallhead, Wise and Kinley (secretary).

28.   These changes had been discussed in January 1929, accepted in June 1930, and finally added to the party constitution in 1931. See *Minutes of the National Executive Committee* (Woodbridge, undated) (hereafter *NEC Mins*), 28 January and 23 February 1931.

29.   *NEC Mins*, 19 November 1930; Howell, *MacDonald's Party*, p. 297.

30.   For Strachey's continued influence at this time, see M. Newman, *John Strachey* (Manchester, 1989), pp. 28–32.

31.   Skidelsky, *Oswald Mosley*, pp. 199–220.

32.   Ibid.

33.   B. Pimlott, *Hugh Dalton* (London, 1995), p. 153.

34.   B. Donoughue and G. W. Jones, *Herbert Morrison: Portrait of a Politician* (London, 2001), p. 158; Howell, *MacDonald's Party*, p. 43.

35.   This maintained a socialist outlook via the influence of Strachey, Bevan and Brown. See Newman, *John Strachey*, p. 34.

36.   Skidelsky, *Oswald Mosley*, pp. 199–245; Labour Party, *Report of the Annual Conference of the Labour Party, 1930*, pp. 200–4; Newman, *John Strachey*, pp. 26–38.

37.   Howell, *MacDonald's Party*, pp. 186–200.

38.   Labour Party, *Report of the Annual Conference of the Labour Party, 1930*, p. 186.

39.   Riddell, *Labour in Crisis*, pp. 56 and 61; Howell, *MacDonald's Party*, pp. 196–8.

40.   See, R. Taylor, *The TUC: From the General Strike to New Unionism* (Basingstoke, 2000), pp. 55–6.

41. H. A. Clegg, *A History of British Trade Unions Since 1889: Volume II, 1911–33* (Oxford, 1985), pp. 478–87.

42. Howell, *MacDonald's Party*, pp. 198–202.

43. Riddell, *Labour in Crisis*, pp. 148–50.

44. Ibid., pp. 110–14; A. J. Morris, *Portrait of a Radical: C. P. Trevelyan, 1870–1975* (Belfast, 1977).

45. Webb is quoted in Donoughue and Jones, *Herbert Morrison*, p. 131. For a less complimentary account, see O. Mosley, *My Life* (London, 1968).

46. C. Wrigley, *Arthur Henderson* (Cardiff, 1990), pp. 165–72.

47. A. Thorpe, *A History of the British Labour Party* (Basingstoke, 1997), p. 73.

48. Marquand, *Ramsay MacDonald*, p. 591.

49. A. Bullock, *Ernest Bevin: A Biography* (London, 2002), p. 167.

50. Wrigley, *Arthur Henderson*, p. 176.

51. *NEC Mins*, 20 August 1931.

52. F. W. Pethick-Lawrence, *Fate Has Been Kind* (London, 1943), p. 166; Pimlott (ed.), *The Political Diary of Hugh Dalton*, p. 151. Pethick-Lawrence also admitted to feeling 'a distinct sense of relief' by the party's decision.

53. Quoted in D. Weinbren, *Generating Socialism: Recollections of Life in the Labour Party* (Stroud, 1997), pp. 86 and 210.

54. Howell, *MacDonald's Party*, pp. 48–51; N. Riddell, 'Arthur Henderson, 1931–32', in K. Jefferys (ed.), *Leading Labour: From Keir Hardie to Tony Blair* (London, 1999), p. 50.

55. For an overview of the rumours and 1931 events, see Donoughue and Jones, *Herbert Morrison*, pp. 162–70.

56. Marquand, *Ramsay MacDonald*, pp. 645–9; Howell, *MacDonald's Party*, pp. 50–2.

57. Ibid.

58. E. A. and G. H. Radice, *Will Thorne: Constructive Militant* (London, 1974), pp. 112–14.

59. Labour Party, *Report of the Annual Conference of the Labour Party, 1931* (London, 1931), pp. 155–9, 176–9 and 244–5.

60. Labour Party, *Labour's Call to Action: The Nation's Opportunity* (London, 1931).

61. Howell, *MacDonald's Party*, p. 330; H. Dalton, *Call Back Yesterday: Memoirs, 1887–1931* (London, 1953), pp. 273–4.

62. Quoted in Taylor, *The TUC*, pp. 58–9.

63. *Report of the Trades Union Congress, 1931* (London, 1931), p. 406.

64. Riddell, *Labour in Crisis*, pp. 121 and 239–52.

65. Minutes of the Roxburgh and Selkirk Divisional Labour Party, 10 October 1931 and 25 December 1932.

66. Minutes of the Hawick Local Labour Party, 25 August 1931.

67. *Minutes of the Gloucester Trades Council and Labour Party*, 9 September 1931.

68. *Minutes of the Wolverhampton Labour Party*, 26 January 1931 (Wakefield, 1986); W. J. Brown, *So Far* (London, 1943), pp. 151–213.

69. Riddell, *Labour in Crisis*, p. 210. Riddell gives Stockport, Gloucester and Cambridgeshire as examples.

70. Marquand, *Ramsay MacDonald*, pp. 651–3; Letter from William Coxon [to Joseph Blackwell], undated, includes letter from Ramsay MacDonald to Coxon, 25 August 1931 (Durham Record Office).

71. Beadle, *A Glorious Century*, pp. 39–42; Riddell, *Labour in Crisis*, p. 121.

72. J. Reynolds and K. Laybourn, *Labour Heartland: A History of the Labour Party in West Yorkshire During the Interwar Years, 1918–39* (Bradford, 1987), p. 92.

73. *Minutes of the Colne Valley Divisional Labour Party*, 29 August 1931.

74. P. Wyncoll, *The Nottingham Labour Movement, 1880–1939* (London, 1985), p. 230.

75. S. Pearce to Denman, 31 August 1931, cited in Howell, *MacDonald's Party*, p. 329; Reynolds and Laybourn, *Labour Heartland*, p. 102.

76. Howell, *MacDonald's Party*, pp. 81–2.

77. Minutes of the Bedwellty Divisional Labour Party, 26 September 1931.

78. *Minutes of the Newport Labour Party*, 4 September 1931.

79.   Minutes of the North Lambeth Divisional Labour Party, 12 September 1931.

80.   *Minutes of the Edinburgh and District Trades and Labour Council*, 28 August 1931; Minutes of the Edinburgh North Conservative Association, 11 November 1931 (Edinburgh City Archive).

81.   Thorpe, *A History of the British Labour Party*, p. 77.

82.   Quoted in Weinbren, *Generating Socialism*, p. 86.

83.   Maxton, McGovern and Wallhead each stood as ILP candidates. Although the AEU and the Patternmakers' Association-nominated Kirkwood and Buchanan, both candidates refused to sign the PLP standing orders.

84.   Reynolds and Laybourn, *Labour Heartland*, pp. 97–103.

85.   A. Flinn, 'Labour's Family: Local Labour Parties, Trade Unions and Trades Councils in Cotton Lancashire, 1931–39', in M. Worley (ed.), *Labour's Grass Roots: Essays on the Activities of Local Labour Parties and Members, 1918–45* (Aldershot, 2005), p. 109.

86.   Thorpe, *A History of the British Labour Party*, p. 78.

87.   Thorpe, *The British General Election*, p. 279.

88.   Labour Party, *Report of the Annual Conference of the Labour Party, 1933*, p. 50.

89.   J. Campbell, *Nye Bevan* (London, 1997), pp. 47–62.

90.   A. Thorpe, 'George Lansbury 1932–35', in Jefferys (ed.), *Leading Labour*, p. 66; C. Attlee, *As it Happened* (London, 1954); K. Harris, *Attlee* (London, 1985), pp. 111–14.

91.   D. Howell, *British Social Democracy: A Study in Development and Decay* (London, 1980), p. 49.

92.   Shepherd, *George Lansbury*, pp. 286–328.

93.   Attlee had previously served as a Labour representative on the Simon Commission, appointed in 1927 to look at developments since the 1919 Government of India Act.

94.   B. Pimlott, *Labour and the Left in the 1930s* (Cambridge, 1977), p. 25. The quotes are from Susan Lawrence and Hugh Dalton.

95.   P. Clarke, *The Cripps Version: The Life of Sir Stafford Cripps, 1889–1952* (London, 2002), pp. 26–39.

96.   Ibid.

97.   Pimlott, *Labour and the Left*, p. 26.

98.   Quoted in Donoughue and Jones, *Herbert Morrison*, pp. 217–18. The quote is from a Dalton diary entry dated 8 October 1932.

99.   Pimlott, *Hugh Dalton*, pp. 206–24.

100.   Figures taken from Labour Party, *Report of the Annual Conference of the Labour Party, 1933*, p. 50. The Labour Party's annual report published detailed figures for membership of each divisional party in the previous year. So, the 1929 report contained the final figures for 1928, etc.

101.   Riddell, *Labour in Crisis*, p. 123.

102.   Labour Party, *Report of the Annual Conference of the Labour Party, 1932* (London, 1932), p. 80.

103.   S. Davies and B. Morley, 'The Reactions of Municipal Voters in Yorkshire to the Second Labour Government, 1929–32', in Worley (ed.), *Labour's Grass Roots*, pp. 132–8. Similar results were evident in Lancashire; see S. Davies and B. Morley, 'The Politics of Place: A Comparative Analysis of Electoral Politics in Four Lancashire Cotton Textile Towns, 1919–39', *Manchester Region History Review*, 14 (2000), pp. 65–6.

104.   Figures given in Donoughue and Jones, *Herbert Morrison*, pp. 654–5. The LCC elections also saw losses for Labour.

105.   Labour Party, *Report of the Annual Conference of the Labour Party, 1931*, pp. 174–6.

106.   Cohen, 'The Independent Labour Party', pp. 209–21.

107.   Quoted in ibid.; Brockway, *Socialism Over Sixty Years*, p. 299.

108.   Quoted in W. Knox, *James Maxton* (Manchester, 1987), pp. 98–9.

109.   Lee, *This Great Journey*, p. 132.

110.   Pimlott, *Labour and the Left*, p. 79; I. Donnachie, 'Scottish Labour in the Depression: The 1930s', in I. Donnachie, C. Harvie and I. S. Wood, *Forward! Labour Politics in Scotland, 1888–1988* (Edinburgh, 1989), p. 61.

111.   W. W. Knox and A. MacKinlay, 'The Re-Making of Scottish Labour in the 1930s', *Twentieth Century British History*, 6, 2 (1995), pp. 174–93.

112. Quoted in ibid., p. 175.
113. Reynolds and Laybourn, *Labour Heartland*, p. 108.
114. My thanks to Gidon Cohen for providing me with this information.
115. See N. Riddell, '"The Age of Cole"? G. D. H. Cole and the British Labour Movement, 1929–33', *Historical Journal*, 38, 4 (1995), pp. 933–57.
116. M. Cole, 'The Society for Socialist Inquiry and Propaganda', in A. Briggs and J. Saville (eds.), *Essays in Labour History, 1918–39* (London, 1977).
117. Quoted in Pimlott, *Labour and the Left*, p. 46.
118. *NEC Mins*, 5 October 1932.
119. P. Seyd, 'Factionalism Within the Labour Party: The Socialist League, 1932–37', in Briggs and Saville (eds.), *Essays in Labour History*, pp. 204–10. Fourteen branches existed in London and its environs (rising to over 40 by 1935), five in Tyneside and four in South Yorkshire.
120. Pimlott, *Labour and the Left*, pp. 49–51; *New Clarion*, 1 April 1933.
121. For Cripps interpretation of class, see Clarke, *The Cripps Version*, pp. 57–9.
122. S. Cripps, 'Can Socialism Come by Constitutional Methods?', in C. Addison, C. R. Attlee et al. (eds.), *Problems of a Socialist Government* (London, 1933), pp. 42–3. See also S. Cripps, *Why This Socialism?* (London, 1934).
123. Pimlott, *Labour and the Left*, pp. 52–3.
124. Herbert Morrison to Sir Stafford Cripps, 15 June 1937, cited in Clarke, *The Cripps Version*, p. 59.
125. Labour Party, *Report of the Annual Conference of the Labour Party, 1932*, pp. 188–94.
126. Pimlott, *Labour and the Left*, p. 46.
127. See Henderson's speech to the 1932 party conference, Labour Party, *Report of the Annual Conference of the Labour Party, 1932*, pp. 204–5.
128. Labour Party, *Report of the Annual Conference of the Labour Party, 1932*, pp. 164–5.
129. N. Riddell, 'Walter Citrine and the British Labour Movement, 1925–35', *History*, 85, 278 (2000), pp. 297–301.
130. Quoted in Howell, *MacDonald's Party*, p. 220; *NEC Mins*, 10 November 1931.
131. Memorandum from Walter Citrine, quoted in H. Pelling, *A History of British Trade Unionism* (London, 1992), p. 199; Howell, *British Social Democracy*, p. 51.
132. *NEC Mins*, 27 January 1932; Labour Party, *Report of the Annual Conference of the Labour Party*, 1932, p. 67.
133. L. Minkin, *The Contentious Alliance: Trade Unions and the Labour Party* (Edinburgh, 1991), pp. 39–40.
134. L. Minkin, *The Labour Party Conference: A Study in the Politics of Intra-Party Democracy* (London, 1978), pp. 18–19.
135. Howell, *British Social Democracy*, p. 52. The report also ensured that any decision to form a minority government had to have the backing of a special party conference; that the prime minister was to chose his/her ministers with three PLP members and the party secretary; and that he/she was subject to the majority decisions of the cabinet. See Labour Party, *Report of the Annual Conference of the Labour Party, 1933*, pp. 8–10.
136. Taylor, *The TUC*, pp. 60–1.
137. R. Toye, *The Labour Party and the Planned Economy, 1931–51* (Woodbridge, 2003), pp. 66–9. Similarly, in a poll carried out by the *New Leader* in March 1932, only Cripps perceived that capitalist collapse was imminent.
138. Labour Party, *Report of the Annual Conference of the Labour Party, 1932*, pp. 204–6.
139. Howell, *British Social Democracy*, p. 69.
140. Labour Party, *Labour's Immediate Programme* (London, 1937).
141. Minkin, *The Contentious Alliance*, pp. 27–48.
142. Clegg, *A History of British Trade Unions*, pp. 540–2; Taylor, *The TUC*, pp. 60–75.
143. W. Citrine, *The Trade Unions in the General Election* (London, 1931), cited in R. Shackleton, 'Trade Unions and the Slump', in B. Pimlott and C. Cook (eds.), *Trade Unions in British Politics* (London, 1982), pp. 128–9.
144. Quoted in Shackleton, 'Trade Unions and the Slump', p. 133.
145. The MFGB affiliated with 800,000 members in 1927, and 400,000 in 1931. In the same years, the United Textile Factory Workers' Association affiliated with 289,866 and 188,875

members. The total affiliated union membership for those years numbered 3,328,936 and 2,024,216. Labour Party, *Report of the Annual Conference of the Labour Party, 1928 and 1932*, pp. 86–109 and pp. 102–17.

146. Labour Party, *Report of the Annual Conference of the Labour Party, 1931*, pp. 176–7.

147. Labour Party, *Labour's Call to Action*; Labour Party, *For Socialism and Peace: The Labour Party's Programme of Action* (London, 1934).

148. Rev. R. L. (Ross Street Unitarian Church, Glasgow) to H. Brailsford, 26 June 1924, cited in C. MacDonald, 'Following the Procession: Scottish Labour, 1918–45', in Worley (ed.), *Labour's Grass Roots*, pp. 44–5.

149. I. Dale (ed.), *Labour Party General Election Manifestos, 1900–97* (London, 2000). Compare, too, the speeches surrounding Frank Hodges' 1922 resolution reiterating Labour's commitment to the nationalisation of the essential means of production, distribution and exchange, wherein the term 'socialism' was not used, with the conference speeches on nationalisation in 1931–2. Labour Party, *Report of the Annual Conference of the Labour Party, 1922*, pp. 222–4.

150. The Labour Party: *County of Durham* (Durham, 1919); *Jack Butler* (Chester-le-Street, 1922); *To the Men and Women Electors of the Seaham Division* (Seaham, undated; 1923); *South Shields Parliamentary Election, 1924* (South Shields, 1924); 'Candidates Election Address', 6 April 1925 (Durham Record Office). See also, *The Labour Candidates* (Sunderland, 1929).

151. Seaham Division (Seaham, 1935); Brandon and Byshottles UDC Election (Durham, 1937).

152. Houghton-le-Spring Labour Party, *Annual Report and Balance Sheet, 1918–38* (Durham Record Office).

153. 'Newport Labour Party Manifesto', 1 November 1919; 'Municipal Elections 1 November 1920: Vote for J. Henry Edwards', *Minutes of the Newport Labour Party*.

154. *Minutes of the Newport Labour Party*, 12 October 1931.

155. See, for example, J. F. Duncan's 'Election Address' to the Moray and Nairn constituency in 1929 (NLS).

156. For example, *Vote for Horrabin* (Peterborough, 1929); Labour Party, *Labour and the Nation*, pp. 5–6.

157. Norwich Labour Party, *To the Electors of Fye Bridge Ward* (Norwich, 1936).

158. The example is from Wrexham, cited in D. Tanner, 'The Pattern of Labour Politics, 1918–39', D. Tanner, C. Williams and D. Hopkin (eds.), *The Labour Party in Wales, 1900–2000* (Cardiff, 2000), p. 129.

159. Thorpe, *A History of the British Labour Party*, p. 82; E. Durbin, *New Jerusalems: The Labour Party and the Economics of Democratic Socialism* (London, 1985); Pimlott, *Labour and the Left*, p. 36.

160. Labour Party, *Report of the Annual Conference of the Labour Party, 1935*, p. 56.

161. Newman, *John Strachey*, pp. 33–6.

162. Toye, *The Labour Party*, pp. 29–33.

163. *Forward!* contained a series of articles discussing economic policy in 1932. G. Walker, *Thomas Johnston* (Manchester, 1988), pp. 116–21.

164. Thorpe, *A History of the British Labour Party*, p. 85.

165. Labour Party, *Report of the Annual Conference of the Labour Party, 1932*, pp. 212–13.

166. Ibid., pp. 214–16.

167. *NEC Mins*, 9 and 15 February, 8 and 22 March 1933; Labour Party, *Report of the Annual Conference of the Labour Party, 1933*, p. 14.

168. Labour Party, *Report of the Annual Conference of the Labour Party, 1933*, pp. 205–10.

169. Ibid., pp. 156–82.

170. Labour Party, *For Socialism and Peace*, pp. 14–22.

171. Ibid., pp. 24–32.

172. Ibid., p. 14.

173. See H. Laski, *Parliamentary Government in England* (London, 1938); Foote, *The Labour Party's Political Thought*, pp. 149–58.

174. Pimlott (ed.), *The Political Diary of Hugh Dalton*, pp. 181–2.

175. M. Taylor, 'Labour and the Constitution', in D. Tanner, P. Thane and N. Tiratsoo (eds.), *Labour's First Century* (Cambridge, 2000), p. 160.

176. Labour Party, *Report of the Annual Conference of the Labour Party, 1932*, p. 51.

177. Pimlott, *Hugh Dalton*, p. 211.

178. Foote, *The Labour Party's Political Thought*, p. 168.

179. Labour Party, *Report of the Annual Conference of the Labour Party, 1934* (London, 1934), p. 158.

180. Ibid., pp. 163–5.

181. Labour Party, *For Socialism and Peace*, p. 9.

182. Labour Party, *Report of the Annual Conference of the Labour Party, 1932*, pp. 228–32.

183. Donoughue and Jones, *Herbert Morrison*, pp. 257–8.

184. Edinburgh and District Trades and Labour Council, Annual Report of the for the year ending 31 March 1934.

185. Labour Party, *Report of the Annual Conference of the Labour Party, 1933*, pp. 185–8.

186. Pethick-Lawrence, *Fate Has Been Kind*, p. 185.

187. Letter from Lansbury to Middleton, 9 August 1934, cited in Shepherd, *George Lansbury*, p. 318; See also, R. Vickers, *The Labour Party and the World: The Evolution of Labour's Foreign Policy, 1900–51* (Manchester, 2004), pp. 107–11.

188. Quoted in Harris, *Attlee*, p. 117.

189. Labour Party, *Report of the Annual Conference of the Labour Party, 1934*, pp. 174–5; Harris, *Attlee*, p. 118.

190. Quoted in Pimlott, *Labour and the Left*, p. 90.

191. Clarke, *The Cripps Version*, pp. 61–4.

192. For an excellent overview, see D. Blaazer, *The Popular Front and the Progressive Tradition: Socialists, Liberals, and the Quest for Unity, 1884–1939* (Cambridge, 1992), pp. 154–72.

193. Quoted in Reynolds and Laybourn, *Labour Heartland*, p. 120.

194. 'Democracy v. Dictatorship', in Labour Party, *Report of the Annual Conference of the Labour Party, 1933*, pp. 277–8.

195. Quoted in Taylor, *The TUC*, pp. 63–4.

196. Quoted in Bullock, *Ernest Bevin*, p. 190.

197. *NEC Mins*, 27 February and 1 March 1934; Meeting of the Three Executives, 28 February and 28 June 1934; Howell, *British Social Democracy*, p. 74.

198. As such, Labour policy was close to the results of the Peace Ballot organised by the League of Nations Union in June 1934. This revealed overwhelming public support for the League, for the reduction of armaments by international agreement, and for sanctions – military and non-military – against an aggressor.

199. Pethick-Lawrence, *Fate Has Been Kind*, pp. 185–6.

200. Walker, *Thomas Johnston*, pp. 130–6.

201. Labour Party, *Report of the Annual Conference of the Labour Party, 1935*, p. 12.

202. Ibid., pp. 153–93.

203. Ibid., p. 153; Shepherd, *George Lansbury*, pp. 318–28; Bullock, *Ernest Bevin*, pp. 190–206.

204. Thorpe, 'The Industrial Meaning of "Gradualism"', p. 113.

205. *Labour Candidate*, February 1933.

206. Labour Party, *Report of the Annual Conference of the Labour Party, 1932*, p. 4.

207. Ibid., p. 172.

208. Quoted in Taylor, *The TUC*, pp. 70–1.

209. Labour Party, *Report of the Annual Conference of the Labour Party, 1932*, p. 31.

210. 'Victory for Socialism', in Labour Party, *Report of the Annual Conference of the Labour Party*, 1933, pp. 290–1.

211. D. E. McHenry, *The Labour Party in Transition, 1931–38* (London, 1938), p. 64.

212. Labour Party, *Report of the Annual Conference of the Labour Party, 1935 and 1937*, pp. 145 and 31.

213. Labour Party, *Party Organisation* (London, 1936).

214. M. A. Hamilton, *The Labour Party Today: What it is and How it Works* (London, 1938), pp. 62–9; also quoted in Weinbren, *Generating Socialism*, p. 167.

215. M. Pinto-Duschinsky, *British Political Finance, 1800–1980* (AEI Studies, 1981), pp. 80–1; Labour Party, *Report of the Annual Conference of the Labour Party, 1933*, pp. 36–7.

216. Labour Party, *Report of the Annual Conference of the Labour Party, 1937*, p. 31.

217. See E. and S. Yeo (eds.), *Popular Culture and Class Conflict, 1590–1914: Explorations in the History of Labour and Leisure* (Brighton, 1981).

218. Beynon and Austrin, *Masters and Servants*, pp. 206–25.

219. Minutes of the Durham Labour Women's Advisory Committee, 1920–37 passim.

220. C. Williams, *Democratic Rhondda: Politics and Society, 1885–1951* (Cardiff, 1996), pp. 109–17.

221. *NEC Mins*, 17 February 1921; *Labour Organiser*, January 1925; Weinbren, *Generating Socialism*, pp. 72–5.

222. *Labour Organiser*, April 1925.

223. Quoted in Weinbren, *Generating Socialism*, p. 34.

224. Donoughue and Jones, *Herbert Morrison*, pp. 71–2 and 214.

225. D. Weinbren, 'Sociable Capital: London's Labour Parties, 1918–45', in Worley (ed.), *Labour's Grass Roots*, p. 200.

226. Minutes of the North Lambeth Labour Party, 13 May 1927.

227. Colne Valley Divisional Labour Party, *Annual Report and Balance Sheet*, 11 February 1939; *Labour Organiser*, October–November 1925.

228. S. G. Jones, *Workers at Play: A Social and Economic History of Leisure, 1918–39* (London, 1986), p. 145.

229. M. Worley, 'For a Proletarian Culture: CPGB Culture in the Third Period, 1928–35', *Socialist History*, 18 (2000) pp. 70–91.

230. Labour Party, *Report of the Annual Conference of the Labour Party, 1935*, p. 59.

231. Colne Valley Divisional Labour Party, *Annual Report and Balance Sheet*, 16 February 1935.

232. See Edinburgh and District Trades and Labour Council, *Annual Reports, 1934–39*.

233. *NEC Mins*, 17 April 1918 and 12 November 1919.

234. Ibid., 10 February 1920. The committee suggested that portable projectors be supplied to party and trade union branches, recommending that moral and/or topical films, such as *Les Misérables*, could be shown.

235. S. G. Jones, *The British Labour Movement and Film, 1918–39* (London, 1987), pp. 137–45; B. Hogenkamp, *Deadly Parallels: Film and the Left in Britain, 1929–39* (London, 1986), pp. 176–91.

236. Furthermore, Conservative central office had established the Conservative and Unionist Film Association, and Conservative relations with the newsreel companies were firmly established. A. Taylor, 'Speaking to Democracy: The Conservative Party and Mass Opinion from the 1920s to the 1950s', in S. Ball and I. Holliday (eds.), *Mass Conservatism: The Conservatives and the Public since the 1880s* (London, 2002), pp. 78–99.

237. *Labour Organiser*, January 1925.

238. Donoughue and Jones, *Herbert Morrison*, p. 213.

239. Weinbren, *Generating Socialism*, pp. 4–11.

240. *Annual Report* of the North Islington Divisional Labour Party, 1934.

241. Minutes of the Merton and Morden Labour Party, 20 April 1937.

242. Minutes of the North Islington Divisional Labour Party, 1935–40, passim.

243. Tanner, 'The Pattern of Labour Politics', pp. 122–3.

244. P. Clarke, 'Introduction', *Minutes of the Colne Valley Divisional Labour Party*.

245. Jones, *Workers at Play*, p. 146.

246. *Labour Organiser*, December 1925.

247. Jones, *Workers at Play*, p. 147.

248. *Labour Organiser*, August 1927.

249. J. E. Cronin, *Labour and Society in Britain, 1918–79* (London, 1984), p. 91.

250. *NEC Mins*, 25 June 1924. The sub-committee on the organisation of youth reported that a questionnaire sent to the party divisions had received 334 replies. These suggested that 99 constituencies contained some form of Labour youth organisation (including five communist and six 'other').

251. Cole, *A History of the Labour Party*, p. 143.

252. *NEC Mins*, 25 June 1924; Labour Party, *Report of the Annual Conference of the Labour Party, 1924*, pp. 23–5.

253. *NEC Mins*, 21 June 1926.

254. Labour Party, *Report of the Annual Conference of the Labour Party, 1933 and 1935*.

255. M. Webb, 'The Rise and Fall of the Labour League of Youth', *Socialist History*, 26 (2004).

256. The quote is from Harry Wickham (Buckingham Labour Party). See Labour Party, *Report of the Annual Conference of the Labour Party, 1933*, p. 147.

257. *Minutes of the Newport Labour Party*, 20 April 1925 and 14 December 1926; *Minutes of the Newport Labour Party Young People's Labour League*, 30 April 1928 and 15 September 1930; *Minutes of the Newport Labour Party Labour League of Youth*, 22 August and 5 September 1934 (LSE).

258. Minutes of the North Lambeth Divisional Labour Party, 14 July and 27 August 1926.

259. Ibid., 19 September and 8 December 1932 (LSE).

260. Weinbren, *Generating Socialism*, pp. 30–6.

261. Ibid., pp. 39–40.

262. Quoted in Webb, 'The Rise and Fall'.

263. Tanner, 'The Pattern of Labour Politics', p. 122.

264. See D. Tanner, 'Labour and its Membership', in Tanner, Thane and Tiratsoo (eds.), *Labour's First Century*, p. 253.

265. Weinbren, *Generating Socialism*, p. 168.

266. Minutes of the Storer Local Labour Party, 1932–9 (Leicestershire Record Office). See also Minutes of the Shepshed Local Labour Party, 1937–51 (Leicestershire Record Office) for similar comments.

267. Norwich Labour Party and Industrial Council, *Executive Report and Balance Sheet, 1937* (Norwich, 1937).

268. J. and B. Braddock, *The Braddocks* (London, 1963), p. 83; Reynolds and Laybourn, *Labour Heartland*, p. 111; Tanner, 'The Pattern of Labour Politics', p. 130.

269. Labour Party, *Report of the Annual Conference of the Labour Party, 1935*, p. 44; Cole, *A History of the Labour Party*, p. 458.

270. Donoughue and Jones, *Herbert Morrison*, pp. 189–91.

Chapter Four

1. C. R. Attlee, *The Labour Party in Perspective* (London, 1937), p. 163.

2. Labour Party, *Report of the Annual Conference of the Labour Party, 1939* (London, 1939), p. 214 (chairman's address).

3. T. Stannage, *Baldwin Thwarts the Opposition: The British General Election of 1935* (London, 1980), p. 150.

4. M. Savage and A. Miles, *The Remaking of the British Working Class* (London, 1994), pp. 87–8.

5. *Ministry of Labour Gazette*, vols. 40–8 (1932–40); W. R. Garside, *British Unemployment, 1919–39* (Cambridge, 1990).

6. B. R. Mitchell and P. Deane, *Abstract of British Historical Statistics* (Cambridge, 1962), p. 306; J. E. Cronin, *Labour and Society in Britain, 1918–79* (London, 1984), p. 53.

7. Cronin, *Labour and Society*, pp. 51–69; S. Pollard, *The Development of the British Economy, 1919–90* (London, 1992), p. 54.

8. A. Thorpe, *Britain in the 1930s* (Oxford, 1992), p. 65.

9. E. Hopkins, *A Social History of the English Working Class, 1815–1945* (London, 1979), p. 227.

10. A. H. Halsey (ed.), *British Social Trends since 1900* (London, 1988), p. 164.

11. E. Hobsbawm, *Industry and Empire: From 1750 to the Present Day* (London, 1990), p. 208.

12. B. Supple, *The History of the British Coal Industry, Volume 4: 1913–1946, The Political Economy of Decline* (Oxford, 1987), pp. 8–9.

13.   H. Francis and D. Smith, *The Fed: A History of the South Wales Miners in the Twentieth Century* (London, 1980), pp. 32–5.

14.   R. McKibbin, *Classes and Cultures: England, 1918–1951* (Oxford, 1998), pp. 106–11.

15.   Savage and Miles, *The Remaking of the British Working Class*, p. 28; G. Routh, *Occupation and Pay in Great Britain, 1906–79* (London, 1980).

16.   Halsey (ed.), *British Social Trends*, pp. 180–2.

17.   Routh, *Occupation and Pay*, pp. 120–1.

18.   Cronin, *Labour and Society*, p. 55.

19.   Routh, *Occupation and Pay*, p. 6.

20.   Savage and Miles, *The Remaking of the British Working Class*, pp. 62–8.

21.   McKibbin, *Classes and Cultures*, p. 185.

22.   Cronin, *Labour and Society*, pp. 74–8.

23.   Thorpe, *Britain in the 1930s*, pp. 97–101; M. Daunton (ed.), *Councillors and Tenants: Local Authority Housing in English Cities, 1919–39* (Leicester, 1984); McKibbin, *Classes and Cultures*, p. 188.

24.   Savage and Miles, *The Remaking of the British Working Class*, pp. 68–72.

25.   McKibbin, *Classes and Cultures*, pp. 419–56; Thorpe, *Britain in the 1930s*, pp. 103–10.

26.   Savage and Miles, *The Remaking of the British Working Class*, pp. 21–40; McKibbin, *Classes and Cultures*, pp. 111–27.

27.   G. D. H. Cole, *A History of the Labour Party from 1914* (London, 1948), p. 480.

28.   Thorpe, *Britain in the 1930s*, p. 110.

29.   *Halifax Daily Courier and Guardian*, 3 November 1930, cited in S. Davies and B. Morley, 'The Reactions of Municipal Voters in Yorkshire to the Second Labour Government, 1929–32', in M. Worley (ed.), *Labour's Grass Roots: Essays on the Activities of Local Labour Parties and Members, 1918–45* (Aldershot, 2005), p. 134. See also D. Weinbren, 'Sociable Capital: London's Labour Parties, 1918–45', in Worley (ed.), *Labour's Grass Roots*, p. 204.

30.   Norwich Labour Party and Industrial Council, *Report and Balance Sheet* (Norwich, 1936 and 1937).

31.   Labour Party, *Report of the Annual Conference of the Labour Party, 1937*, p. 138.

32.   R. C. Whiting, *The View from Cowley: The Impact of Industrialization upon Oxford, 1918–39* (Oxford, 1983), pp. 53–106.

33.   Savage and Miles, *The Remaking of the British Working Class*, p. 88.

34.   R. McKibbin, 'Classes and Cultures: A Postscript', *Mitteilungsblatt des Instituts für soziale Bewegungen*, 27 (2003), p. 154; McKibbin, *Classes and Cultures*, pp. 46–8.

35.   M. Cowling, *The Impact of Labour: The Beginning of Modern British Politics* (Cambridge, 1971).

36.   Thorpe, *Britain in the 1930s*, pp. 86–90.

37.   R. McKibbin, 'Class and Conventional Wisdom: The Conservative Party and the "Public" in Interwar Britain', in his *The Ideologies of Class: Social Relations in Britain, 1890–1950* (Oxford, 1990), pp. 259–93.

38.   P. Williamson, 'The Doctrinal Politics of Stanley Baldwin', in M. Bentley (ed.), *Public and Private Doctrine: Essays in British History Presented to Maurice Cowling* (Cambridge, 1993), pp. 181–208; A. Taylor, 'Speaking to Democracy: The Conservative Party and Mass Opinion from the 1920s to the 1950s', in S. Ball and I. Holliday (eds.), *Mass Conservatism: The Conservatives and the Public since the 1880s* (London, 2002), pp. 79–85.

39.   D. Jarvis, 'The Shaping of Conservative Electoral Hegemony, 1918–39', in J. Lawrence and M. Taylor (eds.), *Party, State and Society: Electoral Behaviour in Britain since 1829* (Aldershot, 1997), pp. 131–51.

40.   This section draws in large part from K. Morgan, 'The Conservatives and Mass Housing, 1918–39', in Ball and Holliday (eds.), *Mass Conservatism*, pp. 58–77.

41.   Thorpe, *Britain in the 1930s*, p. 16.

42.   B. Pimlott (ed.), *The Political Diary of Hugh Dalton, 1918–40, 1945–60* (London, 1986), pp. 190–2.

43.   A. Thorpe, *A History of the British Labour Party* (Basingstoke, 1997), pp. 87–8.

44.   F. W. S. Craig, *British Parliamentary Election Results, 1918–45* (Chichester, 1983).

45.   Labour Party, *Report of the Annual Conference of the Labour Party, 1935*, pp. 257–62. The trade union MPs further comprised two woodworkers, two London Society Compositors, and one each from the boilermakers', ironworkers', dyers', patternmakers', vehicle builders', shop assistants', building workers', pottery workers', bakers', and Typographical workers' unions.

46.   The following table is a list of trade union-sponsored Labour MPs in 1924 and 1935:

	1924	1935
MFGB	40	34
TGWU	6	7
NUGMW	4	6
NUR	3	4
AEU	3	3
Textile Workers	2	0
RCA	1	6
NUDAW	4	5
Other	23	14

47.   Cole, *A History of the Labour Party*, p. 313. In 1929, the divisional parties had sponsored 361 candidates.

48.   See the relevant sections in Labour Party, *Report of the Annual Conference of the Labour Party* for 1935, 1937 and 1939.

49.   D. E. McHenry, *The Labour Party in Transition, 1931–38* (London, 1938), p. 192.

50.   Quoted in B. Donoughue and G. W. Jones, *Herbert Morrison: Portrait of a Politician* (London, 2001), pp. 236–7. For Morrison's relationship with Wilkinson, see B. D. Vernon, *Ellen Wilkinson* (London, 1982), pp. 126–9.

51.   B. Pimlott, *Labour and the Left in the 1930s* (Cambridge, 1977), p. 74.

52.   R. Pearce, 'Clement Attlee 1935–55', in K. Jefferys (ed.), *Leading Labour: From Keir Hardie to Tony Blair* (London, 1999), p. 84.

53.   *Minutes of the National Executive Committee* (Woodbridge, undated) (hereafter *NEC Mins*), 26 November 1935; K. Harris, *Attlee* (London, 1985), p. 121. See also J. Lawson, *A Man's Life* (London, 1944), p. 161, for reference to his good friend Attlee.

54.   Labour Party, *Report of the Annual Conference of the Labour Party, 1939*, p. 224.

55.   D. Howell, *British Social Democracy: A Study in Development and Decay* (London, 1980), p. 103.

56.   L. Minkin, *The Labour Party Conference: A Study in the Politics of Intra-Party Democracy* (London, 1978), p. 368.

57.   Labour Party, *Labour's Immediate Programme* (London, 1937).

58.   J. M. Bellamy and J. Saville (eds.), *Dictionary of Labour Biography, Volume VI* (Basingstoke, 1982), pp. 245–9.

59.   Labour Party, *Report of the Annual Conference of the Labour Party, 1939*, p. 364. The nine female organisers were Mrs Gibb (North Eastern), Mrs Anderson (North Western), Mrs Fenn (Midlands), Miss Tavener (Home and Southern), Miss Somers (London), Mrs Townley (South Western), Miss Francis (Eastern), Mrs Andrews (Wales and Monmouth), and Mrs Lauder (Scotland).

60.   Ibid. The nine male organisers were Mr Lewcock (North Eastern), Mr Wallis (North Western), Mr Connolly (Midlands), Mr Kneeshaw (Home and Southern), Mr Atkinson (London), Mr Jones (South Western), Mr Taylor (Eastern), Mr Morris (Wales and Monmouth), and Mr Woodburn (Scotland). Kneeshaw had moved from the North West to the Home and Southern district by 1937.

61.   Labour Party, *Report of the Annual Conference of the Labour Party, 1939*, p. 92.

62.   C. Wrigley, *British Trade Unions Since 1933* (Cambridge, 2002), p. 8.

63.   Thorpe, *A History of the British Labour Party*, p. 95.

64.   Labour Party, *Report of the Annual Conference of the Labour Party, 1939*, p. 92; Cole, *A History of the Labour Party*, p. 480.

65.   P. Graves, *Labour Women: Women in British Working-Class Politics, 1918–39* (Cambridge, 1994), p. 213; Labour Party, *Report of the Annual Conference of the Labour Party* for 1930, 1932, 1937 and 1940.

66.   Graves, *Labour Women*, pp. 181–219; M. Pugh, *Women and the Women's Movement in Britain, 1914–59* (Basingstoke, 1992), p. 139.

67.   Ibid., pp. 212–15; *NEC Mins*, 20 April 1932.

68.   Graves, *Labour Women*, p. 213; Labour Party, *Report of the Annual Conference of the Labour Party, 1935*, p. 121.

69.   M. Francis, 'Labour and Gender', in D. Tanner, P. Thane and N. Tiratsoo (eds.), *Labour's First Century* (Cambridge, 2000), p. 197.

70.   P. Thane, 'Labour and Welfare', in Tanner, Thane and Tiratsoo (eds.), *Labour's First Century*, p. 93.

71.   Graves, *Labour Women*, pp. 165–78.

72.   Quoted in ibid., p. 172.

73.   Ibid., p. 213; M. Gibb, 'The Labour Party in the North East Between the Wars', *Bulletin of the North East Group for the Study of Labour History*, 18 (1988), p. 12.

74.   Minutes of the Durham Labour Women's Advisory Council, 1920–37, passim.

75.   Minutes of the Bishop Auckland Women's Section of the Labour Party, 1929–32 (Durham Record Office). For the examples given, see entries for 13 March and 10 April 1934.

76.   Minutes of the Seaham Women's Section of the Labour Party, 1939–45 (Durham Record Office).

77.   Minutes of the Crook Labour Party Women's Section, 17 October 1934.

78.   K. Hunt, 'Making Politics in Local Communities', in Worley (ed.), *Labour's Grass Roots*, pp. 80–102.

79.   Ibid. Minutes of the Loughborough Labour Party Women's Section, 1934–40 (Leicestershire Record Office). See, in particular, entries for 24 September 1934, 1 April 1935, 12 October 1936, and 10 January 1938.

80.   D. Tanner, 'Gender, Civic Culture and Politics in South Wales: Explaining Labour Municipal Policy, 1918–39', in Worley (ed.), *Labour's Grass Roots*, p. 182.

81.   Labour Party, *Report of the Annual Conference of the Labour Party* for 1924, 1928, 1933 and 1937, pp. 21–2, 27–8, 45–6 and 51.

82.   Minutes of the Sedgefield Division Federation of Women's Sections, 1934–45 (Durham Record Office), passim.

83.   Minutes of the Merton Labour Party Women's Group, 21 March 1933 (LSE).

84.   M. Savage, *The Dynamics of Working-Class Politics: The Labour Movement in Preston, 1880–1940* (Cambridge, 1987), p. 181.

85.   Labour Party, *Report of the Annual Conference of the Labour Party, 1935*, p. 144.

86.   Graves, *Labour Women*, pp. 213–15.

87.   Minutes of the North Lambeth Divisional Labour Party, 12 and 13 April, and 2 July 1935.

88.   A. Flinn, 'Labour's Family: Local Labour Parties, Trade Unions and Trades Councils in Cotton Lancashire, 1931–39', in Worley (ed.), *Labour's Grass Roots*, pp. 103–24.

89.   Weinbren, 'Sociable Capital', p. 196; S. Davies, *Liverpool Labour: Social and Political Influences on the Development of the Labour Party in Liverpool, 1900–39* (Keele, 1996), pp. 69–73; J. and B. Braddock, *The Braddocks* (London, 1963), p. 85.

90.   Savage, *The Dynamics of Working Class Politics*, pp. 195–8. Savage's suggestion that such a trend fell away over the 1930s as male-dominated trade union affiliates reasserted their dominance does not always readily apply. See Tanner, 'Gender, Civic Culture and Politics', pp. 171–94.

91.   Edinburgh and District Trades and Labour Council, *Annual Report,* 1934 and 1935.

92.   W. W. Knox and A. MacKinlay, 'The Re-Making of Scottish Labour in the 1930s', *Twentieth Century British History*, 6, 2 (1995), pp. 178–81.

93.   J. Marriott, *The Culture of Labourism: The East End Between the Wars* (Edinburgh, 1991), pp. 68–121; H. Beynon and T. Austrin, *Masters and Servants: Class and Patronage in the Making of a Labour Organisation* (London, 1994), pp. 363–70; C. Williams, *Democratic Rhondda: Politics and Society, 1885–1951* (Cardiff, 1996), pp. 205–12.

94.   Labour Party, *Report of the Annual Conference of the Labour Party*, 1930 and 1939, pp. 112–48 and 95. The five in 1929 were Reading, Derby, Faversham, Oldham, and Salford. The 32 in 1938 were Romford, Lewisham East, Harrow, Nelson and Colne, Hendon, Ilford, Twickenham,

Greenwich, Bermondsey West, East Ham South, Deptford, Rotherhithe, East Ham (North), Whitechapel, Newport, Woolwich West, Mitcham, Uxbridge, Dartford, Fulham West, Woolwich East, Lewisham West, Poplar South, Mile End, St Albans, Frome, Croydon South, Norwich, Oldham, Dundee, Southampton and Stockport.

95.   At the same time, Labour needed the support of the borough's large middle-class population if it was to gain political control. To this effect, many of the party leaders and election candidates were middle class (Freda Corbett, Tom Crawford, John Wilmot), and the party slowly built on a local radical tradition that was arguably refired by the outbreak of the Spanish civil war in 1936. In the face of fascist aggression, moreover, Labour succeeded in portraying itself as the defender of the national interest – a political coup that was helped by the fact that Lewisham's two Conservative MPs from 1935 had respective links with Italy and Germany. Sir Philip Dawson was a known admirer of Mussolini, while Sir Assheton Pownell was a member of the Anglo-German Fellowship and a guest at the 1937 Nuremberg rally. See T. Jeffery, 'The Suburban Nation: Politics and Class in Lewisham', in D. Feldman and G. Stedman Jones (eds.), *Metropolis–London: Histories and Representations since 1800* (London, 1989), pp. 189–216.

96.   Labour Party, *Report of the Annual Conference of the Labour Party, 1939*, p. 196.

97.   Weinbren, 'Sociable Capital', p. 205.

98.   Ibid. Norwich Labour Party and Industrial Council, *Report and Balance Sheet* (Norwich, 1936 and 1937).

99.   Labour Party, *Report of the Annual Conference of the Labour Party* for1920, 1921 and 1922, pp. 169–70, 152–4, and 181–4.

100.   N. Riddell, *Labour in Crisis: The Second Labour Government, 1929–31* (Manchester, 1999), pp. 101–2.

101.   Pimlott, *Labour and the Left*, pp. 116–17.

102.   Ibid. Labour Party, *Report of the Annual Conference of the Labour Party, 1933*, pp. 151–4.

103.   Pimlott, *Labour and the Left*, pp. 118–21.

104.   Ibid., pp. 121–5.

105.   Ibid., pp. 111–25.

106.   Ibid., pp. 124–5; Labour Party, *Report of the Annual Conference of the Labour Party, 1936*, p. 247.

107.   See, for example, Minutes of the Darlington Labour Party, 25 May 1937; *Minutes of the Newport Labour Party*, 15 June 1936. Labour Party, *Report of the Annual Conference of the Labour Party, 1937*, pp. 140–1.

108.   H. Dalton, *The Fateful Years: Memoirs, 1931–45* (London, 1957), p. 116; *NEC Mins*, 23 June 1937.

109.   *NEC Mins*, 3 June 1937.

110.   Pimlott (ed.), *The Political Diary of Hugh Dalton*, p. 336.

111.   J. Reynolds and K. Laybourn, *Labour Heartland: A History of the Labour Party in West Yorkshire during the Interwar Years, 1918–39* (Bradford, 1987), pp. 141–3.

112.   Labour Party, *Report of the Annual Conference of the Labour Party, 1937*, pp. 143–56. Greene later joined the British People's Party, and was interned during the Second World War.

113.   Ibid., pp. 149–55.

114.   Labour Party, *The Communist Solar System* (London, 1933).

115.   *NEC Mins*, 22 December 1936 and 4 January 1937; Labour Party, *Report of the Annual Conference of the Labour Party, 1937*, p. 164. Conference voted by 2,116,000 to 331,000 to reaffirm Labour's rejection of the united front with the CPGB.

116.   Braddock, *The Braddocks*, pp. 80–5. Despite this, Braddock's reputation preceded him. He was later arrested and imprisoned for inciting a riot, ultimately fighting his 1932 municipal election campaign from jail.

117.   Vernon, *Ellen Wilkinson*, pp. 141–7; R. Croucher, *We Refuse to Starve in Silence: A History of the National Unemployed Workers' Movement, 1920–46* (London, 1987), pp. 179–82.

118.   See, for a typical example, Labour Party, *Report of the Annual Conference of the Labour Party, 1932*, pp. 167–8.

119.   Labour Party, *Report of the Annual Conference of the Labour Party, 1935*, pp. 38–9 and 143–4.

120. Labour Party, *Report of the Annual Conference of the Labour Party*, 1936 and 1937.

121. Labour Party, *Report of the Annual Conference of the Labour Party, 1939*, p. 214 (chairman's address).

122. Pimlott (ed.), *The Political Diary of Hugh Dalton*, p. 190; *NEC Mins*, 22 and 23 October 1935.

123. Labour Party, *The Labour Party's Call to Power* (London, 1935).

124. Labour Party, *Labour's Immediate Programme*, printed on inside cover.

125. Ibid.; *NEC Mins*, 24 February 1937; Howell, *British Social Democracy*, p. 95.

126. Labour Party, *Labour's Immediate Programme*, pp. 1–7.

127. Labour Party, *Report of the Annual Conference of the Labour Party, 1937*, pp. 181–3.

128. For a critical appraisal of 1930s Labour policy, see A. Booth, 'How Long are Light Years in British Politics? The Labour Party's Economic Ideas in the 1930s', *Twentieth Century British History*, 7, 1 (1996).

129. Howell, *British Social Democracy*, p. 95.

130. R. Toye, *The Labour Party and the Planned Economy, 1931–51* (Woodbridge, 2003), pp. 82–6.

131. Thorpe, *A History of the British Labour Party*, pp. 96–7.

132. Howell, *British Social Democracy*, pp. 95–6.

133. S. Fielding, 'Labourism in the 1940s', *Twentieth Century British History*, 3, 2 (1992), pp. 140–2; Attlee, *The Labour Party in Perspective*, pp. 277–84.

134. Labour Party, *Report of the Annual Conference of the Labour Party* for 1925 and 1937, pp. 65–6 and 44–5; 'Draft Manifesto on Local Elections', *NEC Mins*, 15 January 1925. This was discussed at a meeting of the joint press and publicity department.

135. 'Draft Manifesto on Local Elections'.

136. Labour Party, *Report of the Annual Conference of the Labour Party, 1931*, pp. 44–5.

137. Labour Party, *Report of the Annual Conference of the Labour Party, 1930*, pp. 298–9. These were revised in 1938–9. See Labour Party, *Report of the Annual Conference of the Labour Party, 1939*, pp. 381–3.

138. 'Labour Groups on Local Authorities', in Labour Party, *Report of the Annual Conference of the Labour Party, 1939*, pp. 381–3.

139. Labour Party, *Local Government Speakers' Handbook* (London, 1938), p. 4; Cole, *A History of the Labour Party*, pp. 458–9.

140. A. Thorpe, 'The Consolidation of a Labour Stronghold, 1926–51', in C. Bindfield et al. (eds.), *The History of the City of Sheffield, 1843–1993* (Sheffield, 1993), p. 89.

141. Williams, *Democratic Rhondda*, pp. 96 and 192–212.

142. D. Tanner, 'The Pattern of Labour Politics, 1918–39', in D. Tanner, C. Williams and D. Hopkin (eds.), *The Labour Party in Wales, 1900–2000* (Cardiff, 2000), p. 130.

143. Tanner, 'Gender, Civic Culture and Politics', p. 178.

144. I. Donnachie, 'Scottish Labour in the Depression: The 1930s', in I. Donnachie, C. Harvie and I. S. Wood, *Forward! Labour Politics in Scotland, 1888–1988* (Edinburgh, 1989), p. 59.

145. Reynolds and Laybourn, *Labour Heartland*, pp. 115–16.

146. H. R. S. Phillpott, *Where Labour Rules* (London, 1934), pp. 12–16.

147. Thorpe, 'The Consolidation of a Labour Stronghold', pp. 87–94; Savage, *The Dynamic of Working Class Politics*, p. 31.

148. *Daily Herald*, October 1935, in collection of newspaper cuttings held at the Norfolk Record Office; Norwich Labour Party, *To the Electors of Ber Street Ward* (Norwich, 1936).

149. Phillpott, *Where Labour Rules*, p. 70. See also J. Hill, *Nelson: Politics, Economy, Community* (Keele, 1997), p. 89.

150. Donoughue and Jones, *Herbert Morrison*, pp. 63 and 211. The affiliated membership stood at 255,520, compared to 208,793 in 1931–2.

151. Ibid., pp. 199–209.

152. Quoted in D. Weinbren, *Generating Socialism: Recollections of Life in the Labour Party* (Stroud, 1997), pp. 210 and 218.

153. Minutes of the Islington Borough Labour Party, 19 July 1937 (Wood Green and Hornsey Labour Party Office).

154. L. Baston, 'Labour Local Government, 1900–99', in B. Brivati and R. Heffernan (eds.), *The Labour Party: A Centenary History* (Basingstoke, 2000), p. 452.

155. McHenry, *The Labour Party in Transition*, pp. 212–15.

156. F. Brockway, *Bermondsey Story: The Life of Alfred Salter* (London, 1949), pp. 85–112; S. Goss, *Local Labour and Local Government: A Study of Changing Interests, Politics and Policy in Southwark from 1919 to 1982* (Edinburgh, 1988), p. 25.

157. In 1934, Unemployed Assistance Boards became responsible for relief payments.

158. McHenry, *The Labour Party in Transition*, p. 212.

159. Quoted in Marriott, *The Culture of Labourism*, p. 65.

160. Quoted in Weinbren, 'Sociable Capital', p. 199.

161. N. Branson, *Poplarism, 1919–25: George Lansbury and the Councillors' Revolt* (London, 1985), p. 22.

162. Phillpott, *Where Labour Rules*, p. 37.

163. Braddock, *The Braddocks*, pp. 74–5.

164. Weinbren, *Generating Socialism*, p. 3.

165. C. Williams, 'Labour and the Challenge of Local Government', in Tanner, Williams and Hopkin (eds.), *The Labour Party in Wales*, p. 153.

166. Minutes of the North Lambeth Divisional Labour Party, 11 July 1927 and 11 September 1936.

167. J. J. Rowley, 'Introduction', *Minutes of the Wolverhampton Labour Party* (Wakefield, 1986).

168. Minutes of the Islington Borough Labour Party, 3 December 1936; Colne Valley Divisional Labour Party, *Annual Report and Balance Sheet*, 20 February 1932.

169. Minutes of the Loughborough Borough Labour Party, 24 June 1931.

170. Minutes of the Darlington Labour Party, 27 January 1935.

171. Donoughue and Jones, *Herbert Morrison*, p. 46.

172. Brockway, *Bermondsey Story*, p. 85.

173. J. Baxter et al., *The Making of Barnsley's Labour Movement, 1740–1940* (Rotherham, 1980).

174. Edinburgh and District Trades and Labour Council, *Annual Report, 1933*; McHenry, *The Labour Party in Transition*, p. 218.

175. Labour Party, *Report of the Annual Conference of the Labour Party, 1931*, p. 51.

176. *Minutes of the Newport Labour Party*, 2 December 1920.

177. Ibid., 15 March 1935 and 10 February 1936.

178. Williams, 'Labour and the Challenge of Local Government', p. 158.

179. Weinbren, 'Sociable Capital', p. 209; Tanner, 'Gender, Civic Culture and Politics', p. 175.

180. Reynolds and Laybourn, *Labour Heartland*, pp. 115–16.

181. Thorpe, 'The Consolidation of a Labour Stronghold', pp. 100–2.

182. Weinbren, 'Sociable Capital', p. 205.

183. C. R., Attlee, *Problems of a Socialist Government* (London, 1933), p. 191.

184. See, for example, Labour Party, *What is Fascism?* (London, 1934); Labour Party, *Nazis, Nazism, Nazidom* (London, 1934).

185. G. Webber, 'Patterns of Membership and Support for the British Union of Fascists', *Journal of Contemporary History*, 19 (1984), pp. 575–606; R. Thurlow, *Fascism in Britain: From Oswald Mosley's Blackshirts to the National Front* (London, 1998), pp. 61–113.

186. *NEC Mins*, June–July 1934.

187. Donoughue and Jones, *Herbert Morrison*, p. 223.

188. J. Swift, *Labour in Crisis: Clement Attlee and the Labour Party in Opposition, 1931–40* (Basingstoke, 2001), pp. 135–7.

189. Labour Party, *Report of the Annual Conference of the Labour Party, 1936* (London, 1936).

190. Donoughue and Jones, *Herbert Morrison*, p. 224.

191. M. Newman, 'Democracy versus Dictatorship: Labour's Role in the Struggle against British Fascism, 1933–36', *History Workshop*, 5 (1978), pp. 67–85.

192. Quoted in Weinbren, *Generating Socialism*, p. 113.

193.   Brockway, *Bermondsey Story*, pp. 204–6. The proactive response of the Trades and Labour Council eventually led Salter to resign in protest.

194.   Reynolds and Laybourn, *Labour Heartland*, pp. 121–2.

195.   This was often organised by the CPGB; see N. Barrett, 'A Bright Shining Star: The CPGB and Anti-Fascist Activism in the 1930s', *Science and Society*, 16, 1 (1997).

196.   *Minutes of the Newport Labour Party*, 1 January and 12 January 1934. There was, of course, some crossover of personnel between the ILP and Mosley's New Party and, later, the BUF.

197.   The best overview is T. Buchanan, *The Spanish Civil War and the British Labour Movement* (Cambridge, 1991).

198.   *NEC Mins*, 28 August, 4 and 9 September 1936.

199.   R. Vickers, *The Labour Party and the World: The Evolution of Labour's Foreign Policy, 1900–51* (Manchester, 2004), p. 120.

200.   Labour Party, *Report of the Annual Conference of the Labour Party, 1937*, p. 6.

201.   Vickers, *The Labour Party and the World*, p. 121; C. Attlee, *As it Happened* (London, 1954), p. 111; Dalton, *The Fateful Years*, pp. 95–6; E. Shinwell, *Conflict Without Malice* (London, 1955), pp. 140–1.

202.   T. Buchanan, *Britain and the Spanish Civil War* (Cambridge, 1997), pp. 78–80.

203.   A. Flinn, 'Irish Catholics in South East Lancashire: A Conflict of Loyalties?', *Manchester Region History Review*, 14 (2000).

204.   Minutes of the Islington Borough Labour Party and Trades Council, 30 April 1939.

205.   *Minutes of the Birmingham Borough Labour Party* (Wakefield, 1986).

206.   B. Pimlott, *Hugh Dalton* (London, 1995), pp. 232–5.

207.   Shinwell, *Conflict Without Malice*, pp. 140–1; Labour Party, *Report of the Annual Conference of the Labour Party, 1936*, pp. 169–71.

208.   Blaydon Divisional Labour Party, *Annual Report and Balance Sheet, 1936* (Durham Record Office).

209.   *NEC Mins*, 7–9 October 1936; Labour Party, *Report of the Annual Conference of the Labour Party, 1936*, pp. 181–207; Cole, *A History of the Labour Party*, pp. 326–9.

210.   Swift, *Labour in Crisis*, p. 103–5. Indeed, a brigade was named after the Labour leader.

211.   *NEC Mins*, 23 June 1937; Labour Party, *Report of the Annual Conference of the Labour Party, 1937*, pp. 6–14.

212.   Labour Party, *Report of the Annual Conference of the Labour Party, 1939*, p. 6.

213.   Edinburgh and District Trades and Labour Council, *Annual Report, 1937*; Tanner, 'The Pattern of Labour Politics', p. 129; Reynolds and Laybourn, *Labour Heartland*, p. 139.

214.   Quoted in Weinbren, *Generating Socialism*, p. 101.

215.   Minutes of the Islington Borough Labour Party, 4 May 1937 and 22 January 1939.

216.   Labour Party, *Report of the Annual Conference of the Labour Party, 1939*, p. 6.

217.   C. Fleay and M. L. Sanders, 'The Labour Spain Committee: Labour Party Policy and the Spanish Civil War', *The Historical Journal*, 28, 1 (1985).

218.   K. Morgan, *Against Fascism and War: Ruptures and Continuities in British Communist Politics, 1935–41* (Manchester, 1989).

219.   See, for example, Ellen Wilkinson's speech to the 1933 Labour conference. Labour Party, *Report of the Annual Conference of the Labour Party, 1933*, p. 221.

220.   D. Blaazer, *The Popular Front and the Progressive Tradition: Socialists, Liberals, and the Quest for Unity, 1884–1939* (Cambridge, 1992), pp. 160–92; Pimlott, *Labour and the Left*, pp. 77–108; P. Corthorn, 'The Labour Party and the League of Nations: The Socialist League's Role in the Sanctions Crisis of 1935', *Twentieth Century British History*, 13, 1 (2002), pp. 62–85.

221.   Cole, *A History of the Labour Party*, p. 349; Blaazer, *The Popular Front*, p. 170.

222.   Ibid., p. 348.

223.   F. Brockway, *Inside the Left* (London, 1942), p. 264; Pimlott, *Labour and the Left*, pp. 94–5.

224.   Pimlott, *Labour and the Left*, p. 96.

225.   Labour Party, *Report of the Annual Conference of the Labour Party, 1937*, p. 26.

226.   *NEC Mins*, 27 January and 24 March 1937.

227.   Cole, *A History of the Labour Party*, p. 349.

228.   Quoted in Blaazer, *The Popular Front*, p. 179.

229.   Howell, *British Social Democracy*, p. 91; *NEC Mins*, 5 May 1938.

230. *NEC Mins*, 13 January 1939.

231. Labour Party, *Report of the Annual Conference of the Labour Party, 1939*, pp. 46–8.

232. *NEC Mins*, 25 January and 22 March 1939.

233. Labour Party, *Report of the Annual Conference of the Labour Party, 1937*, p. 162.

234. Howell, *British Social Democracy*, p. 90–1.

235. H. Francis, *Miners Against Fascism: Wales and the Spanish Civil War* (London, 1984).

236. Tanner, 'The Pattern of Labour Politics', pp. 129–30; Minutes of the Bedwellty Divisional Labour Party, 23 January 1937.

237. Quoted in Weinbren, *Generating Socialism*, p. 135.

238. Flinn, 'Labour's Family', pp. 113–19. See, for other parties giving open support to the united or popular front, Blaydon Labour Party, *Annual Report and Balance Sheet, 1936* (Durham Record Office); *Minutes of the Gloucester Trades Council and Labour Party*, 5 March 1939.

239. Thorpe, *A History of the British Labour Party*, p. 93; Whiting, *The View from Cowley*, pp. 168–70.

240. Pimlott, *Labour and the Left*, pp. 56–8.

241. Weinbren, *Generating Socialism*, p. 139.

242. Ibid.

243. Minutes of the Hornsey Labour Party, 28 February 23 August, 28 November 1938 and 6 February 1939; Minutes of the Highgate Ward Labour Party, 27 June 1935, 18 February, 17 June 1936 (Wood Green and Hornsey Labour Party Office).

244. Labour Party, *Report of the Annual Conference of the Labour Party, 1937*, pp. 160–4.

245. Quoted in Pimlott, *Labour and the Left*, p. 102.

246. Howell, *British Social Democracy*, p. 91.

247. Minutes of the North Lambeth Divisional Labour Party, 19 March and 30 April 1937.

248. F. E. Bealey et al., *Constituency Politics: A Study of Newcastle-under-Lyme* (London, 1965), p. 87.

249. P. Wyncoll, *The Nottingham Labour Movement, 1880–1939* (London, 1985), p. 241.

250. Williams, *Democratic Rhondda*, pp. 200–2.

251. *Minutes of the Newport Labour Party*, 28 February, 4 May, 11 September 1936, 8 February, 12 July 1937 and 23 January 1939.

252. Knox and MacKinlay, 'The Re-Making of Scottish Labour', pp. 176–9 and 188–93.

253. Reynolds and Laybourn, *Labour Heartland*, pp. 141–4.

254. *Minutes of the Peterborough Divisional Labour Party*, 13 March 1937; Minutes of the Darlington Labour Party, 22 May 1933, 13 August 1936 and 27 February 1939; G. J. Barnsby, *Socialism in Birmingham and the Black Country, 1850–1939* (Wolverhampton, 1998), p. 542; Houghton-le-Spring Labour Party, *Annual Report and Balance Sheet, 1933*; Wyncoll, *The Nottingham Labour Movement*, pp. 242–3.

255. 'An Appeal to the Movement', in Labour Party, *Report of the Annual Conference of the Labour Party, 1937*, pp. 25–6.

256. Labour Party, *Labour and Popular Front* (London, 1938), pp. 4–6.

257. Pimlott, *Labour and the Left*, pp. 153 and 173.

258. Blaazer, *The Popular Front*, p. 182.

259. Dalton, *The Fateful Years*, pp. 63–4; *NEC Mins*, 4 March 1935; R. Taylor, *The TUC*, pp. 61–6.

260. J. Campbell, *Nye Bevan* (London, 1997), pp. 75–6.

261. Labour Party, *Report of the Annual Conference of the Labour Party, 1937*, pp. 208–9.

262. *NEC Mins*, 4 March, 28 August, 18 September and 2 October 1936.

263. NCL, *Labour and the Defence of Peace* (London, 1936).

264. Labour Party, *Report of the Annual Conference of the Labour Party, 1936*, pp. 192–206; Donoughue and Jones, *Herbert Morrison*, pp. 262–3; Harris, *Attlee*, p. 128.

265. Howell, *British Social Democracy*, p. 99; Harris, *Attlee*, p. 136.

266. Labour Party, *Report of the Annual Conference of the Labour Party, 1937*, pp. 3–4 and 138.

267. *NEC Mins*, 21 September 1938.

268. A. Reekes, *The Rise of Labour, 1899–1951* (Basingstoke, 1991), pp. 104–5. The quote is from Attlee's speech of 3 October 1938.

269. Labour Party, *Report of the Annual Conference of the Labour Party, 1939*, pp. 13–4.

270. Pimlott, *Labour and the Left*, pp. 163–9.

271. Minutes of the North Lambeth Divisional Labour Party, 26 July 1935.

272. Donoughue and Jones, *Herbert Morrison*, p. 265.

273. Reynolds and Laybourn, *Labour Heartland*, p. 145; Hill, *Nelson*, pp. 94–5; Thorpe, 'The Consolidation of a Labour Stronghold', p. 106; *Minutes of the Newport Labour Party*, 20 April 1938.

274. 'The Labour Movement and National Voluntary Service', Labour Party, *Report of the Annual Conference of the Labour Party, 1939*, p. 20.

275. Colne Valley Divisional Labour Party, *Annual Report and Balance Sheet*, 10 February 1940.

Conclusion

1. Labour Party, *Report of the Annual Conference of the Labour Party, 1937* (London, 1937), p. 137 (chairman's address).

2. Letter from E. Bevin to G. D. H. Cole, 31 December 1935, quoted in A. Bullock, *Ernest Bevin: A Biography* (London, 2002), p. 188.

3. C. R. Attlee, *The Labour Party in Perspective* (London, 1937), p. 93.

4. See, for example, R. Miliband, *Parliamentary Socialism: A Study in the Politics of Labour* (London, 1961); K. Coates, *The Labour Party and the Struggle for Socialism* (Cambridge, 1975); T. Forester, *The Labour Party and the Working Class* (London, 1975).

5. Blaydon Labour Party, *Annual Report and Balance Sheet, 1938* (Durham Record Office).

Bibliography

UNPUBLISHED DOCUMENTS

Mathers (George) Papers (National Library of Scotland)
Minutes of the Bedford Constituency Labour Party (London School of Economics)
Minutes of the Bedwellty Divisional Labour Party (Gwent Record Office)
Minutes of the Bishop Auckland Women's Section of the Labour Party (Durham Record Office)
Minutes of the Chepstow and District Labour Party (Gwent Record Office)
Minutes of the Crook Labour Party Women's Section (Durham Record Office)
Minutes of the Dalkeith Local Labour Party (National Library of Scotland)
Minutes of the Darlington Labour Party (Durham Record Office)
Minutes of the Durham Labour Women's Advisory Council (Durham Record Office)
Minutes of the East Grinstead Labour Party (London School of Economics)
Minutes of the Edinburgh North Conservative Association (Edinburgh City Archive)
Minutes of the Gateshead Socialist League (Tyne and Wear Archive Service)
Minutes of the Harborough Conservative and Unionist Association Women' Branch (Leicestershire Record Office)
Minutes of the Harborough Division Liberal Association (Leicestershire Record Office)
Minutes of the Hawick Local Labour Party Women's Section (National Library of Scotland)
Minutes of the Hebburn Labour Party and Trades Council (Durham Record Office)
Minutes of the Highgate Ward Labour Party (Wood Green and Hornsey Labour Party Office)
Minutes of the Hornsey Divisional Labour Party (Wood Green and Hornsey Labour Party Office)
Minutes of the Islington Borough Labour Party (Wood Green and Hornsey Labour Party Office)
Minutes of the Leith Divisional Labour Party (National Library of Scotland)
Minutes of the Leicestershire Liberal Association (Leicestershire Record Office)
Minutes of the Loughborough Borough Labour Party (Leicestershire Record Office)
Minutes of the Loughborough Constituency Labour Party (Leicestershire Record Office)
Minutes of the Loughborough Labour Party Women's Section (Leicestershire Record Office)
Minutes of the Merton and Morden Labour Party (London School of Economics)
Minutes of the Merton Labour Party Women's Group (London School of Economics)
Minutes of the North Islington Divisional Labour Party (Wood Green and Hornsey Labour Party Office)
Minutes of the North Lambeth Divisional Labour Party (London School of Economics)
Minutes of the Nottingham South Divisional Labour Party (Nottingham Record Office)
Minutes of the Peebles and South Midlothian Divisional Labour Party (National Library of Scotland)
Minutes of the Roxburgh and Selkirk Divisional Labour Party (National Library of Scotland)
Minutes of the Scottish Liberal Federation (National Library of Scotland)
Minutes of the Seaham Women's Section of the Labour Party (Durham Record Office)
Minutes of the Sedgefield Division Federation of Women's Sections (Durham Record Office)
Minutes of the Shepshed Local Labour Party (Leicestershire Record Office)
Minutes of the Storer Local Labour Party (Leicestershire Record Office)
Miscellaneous Papers (Durham Record Office)
Norwich Labour Papers (Norfolk Record Office)
Shotton Papers (Durham Record Office)
Woodburn Papers (National Library of Scotland)

PRINTED MATERIALS, DOCUMENTS AND MICROFILM

Ball, S. (ed.), *Parliament and Politics in the Age of Churchill and Attlee: The Headlam Diaries, 1935–51* (Cambridge, 2000)
Bealey, F. (ed.), *The Social and Political Thought of the Labour Party* (London, 1970)
Birmingham Borough Labour Party, *Minutes, 1906–51* (Wakefield, 1986)

Blaydon Divisional Labour Party, *Annual Report and Balance Sheet*, 1919–36 (Durham, 1919–36)
Cole, M. I. (ed.), *Beatrice Webb's Diaries*, 1912–24 and 1924–32 (London, 1952 and 1956)
Colne Valley Divisional Labour Party, *Minutes, Annual Reports and Papers, 1891–1951* (Wakefield, 1986)
Dale, I. (ed.), *Labour Party General Election Manifestos, 1900–97* (London, 2000)
Edinburgh and District Trades and Labour Council, *Minutes, Annual Reports and Papers, 1859–1951* (Wakefield, 1986)
Gloucester (Trades Council and) Labour Party, *Minutes, 1899–1951* (Wakefield, 1986)
Houghton-le-Spring Labour Party, *Annual Report and Balance Sheet, 1918–38* (Durham, 1918–38)
Labour Party, *Labour Party Foundation Conference and Annual Reports, 1900–05* (London, 1967)
—— *Minutes of the National Executive Committee, 1900–39* (Woodbridge, undated)
—— *Report of the Annual Conference of the Labour Party Conference Report, 1907* (London, 1907)
—— *Report of the Annual Conference of the Labour Party, 1918–40* (London, 1918–40)
Newcastle Labour Party, *Annual Report and Balance Sheet, 1918–20* (Newcastle, 1919 and 1920)
Newport Labour Party, *Minutes, Annual Reports and Papers, 1912–77* (Wakefield, 1999)
Norwich Labour Party and Industrial Council, *Executive Report and Balance Sheet, 1918–40* (Norwich, 1918–40)
Penistone and Holmfirth Labour Party, *Minutes, 1909–51* (Wakefield, 1986)
Peterborough Divisional Labour Party, *Minutes, 1900–51* (Wakefield, 1986)
Pimlott, B. (ed.), *The Political Diary of Hugh Dalton, 1918–40, 1945–60* (London, 1986)
South Shields Labour Party, *Minutes, Annual Reports and Papers, 1912–51* (Wakefield, 1986)
Sunderland Labour Party, *Annual Report and Balance Sheet, 1920* (1920)
TUC, *Report of the Trades Union Congress, 1918–40* (London, 1918–40)
Wolverhampton Labour Party, *Minutes, 1907–51* (Wakefield, 1986)

CONTEMPORARY BOOKS, PAMPHLETS AND LEAFLETS

Addison, C., C. R. Attlee et al. (eds.), *Problems of a Socialist Government* (London, 1933)
Attlee, C. R., *The Labour Party in Perspective* (London, 1937)
Chester-le-Street Labour Party, *Jack Butler* (1922)
Cripps, S., *Why This Socialism?* (London, 1934)
Dalton, H., *Practical Socialism for Britain* (London, 1935)
Durham Labour Party, *The Labour Party: County of Durham* (Durham, 1919)
Edinburgh Labour Party, *Parliamentary General Election, 1929 – South Edinburgh Division* (Edinburgh, 1929)
Hamilton, M. A., *The Labour Party Today: What it is and How it Works* (London, 1938)
Jarrow Labour Party, *Election Special* (Jarrow, 1935)
Labour Party, *The Communist Solar System* (London, 1933)
—— *For Socialism and Peace: The Labour Party's Programme of Action* (London, 1934)
—— *Labour and the Nation* (London, 1928)
—— *Labour and the New Social Order* (London, 1918)
—— *Labour and Popular Front* (London, 1938)
—— *Labour's Appeal to the People* (London, 1924)
—— *Labour's Appeal to the Nation* (London, 1929)
—— *Labour's Call to Action: The Nation's Opportunity* (London, 1931)
—— *Labour's Call to the People* (London, 1918)
—— *Labour's Call to the People* (London, 1922)
—— *Labour's Immediate Programme* (London, 1937)
—— *Local Government Speakers' Handbook* (London, 1938)
—— *Nazis, Nazism, Nazidom* (London, 1934)
—— *Party Organisation* (London, 1936 edition)
—— *The Labour Party's Call to Power* (London, 1935)
—— *Unemployment: A Labour Policy* (London, 1920)
—— *What is Fascism?* (London, 1934)
—— *Why Women Should Vote Labour* (undated [1929])
—— *Women and the Labour Party* (London, 1918)

Laski, H., *Parliamentary Government in England* (London, 1938)
Lenin, V. I. *Left Wing Communism* (London, [1920] 1942 version),
London Labour Party, *Labour Party Organisation in London* (London, 1930)
MacDonald, R., *Socialism* (London, 1907)
—— *Socialism After the War* (London, 1917)
National Council and Labour, *International Policy and Defence* (London, 1937)
—— *Labour and the Defence of Peace* (London, 1936)
—— *Labour and the International Situation* (London, 1938)
Newport Labour Party, *Newport Labour Party Manifesto* (Newport, 1919)
—— *The Tolybont Water Scheme* (Newport, 1920)
Norwich Labour Party, *To the Electors of Ber Street Ward* (Norwich, 1936)
—— *To the Electors of Fye Bridge Ward* (Norwich, 1923)
—— *To the Electors of Fye Bridge Ward* (Norwich, 1936)
—— *To The Electors of Thorpe Ward* (Norwich, 1933)
—— *Workers! Vote for Witard* (Norwich, 1909)
Peterborough Labour Party, *Vote for Horrabin* (Peterborough, 1929)
Phillpott, H. R. S., *Where Labour Rules* (London, 1934)
Scanlon, J., *Decline and Fall of the Labour Party* (London, 1932)
Seaham Labour Party, *General Election – 1929, Seaham Parliamentary Division*
—— *To the Men and Women Electors of the Seaham Division* (Seaham, 1923)
—— *Seaham Division* (Seaham, 1935)
Sheffield Labour Party, *Labour Has Kept Faith in the Ratepayers* (1931)
—— *Vote For Thraves!* (1922)
South Shields Labour Party, *South Shields Parliamentary Election, 1924* (South Shields, 1924)
Strachey, J., *Revolution By Reason* (London, 1925)
—— *The Menace of Fascism* (London, 1933)
Sunderland Labour Party, *The Labour Candidates* (Sunderland, 1929)
Tiverton Conservative Association, *Electors, Which Will You Have?* (undated)
Tracey, H. (ed.), *The British Labour Party: Its History, Growth, Policy and Leaders* (London, 1948, three volumes)
Wallsend Labour Party, *Parliamentary Borough of Wallsend* (1931)
Wertheimer, E., *Portrait of the Labour Party* (London, 1929)

NEWSPAPERS AND JOURNALS

Daily Herald
Daily Worker
Darlington Labour Party News
Edinburgh Evening News
Labour Candidate
Labour Elector
Labour Organiser
Labour Press Service
Ministry of Labour Gazette
New Clarion
New Leader
North Norfolk Elector
Seaham Harbour Labour News
The Labour Sentinel
The Seaham Elector
The Socialist
The Times
Tribune

AUTOBIOGRAPHIES, BIOGRAPHIES AND MEMOIRS

Andrews, E., *A Woman's Work is Never Done* (Rhondda, 1948)
Attlee, C. R., *As it Happened* (London, 1954)
Benn, C., *Keir Hardie* (London, 1992)

Blaxland, G., *J. H. Thomas: A Life for Unity* (London, 1964)
Bondfield, M., *A Life's Work* (London, 1948)
Braddock, J. and B. *The Braddocks* (London, 1963)
Brockway, F., *Inside the Left* (London, 1942)
—— *Socialism Over Sixty Years: The Life of Jowett of Bradford* (London, 1946)
—— *Bermondsey Story: The Life of Alfred Salter* (London, 1949)
Brown, W. J., *So Far* (London, 1943)
Bullock, A., *Ernest Bevin: A Biography* (London, 2002)
Burgess, S., *Stafford Cripps: A Political Life* (London, 1999)
Burridge, T., *Clement Attlee* (London, 1985)
Campbell, J., *Nye Bevan: A Biography* (London, 1997)
Citrine, W., *Men and Work: An Autobiography* (London, 1964)
Clarke, P., *The Cripps Version: The Life of Sir Stafford Cripps, 1889–1952* (London, 2002)
Cline, C. A., *E. D. Morel* (Belfast, 1980)
Clynes, J. R., *Memoirs, 1869–1924* (London, 1937)
—— *Memoirs, 1924–37* (London, 1938)
Dalton, H., *Call Back Yesterday: Memoirs, 1887–1931* (London, 1953)
—— *Those Fateful Years: Memoirs, 1931–45* (London, 1957)
Davies, P., *A. J. Cook* (Manchester, 1987)
Donoughue, B., and G. W. Jones, *Herbert Morrison: Portrait of a Politician* (London, 2001 edition)
Foot, M., *Aneurin Bevan, 1897–1945: Volume I* (London 1962)
Graham, T., *Willie Graham* (London, 1948)
Hamilton, M. A., *Arthur Henderson* (London, 1938)
Harris, K., *Attlee* (London, 1985)
Hodgkinson, G., *Sent to Coventry* (London, 1970)
Hollis, P., *Jennie Lee: A Life* (Oxford, 1997)
Johnston, T., *Memories* (London, 1952)
Jones, J., *My Lively Life* (London, 1928)
Jones, R. A., *Arthur Ponsonby: The Politics of Life* (London, 1989)
Knox, W., *James Maxton* (Manchester, 1987)
Kramnick, I., and B. Sheerman, *Harold Laski: A Life on the Left* (London, 1993)
Lansbury, G., *My Life* (London, 1928)
—— *Looking Backwards and Forwards* (London, 1935)
Lawson, J., *A Man's Life* (London, 1944 edition)
Laybourn, K., *Philip Snowden: A Biography, 1864–1937* (Aldershot, 1988)
Lee, J., *This Great Journey* (London, 1963)
Leventhal, F., *Arthur Henderson* (Manchester, 1989)
Manning, L., *A Life for Education: An Autobiography* (London, 1970)
Marquand, D., *Ramsay MacDonald* (London, 1977)
Marwick, A., *Clifford Allen: The Open Conspirator* (Edinburgh, 1964)
McGovern, J., *Neither Fear Nor Favour* (London, 1960)
Mitchell, H., *The Hard Way Up: The Autobiography of Hannah Mitchell* (London, 1977)
Morgan, K., *Harry Pollitt* (Manchester, 1993)
Morgan, K. O., *Keir Hardie: Radical and Socialist* (London, 1975)
Morris, A. J. A., *Portrait of a Radical: C. P. Trevelyan, 1870–1975* (Belfast, 1977)
Morrison, H., *An Autobiography* (London, 1960)
Mosley, N., *Rules of the Game: Sir Oswald and Cynthia Mosley, 1896–1933* (London, 1982)
Mosley, O., *My Life* (London, 1968)
Newman, M., *John Strachey* (Manchester, 1989)
Paton, J., *Left Turn! The Autobiography of John Paton* (London, 1936)
Paynter, W., *My Generation* (London, 1972)
Pethick-Lawrence, F., *Fate Has Been Kind* (London, 1943)
Philips Price, M., *My Three Revolutions* (London, 1969)
Pimlott, B., *Hugh Dalton* (London, 1995 edition)
Pole, D. G., *War Letters and Autobiography* (London, 1961)
Radice, E. A. and G. H., *Will Thorne: Constructive Militant* (London, 1974),

Rowbotham, S., *A New World for Women: Stella Brown – Socialist Feminist* (London, 1977)
Schneer, J., *Ben Tillett* (London, 1982)
—— *George Lansbury* (Manchester, 1990)
Shepherd, J., *George Lansbury: At the Heart of Old Labour* (Oxford, 2002)
Shinwell, E., *Conflict Without Malice* (London, 1955)
Skidelsky, R., *Oswald Mosley* (London, 1975)
Smillie, R., *My Life for Labour* (London, 1924)
Snowden, P., *An Autobiography* (London, 1934)
Thomas, H., *John Strachey* (London, 1973)
Thomas, J. H., *My Story* (London, 1937)
Vernon, B. D., *Ellen Wilkinson* (London, 1982)
Walker, G., *Thomas Johnston* (Manchester, 1988)
Wedgwood, C. V., *The Last of the Radicals: Josiah Wedgwood MP* (London, 1951)
Wedgwood, J., *Memoirs of a Fighting Life* (London, 1941)
Weiler, P., *Ernest Bevin* (Manchester, 1993)
Wood, I., *John Wheatley* (Manchester, 1989)
Wright, A., *R. H. Tawney* (Manchester, 1987)
Wrigley, C., *Arthur Henderson* (Cardiff, 1990)

BOOKS

Addison, P., *The Road to 1945* (London, 1975)
Adelman, P., *The Rise of the Labour Party, 1880–1945* (London, 1972)
Anderson, G. D., *Fascists, Communists and the National Government: Civil Liberties in Great Britain, 1931–37* (Columbia, 1983)
Bagwell, P., *The Railwaymen: The History of the National Union of Railwaymen* (London, 1963)
Ball, S., and A. Seldon (eds.), *Conservative Century: The Conservative Party since 1900* (Oxford, 1994)
Ball, S., and I. Holliday (eds.), *Mass Conservatism: The Conservatives and the Public since the 1880s* (London, 2002)
Barrow, L., and I. Bullock (eds.), *Democratic Ideas and the British Labour Movement, 1880–1914* (Cambridge, 1996)
Barnsby, G. J., *Socialism in Birmingham and the Black Country, 1850–1939* (Wolverhampton, 1998)
Baxter, J., and others, *The Making of the Barnsley Labour Movement, 1740–1940* (Rotherham, 1980)
Beadle, J., *A Glorious Century: One Hundred Years of the Derby Labour Party* (Derby, 2000)
Bealey, F., J. Blondel and W. P. McCann, *Constituency Politics: A Study of Newcastle-under-Lyme* (London, 1965)
Bellamy, J. M., J. Saville et al. (eds.), *Dictionary of Labour Biography, Volumes I–XI* (Basingstoke, 1972–2003)
Bennett, *'A Most Extraordinary and Mysterious Business': The Zinoviev Letter of 1924* (London, 1999)
Bentley, M. (ed.), *Public and Private Doctrine: Essays in British History Presented to Maurice Cowling* (Cambridge, 1993)
Berger, S., *The British Labour Party and the German Social Democrats, 1900–31* (Oxford, 1994)
Berger S., and D. Broughton (eds.), *The Force of Labour: The Western European Labour Movement and the Working Class in the Twentieth Century* (Oxford, 1995)
Beynon H., and T. Austrin, *Masters and Servants: Class and Patronage in the Making of a Labour Organisation* (London, 1994)
Biagini, E., and A. Reid (eds.), *Currents of Radicalism: Popular Radicalism, Organised Labour and Party Politics in Britain, 1850–1914* (Cambridge, 1991)
Bindfield C., et al. (eds.), *The History of the City of Sheffield, 1843–1993* (Sheffield 1993)
Black, L., *Old Labour, New Britain? The Political Culture of the Left in Affluent Britain, 1951–64* (London, 2002)
Blaazer, D., *The Popular Front and the Progressive Tradition: Socialists, Liberals, and the Quest for Unity, 1884–1939* (Cambridge, 1992)

Bourke, J., *Working Class Cultures in Britain, 1890–1960: Gender, Class and Ethnicity* (London, 1994)

Branson, N., *Poplarism, 1919–25: George Lansbury and the Councillors' Revolt* (London, 1985)

Briggs, A., and J. Saville (eds.), *Essays in Labour History: Volume II, 1886–1923* (London, 1971)

—— *Essays in Labour History: Volume III 1918–39* (London, 1977)

Brivati B., and R. Heffernan (eds.), *The Labour Party: A Centenary History* (Basingstoke, 2000)

Brown, K. D (ed.), *Essays in Anti-Labour History: Responses to the Rise of Labour in Britain* (London, 1974)

—— (ed.), *The First Labour Party, 1906–14* (London, 1985)

Buchanan, T., *The Spanish Civil War and the British Labour Movement* (Cambridge, 1991)

—— *Britain and the Spanish Civil War* (Cambridge, 1997)

Butler, D., and J. Freeman, *British Political Facts, 1900–69* (London, 1969)

Callaghan, J., *Socialism in Britain since 1884* (Oxford, 1990)

Callaghan, J., S. Fielding and S. Ludlam (eds.), *Interpreting the Labour Party: Approaches to Labour Politics and History* (Manchester, 2003)

Campbell, A., *The Scottish Miners, 1874–1938, Volume II: Trade Unions and Politics* (Ashgate, 2000)

Cherry, S., *Doing Different? Politics and the Labour Movement in Norwich, 1880–1914* (Norwich, 1989)

Clark, D., *Colne Valley: Radicalism to Socialism: The Portrait of a Northern Constituency in the Formative Years of the Labour Party, 1890–1910* (London, 1981)

—— *We Do Not Want the Earth: The History of South Shields Labour Party* (Whitley Bay, 1992)

Clarke, P. F., *Lancashire and the New Liberalism* (Cambridge, 1971)

Clegg, H. A., *A History of British Trade Unions since 1889: Volume II, 1911–33* (Oxford, 1985)

Cline, C. A., *Recruits to Labour: The British Labour Party, 1914–31* (New York, 1963)

Clinton, A., *The Trade Union Rank and File: Trades Councils in Britain, 1900–40* (Manchester, 1976)

Coates, K., *The Labour Party and the Struggle for Socialism* (Cambridge, 1975)

Cole, G. D. H., *A History of the Labour Party from 1914* (London, 1948)

Collette, C., *For Labour and or Women: The Women's Labour League, 1906–18* (Manchester, 1989)

Cook, C., and I. Taylor (eds.), *The Labour Party: An Introduction to its History, Structure and Politics* (London, 1980)

Cook, C., and J. Stevenson, *The Slump: Society and Politics in the Depression* (London, 1989)

Cowling, M., *The Impact of Labour: The Beginning of Modern British Politics* (Cambridge, 1971)

Craig, F. W. S., *British Parliamentary Election Results, 1918–45* (Chichester, 1983)

Crick, M., *The History of the Social Democratic Federation* (Keele, 1994)

Cronin, J. E., *Labour and Society in Britain, 1918–79* (London, 1984)

Croucher, C., *We Refuse to Starve in Silence A History of the National Unemployed Workers' Movement, 1920–46* (London, 1987)

Davies, A. J., *To Build a New Jerusalem: The British Labour Party from Keir Hardie to Tony Blair* (London, 1992)

Davies, S., *Liverpool Labour: Social and Political Influences on the Development of the Labour Party in Liverpool, 1900–39* (Keele, 1996)

Davies, S., and B. Morley, *County Borough Elections in England, 1918–38* (eight volumes, Aldershot, 1999 onwards)

Daunton, M. (ed.), *Councillors and Tenants: Local Authority Housing in English Cities, 1919–39* (Leicester, 1984)

Donnachie, I., C. Harvie and Ian S. Wood (eds.), *Forward! Labour Politics in Scotland, 1888–1988* (Edinburgh, 1989)

Dowse, R., *Left in the Centre: The Independent Labour Party, 1893–1940* (London, 1966)

Durbin, E., New Jerusalems: *The Labour Party and the Economics of Democratic Socialism* (London, 1985)

Feldman D. and G. Stedman Jones (eds.), *Metropolis–London: Histories and Representations since 1800* (London, 1989)

Fielding, S., *The Labour Party: Continuity and Change in the Making of 'New' Labour* (Basingstoke, 2003)

Fielding, S., P. Thompson, N. Tiratsoo, *'England Arise!' The Labour Party and Popular Politics in 1940s Britain* (Manchester, 1995)

Foote, G., *The Labour Party's Political Thought: A History* (Basingstoke, 1997, third edition)

Forester, T., *The Labour Party and the Working Class* (London, 1975)

Francis, H., *Miners Against Fascism: Wales and the Spanish Civil War* (London, 1984)

Francis, H., and D. Smith, *The Fed: A History of the South Wales Miners in the Twentieth Century* (London, 1980)

Garside, W. R., *The Durham Miners, 1919–60* (London, 1971)

—— *British Unemployment, 1919–39* (Cambridge, 1990)

Goss, S., *Local Labour and Local Government: A Study of Changing Interests, Politics and Policy in Southwark from 1919 to 1982* (Edinburgh, 1988)

Graves, P., *Labour Women: Women in British Working Class Politics, 1918–39* (Cambridge, 1994)

Griffiths, T., *The Lancashire Working Class c. 1880–1930* (Oxford, 2001)

Gupta, P. S., *Imperialism and the British Labour Movement, 1914–64* (London, 1975)

Halsey, A. H. (ed.), *British Social Trends since 1900* (London, 1988)

Hannam, J., and K. Hunt, *Socialist Women: Britain, 1880s to 1920s* (London, 2002)

Hill, J., *Nelson: Politics, Economy, Community* (Keele, 1997)

Hinton, J., *Labour and Socialism: A History of the British Labour Movement, 1867–1874* (Brighton, 1974)

Hobsbawm, E., *Worlds of Labour: Further Studies in the History of Labour* (London, 1984)

—— *Industry and Empire: From 1750 to the Present Day* (London, 1990 edition)

Hogenkamp, B., *Deadly Parallels: Film and the Left in Britain, 1929–39* (London, 1986)

Holford, J., *Reshaping Labour: Organisation, Work and Politics – Edinburgh in the Great War and After* (London, 1988)

Hollis, P., *Ladies Elect: Women in English Local Government, 1865–1914* (London, 1987)

Hopkins, E., *A Social History of the English Working Class, 1815–1945* (London, 1979)

Horne, J. N., *Labour at War: Britain and France, 1914–18* (Oxford, 1991)

Howell, D., *British Social Democracy: A Study in Development and Decay* (London, 1980)

—— *British Workers and the Independent Labour Party, 1888–1906* (Manchester, 1983)

—— *A Lost Left: Three Studies in Socialism and Nationalism* (Manchester, 1986)

—— *MacDonald's Party: Labour Identities and Crisis, 1922–31* (Oxford, 2002)

Howell-Thomas, D., *Socialism in West Sussex: A History of the Chichester Constituency Labour Party* (Chichester, undated)

Ipswich Labour Party, *Ipswich Labour Party, 1923–83* (Ipswich, 1983)

Jefferys, K. (ed.), *Leading Labour: From Keir Hardie to Tony Blair* (London, 1999)

Jones, S. G., *Workers at Play: A Social and Economic History of Leisure, 1918–39* (London, 1986)

—— *The British Labour Movement and Film, 1918–39* (London, 1987)

Kingsford, P., *The Hunger Marchers in Britain, 1920–40* (London, 1982)

Kinnear, M., *The British Voter: An Atlas and Survey since 1885* (London, 1981)

Kirk, N., *Change, Continuity and Class: Labour in British Society, 1850–1920* (Manchester, 1998)

Lancaster, B., *Radicalism, Co-operation and Socialism: Leicester Working Class Politics, 1860–1906* (London, 1988)

Lancaster, B., and T. Mason (eds.), *Life and Labour in a Twentieth Century City: The Experience of Coventry* (Coventry, undated)

Lawrence, J., *Speaking for the People: Party, Language and Popular Politics in England, 1867–1914* (Cambridge, 1990)

Lawrence, J., and M. Taylor (eds.), *Party, State and Society: Electoral Behaviour in Britain since 1829* (Aldershot, 1997)

Laybourn, K., *The Rise of Labour: The British Labour Party, 1890–1979* (London, 1988)

—— *Britain on the Breadline: A Social and Political History of Britain, 1918–1939* (Gloucestershire, 1990)

—— *The General Strike of 1926* (Manchester, 1993)

—— *A Century of Labour: A History of the Labour Party* (Gloucestershire, 2000)

Laybourn, K., and J. Reynolds, *Liberalism and the Rise of Labour, 1890–1918* (London, 1984)

Lyman, R. W., *The First Labour Government, 1924* (London, 1958)

Macdonald, C., *The Radical Thread: Political Change in Scotland: Paisley Politics, 1885–1924* (East Lothian, 2000)

Macfarlane, L. J., *The British Communist Party: Its Origins and Development until 1929* (London, 1966)

Macintyre, S., *A Proletarian Science: Marxism in Britain, 1917–33* (London, 1980)

Marriott, J., *The Culture of Labourism: The East End Between the Wars* (Edinburgh, 1991)

Matthew, D., *From Two Boys and a Dog to Political Power: The Labour Party in the Lowestoft Constituency, 1918–45* (Lowestoft, 1979)

McHenry, D. E., *The Labour Party in Transition, 1931–38* (London, 1938)

McKibbin, R., *The Evolution of the Labour Party, 1900–24* (Oxford, 1974)

—— *The Ideologies of Class: Social Relations in Britain, 1890–1950* (Oxford, 1990)

—— *Classes and Cultures: England, 1918–1951* (Oxford, 1998)

McKinlay, A., and R. J. Morris (eds.), *The ILP on Clydeside, 1893–1932: From Foundation to Disintegration* (Manchester, 1991)

McLean, I., *The Legend of Red Clydeside* (Edinburgh, 1983)

Middlemass, R. K., *The Clydesiders: A Left Wing Struggle for Parliamentary Power* (London, 1965)

Miliband, R., *Parliamentary Socialism: A Study in the Politics of Labour* (London, 1961)

Minkin, L., *The Labour Party Conference: A Study in the Politics of Intra-Party Democracy* (London, 1978)

—— *The Contentious Alliance: Trade Unions and the Labour Party* (Edinburgh, 1991)

Mitchell B. R., and P. Deane, *Abstract of British Historical Statistics* (Cambridge, 1962)

Morgan, K., *Against Fascism and War Ruptures and Continuities in British Communist Politics, 1935–41* (Manchester, 1989)

—— *Consensus and Disunity: The Lloyd George Coalition Government, 1918–22* (Oxford, 1979)

Morgan, K. O., *Labour in Power, 1945–51* (Oxford, 1984)

Mowat, C. L., *Britain Between the Wars, 1918–40* (London, 1968 edition)

Newens, S., *A Brief History of the Labour Party in the Eastern Region* (Harlow, 2000)

Peele, G., and C. Cook (eds.), *The Politics of Reappraisal, 1918–39* (Oxford, 1975)

Pelling, H., *A Short History of the Labour Party* (London, 1961)

—— *The Origins of the Labour Party, 1880–1900* (Oxford, 1965)

—— *Popular Politics and Society in Late Victorian Britain* (Basingstoke, 1967)

—— *Social Geography of British Elections, 1885–1910* (London, 1968)

—— *A History of British Trade Unionism* (London, 1992 edition)

Pimlott, B., *Labour and the Left in the 1930s* (Cambridge, 1977)

Pimlott, B., and C. Cook (eds.), *Trade Unions in British Politics* (London, 1982)

Pinto-Duschinsky, M., *British Political Finance, 1800–1980* (AEI Studies, 1981)

Pollard, S., *The Development of the British Economy, 1919–90* (London, 1992 edition)

Price, R., *Labour in British Society: An Interpretive History* (London, 1990)

Pugh, M., *Women and the Women's Movement in Britain, 1914–59* (Basingstoke, 1992)

Reekes, A., *The Rise of Labour, 1899–1951* (Basingstoke, 1991)

Reynolds, J., and K. Laybourn, *Labour Heartland: A History of the Labour Party in West Yorkshire during the Interwar Years, 1918–39* (Bradford, 1987)

Riddell, N., *Labour in Crisis: The Second Labour Government, 1929–31* (Manchester, 1999)

Routh, G., *Occupation and Pay in Great Britain, 1906–79* (London, 1980)

Savage, M., *The Dynamics of Working Class Politics: The Labour Movement in Preston, 1880–1940* (Cambridge, 1987)

Savage, M., and A. Miles, *The Remaking of the British Working Class* (London, 1994)

Shaw, E., *Discipline and Discord in the Labour Party* (Manchester, 1988)

Skidelsky, R., *Politicians and the Slump: The Labour Government of 1929–31* (London, 1967)

Smyth, J. J., *Labour in Glasgow, 1896–1936* (East Lothian, 2000)

Stedman Jones, G., *Languages of Class: Studies in English Working Class History, 1832–1982* (Cambridge, 1983)

Stannage, T., *Baldwin Thwarts the Opposition: The British General Election of 1935* (London, 1980)

Sunderland Labour Party, *Adventure into the Past* (Sunderland, 1954)

Supple, B., *The History of the British Coal Industry, Volume 4: 1913–1946, The Political Economy of Decline* (Oxford, 1987)

Swift, J., *Labour in Crisis: Clement Attlee and the Labour Party in Opposition, 1931–40* (Basingstoke, 2001)

Tanner, D., *Political Change and the Labour Party, 1900–18* (Cambridge, 1990)

Tanner, D., C. Williams and D. Hopkin (eds.), *The Labour Party in Wales, 1900–2000* (Cardiff, 2000)

Tanner, D., P. Thane and N. Tiratsoo (eds.), *Labour's First Century* (Cambridge, 2000)

Taylor, R., *The TUC: From the General Strike to New Unionism* (Basingstoke, 2000)

Thompson, P., *Socialists, Liberals and Labour: The Struggle for Labour, 1885–1914* (London, 1967)

Thorpe, A., *The British General Election of 1931* (Oxford, 1991)

—— *Britain in the 1930s* (Oxford, 1992)

—— *A History of the British Labour Party* (Basingstoke, 1997)

—— *The British Communist Party and Moscow, 1920–43* (Manchester, 2000)

Thurlow, R., *Fascism in Britain: From Oswald Mosley's Blackshirts to the National Front* (London, 1998)

Toye, R., *The Labour Party and the Planned Economy, 1931–51* (Woodbridge, 2003)

Vickers, R., *The Labour Party and the World: The Evolution of Labour's Foreign Policy, 1900–51* (Manchester, 2004)

Waites, B., *A Class Society at War, 1914–18* (Leamington Spa, 1987)

Waller, P. J., *Democracy and Sectarianism: A Political and Social History of Liverpool, 1868–1939* (Liverpool, 1939)

Waller, R. J., *The Dukeries Transformed: The Social and Political Development of a Twentieth Century Coalfield* (Oxford, 1983)

Ward, P., *Red Flag and Union Jack: Englishness, Patriotism and the British Left, 1891–1924* (Woodbridge, 1998)

Weinbren, D., *Generating Socialism: Recollections of Life in the Labour Party* (Stroud, 1997)

Whiting, R. C., *The View from Cowley: The Impact of Industrialization upon Oxford, 1918–39* (Oxford, 1983)

Williams, C., *Democratic Rhondda: Politics and Society, 1885–1951* (Cardiff, 1996)

Williamson, P., *National Crisis and National Government: British Politics, the Economy and Empire, 1926–32* (Cambridge, 1992)

Winter, J. (ed.), *The Working Class in Modern British History: Essays in Honour of Henry Pelling* (Cambridge, 1983)

Winter, J. M., *Socialism and the Challenge of War: Ideas and Politics in Britain, 1912–28* (London, 1974)

Woodhouse, T., *Nourishing the Liberty Tree: Liberals and Labour in Leeds, 1880–1914* (Keele, 1996)

Worley, M., *Class Against Class: The Communist Party of Great Britain between the Wars* (London, 2002)

—— (ed.), *Labour's Grass Roots: Essays on the Activities of Local Labour Parties and Members, 1918–45* (Aldershot, 2005)

Wrigley, C. (ed.), *A History of British Industrial Relations, 1914–45* (Brighton, 1987)

—— *Lloyd George and the Challenge of Labour: The Post War Coalition, 1918–22* (Hemel Hempstead, 1990)

—— (ed.), *Challenges of Labour: Central and Western Europe, 1917–20* (London, 1993)

—— *British Trade Unions Since 1933* (Cambridge, 2002)

Wrigley, C., and J. Shepherd (eds.), *On the Move: Essays in Labour and Transport History Presented to Philip Bagwell* (London, 1991)

Wyncoll, P., *The Nottingham Labour Movement, 1880–1939* (London, 1985)

Yeo, E and S. (eds.), *Popular Culture and Class Conflict, 1590–1914: Explorations in the History of Labour and Leisure* (Brighton, 1981)

Young, K., *Local Politics and the Rise of Party: The London Municipal Society and then Conservative Intervention in Local Elections, 1894–1963* (Leicester, 1975)

ARTICLES AND CHAPTERS

Adams, T., 'Labour and the First World War: Economy, Politics and the Erosion of Local Peculiarity?', *The Journal of Regional and Local Studies*, 10, 1 (1990)
—— 'Labour Vanguard, Tory Bastion, or the Triumph of New Liberalism? Manchester Politics 1900 to 1914 in Comparative Perspective', *Manchester Region History Review*, 14 (2000)
Ball, S., 'Local Conservatism and the Evolution of the Party Organization', in S. Ball and A. Seldon (eds.), *Conservative Century: The Conservative Party since 1900* (Oxford, 1994)
Ball, S., and I. Holliday, 'Mass Conservatism: An Introduction', in S. Ball and I. Holliday (eds.), *Mass Conservatism: The Conservatives and the Public since the 1880s* London, 2002)
Ball, S., A. Thorpe, M. Worley, 'Elections, Leaflets and Whist Drives: Constituency Party Members in Britain between the Wars', in M. Worley (ed.), *Labour's Grass Roots: Essays on the Activities of Local Labour Parties and Members, 1918–45* (Aldershot, 2005)
Barrett, N., 'A Bright Shining Star: The CPGB and Anti-Fascist Activism in the 1930s', *Science and Society*, 16, 1 (1997)
Baston, L., 'Labour Local Government, 1900–99', in B. Brivati and R. Heffernan (eds.), *The Labour Party: A Centenary History* (Basingstoke, 2000)
Berger, S., 'The British and German Labour Movements before the Second World War', *Twentieth Century British History*, 3, 3 (1992)
—— 'The Decline of Liberalism and the Rise of Labour – The Regional Approach', *Parliamentary History*, 12, 1 (1993)
Bernstein, G. L., 'Liberalism and the Progressive Alliance in the Constituencies, 1900–14: Three Case Studies', *Historical Journal*, 26, 3 (1983)
Black, L., 'Still at the Penny-Farthing Stage in a Jet-Propelled Era: Branch Life in 1950s Socialism', *Labour History Review*, 65, 2 (2000)
—— 'Labour at 100', *Mitteilungsblatt des Instituts für soziale Bewegungen*, 27 (2002)
—— '"What Kind of People are You?" Labour, the People, and the "New Political History"', in J. Callaghan, S. Fielding and S. Ludlum (eds.), *Interpreting the Labour Party: Approaches to Labour Politics and History* (Manchester, 2003)
Booth, A., 'How Long are Light Years in British Politics? The Labour Party's Economic Ideas in the 1930s', *Twentieth Century British History*, 7, 1 (1996)
Boughton, J., 'Working Class Conservatism and the Rise of Labour: A Case Study of Birmingham in the 1920s', *The Historian* (Autumn, 1998)
Callcott, M., 'Sidney Webb, Ramsay MacDonald, Emmanuel Shinwell and the Durham Constituency of Seaham', *Bulletin of the North East Group for the Study of Labour History*, 11 (1977)
—— 'The Nature and Extent of Political Change in the Interwar Years: The Example of County Durham', *Northern History*, 16 (1980)
—— 'Labour Women in North East England', in *North East Labour History*, 17 (1983)
Catterall, P., 'Morality and Politics: The Free Churches and the Labour Party between the Wars', *The Historical Journal*, 36, 3 (1993)
Childs, M., 'Labour Grows Up: The Electoral System, Political Generations, and British Politics, 1890–1929', *Twentieth Century British History*, 6, 2 (1995)
Cohen, G., 'The Independent Labour Party, Disaffiliation, Revolution and Standing Orders', *History*, 86, 282 (2001)
Cole, M., 'The Society for Socialist Inquiry and Propaganda', in A. Briggs and J. Saville (eds.), *Essays in Labour History, 1918–39* (London, 1977)
Collette, C., 'Questions of Gender: Labour and Women', in B. Brivati and R. Heffernan (eds.), *The Labour Party: A Centenary History* (Basingstoke, 2000)
Cook, C., 'Liberals, Labour and Local Elections', in G. Peele and C. Cook (eds.), *The Politics of Reappraisal, 1918–39* (Oxford, 1975)
Cook, C., 'Labour's Electoral Base' in C. Cook and I. Taylor (eds.), *The Labour Party: An Introduction to its History, Structure and Politics* (London, 1980)
Corthorn, P., 'The Labour Party and the League of Nations: The Socialist League's Role in the Sanctions Crisis of 1935', *Twentieth Century British History*, 13, 1 (2002)
Cox, D., 'The Rise of the Labour Party in Leicester', unpublished MA thesis (University of Leicester, 1959)

Dare, R., 'Instinct and Organisation: Intellectuals and British Labour after 1931', *History*, 26 (1983)

Davies, S., and B. Morley, 'The Politics of Place: A Comparative Analysis of Electoral Politics in Four Lancashire Cotton Textile Towns, 1919–39', *Manchester Region History Review*, 14 (2000)

—— 'The Reactions of Municipal Voters in Yorkshire to the Second Labour Government, 1929–32', in M. Worley (ed.), *Labour's Grass Roots: Essays on the Activities of Local Labour Parties and Members, 1918–45* (Aldershot, 2005)

Donnachie, I., 'Scottish Labour in the Depression: The 1930s', in I. Donnachie, C. Harvie and I. S. Wood (eds.), *Forward! Labour Politics in Scotland, 1888–1988* (Edinburgh, 1989)

Douglas, R., 'Labour in Decline, 1910–14', in K. Brown (ed.), *Essays in Anti-Labour History: Responses to the Rise of Labour in Britain* (London, 1974)

Doyle, B. M., 'Urban Liberalism and the "Lost Generation": Politics and Middle Class Culture in Norwich, 1900–35', *Historical Journal*, 38, 3 (1995)

Epstein, L. D., 'British Class Consciousness and the Labour Party', *Journal of British Studies*, 1, 2 (1962)

Evans, N., and D. Jones, '"To Help Forward the Great Work of Humanity": Women in the Labour Party in Wales', in D. Tanner, C. Williams and D. Hopkin (eds.), *The Labour Party Wales, 1900–2000* (Cardiff, 2000)

Fenley, A., 'Labour and the Trade Unions', in C. Cook and I. Taylor (eds.), *The Labour Party: An Introduction to its History, Structure and Politics* (London, 1980)

Fielding, S., 'Labourism in the 1940s', *Twentieth Century British History*, Vol 3 No 2 (1992), p. 145.

—— '"Labourism" and Locating the British Labour Party within the British Left', *Working Papers in Contemporary History and Politics*, Working Paper No. 11 (Salford, undated)

—— '"New" Labour and the "New" Labour History', *Mitteilungsblatt des Instituts für soziale Bewegungen*, 27 (2002)

Fielding, S., and D. McHugh, 'The *Progressive Dilemma* and the Social Democratic Perspective', in J. Callaghan, S. Fielding and S. Ludlam, *Interpreting the Labour Party: Approaches to Labour Politics and History* (Manchester, 2003)

Fleay, C., and M. L. Sanders, 'The Labour Spain Committee: Labour Party Policy and the Spanish Civil War', *The Historical Journal*, 28, 1 (1985)

Flinn, A., 'Irish Catholics in South East Lancashire: A Conflict of Loyalties?', *Manchester Region History Review*, 14 (2000)

—— 'Labour's Family: Local Labour Parties, Trade Unions and Trades Councils in Cotton Lancashire, 1931–39', in M. Worley (ed.), *Labour's Grass Roots: Essays on the Activities of Local Labour Parties and Members, 1918–45* (Aldershot, 2005)

Foster, J., 'Working Class Mobilisation on the Clyde, 1917–20', in C. Wrigley (ed.), *Challenges of Labour:Central and Western Europe, 1917–20* (London, 1993)

Fowler, A., 'Lancashire to Westminster – A Study of Cotton Union Officials and British Labour, 1910–39', *Labour History Review*, 64, 1 (1999)

Francis, M., 'Labour and Gender', in D. Tanner et al. (eds.), *Labour's First Century* (Cambridge, 2000)

Gibb, M., 'The Labour Party in the North East Between the Wars', *Bulletin of the North East Group for the Study of Labour History*, 18 (1988)

Gillespie, J., 'Poplarism and Proletarianism: Unemployment and Labour Politics in London, 1918–34', in D. Feldman and G. Stedman Jones (eds.), *Metropolis–London: Histories and Representations since 1800* (London, 1989)

Harris, J., 'Labour's Political and Social Thought', in D. Tanner, P. Thane and N. Tiratsoo (eds.), *Labour's First Century* (Cambridge, 2000)

Harrison, B., 'Oxford and the Labour Movement', *Twentieth Century British History*, 2, 3 (1991)

Harrison, R., 'The War Emergency Workers' National Committee', in A. Briggs and J. Saville (eds.), *Essays in Labour History, 1886–1923* (London, 1971)

Hastings, R. P. 'The Birmingham Labour Movement, 1918–45', *Midland History*, 5 (1979–80)

Harvie, C., 'Before the Breakthrough, 1886–1922', in I. Donnachie, C. Harvie and Ian S. Wood (eds.), *Forward! Labour Politics in Scotland, 1888–1988* (Edinburgh, 1989)

Henry, J., 'Salford Labour: A Party in Waiting, 1919–32', *Manchester Region History Review*, 14 (2000)

Howard, C., 'Expectations Born to Death: Local Labour Party Expansion in the 1920s', in J. Winter (ed.), *The Working Class in Modern British History: Essays in Honour of Henry Pelling* (Cambridge, 1983)

Howell, D., 'Beyond "The Stereotypes": The Independent Labour Party, 1922–32', *Scottish Labour History*, 29 (1994)

—— '"I Loved My Union and My Country": Jimmy Thomas and the Politics of Railway Trade Unionism', *Twentieth Century British History*, 6, 2 (1995)

Hunt, K., 'Making Politics in Local Communities', in M. Worley (ed.), *Labour's Grass Roots: Essays on the Activities of Local Labour Parties and Members, 1918–45* (Aldershot, 2005)

Jarvis, D., 'The Shaping of Conservative Electoral Hegemony, 1918–39', in J. Lawrence and M. Taylor (eds.), *Party, State and Society: Electoral Behaviour in Britain since 1829* (Aldershot, 1997)

Jeffery, T., 'The Suburban Nation: Politics and Class in Lewisham', in D. Feldman and G. Stedman Jones (eds.), *Metropolis–London: Histories and Representations since 1800* (London, 1989)

Johnson, G., 'Social Democracy and Labour Politics in Britain, 1892–1911', *History*, 277 (2000)

Jones, T., 'Labour's Constitution and Public Ownership: From Old Clause IV to New Clause IV', in B. Brivati and R. Heffernan (eds.), *The Labour Party: A Centenary History* (Basingstoke, 2000)

Knox, W., '"Ours is Not an Ordinary Parliamentary Movement: 1922–26', in A. McKinlay and R. J. Morris (eds.), *The ILP on Clydeside, 1893–1932: From Foundation to Disintegration* (Manchester, 1991)

Knox, W. and A. MacKinlay, 'The Re-Making of Scottish Labour in the 1930s', *Twentieth Century British History*, 6, 2 (1995)

Lawrence, J., 'The Complexities of English Progressivism: Wolverhampton Politics in the Early Twentieth Century', *Midland History*, 24 (1999)

Laybourn, K. 'The Rise of Labour and the Decline of Liberalism: The State of the Debate', *History*, 80 (1995)

Lindley, T., 'The Barnsley Labour Party 1918 to 1945', *Bulletin of the Society for the Study of Labour History*, 39 (1978)

Lyman, R. W., 'The British Labour Party: The Conflict between Socialist Ideals and Practical Politics between the Wars', *Journal of British Studies*, 5, 1 (1965)

Lynn, P., 'The Influence of Class and Gender: Female Political Organisation in County Durham During the Interwar Years', *North east Labour History*, 31 (1997)

MacDonald, C., 'Following the Procession: Scottish Labour, 1918–45', in M. Worley (ed.), *Labour's Grass Roots: Essays on the Activities of Local Labour Parties and Members, 1918–45* (Aldershot, 2005)

Mansfield, N., 'Farmworkers and Local Conservatism in South West Shropshire, 1916–23', in S. Ball and I. Holliday (eds.), *Mass Conservatism The Conservatives and the Public since the 1880s* (London, 2002)

Mathers, H., 'The City of Sheffield, 1893–1926', in C. Bindfield et al. (eds.), *The History of the City of Sheffield, 1843–1993* (Sheffield 1993)

Matthew, H. C. G., R. I. McKibbin and J. Kay, 'The Franchise Factor in the Rise of the Labour Party', *English Historical Review*, 91 (1976)

May, E., *The Mosaic of Labour Politics, 1900–18*, in D. Tanner, C. Williams, D. Hopkin (eds.), *Labour in Wales, 1900–2000* (Cardiff, 2000)

McHugh, D., 'The Labour Party in Manchester and Salford Before the First World War: A Case of Unequal Development', *Manchester Region History Review*, 14 (2000)

—— 'Labour, the Liberals and the Progressive Alliance in Manchester, 1900–14', *Northern History*, 39, 1 (2002)

McKibbin, R., 'The Economic Policy of the Second Labour Government, 1929–31', *Past and Present*, 65 (1975)

—— 'Arthur Henderson as Labour Leader', *International Review of Labour History*, 23 (1978)

—— 'Why Was There No Marxism in Great Britain', in R. McKibbin, *The Ideologies of Class: Social Relations in Britain, 1890–1950* (Oxford, 1990)

—— 'Class and Conventional Wisdom: The Conservative Party and the "public" in Interwar Britain', R. McKibbin, *The Ideologies of Class: Social Relations in Britain, 1890–1950* (Oxford, 1990)

—— 'Classes and Cultures: A Postscript', *Mitteilungsblatt des Instituts für soziale Bewegungen*, 27 (2003)

McKinlay, A., '"Doubtful Wisdom and Uncertain Promise": Strategy, Ideology and Organisation, 1918–22', in A. McKinlay and R. J. Morris, *The ILP on Clydeside, 1893–1932: From Foundation to Disintegration* (Manchester, 1991)

McKinlay A., and J. J. Smyth, 'The End of "the Agitator Workman": 1926–1932', in A. McKinlay and R. J. Morris, *The ILP on Clydeside, 1893–1932: From Foundation to Disintegration* (Manchester, 1991)

Morgan, K., 'The Conservative and Mass Housing, 1918–39', in S. Ball and I. Holliday (eds.), *Mass Conservatism The Conservatives and the Public since the 1880s* (London, 2002)

Morris, R. J., 'The ILP, 1893–1932: Introduction', A. McKinlay and R. J. Morris, *The ILP on Clydeside, 1893–1932: From Foundation to Disintegration* (Manchester, 1991)

Newman, M., 'Democracy versus Dictatorship: Labour's Role in the Struggle against British Fascism, 1933–36', *History Workshop*, 5 (1978)

Olechnowicz, A., 'Union First, Politics After: Oldham Cotton Unions and the Labour Party Before 1914', *Manchester Region History Review*, 14 (2000)

Pearce, R., 'Clement Attlee 1935–55', in K. Jefferys (ed.), *Leading Labour: From Keir Hardie to Tony Blair* (London, 1999)

Perry, M., 'The Jarrow Crusade's Return: The "New Labour Party" of Jarrow and Ellen Wilkinson MP', *Northern History*, 39 (2002)

Potts, A., 'Forty Years On: The Labour Party in Sunderland', *North East Labour History*, 24 (1980)

Pugh, M., '"Class Traitors": Conservative Recruits to Labour, 1900–30', *English Historical Review*, 113 (1998)

—— 'The Rise of Labour and the Political Culture of Conservatism, 1890–1945', *History*, 87, 288 (2002)

Riddell, N., '"The Age of Cole"? G. D. H. Cole and the British Labour Movement, 1929–33', *Historical Journal*, 38, 4 (1995)

—— 'Arthur Henderson, 1931–32', in K. Jefferys (ed.), *Leading Labour: From Keir Hardie to Tony Blair* (London, 1999)

—— 'Walter Citrine and the British Labour Movement, 1925–35', *History*, 85, 278 (2000)

Roberts, D., 'Labour in Office: 1924–31', in C. Cook and I. Taylor (eds.), *The Labour Party: An Introduction to its History, Structure and Politics* (London, 1980)

Robertson, N., 'The Political Dividend: Co-operative Parties in the Midlands, 1917–39', in M. Worley (ed.), *Labour's Grass Roots: Essays on the Activities of Local Labour Parties and Members, 1918–45* (Aldershot, 2005)

Savage, M., 'The Rise of the Labour Party in Local Perspective', *The Journal of Regional and Local Studies*, 10, 1 (1990)

—— 'Urban Politics and the Rise of the Labour Party, 1919–39', in L. Jamieson and H. Corr (eds.), *State, Private Life and Political Change* (New York, 1990)

Seyd, P., 'Factionalism Within the Labour Party: The Socialist League, 1932–37', in A. Briggs and J. Saville (eds.), *Essays in Labour History, 1918–39* (London, 1977)

Shackleton, R., 'Trade Unions and the Slump', in B. Pimlott and C. Cook (eds.), *Trade Unions in British Politics* (London, 1982)

Shepherd, J., 'Labour and Trade Unions: Lansbury, Ernest Bevin and the Leadership Crisis of 1935', in C. Wrigley, and J. Shepherd (eds.), *On the Move: Essays in Labour and Transport History Presented to Philip Bagwell* (London, 1991)

Sheppard, M. G., and J. Halstead, 'Labour's Municipal Election Performance in Provincial England and Wales, 1901–13', *Bulletin of the Society for the Study of Labour History*, 39 (1979)

Smith, J., 'The Labour Tradition in Glasgow and Liverpool', *History Workshop*, 17 (1984)

Tanner, D., 'Elections, Statistics, and the Rise of the Labour Party, 1906–31', *The Historical Journal*, 34, 4 (1991)

—— 'The Parliamentary Electoral System, the "Fourth" Reform Act and the Rise of Labour in England and Wales', *Bulletin of the Institute of Historical Research*, 3 (1983)

—— 'The Development of British Socialism, 1900–18', *Parliamentary History*, 16 (1997)

—— 'Class Voting and Radical Politics: The Liberal and Labour Party', in J. Lawrence and M. Taylor, *Party, State and Society: Electoral Behaviour in Britain since 1829* (Aldershot, 1997)

—— 'Labour and its Membership', in D. Tanner, P. Thane and N. Tiratsoo (eds.), *Labour's First Century* (Cambridge, 2000)

—— 'The Pattern of Labour Politics, 1918–39', in D. Tanner, C. Williams and D. Hopkin (eds.), *The Labour Party in Wales, 1900–2000* (Cardiff, 2000)

—— 'Gender, Civic Culture and Politics in South Wales: Explaining Labour Municipal Policy, 1918–39', in M. Worley (ed.), *Labour's Grass Roots: Essays on the Activities of Local Labour Parties and Members, 1918–45* (Aldershot, 2005)

Taylor, A., 'Speaking to Democracy: The Conservative Party and Mass Opinion from the 1920s to the 1950s', in S. Ball and I. Holliday, *Mass Conservatism: The Conservatives and the Public since the 1880s* (London, 2002)

Taylor, M., 'Labour and the Constitution', in D. Tanner, P. Thane and N. Tiratsoo (eds.), *Labour's First Century* (Cambridge, 2000)

Taylor, R., 'Out of the Bowels of the Movement: The Trade Unions and the Origins of the Labour Party, 1900–18', in B. Brivati and R. Heffernan (eds.), *The Labour Party: A Centenary History* (Basingstoke, 2000)

Teanby, K., 'Leftism in the Doncaster Labour Party, 1921–26', *Bulletin of the Society for the Study of Labour History*, 39 (1978)

Thane, P., 'The Women of the British Labour Party and Feminism, 1906–45', in H. L. Smith (ed.), *British Feminism and the Twentieth Century* (Aldershot, 1990)

—— 'Labour and Welfare', in D. Tanner, P. Thane and N. Tiratsoo (eds.), *Labour's First Century* (Cambridge, 2000)

Thorpe, A., 'Arthur Henderson and the British Political Crisis of 1931', *Historical Journal*, 31 (1988)

—— 'J. H. Thomas and the Rise of Labour in Derby, 1880–1945', *Midland History*, 15 (1990)

—— '"I Am in the Cabinet": J. H. Thomas's Decision to Join the National Government in 1931', *Historical Research*, 64 (1991)

—— 'The Consolidation of a Labour Stronghold, 1926–51', in C. Bindfield et al. (eds.), *The History of the City of Sheffield, 1843–1993* (Sheffield 1993)

—— 'The Industrial Meaning of "Gradualism": The Labour Party and Industry, 1918–31', *Journal of British Studies*, 35 (1996)

—— 'George Lansbury 1932–35', in K. Jefferys (ed.), *Leading Labour: From Keir Hardie to Tony Blair* (London, 1999)

—— 'The Membership of the Communist Party of Great Britain, 1920–45', *The Historical Journal*, 43, 3 (2000)

Tiratsoo, N., 'Labour and the Electorate', in D. Tanner et al, *Labour's First Century* (Cambridge, 2000)

Tomlinson, J., 'Labour and the Economy', in D. Tanner, P. Thane and N. Tiratsoo (eds.), *Labour's First Century* (Cambridge, 2000)

Webb, M., 'The Rise and Fall of the Labour League of Youth', *Socialist History*, 26 (2004)

Webber, G., 'Patterns of Membership and Support for the British Union of Fascists', *Journal of Contemporary History*, 19 (1984)

Weinbren, D., 'Labour's Roots and Branches: The Labour Oral History Project', *Oral History Journal*, 24, 1 (1996)

—— 'Building Communities, Constructing Identities: The Rise of the Labour Party in London', *London Journal*, 23, 1 (1998)

—— 'Sociable Capital: London's Labour Parties, 1918–45', in M. Worley (ed.), *Labour's Grass Roots: Essays on the Activities of Local Labour Parties and Members, 1918–45* (Aldershot, 2005)

Williams, A., 'The Labour Party's Attitude to the Soviet Union, 1927–35: An Overview with Specific Reference to Unemployment Policy and Peace', *Journal of Contemporary History*, 22,1 (1987)

Williams, C., 'Britain', in S. Berger and D. Broughton (eds.), *The Force of Labour: The Western European Labour Movement and the Working Class in the Twentieth Century* (Oxford, 1995)

——— 'Labour and the Challenge of Local Government', in D. Tanner, C. Williams and D. Hopkin (eds.), *The Labour Party in Wales, 1900–2000* (Cardiff, 2000)

Williamson, P., 'The Doctrinal Politics of Stanley Baldwin', in M. Bentley (ed.), *Public and Private Doctrine: Essays in British History Presented to Maurice Cowling* (Cambridge, 1993)

Wood, I. S., 'Hope Deferred: Labour in Scotland in the 1920s', in I. Donnachie, C. Harvie and I. S. Wood (eds.), *Forward! Labour Politics in Scotland, 1888–1988* (Edinburgh, 1989)

Worley, M., 'For a Proletarian Culture: CPGB Culture in the Third Period, 1928–35', *Socialist History*, 18 (2000)

Wrigley, C., 'The Trade Unions between the Wars', in C. Wrigley (ed.), *A History of British Industrial Relations, 1914–45* (Brighton, 1987)

——— 'Explaining Why So Many as well as So Few: Some Aspects of the Development of the Labour Party in Small Towns and Rural Areas', *The Journal of Regional and Local Studies*, 10, 1 (1990)

——— 'The State and the Challenge of Labour in Britain, 1917–20', in C. Wrigley (ed.), *Challenges of Labour: Central and Western Europe, 1917–20* (London, 1993)

——— 'James Ramsay MacDonald, 1922–31', in K. Jefferys (ed.), *Leading Labour: From Keir Hardie to Tony Blair* (London, 1999)

Yeo, S., 'The New Life: The Religion of Socialism in Britain, 1883–96', *History Workshop*, 4 (1977)

Index